THE

MINISTER'S

TOPICAL BIBLE

King James Version

Compiled by Derwin B. Stewart

THE MINISTER'S TOPICAL BIBLE

King James Version

Copyright © 1997 by Derwin B. Stewart
Printed in the United States of America
The Minister's Topical Bible – King James Version
ISBN: 1-56229-104-1

First Printing - 1997
Second Printing - 1998
Third Printing - 2000

Pneuma Life Publishing
P. O. Box 1127
Rockville, MD 20849-1127 U.S.A.
(301) 251-4470
(800) 727-3218

Internet: http://www.pneumalife.com

Contributors

Derwin B. Stewart, The Minister's Topical Bible

As the Founder and President of Pneuma Life Publishing, Mr. Stewart is committed to supporting pastors, ministers, and laity with literature to develop the whole man. He attended Bakersfield College and Oral Roberts University majoring in English and Psychology.

Author/Complier, *The Believer's Topical Bible, The Minister's Topical Bible, The Women's Topical Bible, The Men's Topical Bible,* and *Inevitable Success*

Leonard Lovett, Ph.D., Article: *Ethics for Those Who Minister*

Dr. Leonard Lovett is a native of Pompano Beach Florida who currently resides in Alexandria, Virginia. He is a graduate of Morehouse College and Crozer Theological Seminary and earned a Doctor of Philosophy degree in Ethics and Society from Emory University. with over two decades of pastoral ministry between Philadelphia, Atlanta, and Los Angeles, Dr. Lovett is currently CEO of Seminex Ministries, wherein he serves as a consultant to metropolitan-based churches. Dr. Lovett is also an independent Research Scholar. He is in demand throughout North America and abroad as a lecturer at churches and within the academic community and is currently a member of the National Council of Churches' Faith and Order Commission.

Author, *Opening the Front Door of Your Church, Widen the Front Door as You Close the Back of Your Church*

Dr. Myles Munroe, Leadership Quotes, Article: *What is Leadership?*

An international teacher, speaker, lecturer, evangelist, and advisor, Dr. Myles Munroe is founder and president of Bahamas Faith Ministries International, an all-encompassing network of ministries headquartered in Nassau, Bahamas. Dr. Munroe holds Bachelor of Arts degrees in Education, Fine Arts, and Theology from Oral Roberts University and a Master of Arts degree in Administration from the University of Tulsa. In 1990, Dr. Munroe received an honorary doctorate degree from Oral Roberts University.

Author, *Becoming A Leader, Single-Married-Separated and Life after Divorce, Understanding Your Potential, Releasing Your Potential, In Pursuit of Purpose,* and *Maximizing Your Potential*

Dedication

This book is dedicated to those who are
faithful proclaimers of the Word of God.

TABLE OF CONTENTS

Dedication
Ethics for Those Who Minister 1
What is Leadership? 13

Personal Life

THE MINISTER'S RELATIONSHIP WITH GOD

Fellowship with God 19
Praising God 19
Worshipping God 23
Fear of the Lord 25
Trusting God 26
Faith in God and His Word 28
    Great Faith 28
    Principles of Faith 29
    Faith in Action 30
    A Lifestyle of Faith 31
    through Faith 32
    Obtaining Faith 32
    According to Your Faith 32
    Doubt and Unbelief 33
The Will of God 35
    Obedience to God's Will (God's Word) 35
    Praying in Agreement with His Will 35
    Submitting to God's Will 36
    God is Willing to Bless, Heal and Save You 37

THE MINISTER IN RELATIONSHIPS

Family of God 39
Angels 39
    Angels Protect the Children of God 39
    Angels Travel Back and Forth between Heaven and Earth 40
    Angels Respond to the Spoken Word of God 40
    Angels Are Assigned to Different Believers 40
    Angels Engage in Spiritual Warfare 40
    Angels Will Accompany Christ when He Returns (The Rapture) 41
    Angels Are Infinite in Number 41
    Angels Minister to God's Children 41
    Angels Are Not to Be Worshipped 42
    Angels Can Disguise Themselves as Human Beings 42
    Angels Are Under the Authority of God 42
    Angels Will Separate the Believers from the Unbelievers 42
Fellowship with Believers 42
Marriage 44

Husbands 44
Wives 45
Child-Parent Relationship 46
Raising Children 46
Physically Correcting Your Children 47
Being Fair to Your Children 47
Teaching Your Children the Word of God 47
Friends 48
Avoiding or Breaking Bad Relationships 50

THE MINISTER'S CHARACTER

Keeping Your Word (Promises, Vows, and Commitments) 53
Honesty 53
Being Honest with Yourself 55
Accepting Advice and Positive Criticism 55
Learning to Control the Words that You Speak 56
Avoid Speaking Evil, Useless and Meaningless Words 57
Evil Words are Destructive 58
Don't Talk too Much 58
A Fool Talks too Much 58
You Will Be Judged by the Words that You Speak 59
Think Before You Speak 59
Speaking Positive Words 60
Speaking Words of Wisdom and Integrity 60
Speaking the Right Words at the Appropriate Time 61
Speaking Knowledgeable Words 61
Becoming Bold in Christ 62

THE MINISTER'S ATTITUDE

Meekness 65
Overcoming Pride 67
God Hates Pride 68
Pride Will Cause You to Fall 69
Being Prideful Starts Trouble 69
Controlling Anger 69
Overcoming an Envious Heart 71
Building Your Self-Confidence through Christ 71
Building Your Self-Image through God's Word 72

Ministry

HOW TO HAVE CHURCH OR MINISTRY GROWTH

Be a Vessel of Power 75
Remain Humble 75
Love Everyone 76

PREACHING THE GOSPEL

To the World 79
Use Words of Simplicity and Humility 81

Preach the Gospel with Pure Motives 82

How To's in Ministry

How to Handle a Successful Ministry 85
How to Persevere in a Struggling Ministry 87
How to Qualify Potential Associate Ministers and Staff 89
How to Handle Persecution from the World and the Church 91

Hindrances

Pleasing God vs. Pleasing Man 93
Fear of Man 94
Trusting in Man or an Organization 94
Flattery 95

What Makes a Church or Ministry Fail

Not Flowing in the Holy Spirit 97
Not Continuously Praying 98
Living in Sin 98
Being Prideful 99
Not Controlling Your Sexual Desires 99
Judging Members by Their Money, Race, or Association 100
Not Confronting Sin in Your Staff and Church 101
    Make Sure Your Life is in Order Before Confronting Anyone 102
    Always Confront Sin in the Spirit of Love 102
    Examples of Godly Confrontation 103
Allowing False Brothers/Teachers to Minister at Your Church
or Be Members of Your Staff 104
    Recognizing False Brother and Teachers 104
    Test and Confront False Brothers and Teachers 107

The Root Cause for Ministry Conflicts and Church Splits

Strife 109
    Causes of Strife 109
    Stopping Strife 110
Contention 110
    A Contentious Woman 111
    A Contentious Man 111
Gossip 111
Slander 112
Envy 113
Lying 114
Judgmental Attitudes 115

Spiritual Discernment

Spiritual Eyes and Ears 117
Spiritual Blindness and Deafness 118
Discernment 119

Discerning Good and Evil 119
Discernment from God's Word 120
Deception 120
    Being Deceived by Others 120
    Self-Deception 122
    Deceived by Darkness 123
The Strategies of satan (the devil) 124
    satan's most infamous strategy is lying 124
    satan's seeks to steal, kill, and destroy 124
    satan is the inventor of sin 124
    satan tries to steal the Word of God out of the heart of man 124
    satan tries to put evil thoughts into your mind 125
    satan tries to deceive people into false religions, cults, and the like 125
    satan tempts you 126
    satan condemns believers of the past 126
    satan tries to convince people that God is angry with them 126
    satan tries to control minds 127
    satan tries to control life-styles 127
    satan delays prayers 127
    satan tries to prevent people from receiving Christ 127
    satan is in constant warfare with God's army 127
    satan causes manifold problems 128
Laying on of Hands 128
    Miracles of Jesus 128
    Spiritual Gifts 128
    Blessings 129
    Miracles of the Disciples 129
    Transference of Spirits 130
False Prophets 130
Judging Prophecy 133

THE MINISTER IN COUNSELING

Wisdom 135
    How to Obtain Wisdom 135
    Wisdom Comes from God 135
    True Wisdom 136
    Pursue Wisdom 136
    Wisdom Enters the Heart 137
    Wisdom is Valuable 137
    Wisdom is Found in Counsel 137
    The Benefits of Wisdom 137
    Wisdom in Action 138
Knowledge 138
    God is the Source of Knowledge 138
    Pursue Knowledge 139
    The Benefits of Obtaining Knowledge 140
    The Consequences of Lacking Knowledge 140
    Knowledge from God's Word 140
Understanding 141
    Godly Understanding 142
    Obtaining Understanding 142
Curses 143
    Curses Activated by Disobedience to God's Word 144

Curses Activated by Words 144
How to Break Curses 144
Generational (Hereditary) Sins 145
Casting Out devils/demons 146
Examples of Jesus Casting Out devils 146
Disciples Casting Out devils 148
You Can Cast Out devils 149
Before Casting Out devils 149
Keys to Remember When Casting Out devils 149

Discipleship

SALVATION

The Plan of Salvation 151
How to Obtain Eternal Life through Jesus Christ 151
How to be Saved 151
How to Know You are Really Saved 151
Now that You are Saved 152
Saved by Grace 153
Respecting the Grace of God 153
Sanctification 153
Sanctified by the Word of God 154
Sanctified through Jesus Christ 154
Set Apart from the Sins of the World 155
Righteousness 155
Righteousness through Jesus Christ 155
Believing Unto Righteousness 156
The Word of God is Our Instruction for Righteous Living 156
Man-Made Righteousness 156
Justification 157
Remaining in the Kingdom of God 158
Backslider 158
Compromising Christian 159
A Warning for the Backslider or Compromising Christian 162

LOVE

Characteristics of Love 165
God's Love 166
Loving God 167
Loving Others 168

MATURING IN CHRIST

Forgiveness 171
Patience 172
Remaining Patient in Tribulations 174
Living in Holiness 174
Fruitful Living 176
Peacemaker 177
Overcoming Covetousness 178
The Consequences of Covetousness 179

ix

COMMITTING TO CHRIST

Seeking God 181
    Seek After God with Your Whole Being 183
    Seek God Early in the Morning 183
    Seek God Continuously 183
    The Results of Continuously Seeking God 184
    The Consequences of Not Seeking God 184
Obeying the Word of God 184
    True Obedience 187
Submitting to the Correction of God 187
Dying to Self 188
Following Christ and Carrying Your Cross 189
Being a True Representative of God 190
    Living the Life of Christ Before God and Man 190
    Being a True Representative of God is 191
Fasting 193
    Fasting Gives You Power Over satan 194
    Fasting with Pure Motives 194

OVERCOMING SIN

Sin 195
What Should I Do When I Sin? 196
    Repent 196
    Confess the Sin 198
    Stop Sinning 198
Deliverance from Sin 199
Secret Sins 200
    The Pleasure of Sin is Only Temporary 201
Deliberate and Willful Sin 201
Sowing Sin and Reaping its Consequences 202
Sin Gives satan Entrance into Your Life 203
The Hardships of a Life of Sin 204

RECEIVING GOD'S FORGIVENESS FOR YOUR SINS

Sins Cleansed by the Blood of Jesus 205
God Will Forgive Your Sins 205
God Will Not Remember Your Sins 207
God Will Blot Out Your Sins 207
Overcoming Guilt 207
Overcoming Condemnation 209
    You are Condemned When You 209

DEVELOPING THE WHOLE MAN

The Spirit

God is the Creator of Human Spirits 211
God Has Ultimate Control Over Human Spirits 211
The Body is the Temporary Container for the Human Spirit 212

The Life of the Human Spirit 212
God Communicates with Your Spirit... 212
The Spirit of Man 213
Renewed (Born Again) Spirit 213
Food (God's Word) for the Spirit.. 213
The Word of God Planted in the Heart of Man 215
God's Word Discerns the Heart 216
Thoughts and Words Originate in the Heart of Man 216
Living and Walking in the Spiritual Realm 217
Fruit of the Spirit 217

The Mind

Renewing Your Mind.. 218
Focusing Your Mind on the Word of God 218
Focusing Your Mind on Jesus... 219
Controlling Imaginations and Thoughts 219
Television, Movies, and Music.. 220
    Would Jesus listen to this music, or watch this TV program or movie? 220
    What kind of people or evil spirits are you inviting into your home? 220
    Is it contrary to God's Word? 220
    Is it bringing you closer to Christ? 221
    Is it causing you to compromise and sin? 221
    What are you putting in you heart (through your eyes and ears)? 221
    Are you wasting time? 222
    How do you qualify good TV programs, movies, and music? 222
Controlling Lust 223

The Body

The Temple of the Holy Spirit 225
Sex Before Marriage.. 225
    Sex is Only for Married Couples 226
The Consequences of Fornication 226
Adultery 227
The Consequences of Adultery 227
Homosexuality and Lesbianism 227
Gluttony 228
Biblical Diet... 229
Healing 229
    Provisions for Healing 229
    Preventive Medicine 230
    God's Promises for Healing 230
    Praying for Healing 232
Living a Long and Satisfied Life 233

Teaching

HOLY SPIRIT

Respecting the Holy Spirit 235
Receiving the Baptism of the Holy Spirit 235
The Benefits of Praying in the Holy Spirit 236
Examples of Believers Being Filled with the Holy Spirit 236
The Holy Spirit is the Teacher, Leader, Guide and Counselor 237
The Holy Spirit Living Inside the Believer 238
Sealed by the Holy Spirit 239
The Power of the Holy Spirit 239
The Gifts of the Holy Spirit 240

PRAYER

Praying in the Name of Jesus 241
The Lord's Prayer 242
God Hears Your Prayers 242
Hindrances to Prayer 243
Praying with the Right Attitude and Motives 243
Different Kinds of Prayer 244
Prayer of Agreement 245
Praying in Faith 245
Waiting on God in Prayer 245
Praying in the Holy Spirit 245
Intercessory Prayer 246
Examples of Prayer Warriors 247
Praying Continuously 247

THE BELIEVER'S AUTHORITY

The Superior Power and Authority of Christ 249
You Have Power Over the devil and his demons 250
Spiritual Warfare 251
    The Armor for the Spiritual Realm 251
The Weapons of the Spiritual Realm 252
    The Name of Jesus 252
    The Blood of Jesus 252
    The Sword of the Spirit (The Word of God) 252

Binding and Loosing 253
God's End-Time Army 253
Spiritual Enemies 253
Attacking the Enemy 254

THE BELIEVER'S PLACE AND IDENTITY IN JESUS CHRIST

In Christ 255
By Christ 269
In Him 260
By Him 262
Through Christ 262
Of Christ 263
With Christ 264
By Himself 264
By Whom 265
From Whom 265
In Whom 265
Of Him 266
Through Him 266
With Christ 266
With Him 267

THE NAME OF JESUS

The Different Names of Jesus 269
The Name Above All Names 272
Praying in the Name of Jesus 272
Power in the Name of Jesus 273
Believing in the Name of Jesus 274
Serving in the Name of Jesus 275
Suffering for the Name of Jesus 275

GOD'S WORD

The Integrity of God's Word 277
God's Word is Spiritual Food 279
The Word of God in the Heart 281
    Different Ways the Word of God is Taken Out of the Heart of Man 282
    A Good Heart for the Word of God 283
Meditating on God's Word 284
How to Obtain Promises from God's Word 285
    Confess the Word of God 285
    Remain Patient 285
    Do Not Doubt the Ability of God and His Word 286
The Cleansing of the Word of God 287
Memorizing the Word of God 288
Guidance from God's Word 288
The Spoken Word of God 289
    Is the Sword of the Spirit 289
    Gives Faith to the Believer 289
    Convicts and Converts the Unbeliever 290
    Angers the Sinner 290
    Will Cast Out demon spirits 290
    Puts satan to Flight 290

THE KEYS OF SUCCESS

Direction 291
Favor from God 294
Decisions 294
    Say "No" 294
    Say "Yes" 295
Diligence 295
    Diligence in Work and Business 295
Wise and Godly Counsel 296
Faithfulness 297
Overcoming Laziness 298
Work 299
    Benefits of Working 301
    We Are Commanded to Work 301
    Consequences of Not Working 301
Good Works 301
    Your Works Will Be Judged by Christ 303

PREPARING THE MIND AND HEART TO RECEIVE GOD'S BLESSINGS

God Wants You to Prosper Financially 305
Giving in the Right Attitude 306
True Riches 307
Do Not Put Your Trust or Hope in Money 308
Contentment 309

THE PURPOSE FOR FINANCES

To Spread the Gospel of Jesus Christ 311
To Help the Poor 312

GOD'S FINANCIAL BUSINESS PLAN FOR YOU

Tithing and Offerings 315
Sowing Seeds 316
Reaping the Harvest 317
The End-Time Transfer of Wealth to Christians 317
Loans 318
Co-Signing for Others 319

FACING CHALLENGES AND WINNING

Facing Fear and Winning 321
    Fear is an evil spirit from satan 321
    Fear Brings the Problem to You 321
    Don't Fear! God is with You 321
Facing Death and Winning 322
Facing Enemies and Winning 323
    How to Treat Your Enemies 325
    Do Not Rejoice When Your Enemies Suffer 326
Facing Loneliness and Winning 326

Facing Revenge and Winning 327
    Revenge is God's Job 327
    Do Not Seek Revenge 328
Facing Persecution and Winning 329
Facing Temptation and Winning... 330
Facing Stress and Depression and Winning 332
Facing Anxiety and Worry and Winning 334

JESUS WILL

Jesus Will Give You Love 337
Jesus Will Give You Hope 338
Jesus Will Give You Joy 340
Jesus Will Give You Mercy 342
Jesus Will Give You Peace 345
    Peace through Jesus Christ 346
    Peace from God's Word 347
    How to Have Peace 347
Jesus Will Give You Comfort 348
Jesus Will Deliver You 349
Jesus Will Give You Perseverance... 350

PERTINENT TRUTHS OF THE GOSPEL

Who is God? 353
    God is the Creator of Heaven and Earth 353
    God is Sovereign and Omnipotent 353
    God is the Creator of Mankind 356
The Trinity (The Father, The Son, and The Holy Spirit) 356
How to Reach God 358
How to Love and Please God 359
Who is Jesus? 359
    Jesus is the Mediator between God and Man 360
    Jesus is the Son of God 360
    Jesus is God 361
    Jesus Existed as God Before He Came to Earth 361
    Jesus is the Word of God 363
    Jesus is Wisdom 363
The Pre-Existence of Jesus Christ 363
The Sufferings and Death of Jesus Christ 365
    Prophecies of the Suffering and Death of Jesus Christ 365
    New Testament Fulfillment of Old Testament Prophecies 366
The Shed Blood of Jesus Christ 368
    Redeemed by the Blood 370
    Sins Cleansed by the Blood 370
    The Blood of Jesus as a Spiritual Weapon 370
The Resurrection of Jesus Christ 371
    Prophecies of the Resurrection of Jesus Christ 371
    The Resurrection 371
    Benefits from the Resurrection of Jesus Christ 372
Eternal Life through Jesus Christ 373

The Return of Jesus Christ (The Rapture) 375
    Are You Ready for the Rapture? 376
The Faithfulness of God 376
Confessing Jesus Christ 378
    Jesus Confessing the Word of His Father (God) 379
Confessing the Word of God 379
    The Power of Confession 380
Confessing Sins 380
Idolatry 380
    The Consequences of Committing Idolatry 381
    The Worship of demon spirits 381
    Material and Human gods 381
    Sins Related to Idolatry 382
Unity in the Body of Christ 382
God's Divine Protection 383
Time on Earth 384
    Human Life is Short 384
    Man's Time Compared to God's Time 385
The Final Judgment of Mankind 385
    Jesus Christ is Appointed by God to Judge the World 386
    The Judgment Seat of Christ 387
Heaven 387
    Who's Going to Heaven and Why 387
    What is Heaven Like? 388
    Buildings in Heaven 389
    Fellowship in Heaven 390
Hell 391
    Who is Hell For? 391
    Who's Going to Hell and Why? 392
    How Serious is Hell? 393
    An Example of Hell 393
    What is Hell Like? 394
    Different Levels of Punishment in Hell 394
    The Location of Hell 395
    Hell is a Bottomless Pit 395
satan's Past 396
satan's Eternal Future 397

Daily Bible Reading Plan 401
Prayer Journal 406
Personal Goals 412
Ministry Goals 414
Church Goals 415
Mission Statement 416
Personal Phone Numbers 417
U.S. Area Codes 423
Helpful Toll Free Numbers 424
Travel Mileage Between Cities 425

Ethics for Those Who Minister

Leonard Lovett, Ph.D.

MORAL LEADERSHIP

Those who lead God's people in today's society often find themselves living either in the center or on the edge of the ethical quandary. In a society encumbered by ethical mishaps, a few words–written specifically to ministers–of pastoral wisdom forged on the anvil of pastoral experience may be in order. Immorality in the ministry is a rather complex issue that involves a number of factors. Such delicate factors as one's self-image, identity, and life-style surface as we come under the mirror of scrutiny. The sins that plague us in ministry are often more than just spiritual problems. The interpersonal dynamics of moral failure must be critically assessed if we are to mature and learn from the mistakes of others.

Ministers are often like physicians who care deeply for the patients they treat, but end up dying from the very diseases they are trained to cure. We listen to the sins and failures of others in counseling sessions, but refuse to disclose our pain even to those we believe to be close to us. We search for someone to trust and engage in open disclosure without the fear of having our moral strivings used against us. If we are to be whole in body, mind and spirit it will involve sharing our pain and those deep-seated fears that also increase our stress levels. Moral leadership is not some separate calling in ministry, it lies at the very core of who we are and what we do in leading God's people. According to the wisdom of our Lord, whenever the "blind leads the blind" both can be victimized by falling into a ditch.

THE MINISTER'S RELATIONSHIP WITH GOD

We who serve in ministry must seek to render the best service by being morally, mentally, physically and spiritually sound. We should find

1

a specific time to "practice the presence of God" daily. This may be meditation on Scripture, prayer or finding a quiet place. I have discovered that my day doesn't proceed with as much purpose when I, for whatever reason, forfeit that "quiet time." The great Methodist missionary to India for more than fifty years, the late E. Stanley Jones, described prayer as "entering God's presence for cleansing and decision-making." Communion with God is the fountain and source of renewal and replenishment. We are channels for God's grace and power but not the source. Indeed we are compelled to drink from the "fountains of living water" if we are to lead the people of God.

Physical and Mental

We who serve in ministry must be physically and mentally sound in order to effectively lead the people of God. Find time to engage in some form of exercise compatible with your condition of health. Friends who walk five miles a day in Los Angeles told me about a man who had all kinds of health problems–including heart disease and hypertension. This man, in his early seventies, had been spending major amounts of money on medication, but he had never engaged in any kind of physical exercise. Within months after adopting walking as a daily form of exercise, he dropped all medications and has been told that his hypertension and heart condition has receded. I have been an avid racquetball player since 1979, and recently have become a frequent walker/jogger. I have observed that whenever I am consistently on task with a balanced exercise program, my energy level is high. Occasional use of a vitamin supplement provides astounding energy for most tasks. Diet, rest and proper exercise increases blood circulation and impacts my total energy level. Mental alertness is also one of the positive consequences of a regular fitness program. Exercise helps to relieve us of stress.

Social

Those who are bearers of the Gospel are also social beings. Jesus was a special guest at a wedding in Cana of Galilee. The issue is not whether we are social beings or not, but rather what are the limitations and boundaries imposed on our social behavior. Should we be viewed as "ecclesiastical snobs" or as human beings too "holy" to laugh or play? What are the risks to our ministry when we cross the boundaries of our professional behavior for personal aggrandizement? Yet, the ancient words of Scripture are still appropriate in our time, "Can one take fire in his bosom and not be burned?" As an ethicist, it appears that discernment is the normative key to setting limitations on our social behavior.

Ministers must be discerning at all times. Most of us are aware of ministers who were excellent communicators and motivators but failed because they crossed the ethical boundaries of professionalism and developed inappropriate relationships with those they sought to help. The minister's relationship to those of the opposite sex must be free, guarded and yet responsible. Counseling should take place only in a professional setting. Reputation has to do with *who people say we are*. Character has to do with *who we are*. We must be discerning so that we will not do anything that will violate another as we seek to lead the people of God

I have been in settings where it was social to imbibe a cocktail. My choice was Coca-Cola. I did not superimpose my judgment on those who sipped their cocktail. I was comfortable and unembarrassed as I sipped my Coke. Discernment was the key in making such a decision. I had imposed on my life-style the co-efficiency of consistency and discipline. It is important that my witness be coherent and clear at all times. Most of us are familiar with ministers who crossed the boundaries of social drinking and ended up strung out on alcohol or drugs. Those of us who bear the witness of the claims of Jesus Christ must never surrender our convictions simply to go along with the crowd. I have friends who have paid the price of the loss of their ministry for failing to be discerning and taking a stand.

THE MINISTER AND STEWARDSHIP

A special friend of mine from Savannah, Pastor Ricky R. Temple of the Overcoming Faith Foursquare Church, shared with me some special words of wisdom during a crisis that caught me by surprise. Many problems that face clergy are usually directly or indirectly related to economics–your low salary, your house, taxes or any other so-called culprit. However, it is the lack of financial planning that causes our finances to get out of control. Professional financial planners have established the fact that bankruptcy knows no class, race, occupational or gender boundaries. People at all levels of the income ladder file for bankruptcy. People who are earning six figures go broke as do those making far less. Clearly, the final solution to the problem is not additional income. The solution is developing a personal stewardship plan and perspective that will enable you to proceed from where you are to where you would like to go.

Stewardship planning refers to a process of sorting data about our financial life-style, monitoring our income and spending patterns, establishing goals and devising strategies that enable us to reach specific goals. Such planning involves taking an honest look at our values and goals, learning how to utilize resources that are available to us, and making

3

adjustments in our life-style that result in goal accomplishment. At a more pragmatic level, it involves taking inventory of our assets and liabilities and gaining control of our financial destiny. Try avoiding quick fix schemes or presentations that appear too good to be true. They usually are and seldom are what they appear to be. To gain control you must find a way to determine that your liabilities (debts or what you owe) will not exceed your assets (everything you own and its current value). Credit card debt is our worst enemy. Through experience I have learned that a credit card should only be used if it can be repaid within a thirty day period.

Budgeting is the key to stewardship planning. God expects that we should be responsible managers of the resources we obtain. Make a list of average monthly expenditures and income. After setting up an IRA or some pension plan for future retirement, try saving all professional fees you receive for services rendered. The amount you have saved will surprise you at the end of the year. Discover a way to save money on an automobile. Find out whether leasing or purchasing an automobile is more favorable. Note that many denominations can provide you with a financial planning consultant. Tax efficiency is also good stewardship. Be sure to ask about such things as tax-deferred savings plans. These precautions could send you on your way to a less stressful future.

Avoid flamboyance in life-style. Try to find a happy medium. Keep in mind the people you have been called to serve. Ostentatiousness sends the wrong message to persons who may not have the maturity to appreciate financial blessings.

The goals we set reflect our values. Our values filter through our life-style and send certain messages. In planning your compensation package, make sure you are comfortable with it and that it reflects inflation adjustments and cost of living increases. Try tracking expenses during the fiscal year. In Scripture, money is not the root of evil. Stewardship planning enables us to live life with the deep sense of confidence that we are in control of our financial destiny. Remember, it is the "love" of money that constitutes the root of evil. According to Richard Exley, in Perils of Power, "if money is your motive for ministry you are already corrupt even if you never steal one dime."

THE MINISTER'S RELATIONSHIP TO FAMILY

There is no substitute for a well balanced family life for those who minister. Apart from preaching responsibilities, a minister is at heart a shepherd. Opportunities to touch the lives of people come to us in unlimited ways. Combined with this are the pressures and multiple demands and expectations placed upon we ministers. If you are a pastor, there is always the possibility of subjection to unfair criticism, complaints and various negativities. If things are in disarray at home it adds additional unwanted pressure.

There are some ministers whose life is so bound up in the life of the church that it becomes a sort of competitive second marriage partner. A terrible judgment is to appear successful and high profile in the public arena but receive low marks at home. Situations such as this can become the source of major resentment especially for our spouses. They tend to resent the time taken from family in the name of ministry.

It is such a set of dynamics that sets the stage for temptation. Emotional adultery is usually the consequence of a minister seeking solace, comfort and affirmation almost always from some person bent on compromising ministers. Do not allow temptation to lurk in your bosom; deal with it as soon as possible. Traps are set for ministers–often in seemingly innocent ways–by those who pretend to care for us. Again, the ancient wisdom of Scripture is most appropriate, "Can a man take fire into his bosom and not be burned?"(Proverbs 6:27ff).

After ministering to the point of exhaustion, avoid social settings. When a person is exhausted, their inhibitions are down. In the wilderness satan encountered the man Jesus at the point of physical exhaustion and weakness. I have discovered that I am less sociable after a time of intense ministry. I often need time to recover before interacting with people. At this vulnerable time, the warmth and tenderness of a loving spouse can often bring reassurance and renewal.

There need not be a third party present for an affair to begin. Anything that becomes a substitute for the time that should be shared with one's family constitutes an affair. Affairs do not always occur with another person. An affair occurs when one's attachment to a particular thing prevents both partners in a marital relationship from maximizing their potential. People have affairs with money, clothes or simply "things."

You should plan a regularly scheduled time–preferably weekly–that can be shared only by your immediate family. As a pastor in a hectically paced city, I kept Monday as a time to completely relax and recoup from the previous weekend's services. Ideally you should plan a series of events that can be shared together with your family. It is crucial that you protect your day at all cost. Do not surrender this turf to anyone else. Married clergy need the strength of a stable marriage to keep their ministry viable. Make sure your emotional needs are being met within the boundaries of marriage. Keep in mind that a healthy marriage does not cause temptation to vanish, but it does strengthen both partners to deal with it when it comes your way. A rule of thumb is never trifle with temptation.

We must be able to play and pray with our families and enjoy it. If you have children, they can be a real source of fun. Stress-related illnesses plague us in modern times because we do not know how to enjoy a sunset, or the smell of a rose, or a nature hike. We must be vigilant when it comes to protecting our families from a lack of emotional intimacy; this is the key to a balanced family life. Emotional intimacy in marriage is a healthy sign that both partners are intent on meeting those special needs of their spouses–needs that enhance one's total well-being.

Ministry should never become the "other person" in a marriage. If a person cannot rule their house how can they manage the household of God? I know several friends who are completely out of the ministry because their priorities were mixed when it came to discipline in this area. One cannot be a follower of Jesus without the unique gift of discipline. It is no less true for ministers, lest "after ministering to others we become castaways."

We must also find time to get away from the routine. It is vital that a minister take a vacation. In addition to annual vacations, it is necessary to build in mini-vacations. This may mean leaving on Friday and returning late Saturday evening but it can be a source of renewal and strength in this stress laden vocation called ministry. The God Who called us to ministry wills that we be whole persons. As vessels of honor we can serve the cause of the Kingdom with strength and fervor. Though we have feet of clay. We must not be weary in well doing as we participate with God in reconciling this broken world. Somewhere I came across a dictum that stated: "Live so that as people get to know you better, they will know Christ better."

THE MINISTER'S RELATIONSHIP TO PARISHIONERS

During my first pastorate a banker warned me not to co-sign a $300 note with a brother who had been in attendance for only one month. In post reflection I must confess that my naiveté shaded my decision. I felt that if anyone should have assisted this brother it should have been me. Unfortunately, the brother also read my naiveté and took full advantage of the same. I advanced the brother $300 from my personal savings account. By the middle of the second month–after the loan was made–the brother vanished. Needless to say I was bound by the co-signed agreement to pay the balance of the loan. I made the loan against my better judgment and the counsel of an experienced banker. Psalm 37:21 states that "the wicked borroweth and payeth not again."

In another pastorate, a brother who was about to be evicted from his apartment by another member requested a loan of $1,000 from the church. I had met with both parties to assure them that I was bound by conscience and duty to be impartial to both parties. The member who was landlord stood to lose the rental property due to non-payment of the rent. The renter wanted to buy time in order to secure another dwelling for his family and did not feel responsible for paying the overdue rent. The whole issue became highly controversial with members taking sides. I finally had to declare a moratorium on the whole matter and urged both to resolve the issue in a civil court after both parties refused the counsel I had provided as a pastoral leader. The church advanced the loan in good faith. As soon as the brother moved to a new apartment he transferred his membership in order to escape responsibility for repayment of the loan. After several attempts to collect payment, the brother resorted to insulting us.

Churches would do well to establish and develop a benevolent fund with certain criteria for assisting persons who demonstrate genuine need. Ministers who personally assist members financially may find themselves in serious ethical conflict. The moment you personally loan money to a member it alters the relationship. You have all of a sudden become a banker who expects to collect. What happens when a member will not pay? Experience has shown that when members cannot repay a loan they invariably stop attending the church because they cannot face their debtor in good conscience. The attitude of the minister is no longer one of compassion in many instances, but one of dismay, disappointment and disgust. We tend to argue that since such transactions are done in good faith it logically follows that Christian members will be honest and pay their just debts.

A minister must exercise extreme caution when tempted to transact any form of business that will alter their relationship with parishioners. This also raises other issues that warrant attention. Should there be social distance between the minister and parishioners? If so, how much? Should ministers socialize with their parishioners? To what extent ought a minister be "human" when in the presence of those who follow his/her leadership? There is a rule of wisdom from past experience that warrants examination: After a grueling session of giving oneself in ministry is to avoid crowds and find a quiet time to be alone to settle down. Likewise, couples should seek the comfort of each other after a grueling ministry of giving. Contact with members should be limited until one recovers strength and overcomes exhaustion. There are many stories in the community of faith about ministers who ended up becoming alcoholics or engaging in substance abuse during such times because they did not understandthese boundaries.

An area of concern that requires wisdom and discernment is the expectations imposed upon the minister's spouse by parishioners. In slippery, sloping gray areas such as leading a particular ministry or auxiliary we would do well to proceed with extreme caution in order to avoid conflict of interest. Experience has proven to be invaluable in this area. As a pastor my policy was to allow my wife the freedom to participate in any phase of ministry in the church. To avoid conflict of interest, however, she was not allowed to be the administrator or leader of any ministry auxiliary. Should a dispute develop in an area where your spouse is the leader, whose side will you be on in the final analysis? I have watched great ministries collapse because the pastoral leader was not discerning enough to understand the volatile dynamics and potential for conflict that resides in such an arrangement. On the other hand, I have also observed ministries where spousal leadership appeared to have been working. This issue is relative to particular situations, therefore proceed with extreme caution.

I recently observed a church where the members addressed the pastor by his first name in an attempt to be human and remove certain barriers between pastor and parishioners. It was quite interesting to observe six year olds addressing the pastor by his first name. There may be some wisdom in the saying "familiarity breeds contempt." Ministers should be friendly, yet firm. They should conduct themselves in the presence of their parishioners so as to earn their respect. I have observed pastoral settings where parishioners were too familiar. In such settings we raise the flag of caution. While pastors must not give the impression that they live in glass houses far removed from the common touch, they should never become too familiar with members in their attempt to close the gap. The very people that you "let your hair down with" also expect you to be available to pray for their special concerns. Whatever you are in your private moments is what you really are. Every minister would do well to read Richard Exley's excellent work, Perils of Power, as a basic approach to understanding power, loneliness and avoidance of affairs that often bring down the mighty. Avoid pretense but be "human" in a responsible way.

THE MINISTER'S RELATIONSHIP TO COLLEAGUES

The need for professional ethics toward colleagues is an area that merits attention. Most professions have a guidelines that provide assistance in making decisions. Lawyers, Physicians, Bankers and Legislators are expected to adhere to a strict code of ethics. Ministerial ethics are rarely required for the profession except in an informal way. Over three decades ago, I came across Nolan Harmon's <u>Ministerial Ethics and Etiquette</u>, a classic in the area of personal ethics for ministry. A more recent work is Richard Bondi's <u>Leading God's People</u>, ethics for the practice of ministry. The question often arises: what ought to be my attitude toward those who are in the ministry profession?

Ministers must never undermine the influence of a colleague. In ministry the occasion arises where jealousy raises its ugly head often over inessentials. When a minister speaks in a derogatory manner about a colleague, it diminishes the person engaged in the process. One can always find something positive to say about another person. Try seeking positive assessments of colleagues and be willing to engage in face-to-face constructive criticism.

Ministers should avoid open rivalry with colleagues in ministry. The Kingdom of God is diverse and has room for many expressions. Seek ways to complement a colleague at all times and watch your own stock increase. I have observed competition in ministry get out of control and generate problems of major proportions. We are responsible for the well being of those we relate to in ministry. Be willing to participate in tough love conversations with someone in ministry that you trust, it will save you from future disaster.

Ministers should never brag, especially about material acquisitions. This is "vanity of vanity" says the preacher of the Book of Ecclesiastes. I can't count the number of times I have observed ministers bragging about their clothes, shoes, watches and automobiles. Such behavior often mirrors the values embraced by those who should be bearers of the "good news" of the Gospel.

THE MINISTER AND PARTISAN POLITICS

Since God is neither Republican, Democrat or Independent we need to understand the relationship of the minister to partisan politics. Long before politics became complex and highly sophisticated, Aristotle, the classical Greek philosopher, spoke of it as "the art of achieving the possible." Politics has to do with the art, science and philosophy of the governmental process. Another way of stating it is that politics is that discipline which takes seriously the task of making life more humane through organized means. Religion also focuses on making life more humane. Religion has been commonly defined as the life of God in the soul of

9

humankind; or a system of beliefs and attitudes directed toward a Supreme Being. It appears that by definition religion and politics share a common goal, improving the quality of life for the individual.

The involvement of ministers in partisan politics has always been a sensitive issue. Pastors have faced the issue of their church's tax-exempt status coming under scrutiny. The ranting biblicist and many Christians will utter a resounding "no" to the issue of a Gospel minister's participation in partisan politics. More and more in our times we see pastors involved directly in the political process. The late Rep. Adam Clayton Powell, Sr. balanced the dual hats of politician and pastor. More recently, Rep. William "Bill" Gray, Jr. of Philadelphia and Rep. Floyd Flake of New York are contemporary examples of ministers who are also politicians.

The main issue is not "should ministers be involved in partisan politics?" Rather, to what extent are they already involved in the political process? Every church building that is situated within a city block is not only a spiritual entity, but is also a political entity, subject to zoning laws. A clear reading of the Old Testament reveals the fact that God is a political God. Each time God chose to deal with His people, the covenant between God and His chosen people became the point of reference. A covenant is an agreement–a treaty–and that makes it a political instrument. A covenant has terms, "If you will be my people, I will be your God." The Old Testament is replete with political language–kingships, thrones, rulers, subjects, a people. Cyrus, a ruler, is referred to as God's anointed.

Politics, in and of itself, is no more corrupt than economics or any other aspect of our social existence. While some politicians may be corrupt, there are many Christians who see politics as an arena for Christian service, vocation and witness. God is Lord of the world and that includes the political arena. What a difference it would make in our time if we realized that we are inextricably bound together. In the words of the late Dr. Martin Luther King, Jr. "we are wrapped in a single garment of human destiny." Translated into political language, the political arena cannot be what it should be until Christians begin to enter the halls of power, seize the moment and by participating and acting responsibly, be what they were called to be and where they are really needed. Being a part of community makes us responsible.

We must remember that our primary calling is to communicate the Gospel of Jesus Christ. The minister who enters the political arena must do so at his/her own risk. It must be a matter of conscience. This minister

10

must enter as a "losing winner" and a "winning loser." There will always be a paradoxical tension that propels the Christian in the political arena. One must be prepared to lose on the proposed issue but knowingly willing to win on principle. The late President John F. Kennedy wrote a book during the early portion of his presidency, entitled <u>Profiles in Courage</u>. It should be required reading for everyone in ministry. If politicians can stare into their political graves and survive like a Daniel Webster and a Lucius Cincinnatus Lamar, what about those who proclaim the Gospel and face difficult circumstances?

The minister who enters the political arena must be aware of the provisional nature of politics. The answers provided in politics are at best partial in a fallen world and must never be regarded as final. Senator Mark Hatfield was correct as a Christian legislator when he stated: "for the Christian to say that he will not enter politics because he might lose his faith is the same as for the physician to say that he will not heal men because he might catch their diseases." Since politics itself is not inherently evil or good and is no more than the conduct of public affairs, the presence of believers in such an arena could impact morality in places of public leadership. The minister who enters the political arena must indeed be discerning if the will of God is brought to bear in making a difference in our world.

As matured believers following Jesus Christ, we come to realize that while the world is fallen, i.e. corrupted and tainted by sin, it is still God's very creation and comes under His providence and dominion. Prayer and action should always go together. In Exodus 14:15, at the point where God is about to intervene by way of another miracle in delivering the Israelites from Egypt, Moses is instructed by God to "stop praying" and speak unto the children of Israel that they go forward. Too many of us are praying when we should be acting, and acting when we should be praying . . . . They are mutually complimentary. We are admonished that only those who "do the will of God shall enter the Kingdom of Heaven." (Matthew 7:21) Elsewhere we are admonished that we must be "doers of the word and not hearers only." (James 1:22)

Involvement or non-involvement in the political arena is an amoral concern. It is neither right nor wrong. It is a relative concern. The presence of the Christian Coalition has to be reckoned with whether we agree with their agenda or not. Had there been no Dr. Martin Luther King, Jr., African Americans would not be where we are today in American life. Dr. King viewed his commitment to civil rights as a divine calling and changed the face of a nation. Indeed this is our Father's world and we have been placed in it to minister to it. Without the salt of our witness

11

and action in God's world, decay would destroy it. As lights in a fallen world we are to lead those in darkness to the Light of the world and serve as a sign to an unbelieving generation.

What is Leadership?

by Dr. Myles Munroe

Everyone has the capacity, potential and raw material to become a leader by the design of the Creator. However, it is a tragedy that most of the people on this planet will bury the leader trapped within them in the grave of a follower. In fact, many people die without ever knowing who they really were. This is because most of us are mere products of our environment, lacking the will to change, to develop and maximize our potential and become who we really are. How do you become the leader you were born to be? How do you know when you have become a leader?

As I stated before, becoming a leader isn't easy, but learning to lead is a lot easier than you think it is, because God created you with the capacity to lead. You were born to lead but you must become a leader, just as one may be born a male but must become a man.

Leaders today appear to be an endangered species and in many cases they are being replaced with managers rather than leaders. Others have mistaken being a leader with being a boss. However, it is difficult and perhaps impossible to become something you do not know or cannot define.

Therefore, in this chapter we are going to look at what a leader is, how you can begin your journey to becoming an effective leader and how to refine and further enhance your leadership capacity.

Not an Act of Man

The word "leader" is defined as one who guides by influence, or one who directs, by going before or along with. Regardless of title, you cannot be a leader without followers. In essence, a person who has subordinates but no followers, is not a leader. Subordinates who are not followers may be viewed as a resource to be managed, rather than followers to be led. Simply put, a leader is one who leads others to leadership. He leads himself first and by so doing, inspires others to follow him into leadership.

A leader is one who influences others to follow after him to a common cause or purpose, and possesses the character which inspires their confidence. At the same time, he is a confident servant. Ultimately, a leader is one who becomes himself fully and attempts to express that self totally.

What Makes a Leader

Leaders are not born, but made. Everyone has the capacity and potential to become a leader. But what makes one a leader, and are there distinct characteristics that are common to leadership? A careful study of the lives of effective leaders will reveal some basic ingredients that they all share. They include the following:

1. Purpose

The foundational key to becoming a leader is the discovering and capturing of a sense of purpose for your life. Purpose is the original intent, a reason for the creation or existence of a thing. Discovering personal purpose for your life, is finding reason and meaning for living.

The leader has a clear, guiding vision that engenders persistence and perseverance, even in the face of setbacks and failures. He possesses a strong sense of destiny and significance, with a deep love for life. In scripture, Jesus Christ and Paul had this ingredient and it served as a guiding force in their every action. Jesus stated, "For this cause [purpose] came I into the world." The apostle Paul declared in Philippians 3:13, "But this one thing I do."

2. Passion

A deep controlling desire that makes the leader's commitment to the guiding purpose a love affair with destiny. The leader loves what he does and loves doing it. His work is his life. Jesus expressed this when he stated, "My food is to do the will of my father."

You must have a deep guiding purpose, a clear vision for your life and a sense of significance. Life without purpose is a study in chaos and an exercise in frustration. Purpose provides the fuel for perseverance, persistence and passion.

3. Integrity

This involves self-knowledge, candor, and maturity. "Know thy self," is the inscription over the oracle of Delphi, and it is still the most difficult task any of us face. But until you truly know yourself, your strengths and weaknesses, what you want to do and why you want to do it, you cannot experience any significant success in life. The leader never lies to himself, especially about himself. He knows his flaws and his assets, and deals with them directly. A leader is his own raw material. The leader strives to discover his full potential. The leader is one who knows who he is and accepts himself as worthy and valuable.

Candor is the key to self-knowledge. Candor is based on honesty of thought and action, a steadfast devotion to principle, and fundamental soundness and wholeness. Every leader has a strong spiritual commitment in life. Maturity is also important because every leader needs to have experience and growth through following. He needs to learn to be dedicated, observant and capable of working with others. As a result, he can encourage these qualities in his followers. This ingredient of integrity is one key to becoming a leader.

4. Trust

Integrity is the basis of trust which is a product of leadership. It is the one quality that cannot be acquired; it must be earned. It is given by co-workers and followers; and, without it, the leader cannot function. Trust is a product of time and integrity.

Leaders are individuals whose characters have been tested, proven and established as being faithful and trustworthy. Trustworthiness is a product of character and competence, that is who you are and what you can do. Trustworthiness is the foundation of trust. To become an effective leader you must earn the trust and confidence of others.

5. Curiosity and Daring

To a leader, life is an adventure. Leaders are willing to challenge traditions, experiment with new ideas and explore. A leader is willing to take risks, step out in faith, try new things and challenge convention. He does not worry about failure, knowing he will learn from it.

15

It is important to note that none of the above ingredients are traits you were born with and cannot change. What is true for leaders is true for all of us; we are our own raw material. Only when we know what we're made of and what we want to be, can we begin to live effectively in spite of the challenges against us. Leaders are truly like courageous explorers. They have such a strong sense of purpose and security that they welcome the unknown.

It is vital for people to develop their own sense of themselves and their role in the world, and it is equally vital for them to try new things, to test themselves and their beliefs and principles. The world longs for people who will stand up for what they believe, even if they have to stand alone, because we have confidence in such people. The essence of becoming a leader is knowing and becoming yourself.

A leader is one who has his or her own value system and beliefs, not someone else's. Most people live their lives walking around in borrowed postures, spouting secondhand ideas, trying desperately to fit in rather than to stand out. True leaders are inwardly directed, self-assured, and as a result truly charismatic. To become a leader, you must know and become yourself. Knowing yourself means separating who you are and who you want to be from what the world thinks you are and wants you to be. No one can teach you how to become yourself and to fully express yourself except you.

To become the leader you were born to be, you must discover who you are, find your purpose in life and understand God's design for your existence Nothing is truly yours until you understand it; not even yourself. When you understand, then you know what to do.

This is the distinctive mark of leaders. Therefore, the ingredients of leadership cannot be taught, they must be learned, and the capacity to learn resides within you.

No true leader sets out to become a leader. They are simply people who live their lives and express themselves fully. When that expression is one of value, they become leaders. So the point is not to become a leader. The point is to become yourself, to use yourself completely and to use and maximize all your skills, gifts, energies and anointing in order to make your vision and purpose in life a reality.

Leaders are more concerned with expressing themselves, than with proving themselves. It is this full expression that brings glory to God. It is in this light that everyone can become a leader, and it is important that you strive to discover who you are and God's purpose for your life.

16

An Irish proverb says, "You've got to do your own growing, no matter how tall your grandfather is." God created you separate, unique, special and original. Discover and be yourself, and become a leader.

Leaders, not Managers

In any discussion on the subject of leadership and any attempt to define it, it would be essential that we also distinguish the difference between a "manager" and a "leader." It is important that these concepts are understood because there are many situations where managers have been mistaken for leaders and placed in positions in which they are unable to function and perform, thus frustrating the organization and its' objectives.

This difference can be expressed in the saying, "There are four types of people in the world: those who watch things happen, those who let things happen, those who ask what happened and those who make things happen." Leaders are those who make things happen. Managers are in the other groups. Leaders are those who master the context, managers are those who surrender to it. *All leaders were managers on their way to leadership.* It is the natural path of progression. However, not all managers become leaders.

Jesus speaks of this difference in responsibility in his discourse on the role of a manager in Luke 16. He tells the story of a manager who failed to fulfill his responsibility and was unable to account for his time and resources. In this parable, Jesus states a principle that stresses the conditions of transition from manager to leader. Luke 16:10 and 12 states, "Whoever can be trusted with very little can also be trusted with much, and whoever is dishonest with very little will also be dishonest with much. And if you have not been trustworthy with someone else's property, who will give you property of your own?"

Warren Bennis, professor of Business Administration at the University of California, in his book on leadership recorded some of these differences, and they are enormous and crucial. Study the list below and check your leadership state:

- The manager administers, the leader innovates.
- The manager is a copy, the leader is an original.
- The manager maintains, the leader develops.
- The manager focuses on systems and structure, the leader focuses on people.
- The manager relies on control, the leader inspires trust.

- The manager has a short range view, the leader has a long range perspective.
- The manager asks how and when, the leader ask what and why.
- The manager has his eyes on the bottom line, the leader has his eyes on the horizon.
- The manager imitates, the leader originates.
- The manager accepts the status quo, the leader challenges it.
- The manager is the classical good soldier, the leader is his own person.
- The manager does things right, the leader does the right thing.

Leaders are individuals who have declared independence from the expectations of others and have determined to be true to themselves in the face of a society who wants to homogenize them. If you are to become the leader God intended you to be, then it is necessary to challenge the opinion of others and defy the social straight-jacket that stifles the untapped leader within.

Remember, leadership depends on the ability to make people want to follow voluntarily. They are not made by corporate courses, any more than they are made by college courses. They are made by experience. A true leader is one who discovers himself, his purpose for living and commits to exploring and expressing himself fully to the glory of God. Simply put, a *leader is one who deploys himself and by so doing, inspires others to do the same.*

Therefore, a true leader is more concerned with deployment rather than employment. He does not attempt to clone people or make everyone else over in his image. His deep desire is to help them discover themselves and deploy their abilities, talents, gifts and potential. To him, as long as people have the same goals, it is not important that they have the same personality. The basic function of the leader is to provide an environment that fosters mutual respect and builds a complementary, cohesive team, where each unique strength is made productive and each weakness is made irrelevant.

THE MINISTER'S RELATIONSHIP WITH GOD

Fellowship with God

But the hour cometh, and now is, when the true worshippers shall worship the Father in spirit and in truth: for the Father seeketh such to worship him. God is a Spirit: and they that worship him must worship him in spirit and in truth. John 4:23-24

Let us come before his presence with thanksgiving, and make a joyful noise unto him with psalms. Psalms 95:2

Enter into his gates with thanksgiving, and into his courts with praise: be thankful unto him, and bless his name. Psalms 100:4

For through him we both have access by one Spirit unto the Father.
Ephesians 2:18

In whom we have boldness and access with confidence by the faith of him. Ephesians 3:12

> *God has no favorites but He does have intimates.*
> *- Vance Havner*

Let us therefore come boldly unto the throne of grace, that we may obtain mercy, and find grace to help in time of need. Hebrews 4:16

Having therefore, brethren, boldness to enter into the holiest by the blood of Jesus. Hebrews 10:19

Behold, I stand at the door, and knock: if any man hear my voice, and open the door, I will come in to him, and will sup with him, and he with me. Revelation 3:20

Praising God

I will praise the Lord according to his righteousness: and will sing praise to the name of the Lord most high. Psalms 7:17

19

The Lord is my strength and my shield; my heart trusted in him, and I am helped: therefore my heart greatly rejoiceth; and with my song will I praise him. Psalms 28:7

I will bless the Lord at all times: his praise shall continually be in my mouth. Psalms 34:1

And my tongue shall speak of thy righteousness and of thy praise all the day long. Psalms 35:28

In God we boast all the day long, and praise thy name for ever. Selah.
Psalms 44:8

Great is the Lord, and greatly to be praised in the city of our God, in the mountain of his holiness. Psalms 48:1

O Lord, open thou my lips; and my mouth shall shew forth thy praise.
Psalms 51:15

In God I will praise his word, in God I have put my trust; I will not fear what flesh can do unto me. Psalms 56:4

In God will I praise his word: in the Lord will I praise his word.
Psalms 56:10

My heart is fixed, O God, my heart is fixed: I will sing and give praise.
Psalms 57:7

So will I sing praise unto thy name for ever, that I may daily perform my vows. Psalms 61:8

Because thy lovingkindness is better than life, my lips shall praise thee.
Psalms 63:3

Make a joyful noise unto God, all ye lands: Sing forth the honour of his name: make his praise glorious. Psalms 66:1-2

Let the people praise thee, O God; let all the people praise thee.
Psalms 67:3

Sing unto God, ye kingdoms of the earth; O sing praises unto the Lord; Selah. Psalms 68:32

I will praise the name of God with a song, and will magnify him with thanksgiving. Psalms 69:30

A good leader not only knows where he is going, but he can inspire others to go with him.

Let the heaven and earth praise him, the seas, and everything that moveth therein. Psalms 69:34

Let my mouth be filled with thy praise and with thy honour all the day.
Psalms 71:8

But I will hope continually, and will yet praise thee more and more.
Psalms 71:14

I will praise thee, O Lord my God, with all my heart: and I will glorify thy name for evermore. Psalms 86:12

And the heavens shall praise thy wonders, O Lord: thy faithfulness also in the congregation of the saints. Psalms 89:5

It is a good thing to give thanks unto the Lord, and to sing praises unto thy name, O most High: To shew forth thy lovingkindness in the morning, and thy faithfulness every night, Upon an instrument of ten strings, and upon the psaltery; upon the harp with a solemn sound. For the Lord is great, and greatly to be praised: he is to be feared above all gods.
Psalms 92:1-4

Make a joyful noise unto the Lord, all the earth: make a loud noise, and rejoice, and sing praise. Psalms 98:4

Make a joyful noise unto the Lord, all ye lands. Serve the Lord with gladness: come before his presence with singing. Psalms 100:1-2

Enter into his gates with thanksgiving, and into his courts with praise: be thankful unto him, and bless his name. For the Lord is good; his mercy is everlasting; and his truth endureth to all generations. Psalms 100:4-5

O God, my heart is fixed; I will sing and give praise, even with my glory. Awake, psaltery and harp: I myself will awake early. I will praise thee, O Lord, among the people: and I will sing praises unto thee among the nations. Psalms 108:1-3

Praise ye the Lord. I will praise the Lord with my whole heart, in the assembly of the upright, and in the congregation. Psalms 111:1

Praise ye the Lord. Praise, O ye servants of the Lord, praise the name of the Lord. Blessed be the name of the Lord from this time forth and for evermore. From the rising of the sun unto the going down of the same the Lord's name is to be praised. Psalms 113:1-3

O praise the Lord, all ye nations: praise him, all ye people. For his merciful kindness is great toward us: and the truth of the Lord endureth for ever. Praise ye the Lord. Psalms 117:1-2

Thou art my God, and I will praise thee: thou art my God, I will exalt thee. O give thanks unto the Lord; for he is good: for his mercy endureth for ever. Psalms 118:28-29

I will praise thee with uprightness of heart, when I shall have learned thy righteous judgments. Psalms 119:7

Seven times a day do I praise thee because of thy righteous judgments. Psalms 119:164

Praise the Lord; for the Lord is good: sing praises unto his name; for it is pleasant. Psalms 135:3

I will praise thee with my whole heart: before the gods will I sing praise unto thee. I will worship toward thy holy temple, and praise thy name for thy lovingkindness and for thy truth: for thou hast magnified thy word above all thy name. Psalms 138:1-2

All the kings of the earth shall praise thee, O Lord, when they hear the words of thy mouth. Psalms 138:4

Great is the Lord, and greatly to be praised; and his greatness is unsearchable. Psalms 145:3

Praise ye the Lord: for it is good to sing praises unto our God; for it is pleasant; and praise is comely. Psalms 147:1

Praise ye the Lord. Praise ye the Lord from the heavens: praise him in the heights. Praise ye him, all his angels: praise ye him, all his hosts. Praise ye him, sun and moon: praise him, all ye stars of light. Praise him, ye heavens of heavens, and ye waters that be above the heavens. Let them praise the name of the Lord: for he commanded, and they were created. He hath also stablished them for ever and ever: he hath made a decree which shall not pass. Praise the Lord from the earth, ye dragons, and all deeps: Fire, and hail; snow, and vapour; stormy wind fulfilling his word: Mountains, and all hills; fruitful trees, and all cedars: Beasts, and all cattle; creeping things, and flying fowl: Kings of the earth, and all people; princes, and all judges of the earth: Both young men, and maidens; old men, and children: Let them praise the name of the Lord: for his name alone is excellent; his glory is above the earth and heaven. Psalms 148:1-13

Praise ye the Lord. Praise God in his sanctuary: praise him in the firmament of his power. Praise him for his mighty acts: praise him according to his excellent greatness. Praise him with the sound of the trumpet: praise him with the psaltery and harp. Praise him with the timbrel and dance: praise him with stringed instruments and organs. Praise him upon the loud cymbals: praise him upon the high sounding cymbals. Let every thing that hath breath praise the Lord. Praise ye the Lord.

Psalms 150:1-6

O Lord, thou art my God; I will exalt thee, I will praise thy name; for thou hast done wonderful things; thy counsels of old are faithfulness and truth. Isaiah 25:1

To appoint unto them that mourn in Zion, to give unto them beauty for ashes, the oil of joy for mourning, the garment of praise for the spirit of heaviness; that they might be called trees of righteousness, the planting of the Lord, that he might be glorified. Isaiah 61:3

And said unto him, Hearest thou what these say? And Jesus saith unto them, Yea; have ye never read, Out of the mouth of babes and sucklings thou hast perfected praise? Matthew 21:16

By him therefore let us offer the sacrifice of praise to God continually, that is, the fruit of our lips giving thanks to his name. Hebrews 13:15

And a voice came out of the throne, saying, Praise our God, all ye his servants, and ye that fear him, both small and great. Revelation 19:5

Worshipping God

For thou shalt worship no other god: for the Lord, whose name is Jealous, is a jealous God. Exodus 34:14

Thou, even thou, art Lord alone; thou hast made heaven, the heaven of heavens, with all their host, the earth, and all things that are therein, the seas, and all that is therein, and thou preservest them all; and the host of heaven worshippeth thee. Nehemiah 9:6

All the ends of the world shall remember and turn unto the Lord: and all the kindreds of the nations shall worship before thee. Psalms 22:27

Give unto the Lord the glory due unto his name; worship the Lord in the beauty of holiness. Psalms 29:2

So shall the king greatly desire thy beauty: for he is thy Lord; and worship thou him. Psalms 45:11

All the earth shall worship thee, and shall sing unto thee; they shall sing to thy name. Selah. Psalms 66:4

All nations whom thou hast made shall come and worship before thee, O Lord; and shall glorify thy name. Psalms 86:9

O come, let us worship and bow down: let us kneel before the Lord our maker. Psalms 95:6

Exalt ye the Lord our God, and worship at his footstool; for he is holy.
Psalms 99:5

Exalt the Lord our God, and worship at his holy hill; for the Lord our God is holy. Psalms 99:9

We will go into his tabernacles: we will worship at his footstool.
Psalms 132:7

I will worship toward thy holy temple, and praise thy name for thy lovingkindness and for thy truth: for thou hast magnified thy word above all thy name. Psalms 138:2

Saying, Where is he that is born King of the Jews? for we have seen his star in the east, and are come to worship him. Matthew 2:2

Then saith Jesus unto him, Get thee hence, Satan: for it is written, Thou shalt worship the Lord thy God, and him only shalt thou serve.
Matthew 4:10

And as they went to tell his disciples, behold, Jesus met them, saying, All hail. And they came and held him by the feet, and worshipped him.
Matthew 28:9

And when they saw him, they worshipped him: but some doubted.
Matthew 28:17

But when he saw Jesus afar off, he ran and worshipped him. Mark 5:6

But the hour cometh, and now is, when the true worshippers shall worship the Father in spirit and in truth: for the Father seeketh such to worship him. God is a Spirit: and they that worship him must worship him in spirit and in truth. John 4:23-24

Now we know that God heareth not sinners: but if any man be a worshipper of God, and doeth his will, him he heareth. John 9:31

For we are the circumcision, which worship God in the spirit, and rejoice in Christ Jesus, and have no confidence in the flesh. Philippians 3:3

The four and twenty elders fall down before him that sat on the throne, and worship him that liveth for ever and ever, and cast their crowns be-

---

A true leader is a model for his followers.

fore the throne, saying, Thou art worthy, O Lord, to receive glory and honour and power: for thou hast created all things, and for thy pleasure they are and were created. Revelation 4:10-11

And the four beasts said, Amen. And the four and twenty elders fell down and worshipped him that liveth for ever and ever. Revelation 5:14

Our Lord approved neither idol worship or idle worship but ideal worship in Spirit and truth. - Vance Havner

And all the angels stood round about the throne, and about the elders and the four beasts, and fell before the throne on their faces, and worshipped God, Saying, Amen: Blessing, and glory, and wisdom, and thanksgiving, and honour, and power, and might, be unto our God for ever and ever. Amen. Revelation 7:11-12

And the four and twenty elders, which sat before God on their seats, fell upon their faces, and worshipped God. Revelation 11:16

Saying with a loud voice, Fear God, and give glory to him; for the hour of his judgment is come: and worship him that made heaven, and earth, and the sea, and the fountains of waters. Revelation 14:7

Fear of the Lord

The fear of the Lord is clean, enduring for ever: the judgments of the Lord are true and righteous altogether. Psalms 19:9

The fear of the Lord is the beginning of wisdom: a good understanding have all they that do his commandments: his praise endureth for ever.
Psalms 111:10

Then shalt thou understand the fear of the Lord, and find the knowledge of God. Proverbs 2:5

The fear of the Lord is the beginning of wisdom: and the knowledge of the holy is understanding. Proverbs 9:10

The fear of the Lord prolongeth days: but the years of the wicked shall be shortened. Proverbs 10:27

I fear God, yet I am not afraid of him. - Thomas Browne

In the fear of the Lord is strong confidence: and his children shall have a place of refuge. The fear of the Lord is a fountain of life, to depart from the snares of death. Proverbs 14:26-27

The fear of the Lord is the instruction of wisdom; and before honour is humility. Proverbs 15:33

The fear of the Lord is to hate evil: pride, and arrogancy, and the evil way, and the froward mouth, do I hate. Proverbs 8:13

Better is little with the fear of the Lord than great treasure and trouble therewith. Proverbs 15:16

By mercy and truth iniquity is purged: and by the fear of the Lord men depart from evil. Proverbs 16:6

The fear of the Lord tendeth to life: and he that hath it shall abide satisfied; he shall not be visited with evil. Proverbs 19:23

By humility and the fear of the Lord are riches, and honour, and life.
Proverbs 22:4

Having therefore these promises, dearly beloved, let us cleanse ourselves from all filthiness of the flesh and spirit, perfecting holiness in the fear of God. 2 Corinthians 7:1

Let not thine heart envy sinners: but be thou in the fear of the Lord all the day long. Proverbs 23:17

> *To fear God is to stand in awe of him; to be afraid of God is to run away from him. - Carroll E. Simcox*

Trusting God

The God of my rock; in him will I trust: he is my shield, and the horn of my salvation, my high tower, and my refuge, my saviour; thou savest me from violence. 2 Samuel 22:3

As for God, his way is perfect; the word of the Lord is tried: he is a buckler to all them that trust in him. 2 Samuel 22:31

Wilt thou trust him, because his strength is great? or wilt thou leave thy labour to him? Job 39:11

Offer the sacrifices of righteousness, and put your trust in the Lord.
Psalms 4:5

But let all those that put their trust in thee rejoice: let them ever shout for joy, because thou defendest them: let them also that love thy name be joyful in thee. Psalms 5:11

O Lord my God, in thee do I put my trust: save me from all them that persecute me, and deliver me. Psalms 7:1

And they that know thy name will put their trust in thee: for thou, Lord, hast not forsaken them that seek thee. Psalms 9:10

But I have trusted in thy mercy; my heart shall rejoice in thy salvation. Psalms 13:5

Preserve me, O God: for in thee do I put my trust. Psalms 16:1

We do not usually learn that Christ is all we need until we reach that place where He is all we have! - Vance Havner

The Lord is my rock, and my fortress, and my deliverer; my God, my strength, in whom I will trust; my buckler, and the horn of my salvation, and my high tower. Psalms 18:2

As for God, his way is perfect: the word of the Lord is tried: he is a buckler to all those that trust in him. Psalms 18:30

Judge me, O Lord; for I have walked in mine integrity: I have trusted also in the Lord; therefore I shall not slide. Psalms 26:1

The Lord is my strength and my shield; my heart trusted in him, and I am helped: therefore my heart greatly rejoiceth; and with my song will I praise him. Psalms 28:7

In thee, O Lord, do I put my trust; let me never be ashamed: deliver me in thy righteousness. Psalms 31:1

Many sorrows shall be to the wicked: but he that trusteth in the Lord, mercy shall compass him about. Psalms 32:10

O taste and see that the Lord is good: blessed is the man that trusteth in him. Psalms 34:8

Trust in the Lord, and do good; so shalt thou dwell in the land, and verily thou shalt be fed. Psalms 37:3

Commit thy way unto the Lord; trust also in him; and he shall bring it to pass. Psalms 37:5

Jesus does not say, "There is no storm." He says, "I am here, do not toss but trust." - Vance Havner

Blessed is that man that maketh the Lord his trust, and respecteth not the proud, nor such as turn aside to lies. Psalms 40:4

But I am like a green olive tree in the house of God: I trust in the mercy of God for ever and ever. Psalms 52:8

What time I am afraid, I will trust in thee. Psalms 56:3

Trust in him at all times; ye people, pour out your heart before him: God is a refuge for us. Selah. Psalms 62:8

In thee, O Lord, do I put my trust: let me never be put to confusion.
Psalms 71:1

I will say of the Lord, He is my refuge and my fortress: my God; in him will I trust. Psalms 91:2

They that trust in the Lord shall be as mount Zion, which cannot be removed, but abideth for ever. Psalms 125:1

Trust in the Lord with all thine heart; and lean not unto thine own understanding. Proverbs 3:5

Behold, God is my salvation; I will trust, and not be afraid: for the Lord Jehovah is my strength and my song; he also is become my salvation.
Isaiah 12:2

Faith in God and His Word

1. Great Faith

But Jesus turned him about, and when he saw her, he said, Daughter, be of good comfort; thy faith hath made thee whole. And the woman was made whole from that hour. Matthew 9:22

Then Jesus answered and said unto her, O woman, great is thy faith: be it unto thee even as thou wilt. And her daughter was made whole from that very hour. Matthew 15:28

And he said unto her, Daughter, thy faith hath made thee whole; go in peace, and be whole of thy plague. Mark 5:34

When Jesus heard these things, he marvelled at him, and turned him about, and said unto the people that followed him, I say unto you, I have not found so great faith, no, not in Israel. Luke 7:9

And he said unto them, Where is your faith? And they being afraid wondered, saying one to another, What manner of man is this! for he commandeth even the winds and water, and they obey him. Luke 8:25

As it is written, I have made thee a father of many nations, before him whom he believed, even God, who quickeneth the dead, and calleth those

Great leaders never desire to lead but to serve.

things which be not as though they were. Who against hope believed in hope, that he might become the father of many nations; according to that which was spoken, So shall thy seed be. And being not weak in faith, he considered not his own body now dead, when he was about an hundred years old, neither yet the deadness of Sara's womb: He staggered not at the promise of God through unbelief; but was strong in faith, giving glory to God; And being fully persuaded that, what he had promised, he was able also to perform. Romans 4:17-21

Through faith also Sara herself received strength to conceive seed, and was delivered of a child when she was past age, because she judged him faithful who had promised. Therefore sprang there even of one, and him as good as dead, so many as the stars of the sky in multitude, and as the sand which is by the sea shore innumerable. These all died in faith, not having received the promises, but having seen them afar off, and were persuaded of them, and embraced them, and confessed that they were strangers and pilgrims on the earth. Hebrews 11:11-13

2. Principles of Faith

For verily I say unto you, If ye have faith as a grain of mustard seed, ye shall say unto this mountain, Remove hence to yonder place; and it shall remove; and nothing shall be impossible unto you. Matthew 17:20

And Jesus answering saith unto them, Have faith in God. For verily I say unto you, That whosoever shall say unto this mountain, Be thou removed, and be thou cast into the sea; and shall not doubt in his heart, but shall believe that those things which he saith shall come to pass; he shall have whatsoever he saith. Therefore I say unto you, What things soever ye desire, when ye pray, believe that ye receive them, and ye shall have them. Mark 11:22-24

Then saith he to Thomas, reach hither thy finger, and behold my hands; and reach hither thy hand, and thrust it into my side: and be not faithless, but believing. John 20:27

Jesus saith unto him, Thomas, because thou hast seen me, thou hast believed: blessed are they that have not seen, and yet have believed.
John 20:29

And he that doubteth is damned if he eat, because he eateth not of faith: for whatsoever is not of faith is sin. Romans 14:23

While we look not at the things which are seen, but at the things which are not seen: for the things which are seen are temporal; but the things which are not seen are eternal. 2 Corinthians 4:18

29

For we walk by faith, not by sight. 2 Corinthians 5:7

Let us hold fast the profession of our faith without wavering; for he is faithful that promised. Hebrews 10:23

Now faith is the substance of things hoped for, the evidence of things not seen. Hebrews 11:1

Through faith we understand that the worlds were framed by the word of God, so that things which are seen were not made of things which do appear. Hebrews 11:3

Knowing this, that the trying of your faith worketh patience. James 1:3

Whom having not seen, ye love; in whom, though now ye see him not, yet believing, ye rejoice with joy unspeakable and full of glory. Receiving the end of your faith, even the salvation of your souls. 1 Peter 1:8-9

> *Nothing is more disastrous than to study faith, analyze faith, make noble resolves of faith, but never actually make the leap of faith. - Vance Havner*

3. Faith in Action

But let him ask in faith, nothing wavering. For he that wavereth is like a wave of the sea driven with the wind and tossed. For let not that man think that he shall receive any thing of the Lord. A double minded man is unstable in all his ways. James 1:6-8

What doth it profit, my brethren, though a man say he hath faith, and have not works? can faith save him? If a brother or sister be naked, and destitute of daily food, And one of you say unto them, Depart in peace, be ye warmed and filled; notwithstanding ye give them not those things which are needful to the body; what doth it profit? Even so faith, if it hath not works, is dead, being alone. Yea, a man may say, Thou hast faith, and I have works: shew me thy faith without thy works, and I will shew thee my faith by my works. Thou believest that there is one God; thou doest well: the devils also believe, and tremble. But wilt thou know, O vain man, that faith without works is dead? Was not Abraham our father justified by works, when he had offered Isaac his son upon the altar? Seest thou how faith wrought with his works, and by works was faith made perfect? And the scripture was fulfilled which saith, Abraham

---

Leadership has very little to do with what you do and is fundamentally a matter of becoming who you are.

---

believed God, and it was imputed unto him for righteousness: and he was called the Friend of God. Ye see then how that by works a man is justified, and not by faith only. Likewise also was not Rahab the harlot justified by works, when she had received the messengers, and had sent them out another way? For as the body without the spirit is dead, so faith without works is dead also. James 2:14-26

> *It's not how much you know, but it is what you do with what you know. - Ramiro Angulo*

Now in the morning as he returned into the city, he hungered. And when he saw a fig tree in the way, he came to it, and found nothing thereon, but leaves only, and said unto it, Let no fruit grow on thee henceforward for ever. And presently the fig tree withered away. And when the disciples saw it, they marvelled, saying, How soon is the fig tree withered away!
Matthew 21:18-20

And seeing a fig tree afar off having leaves, he came, if haply he might find any thing thereon: and when he came to it, he found nothing but leaves; for the time of figs was not yet. And Jesus answered and said unto it, No man eat fruit of thee hereafter for ever. And his disciples heard it. Mark 11:13-14

And in the morning, as they passed by, they saw the fig tree dried up from the roots. And Peter calling to remembrance saith unto him, Master, behold, the fig tree which thou cursedst is withered away.
Mark 11:20-21

Above all, taking the shield of faith, wherewith ye shall be able to quench all the fiery darts of the wicked. Ephesians 6:16

Fight the good fight of faith, lay hold on eternal life, whereunto thou art also called, and hast professed a good profession before many witnesses.
1 Timothy 6:12

But whoso hath this world's good, and seeth his brother have need, and shutteth up his bowels of compassion from him, how dwelleth the love of God in him? My little children, let us not love in word, neither in tongue; but in deed and in truth. 1 John 3:17-18

4. A Lifestyle of Faith

For therein is the righteousness of God revealed from faith to faith: as it is written, The just shall live by faith. Romans 1:17

31

But that no man is justified by the law in the sight of God, it is evident: for, The just shall live by faith. Galatians 3:11

Now the just shall live by faith: but if any man draw back, my soul shall have no pleasure in him. Hebrews 10:38

5. Through Faith

By whom also we have access by faith into this grace wherein we stand, and rejoice in hope of the glory of God. Romans 5:2

For by grace are ye saved through faith; and that not of yourselves: it is the gift of God. Ephesians 2:8

That the blessing of Abraham might come on the Gentiles through Jesus Christ; that we might receive the promise of the Spirit through faith.
Galatians 3:14

6. Obtaining Faith

Looking unto Jesus the author and finisher of our faith; who for the joy that was set before him endured the cross, despising the shame, and is set down at the right hand of the throne of God. Hebrews 12:2

So then faith cometh by hearing, and hearing by the word of God.
Romans 10:17

For I say, through the grace given unto me, to every man that is among you, not to think of himself more highly than he ought to think; but to think soberly, according as God hath dealt to every man the measure of faith. Romans 12:3

We having the same spirit of faith, according as it is written, I believed, and therefore have I spoken; we also believe, and therefore speak.
2 Corinthians 4:13

7. According to Your Faith

Then touched he their eyes, saying, According to your faith be it unto you. Matthew 9:29

Then Jesus answered and said unto her, O woman, great is thy faith: be it unto thee even as thou wilt. And her daughter was made whole from that very hour. Matthew 15:28

And he said unto her, Daughter, thy faith hath made thee whole; go in peace, and be whole of thy plague. Mark 5:34

And Jesus said unto him, Go thy way; thy faith hath made thee whole. And immediately he received his sight, and followed Jesus in the way.
Mark 10:52

8. Doubt and Unbelief

a. Examples of Doubt and Unbelief

And he could there do no mighty work, save that he laid his hands upon a few sick fold, and healed them. And he marvelled because of their unbelief. And he went round about the villages, teaching.
Mark 6:5-6

He staggered not at the promise of God through unbelief; but was strong in faith, giving glory to God; Romans 4:20

Well; because of unbelief they were broken off, and thou standest by faith. Be not highminded, but fear: Romans 11:20

That is true. But they were broken (pruned) off because of their unbelief—their lack of real faith, and you are established through faith—because you do believe. So do not become proud and conceited, but rather stand in awe and be reverently afraid. Romans 11:20 AMP

> *Negative, uncertain, doubtful living poisons the body, mind, and spirit; fills insane asylums, penitentiaries, graves, and hell itself. - Vance Havner*

Take heed, brethren, lest there be in any of you an evil heart of unbelief, in departing from the living God. Hebrews 3:12

[Therefore beware,] brethren; take care lest there be in any one of you a wicked, unbelieving heart—which refuses to cleave to, trust in and rely on Him—leading you to turn away and desert or stand aloof from the living God. Hebrews 3:12 AMP

The only limit to our realization of tomorrow will be our doubts of today. Let us move forward with strong and active faith.
- Franklin D. Roosevelt

b. Doubt and Unbelief Stop the Power of God in Your Life

And he did not many mighty works there because of their unbelief.
Matthew 13:58

And Jesus rebuked the devil; and he departed out of him: and the child was cured from that very hour. Then came the disciples to Jesus apart, and said, Why could not we cast him out? And Jesus said unto them, Because of your unbelief: for verily I say unto you, If ye have faith as a grain of mustard seed, ye shall say unto this mountain, Remove hence to yonder place; and it shall remove; and nothing shall be impossible unto you. Matthew 17:18-20

So we see that they could not enter in because of unbelief.
Hebrews 3:19

So we see that they were not able to enter [into His rest] because of their unwillingness to adhere to and trust and rely on God— unbelief had shut them out. Hebrews 3:19 AMP

Doubt's number one tactic is to invade your mind with thoughts and imaginations that are contrary to the Word of God or to your prayer of faith. Resist doubt every time it comes to you and audibly confess God's Word.

c. Doubt and Unbelief Frustrate God

Afterward he appeared unto the eleven as they sat at meat, and upbraided them with their unbelief and hardness of heart, because they believed not them which had seen him after he was risen. Mark 16:14

If then God so clothe the grass, which is to day in the field, and to morrow is cast into the oven; how much more will he clothe you, O ye of little faith? And seek not ye what ye shall eat, or what ye shall drink, neither be ye of doubtful mind. Luke 12:28-29

But let him ask in faith, nothing wavering. For he that wavereth is like a wave of the sea driven with the wind and tossed. For let not that man think that he shall receive any thing of the Lord. A double minded man is unstable in all his ways. James 1:6-8

Leaders are simply people who dare to be themselves and are able to express themselves fully.

Only it must be in faith that he asks, with no wavering—no hesitating, no doubting. For the one who wavers (hesitates, doubts) is like the billowing surge out at sea, that is blown hither and thither and tossed by the wind. For truly, let not such a person imagine that he will receive anything [he asks for] from the Lord, [For being as he is] a man of two minds—hesitating, dubious, irresolute—[he is] unstable and unreliable and uncertain about everything (he thinks, feels, decides). James 1:6-8 AMP

And immediately Jesus stretched forth his hand, and caught him, and said unto him, O thou of little faith, wherefore didst thou doubt?

Matthew 14:31

The Will of God

1. Obedience to God's Will (God's Word)

For whosoever shall do the will of God, the same is my brother, and my sister, and mother. Mark 3:35

For whosoever shall do the will of my Father which is in heaven, the same is my brother, and sister, and mother. Matthew 12:50

And that servant, which knew his lord's will, and prepared not himself, neither did according to his will, shall be beaten with many stripes.

Luke 12:47

If any man will do his will, he shall know of the doctrine, whether it be of God, or whether I speak of myself. John 7:17

Now we know that God heareth not sinners: but if any man be a worshipper of God, and doeth his will, him he heareth. John 9:31

Not with eyeservice, as menpleasers; but as the servants of Christ, doing the will of God from the heart; Ephesians 6:6

For ye have need of patience, that, after ye have done the will of God, ye might receive the promise. Hebrews 10:36

And the world passeth away, and the lust thereof: but he that doeth the will of God abideth for ever. 1 John 2:17

2. Praying in Agreement With His Will

And this is the confidence that we have in him, that, if we ask any thing according to his will, he heareth us: And if we know that he hear us,

35

whatsoever we ask, we know that we have the petitions that we desired of him. 1 John 5:14-15

Prayer is not overcoming God's reluctance: it is laying hold of His highest willingness. - Richard Chenevix

And he that searcheth the hearts knoweth what is the mind of the Spirit, because he maketh intercession for the saints according to the will of God. Romans 8:27

But I know, that even now, whatsoever thou wilt ask of God, God will give it thee. John 11:22

3. Submitting to God's Will

And he went a little further, and fell on his face, and prayed, saying, O my Father, if it be possible, let this cup pass from me: nevertheless not as I will, but as thou wilt. Matthew 26:39

Thy kingdom come. Thy will be done in earth, as it is in heaven.
Matthew 6:10

And he said to them all, If any man will come after me, let him deny himself, and take up his cross daily, and follow me. Luke 9:23

And be not conformed to this world: but be ye transformed by the renewing of your mind, that ye may prove what is that good, and acceptable, and perfect, will of God. Romans 12:2

And this they did, not as we hoped, but first gave their own selves to the Lord, and unto us by the will of God. 2 Corinthians 8:5

Who gave himself for our sins, that he might deliver us from this present evil world, according to the will of God and our Father: Galatians 1:4

For it is God which worketh in you both to will and to do of his good pleasure. Philippians 2:13

Epaphras, who is one of you, a servant of Christ, saluteth you, always labouring fervently for you in prayers, that ye may stand perfect and complete in all the will of God. Colossians 4:12

For this is the will of God, even your sanctification, that ye should abstain from fornication: 1 Thessalonians 4:3

Rejoice evermore. **Pray** without ceasing. **In** every thing give thanks: for this is the will of God in Christ Jesus concerning you.
1 Thessalonians 5:16-18

For so is the will of God, that with well doing ye may put to silence the ignorance of foolish men: 1 Peter 2:15

In His will is our peace. - Dante Alighieri

That he no longer should live the rest of his time in the flesh to the lusts of men, but to the will of God. 1 Peter 4:2

Wherefore let them that suffer according to the will of God commit the keeping of their souls to him in well doing, as unto a faithful Creator.

1 Peter 4:19

The Lord is not slack concerning his promise, as some men count slackness; but is longsuffering to us-ward, not willing that any should perish, but that all should come to repentance. 2 Peter 3:9

4. God is Willing to Bless, Heal and Save You

But I know, that even now, whatsoever thou wilt ask of God, God will give it thee. John 11:22

And Jesus answered and said unto him, What wilt thou that I should do unto thee? The blind man said unto him, Lord, that I might receive my sight. And Jesus said unto him, Go thy way; thy faith hath made thee whole. And immediately he received his sight, and followed Jesus in the way. Mark 10:51-52

And it came to pass, when he was in a certain city, behold a man full of leprosy: who seeing Jesus fell on his face, and besought him, saying, Lord, if thou wilt, thou canst make me clean. And he put forth his hand, and touched him, saying, I will; be thou clean. And immediately the leprosy departed him. Luke 5:12-13

Wherein God, willing more abundantly to shew unto the heirs of promise the immutability of his counsel, confirmed it by an oath:

Hebrews 6:17

The Lord is not slack concerning his promise, as some men count slackness; but is longsuffering to us-ward, not willing that any should perish, but that all should come to repentance. 2 Peter 3:9

THE MINISTER IN RELATIONSHIPS

Family of God

For as many as are led by the Spirit of God, they are the sons of God. For ye have not received the spirit of bondage again to fear; but ye have received the Spirit of adoption, whereby we cry, Abba, Father. The Spirit itself beareth witness with our spirit, that we are the children of God: And if children, then heirs; heirs of God, and joint-heirs with Christ; if so be that we suffer with him, that we may be also glorified together.

Romans 8:14-17

And will be a Father unto you, and ye shall be my sons and daughters, saith the Lord Almighty. 2 Corinthians 6:18

And because ye are sons, God hath sent forth the Spirit of his Son into your hearts, crying, Abba, Father. Wherefore thou art no more a servant, but a son; and if a son, then an heir of God through Christ.

Galatians 4:6-7

Having predestinated us unto the adoption of children by Jesus Christ to himself, according to the good pleasure of his will, Ephesians 1:5

For this cause I bow my knees unto the Father of our Lord Jesus Christ, Of whom the whole family in heaven and earth is named,

Ephesians 3:14-15

But ye are a chosen generation, a royal priesthood, an holy nation, a peculiar people; that ye should shew forth the praises of him who hath called you out of darkness into his marvellous light. 1 Peter 2:9

Angels

1. Angels Protect the Children of God

And when the morning arose, then the angels hastened Lot, saying, Arise, take thy wife, and thy two daughters, which are here; lest thou be consumed in the iniquity of the city. And while he lingered, the men laid hold upon his hand, and upon the hand of his wife, and upon the hand of his two daughters; the Lord being merciful unto him: and they brought him forth, and set him without the city. Genesis 19:15-16

For he shall give his angels charge over thee, to keep thee in all thy ways. Psalms 91:11

And saith unto him, If thou be the Son of God, cast thyself down: for it is written, He shall give his angels charge concerning thee: and in their hands they shall bear thee up, lest at any time thou dash thy foot against a stone. Matthew 4:6

For it is written, He shall give his angels charge over thee, to keep thee:
Luke 4:10

2. Angels Travel Back and Forth between Heaven and Earth

And he dreamed, and behold a ladder set up on the earth, and the top of it reached to heaven: and behold the angels of God ascending and descending on it. Genesis 28:12

And he saith unto him, Verily, verily, I say unto you, Hereafter ye shall see heaven open, and the angels of God ascending and descending upon the Son of man. John 1:51

3. Angels Respond to the Spoken Word of God

Bless the Lord, ye his angels, that excel in strength, that do his commandments, hearkening unto the voice of his word. Psalms 103:20

4. Angels Are Assigned to Different Believers

Take heed that ye despise not one of these little ones; for I say unto you, That in heaven their angels do always behold the face of my Father which is in heaven. Matthew 18:10

5. Angels Engage in Spiritual Warfare

And there was war in heaven: Michael and his angels fought against the dragon; and the dragon fought and his angels, Revelation 12:7

You become a leader when you decide not to be a copy but an original.

And the great dragon was cast out, that old serpent, called the Devil, and Satan, which deceiveth the whole world: he was cast out into the earth, and his angels were cast out with him. Revelation 12:9

6. Angels Will Accompany Christ When He Returns to Earth (the Rapture)

When the Son of man shall come in his glory, and all the holy angels with him, then shall he sit upon the throne of his glory: Matthew 25:31

Whosoever therefore shall be ashamed of me and of my words in this adulterous and sinful generation; of him also shall the Son of man be ashamed, when he cometh in the glory of his Father with the holy angels.
Mark 8:38

7. Angels Are Infinite in Number

Praise ye him, all his angels: praise ye him, all his hosts. Psalms 148:2

Thinkest thou that I cannot now pray to my Father, and he shall presently give me more than twelve legions of angels? Matthew 26:53

But ye are come unto mount Sion, and unto the city of the living God, the heavenly Jerusalem, and to an innumerable company of angels.
Hebrews 12:22

And I beheld, and I heard the voice of many angels round about the throne and the beasts and the elders: and the number of them was ten thousand times ten thousand, and thousands of thousands;
Revelation 5:11

The chariots of God are twenty thousand, even thousands of angels: the Lord is among them, as in Sinai, in the holy place. Psalms 68:17

8. Angels Minister to God's Children

And he was there in the wilderness forty days, tempted of Satan; and was with the wild beasts; and the angels ministered unto him. Mark 1:13

Who maketh his angels spirits; his ministers a flaming fire: Psalms 104:4

Then the devil leaveth him, and, behold, angels came and ministered unto him. Matthew 4:11

And of the angels he saith, Who maketh his angels spirits, and his ministers a flame of fire. Hebrews 1:7

9. Angels Are Not To Be Worshiped

Let no man beguile you of your reward in a voluntary humility and worshipping of angels, intruding into those things which he hath not seen, vainly puffed up by his fleshly mind, Colossians 2:18

10. Angels Can Disguise Themselves as Human Beings

Be not forgetful to entertain strangers: for thereby some have entertained angels unawares. Hebrews 13:2

11. Angels Are Under the Authority of God

Who is gone into heaven, and is on the right hand of God; angels and authorities and powers being made subject unto him. 1 Peter 3:22

12. Angels Will Separate the Believers from the Unbelievers

The enemy that sowed them is the devil; the harvest is the end of the world; and the reapers are the angels. Matthew 13:39

The Son of man shall send forth his angels, and they shall gather out of his kingdom all things that offend, and them which do iniquity;
Matthew 13:41

So shall it be at the end of the world: the angels shall come forth, and sever the wicked from among the just, Matthew 13:49

And then shall he send his angels, and shall gather together his elect from the four winds, from the uttermost part of the earth to the uttermost part of heaven. Mark 13:27

And to you who are troubled rest with us, when the Lord Jesus shall be revealed from heaven with his mighty angels. 2 Thessalonians 1:7

Fellowship with Believers

Behold, how good and how pleasant it is for brethren to dwell together in unity! Psalms 133:1

Now I beseech you, brethren, by the name of our Lord Jesus Christ, that ye all speak the same thing, and that there be no divisions among you; but that ye be perfectly joined together in the same mind and in the same judgment. 1 Corinthians 1:10

If therefore the whole church be come together into one place, and all speak with tongues, and there come in those that are unlearned, or unbelievers, will they not say that ye are mad? 1 Corinthians 14:23

For, brethren, ye have been called unto liberty; only use not liberty for an occasion to the flesh, but by love serve one another. Galatians 5:13

Till we all come in the unity of the faith, and of the knowledge of the Son of God, unto a perfect man, unto the measure of the stature of the fulness of Christ. Ephesians 4:13

And be ye kind one to another, tenderhearted, forgiving one another, even as God for Christ's sake hath forgiven you. Ephesians 4:32

Submitting yourselves one to another in the fear of God.Ephesians 5:21

Only let your conversation be as it becometh the gospel of Christ: that whether I come and see you, or else be absent, I may hear of your affairs, that ye stand fast in one spirit, with one mind striving together for the faith of the gospel. Philippians 1:27

Fulfil ye my joy, that ye be likeminded, having the same love, being of one accord, of one mind. Philippians 2:2

Nevertheless, whereto we have already attained, let us walk by the same rule, let us mind the same thing. Philippians 3:16

And let the peace of God rule in your hearts, to the which also ye are called in one body; and be ye thankful. Colossians 3:15

And the Lord make you to increase and abound in love one toward another, and toward all men, even as we do toward you.
1 Thessalonians 3:12

But as touching brotherly love ye need not that I write unto you: for ye yourselves are taught of God to love one another. 1 Thessalonians 4:9

Wherefore comfort yourselves together, and edify one another, even as also ye do. 1 Thessalonians 5:11

Seeing ye have purified your souls in obeying the truth through the Spirit unto unfeigned love of the brethren, see that ye love one another with a pure heart fervently. 1 Peter 1:22

Finally, be ye all of one mind, having compassion one of another, love as brethren, be pitiful, be courteous. 1 Peter 3:8

Use hospitality one to another without grudging. 1 Peter 4:9

But if we walk in the light, as he is in the light, we have fellowship one with another, and the blood of Jesus Christ his Son cleanseth us from all sin. 1 John 1:7

Marriage

Therefore shall a man leave his father and his mother, and shall cleave unto his wife: and they shall be one flesh. Genesis 2:24

> *Husband and wives who would live happily ever after learn early to give and take, to reach agreements by mutual consent. - Vance Havner*

But from the beginning of the creation God made them male and female. For this cause shall a man leave his father and mother, and cleave to his wife; And they twain shall be one flesh: so then they are no more twain, but one flesh. What therefore God hath joined together, let not man put asunder. Mark 10:6-9

1. Husbands

Let thy fountain be blessed: and rejoice with the wife of thy youth. Let her be as the loving hind and pleasant roe; let her breasts satisfy thee at all times; and be thou ravished always with her love. Proverbs 5:18-19

Whoso findeth a wife findeth a good thing, and obtaineth favour of the Lord. Proverbs 18:22

Houses and riches are the inheritance of fathers and a prudent wife is from the Lord. Proverbs 19:14

Who can find a virtuous woman? for her price is far above rubies.
Proverbs 31:10

Give her of the fruit of her hands; and let her own works praise her in the gates. Proverbs 31:31

Live joyfully with the wife whom thou lovest all the days of the life of thy vanity, which he hath given thee under the sun, all the days of thy vanity: for that is thy portion in this life, and in thy labour which thou takest under the sun. Ecclesiastes 9:9

> *Success in marriage consist not only in finding the right mate, but also in being the right mate. - Anonymous*

Yet ye say, Wherefore? Because the Lord hath been witness between thee and the wife of thy youth, against whom thou hast dealt treacher-

---

We are all capable of leadership by design, but we cannot lead correctly and effectively unless we are led by His Spirit.

---

ously: yet is she thy companion, and the wife of thy covenant. And did not he make one? Yet had he the residue of the spirit. And wherefore one? That he might seek a godly seed. Therefore take heed to your spirit, and let none deal treacherously against the wife of his youth. For the Lord, the God of Israel, saith that he hateth putting away: for one covereth violence with his garment, saith the Lord of hosts: therefore take heed to your spirit, that ye deal not treacherously. Malachi 2:14-16

Let the husband render unto the wife due benevolence: and likewise also the wife unto the husband. The wife hath not power of her own body, but the husband: and likewise also the husband hath not power of his own body, but the wife. Defraud ye not one the other, except it be with consent for a time, that ye may give yourselves to fasting and prayer; and come together again, that Satan tempt you not for your incontinency. But I speak this by permission, and not of commandment. 1 Corinthians 7:3-6

But I would have you know, that the head of every man is Christ; and the head of the woman is the man; and the head of Christ is God.
1 Corinthians 11:3

Wives, submit yourselves unto your own husbands, as unto the Lord. For the husband is the head of the wife, even as Christ is the head of the church: and he is the saviour of the body. Ephesians 5:22-23

Wives, submit yourselves unto your own husbands, as it is fit in the Lord. Husbands, love your wives, and be not bitter against them.
Colossians 3:18-19

Fathers, provoke not your children to anger, lest they be discouraged.
Colossians 3:21

2. Wives

A virtuous woman is a crown to her husband: but she that maketh ashamed is as rottenness in his bones. Proverbs 12:4

Every wise woman buildeth her house: but the foolish plucketh it down with her hands. Proverbs 14:1

Whoso findeth a wife findeth a good thing, and obtaineth favour of the Lord. Proverbs 18:22

House and riches are the inheritance of fathers and a prudent wife is from the Lord. Proverbs 19:14

Who can find a virtuous woman? for her price is far above rubies.
Proverbs 31:10

Give her of the fruit of her hands; and let her own works praise her in the gates. Proverbs 31:31

Let the husband render unto the wife due benevolence: and likewise also the wife unto the husband. The wife hath not power of her own body, but the husband: and likewise also the husband hath not power of his own body, but the wife. Defraud ye not one the other, except it be with consent for a time, that ye may give yourselves to fasting and prayer; and come together again, that Satan tempt you not for your incontinency. But I speak this by permission, and not of commandment. 1 Corinthians 7:3-6

But I would have you know, that the head of every man is Christ; and the head of the woman is the man; and the head of Christ is God.
1 Corinthians 11:3

Wives, submit yourselves unto your own husbands, as unto the Lord. For the husband is the head of the wife, even as Christ is the head of the church: and he is the saviour of the body. Ephesians 5:22-23

Wives, submit yourselves unto your own husbands, as it is fit in the Lord. Husbands, love your wives, and be not bitter against them.
Colossians 3:18-19

Child-Parent Relationship

1. Raising Children

A good man leaveth an inheritance to his children's children: and the wealth of the sinner is laid up for the just. Proverbs 13:22

Children's children are the crown of old men; and the glory of children are their fathers. Proverbs 17:6

The father of the righteous shall greatly rejoice: and he that begetteth a wise child shall have joy of him. Proverbs 23:24

One that ruleth well his own house, having his children in subjection with all gravity; For if a man know not how to rule his own house, how shall he take care of the church of God? 1 Timothy 3:4-5

But if any provide not for his own, and specially for those of his own house, he hath denied the faith, and is worse than an infidel.
1 Timothy 5:8

The most important thing a father can do for his children is to love their mother. - Theodore M. Hesburgh

2. Physically Correcting Your Children

He that spareth his rod hateth his son: but he that loveth him chasteneth him betimes. Proverbs 13:24

Foolishness is bound in the heart of a child; but the rod of correction shall drive it far from him. Proverbs 22:15

Withhold not correction from the child: for if thou beatest him with the rod, he shall not die. Thou shalt beat him with the rod, and shalt deliver his soul from hell. Proverbs 23:13-14

The rod and reproof give wisdom: but a child left to himself bringeth his mother to shame. Proverbs 29:15

Correct thy son, and he shall give thee rest; yea, he shall give delight unto thy soul. Proverbs 29:17

3. Being Fair to Your Children

And, ye fathers, provoke not your children to wrath: but bring them up in the nurture and admonition of the Lord. Ephesians 6:4

Fathers, provoke not your children to anger, lest they be discouraged.
Colossians 3:21

4. Teaching Your Children the Word of God

And these words, which I command thee this day, shall be in thine heart: And thou shalt teach them diligently unto thy children, and shalt talk of them when thou sittest in thine house, and when thou walkest by the way, and when thou liest down, and when thou risest up. And thou shalt bind them for a sign upon thine hand, and they shall be as frontlets between thine eyes. And thou shalt write them upon the posts of thy house, and on thy gates. Deuteronomy 6:6-9

For I know him, that he will command his children and his household after him, and they shall keep the way of the Lord, to do justice and judgment; that the Lord may bring upon Abraham that which he hath spoken of him. Genesis 18:19

And thou shalt shew thy son in that day, saying, This is done because of that which the Lord did unto me when I came forth out of Egypt.
Exodus 13:8

My father could talk it, and, by the grace of God, he lived it. He had not only a talking but a "walking" knowledge of the Scriptures. - Vance Havner

47

Only take heed to thyself, and keep thy soul diligently, lest thou forget the things which thine eyes have seen, and lest they depart from thy heart all the days of thy life: but teach them thy sons, and thy sons' sons; Specially the day that thou stoodest before the Lord thy God in Horeb, when the Lord said unto me, Gather me the people together, and I will make them hear my words, that they may learn to fear me all the days that they shall live upon the earth, and that they may teach their children.
Deuteronomy 4:9-10

And ye shall teach them your children, speaking of them when thou sittest in thine house, and when thou walkest by the way, when thou liest down, and when thou risest up. Deuteronomy 11:19

And if it seem evil unto you to serve the Lord, choose you this day whom ye will serve; whether the gods which your fathers served that were on the other side of the flood, or the gods of the Amorites, in whose land ye dwell: but as for me and my house, we will serve the Lord. Joshua 24:15

We will not hide them from their children, shewing to the generation to come the praises of the Lord, and his strength, and his wonderful works that he hath done. For he established a testimony in Jacob, and appointed a law in Israel, which he commanded our fathers, that they should make them known to their children: That the generation to come might know them, even the children which should be born; who should arise and declare them to their children: That they might set their hope in God, and not forget the works of God, but keep his commandments: Psalms 78:4-7

Train up a child in the way he should go: and when he is old, he will not depart from it. Proverbs 22:6

Train your child in the way in which you know you should have gone yourself. - Charles H. Spurgeon

And all thy children shall be taught of the Lord; and great shall be the peace of thy children. Isaiah 54:13

Friends

A friend loveth at all times, and a brother is born for adversity.
Proverbs 17:17

A man that hath friends must shew himself friendly: and there is a friend that sticketh closer than a brother. Proverbs 18:24

> **Leadership is the ability of one person to influence others.**

The man of many friends [a friend of all the world] will prove himself a bad friend, but there is a friend who sticks closer than a brother.

Proverbs 18:24 AMP

A man of many companions may come to ruin, but there is a friend who sticks closer than a brother. Proverbs 18:24 NIV

Wealth maketh many friends; but the poor is separated from his neighbour. Proverbs 19:4

A friend is the one who comes in when the whole world has gone out. - Anonymous

Two are better than one; because they have a good reward for their labour. For if they fall, the one will lift up his fellow: but woe to him that is alone when he falleth; for he hath not another to help him up. Again, if two lie together, then they have heat: but how can one be warm alone? And if one prevail against him, two shall withstand him; and a threefold cord is not quickly broken. Ecclesiastes 4:9-12

Many will entreat the favour of the prince: and every man is a friend to him that giveth gifts. Proverbs 19:6

To him that is afflicted pity should be shewed from his friend; but he forsaketh the fear of the Almighty. Job 6:14

He that loveth pureness of heart, for the grace of his lips the king shall be his friend. Proverbs 22:11

Faithful are the wounds of a friend; but the kisses of an enemy are deceitful. Proverbs 27:6

Ointment and perfume rejoice the heart: so doth the sweetness of a man's friend by hearty counsel. Thine own friend, and thy father's friend, forsake not; neither go into thy brother's house in the day of thy calamity: 'for better is a neighbour that is near than a brother far off.

Proverbs 27:9-10

A real friend covers your sins and protects your reputation in public and rebukes and admonishes you in private.

Iron sharpeneth iron; so a man sharpeneth the countenance of his friend.

Proverbs 27:17

Greater love hath no man than this, that a man lay down his life for his friends. Ye are my friends, if ye do whatsoever I command you.

John 15:13-14

Henceforth I call you not servants; for the servant knoweth not what his lord doeth: but I have called you friends; for all things that I have heard of my Father I have made known unto you. John 15:15

And the scripture was fulfilled which saith, Abraham believed God, and it was imputed unto him for righteousness: and he was called the Friend of God. James 2:23

> *Insomuch as any one pushes you nearer to God, he or she is your friend. - Anonymous*

Avoiding or Breaking Bad Relationships

Blessed is the man that walketh not in the counsel of the ungodly, nor standeth in the way of sinners, nor sitteth in the seat of the scornful.
Psalms 1:1

Depart from me, ye evildoers: for I will keep the commandments of my God. Psalms 119:115

Forsake the foolish, and live; and go in the way of understanding.
Proverbs 9:6

The thoughts of the righteous are right: but the counsels of the wicked are deceit. Proverbs 12:5

He that tilleth his land shall be satisfied with bread: but he that followeth vain persons is void of understanding. Proverbs 12:11

He that walketh with wise men shall be wise: but a companion of fools shall be destroyed. Proverbs 13:20

Go from the presence of a foolish man, when thou perceivest not in him the lips of knowledge. Proverbs 14:7

Better it is to be of an humble spirit with the lowly, than to divide the spoil with the proud. Proverbs 16:19

A violent man enticeth his neighbour, and leadeth him into the way that is not good. Proverbs 16:29

The man that wandereth out of the way of understanding shall remain in the congregation of the dead. Proverbs 21:16

Make no friendship with an angry man; and with a furious man thou shalt not go. Lest thou learn his ways, and get a snare to thy soul.
Proverbs 22:24-25

Be not thou envious against evil men, neither desire to be with them.
Proverbs 24:1

My son, fear thou the Lord and the king: and meddle not with them that are given to change. Proverbs 24:21

For their calamity shall rise suddenly; and who knoweth the ruin of them both? Proverbs 24:22

Whoso keepeth the law is a wise son: but he that is a companion of riotous men shameth his father. Proverbs 28:7

Whoso loveth wisdom rejoiceth his father: but he that keepeth company with harlots spendeth his substance. Proverbs 29:3

I sat not in the assembly of the mockers, nor rejoiced; I sat alone because of thy hand: for thou hast filled me with indignation. Jeremiah 15:17

Blessed are ye, when men shall hate you, and when they shall separate you from their company, and shall reproach you, and cast out your name as evil, for the Son of man's sake. Luke 6:22

Then spake Jesus again unto them, saying, I am the light of the world: he that followeth me shall not walk in darkness, but shall have the light of life. John 8:12

I am come a light into the world, that whosoever believeth on me should not abide in darkness. John 12:46

I wrote unto you in an epistle not to company with fornicators: Yet not altogether with the fornicators of this world, or with the covetous, or extortioners, or with idolaters; for then must ye needs go out of the world. But now I have written unto you not to keep company, if any man that is called a brother be a fornicator, or covetous, or an idolater, or a railer, or a drunkard, or an extortioner; with such an one no not to eat.
1 Corinthians 5:9-11

Ye cannot drink the cup of the Lord, and the cup of devils: ye cannot be partakers of the Lord's table, and of the table of devils.
1 Corinthians 10:21

Be not deceived: evil communications corrupt good manners.
1 Corinthians 15:33

Be ye not unequally yoked together with unbelievers: for what fellowship hath righteousness with unrighteousness? and what communion hath light with darkness? And what concord hath Christ with Belial? or what part hath he that believeth with an infidel? 2 Corinthians 6:14-15

51

And what agreement hath the temple of God with idols? for ye are the temple of the living God; as God hath said, I will dwell in them, and walk in them; and I will be their God, and they shall be my people. Wherefore come out from among them, and be ye separate, saith the Lord, and touch not the unclean thing; and I will receive you, And will be a Father unto you, and ye shall be my sons and daughters, saith the Lord Almighty. 2 Corinthians 6:16-18

And have no fellowship with the unfruitful works of darkness, but rather reprove them. Ephesians 5:11

If ye then be risen with Christ, seek those things which are above, where Christ sitteth on the right hand of God. Colossians 3:1

Abstain from all appearance of evil. 1 Thessalonians 5:22

Ye adulterers and adulteresses, know ye not that the friendship of the world is enmity with God? whosoever therefore will be a friend of the world is the enemy of God. James 4:4

Salt seasons, purifies, preserves. But somebody ought to remind us that salt also irritates. Real living Christianity rubs this world the wrong way. - Vance Havner

---

Leadership is first being, then doing.

THE MINISTER'S CHARACTER

Keeping Your Word (Promises, Vows and Commitments)

If a man vow a vow unto the Lord, or swear an oath to bind his soul with a bond; he shall not break his word, he shall do according to all that proceedeth out of his mouth. Numbers 30:2

When thou shalt vow a vow unto the Lord thy God, thou shalt not slack to pay it: for the Lord thy God will surely require it of thee; and it would be sin in thee. Deuteronomy 23:21

That which is gone out of thy lips thou shalt keep and perform; even a freewill offering, according as thou hast vowed unto the Lord thy God, which thou hast promised with thy mouth. Deuteronomy 23:23

Say not unto thy neighbour, Go, and come again, and to morrow I will give; when thou hast it by thee. Proverbs 3:28

It is a snare to the man who devoureth that which is holy, and after vows to make inquiry. Proverbs 20:25

It is a snare to a man to utter a vow [of consecration] rashly, and not until afterward inquire [whether he can fulfill it]. Proverbs 20:25 AMP

When thou vowest a vow unto God, defer not to pay it; for he hath no pleasure in fools: pay that which thou hast vowed. Better is it that thou shouldest not vow, than that thou shouldest vow and not pay.

Ecclesiastes 5:4-5

Honesty

He that walketh uprightly, and worketh righteousness, and speaketh the truth in his heart. Psalms 15:2

These are the things that ye shall do; Speak ye every man the truth to his neighbour; execute the judgment of truth and peace in your gates.

Zechariah 8:16

53

He that speaketh truth sheweth forth righteousness: but a false witness deceit. Proverbs 12:17

But that on the good ground are they, which in an honest and good heart, having heard the word, keep it, and bring forth fruit with patience.
Luke 8:15

Wherefore, brethren, look ye out among you seven men of honest report, full of the Holy Ghost and wisdom, whom we may appoint over this business. Acts 6:3

> *Your lifestyle may be the only Christ that some
> people may ever see or read about.*

Providing for honest things, not only in the sight of the Lord, but also in the sight of men. 2 Corinthians 8:21

Not slothful in business; fervent in spirit; serving the Lord. Romans 12:11

Recompense to no man evil for evil. Provide things honest in the sight of all men. Romans 12:17

Let us walk honestly, as in the day; not in rioting and drunkenness, not in chambering and wantonness, not in strife and envying. Romans 13:13

Now I pray to God that ye do no evil; not that we should appear approved, but that ye should do that which is honest, though we be as reprobates. 2 Corinthians 13:7

Honesty is doing what is right when no one else is around.

If so be that ye have heard him, and have been taught by him, as the truth is in Jesus. Ephesians 4:21

That ye may walk honestly toward them that are without, and that ye may have lack of nothing. 1 Thessalonians 4:12

Pray for us: for we trust we have a good conscience, in all things willing to live honestly. Hebrews 13:18

Having your conversation honest among the Gentiles: that, whereas they speak against you as evildoers, they may by your good works, which they shall behold, glorify God in the day of visitation. 1 Peter 2:12

Leadership is first being, then doing.

Being Honest with Yourself

Take heed to yourselves, that your heart be not deceived, and ye turn aside, and serve other gods, and worship them. Deuteronomy 11:16

Thus saith the Lord; Deceive not yourselves, saying, The Chaldeans shall surely depart from us: for they shall not depart. Jeremiah 37:9

Let no man deceive himself. If any man among you seemeth to be wise in this world, let him become a fool, that he may be wise.
1 Corinthians 3:18

For if a man think himself to be something, when he is nothing, he deceiveth himself. Galatians 6:3

But be ye doers of the word, and not hearers only, deceiving your own selves. James 1:22

If any man among you seem to be religious, and bridleth not his tongue, but deceiveth his own heart, this man's religion is vain. James 1:26

And shall receive the reward of unrighteousness, as they that count it pleasure to riot in the day time. Spots they are and blemishes, sporting themselves with their own deceivings while they feast with you.
2 Peter 2:13

If we say that we have fellowship with him, and walk in darkness, we lie, and do not the truth. 1 John 1:6

If we say that we have no sin, we deceive ourselves, and the truth is not in us. 1 John 1:8

He that committeth sin is of the devil; for the devil sinneth from the beginning. For this purpose the Son of God was manifested, that he might destroy the works of the devil. **W**hosoever is born of God doth not commit sin; for his seed remaineth in him: and he cannot sin, because he is born of God. **I**n this the children of God are manifest, and the children of the devil: whosoever doeth not righteousness is not of God, neither he that loveth not his brother. 1 John 3:8-10

Be not deceived; God is not mocked: for whatsoever a man soweth, that shall he also reap. Galatians 6:7

Accepting Advice and Positive Criticism

A wise man will hear, and will increase learning; and a man of understanding shall attain unto wise counsels. Proverbs 1:5

But whoso hearkeneth unto me shall dwell safely, and shall be quiet from fear of evil. Proverbs 1:33

Hear, O my son, and receive my sayings; and the years of thy life shall be many. Proverbs 4:10

Hear instruction, and be wise, and refuse it not. Proverbs 8:33

He is in the way of life that keepeth instruction: but he that refuseth reproof erreth. Proverbs 10:17

Whoso loveth instruction loveth knowledge: but he that hateth reproof is brutish. Proverbs 12:1

Poverty and shame shall be to him that refuseth instruction: but he that regardeth reproof shall be honoured. Proverbs 13:18

The ear that heareth the reproof of life abideth among the wise. He that refuseth instruction despiseth his own soul: but he that heareth reproof getteth understanding. Proverbs 15:31-32

A reproof entereth more into a wise man than an hundred stripes into a fool. Proverbs 17:10

Hear counsel, and receive instruction, that thou mayest be wise in thy latter end. Proverbs 19:20

Buy the truth, and sell it not; also wisdom, and instruction, and understanding. Proverbs 23:23

For the commandment is a lamp; and the law is light; and reproofs of instruction are the way of life. Proverbs 6:23

Learn to Control the Words that You Speak

Set a watch, O Lord, before my mouth; keep the door of my lips.
Psalms 141:3

I said, I will take heed to my ways, that I sin not with my tongue: I will keep my mouth with a bridle, while the wicked is before me.
Psalms 39:1

In the multitude of words there wanteth not sin: but he that refraineth his lips is wise. Proverbs 10:19

He that keepeth his mouth keepeth his life: but he that openeth wide his lips shall have destruction. Proverbs 13:3

Thou has proved mine heart; thou hast visited me in the night; thou has tried me, and shalt find nothing; I am purposed that my mouth shall not transgress. Psalms 17:3

A soft answer turneth away wrath: but grievous words stir up anger.
Proverbs 15:1

The secret of a governable tongue is not self-control but Christ-control. - G. S.

1. Avoid Speaking Evil, Useless and Meaningless Words

All the while my breath is in me, and the spirit of God is in my nostrils; My lips shall not speak wickedness, nor my tongue utter deceit.
Job 27:3-4

Keep thy tongue from evil, and thy lips from speaking guile.
Psalms 34:13

For he that will love life, and see good days, let him refrain his tongue from evil, and his lips that they speak no guile. 1 Peter 3:10

That ye put off concerning the former conversation the old man, which is corrupt according to the deceitful lusts. Ephesians 4:22

Let all bitterness, and wrath, and anger, and clamour, and evil speaking, be put away from you, with all malice. Ephesians 4:31

Neither filthiness, nor foolish talking, nor jesting, which are not convenient: but rather giving of thanks. Ephesians 5:4

O Timothy, keep that which is committed to thy trust, avoiding profane and vain babblings, and oppositions of science falsely so called: Which some professing have erred concerning the faith. Grace be with thee. Amen. 1 Timothy 6:20-21

But shun profane and vain babblings: for they will increase unto more ungodliness. 2 Timothy 2:16

Speak not evil one of another, brethren. He that speaketh evil of his brother, and judgeth his brother, speaketh evil of the law, and judgeth the law: but if thou judge the law, thou art not a doer of the law, but a judge.
James 4:11

Be not deceived: evil communications corrupt good manners.
1 Corinthians 15:33

2. Evil Words are Destructive

An hypocrite with his mouth destroyeth his neighbour: but through knowledge shall the just be delivered. Proverbs 11:9

The wicked is snared by the transgression of his lips: but the just shall come out of trouble. Proverbs 12:13

There is that speaketh like the piercings of a sword; but the tongue of the wise is health. Proverbs 12:18

Real spiritual maturity is evident by a controlled tongue. But hypocrisy can be disguised by fluent scripture quotation, spiritual cliches, religious mannerism, and emotionalism.

3. Don't Talk too Much

He that hath knowledge spareth his words: and a man of understanding is of an excellent spirit. Even a fool, when he holdeth his peace, is counted wise: and he that shutteth his lips is esteemed a man of understanding.
Proverbs 17:27-28

Whoso keepeth his mouth and his tongue keepeth his soul from troubles.
Proverbs 21:23

Talk no more so exceeding proudly; let not arrogancy come out of your mouth: for the Lord is a God of knowledge, and by him actions are weighed. Isaiah 2:3

But let your communication be, Yea, yea; Nay, nay: for whatsoever is more than these cometh of evil. Matthew 5:37

The best time for you to hold your tongue is the time you feel you must say something or bust. - Josh Billings

4. A Fool Talks too Much

A fool uttereth all his mind: but a wise man keepeth it in till afterwards.
Proverbs 29:11

The heart of him that hath understanding seeketh knowledge: but the mouth of fools feedeth on foolishness. Proverbs 15:14

An important ingredient of the leadership function is the ability to draw the best out of other people.

A fool's lips enter into contention, and his mouth calleth for strokes. **A** fool's mouth is his destruction, and his lips are the snare of his soul.

Proverbs 18:6-7

The words of a wise man's mouth are gracious; but the lips of a fool will swallow up himself. **T**he beginning of the words of his mouth is foolishness: and the end of his talk is mischievous madness. **A** fool also is full of words: a man cannot tell what shall be; and what shall be after him, who can tell him? Ecclesiastes 10:12-14

> *Better to remain silent and be thought a fool than to speak and to remove all doubt. - Abraham Lincoln*

5. You Will Be Judged by the Words that You Speak

But I say unto you, That every idle word that men shall speak, they shall give account thereof in the day of judgment. **F**or by thy words thou shalt be justified, and by thy words thou shalt be condemned.

Matthew 12:36-37

> *In times like the present, men should utter nothing for which the would not willingly be responsible through time and eternity. - Abraham Lincoln*

6. Think Before You Speak

The heart of the righteous studieth to answer: but the mouth of the wicked poureth out evil things. Proverbs 15:28

The heart of the wise teacheth his mouth, and addeth learning to his lips.

Proverbs 16:23

He that answereth a matter before he heareth it, it is folly and shame unto him. Proverbs 18:13

Seest thou a man that is hasty in his words? there is more hope of a fool than of him. Proverbs 29:20

Be not rash with thy mouth, and let not thine heart be hasty to utter any thing before God: for God is in heaven, and thou upon earth: therefore let thy words be few. Ecclesiastes 5:2

But foolish and unlearned questions avoid, knowing that they do gender strifes. 2 Timothy 2:23

> *Besser stumm als dumm—Better silent than stupid.*
> *- German Proverb*

59

7. Speaking Positive Words

Hear; for I will speak of excellent things; and the opening of my lips shall be right things. For my mouth shall speak truth; and wickedness is an abomination to my lips. All the words of my mouth are in righteousness; there is nothing froward or perverse in them. Proverbs 8:6-8

The mouth of a righteous man is a well of life: but violence covereth the mouth of the wicked. Proverbs 10:11

The tongue of the just is as choice silver: the heart of the wicked is little worth. The lips of the righteous feed many: but fools die for want of wisdom. Proverbs 10:20-21

The mouth of the just bringeth forth wisdom: but the froward tongue shall be cut out. Proverbs 10:31

Heaviness in the heart of man maketh it stoop: but a good word maketh it glad. Proverbs 12:25

A wholesome tongue is a tree of life: but perverseness therein is a breach in the spirit. Proverbs 15:4

The angels of heaven and the demons of hell bring to past whatever you speak out of your mouth. The angels respond to the Word of God and demons respond to negative, vain, and destructive words.

Pleasant words are as an honeycomb, sweet to the soul, and health to the bones. Proverbs 16:24

8. Speaking Words of Wisdom and Integrity

The words of wise men are heard in quiet more than the cry of him that ruleth among fools. Ecclesiastes 9:17

The words of a wise man's mouth are gracious; but the lips of a fool will swallow up himself. Ecclesiastes 10:12

For I will give you a mouth and wisdom, which all your adversaries shall not be able to gainsay nor resist. Luke 21:15

Sound speech, that cannot be condemned; that he that is of the contrary part may be ashamed, having no evil thing to say of you. Titus 2:8

Blessed is the man who, having nothing to say, abstains from giving wordy evidence of the fact. - George Eliot

Who is a wise man and endued with knowledge among you? let him shew out of a good conversation his works with meekness of wisdom.

James 3:13

9. Speaking the Right Words at the Appropriate Time

The lips of the righteous know what is acceptable: but the mouth of the wicked speaketh frowardness. Proverbs 10:32

A man hath joy by the answer of his mouth: and a word spoken in due season, how good is it! Proverbs 15:23

My son, if thine heart be wise, my heart shall rejoice, even mine. Yea, my reins shall rejoice, when thy lips speak right things.

Proverbs 23:15-16

A word fitly spoken is like apples of gold in pictures of silver.

Proverbs 25:11

To every thing there is a season, and a time to every purpose under the heaven: **A** time to rend, and a time to sew; a time to keep silence, and a time to speak; Ecclesiastes 3:1-7

The Lord God hath given me the tongue of the learned, that I should know how to speak a word in season to him that is weary: he wakeneth morning by morning, he wakeneth mine ear to hear as the learned.

Isaiah 50:4

Let your speech be alway with grace, seasoned with salt, that ye may know how ye ought to answer every man. Colossians 4:6

10. Speaking Knowledgeable Words

The tongue of the wise useth knowledge aright: but the mouth of fools poureth out foolishness. Proverbs 15:2

The lips of the wise disperse knowledge: but the heart of the foolish doeth not so. Proverbs 15:7

There is gold, and a multitude of rubies: but the lips of knowledge are a precious jewel. Proverbs 20:15

Should a wise man utter vain knowledge, and fill his belly with the east wind? Job 15:2

My words shall be of the uprightness of my heart: and my lips shall utter knowledge clearly. Job 33:3

Job hath spoken without knowledge, and his words were without wisdom. Job 34:35

Therefore doth Job open his mouth in vain; he multiplieth words without knowledge. Job 35:16

For truly my words shall not be false: he that is perfect in knowledge is with thee. Job 36:4

That thou mayest regard discretion, and that thy lips may keep knowledge. Proverbs 5:2

For the priest's lips should keep knowledge, and they should seek the law at his mouth: for he is the messenger of the Lord of hosts.
Malachi 2:7

Who is a wise man and endued with knowledge among you? let him shew out of a good conversation his works with meekness of wisdom.
James 3:13

Becoming Bold in Christ

I will speak of thy testimonies also before kings, and will not be ashamed.
Psalms 119:46

The wicked flee when no man pursueth: but the righteous are bold as a lion. Proverbs 28:1

A boldness in Christ should be accompanied by wisdom, divine timing, and a spirit of love.

Whosoever therefore shall be ashamed of me and of my words in this adulterous and sinful generation; of him also shall the Son of man be ashamed, when he cometh in the glory of his Father with the holy angels.
Mark 8:38

In whom we have boldness and access with confidence by the faith of him. Ephesians 3:12

And for me, that utterance may be given unto me, that I may open my mouth boldly, to make known the mystery of the gospel, For which I am an ambassador in bonds: that therein I may speak boldly, as I ought to speak. Ephesians 6:19-20

Inspiration is the opposite of intimidation and is absent of manipulation.

And many of the brethren in the Lord, waxing confident by my bonds, are much more bold to speak the word without fear. Philippians 1:14

Wherefore, though I might be much bold in Christ to enjoin thee that which is convenient. Philemon 1:8

Let us therefore come boldly unto the throne of grace, that we may obtain mercy, and find grace to help in time of need. Hebrews 4:16

Having therefore, brethren, boldness to enter into the holiest by the blood of Jesus. Hebrews 10:19

So that we may boldly say, The Lord is my helper, and I will not fear what man shall do unto me. Hebrews 13:6

Herein is our love made perfect, that we may have boldness in the day of judgment: because as he is, so are we in this world. 1 John 4:17

THE MINISTER'S ATTITUDE

Meekness

Now the man Moses was very meek, above all the men which were upon the face of the earth. Numbers 12:3

The meek shall eat and be satisfied: they shall praise the Lord that seek him: your heart shall live for ever. Psalms 22:26

The meek will he guide in judgment: and the meek will he teach his way.
Psalms 25:9

But the meek shall inherit the earth; and shall delight themselves in the abundance of peace. Psalms 37:11

And in thy majesty ride prosperously because of truth and meekness and righteousness; and thy right hand shall teach thee terrible things.
Psalms 45:4

When God arose to judgment, to save all the meek of the earth. Selah.
Psalms 76:9

The Lord lifteth up the meek: he casteth the wicked down to the ground.
Psalms 147:6

For the Lord taketh pleasure in his people: he will beautify the meek with salvation. Psalms 149:4

But with righteousness shall he judge the poor, and reprove with equity for the meek of the earth: and he shall smite the earth with the rod of his mouth, and with the breath of his lips shall he slay the wicked.
Isaiah 11:4

The meek also shall increase their joy in the Lord, and the poor among men shall rejoice in the Holy One of Israel. Isaiah 29:19

The Spirit of the Lord God is upon me; because the Lord hath anointed me to preach good tidings unto the meek; he hath sent me to bind up the brokenhearted, to proclaim liberty to the captives, and the opening of the prison to them that are bound. Isaiah 61:1

Seek ye the Lord, all ye meek of the earth, which have wrought his judgment; seek righteousness, seek meekness: it may be ye shall be hid in the day of the Lord's anger. Zephaniah 2:3

Blessed are the meek: for they shall inherit the earth. Matthew 5:5

Take my yoke upon you, and learn of me; for I am meek and lowly in heart: and ye shall find rest unto your souls. Matthew 11:29

Tell ye the daughter of Sion, Behold, thy King cometh unto thee, meek, and sitting upon an ass, and a colt the foal of an ass. Matthew 21:5

What will ye? shall I come unto you with a rod, or in love, and in the spirit of meekness? 1 Corinthians 4:21

Now I Paul myself beseech you by the meekness and gentleness of Christ, who in presence am base among you, but being absent am bold toward you. 2 Corinthians 10:1

But the fruit of the Spirit is love, joy, peace, longsuffering, gentleness, goodness, faith, Meekness, temperance: against such there is no law.
Galatians 5:22-23

Brethren, if a man be overtaken in a fault, ye which are spiritual, restore such an one in the spirit of meekness; considering thyself, lest thou also be tempted. Galatians 6:1

With all lowliness and meekness, with longsuffering, forbearing one another in love. Ephesians 4:2

Put on therefore, as the elect of God, holy and beloved, bowels of mercies, kindness, humbleness of mind, meekness, longsuffering.
Colossians 3:12

But thou, O man of God, flee these things; and follow after righteousness, godliness, faith, love, patience, meekness. 1 Timothy 6:11

To speak evil of no man, to be no brawlers, but gentle, shewing all meekness unto all men. Titus 3:2

Wherefore lay apart all filthiness and superfluity of naughtiness, and receive with meekness the engrafted word, which is able to save your souls. James 1:21

A title and position do not guarantee performance and productivity.

Who is a wise man and endued with knowledge among you? let him shew out of a good conversation his works with meekness of wisdom.

James 3:13

But let it be the hidden man of the heart, in that which is not corruptible, even the ornament of a meek and quiet spirit, which is in the sight of God of great price. 1 Peter 3:4

But sanctify the Lord God in your hearts: and be ready always to give an answer to every man that asketh you a reason of the hope that is in you with meekness and fear. 1 Peter 3:15

Overcoming Pride

Hear ye, and give ear; be not proud: for the Lord hath spoken.

Jeremiah 13:15

Look on every one that is proud, and bring him low; and tread down the wicked in their place. Job 40:12

Thou hast rebuked the proud that are cursed, which do err from thy commandments. Psalms 119:21

An high look, and a proud heart, and the plowing of the wicked, is sin.

Proverbs 21:4

Seest thou a man wise in his own conceit? there is more hope of a fool than of him. Proverbs 26:12

> *The wonderful thing about cockiness is that it can be overcome by a little maturity. - Delton Trueblood*

Woe unto them that are wise in their own eyes, and prudent in their own sight! Isaiah 5:21

And Jesus called a little child unto him, and set him in the midst of them, And said, Verily I say unto you, Except ye be converted, and become as little children, ye shall not enter into the kingdom of heaven. Whosoever therefore shall humble himself as this little child, the same is greatest in the kingdom of heaven. Matthew 18:2-4

But he that is greatest among you shall be your servant. And whosoever shall exalt himself shall be abased; and he that shall humble himself shall be exalted. Matthew 23:11-12

And he sat down, and called the twelve, and saith unto them, If any man desire to be first, the same shall be last of all, and servant of all.

Mark 9:35

67

For I say, through the grace given unto me, to every man that is among you, not to think of himself more highly than he ought to think; but to think soberly, according as God hath dealt to every man the measure of faith. Romans 12:3

Be of the same mind one toward another. Mind not high things, but condescend to men of low estate. Be not wise in your own conceits.
Romans 12:16

That, according as it is written, He that glorieth, let him glory in the Lord. 1 Corinthians 1:31

Let no man deceive himself. If any man among you seemeth to be wise in this world, let him become a fool, that he may be wise.
1 Corinthians 3:18

Charity suffereth long, and is kind; charity envieth not; charity vaunteth not itself, is not puffed up. 1 Corinthians 13:4

Not that we are sufficient of ourselves to think any thing as of ourselves; but our sufficiency is of God. 2 Corinthians 3:5

But we have this treasure in earthen vessels, that the excellency of the power may be of God, and not of us. 2 Corinthians 4:7

God knows best; he hasn't arranged your anatomy so as to make it easy for you to pat yourself on the back. - Anonymous

But he that glorieth, let him glory in the Lord. 2 Corinthians 10:17

If I must needs glory, I will glory of the things which concern mine infirmities. 2 Corinthians 11:30

But God forbid that I should glory, save in the cross of our Lord Jesus Christ, by whom the world is crucified unto me, and I unto the world.
Galatians 6:14

Humble yourselves in the sight of the Lord, and he shall lift you up.
James 4:10

Let nothing be done through strife or vainglory; but in lowliness of mind let each esteem other better than themselves. Philippians 2:3

Don't talk about yourself; it will be done when you leave.
- Wilson Mizner

1. God Hates Pride

Though the Lord be high, yet hath he respect unto the lowly: but the proud he knoweth afar off. Psalms 138:6

The fear of the Lord is to hate evil: pride, and arrogancy, and the evil way, and the froward mouth, do I hate. Proverbs 8:13

And he said unto them, Ye are they which justify yourselves before men; but God knoweth your hearts: for that which is highly esteemed among men is abomination in the sight of God. Luke 16:15

But he giveth more grace. Wherefore he saith, God resisteth the proud, but giveth grace unto the humble. Submit yourselves therefore to God. Resist the devil, and he will flee from you. James 4:6-7

Likewise, ye younger, submit yourselves unto the elder. Yea, all of you be subject one to another, and be clothed with humility: for God resisteth the proud, and giveth grace to the humble. 1 Peter 5:5

> *God sends no one away empty except those who are full of themselves. - D. L. Moody*

2. Pride Will Cause You to Fall

Pride goeth before destruction, and an haughty spirit before a fall. Better it is to be of an humble spirit with the lowly, than to divide the spoil with the proud. Proverbs 16:18-19

Before destruction the heart of man is haughty, and before honour is humility. Proverbs 18:12

A man's pride shall bring him low: but honour shall uphold the humble in spirit. Proverbs 29:23

Wherefore let him that thinketh he standeth take heed lest he fall.
1 Corinthians 10:12

3. Being Prideful Starts Trouble

Only by pride cometh contention: but with the well advised is wisdom.
Proverbs 13:10

He that is of a proud heart stirreth up strife: but he that putteth his trust in the Lord shall be made fat. He that trusteth in his own heart is a fool: but whoso walketh wisely, he shall be delivered. Proverbs 28:25-26

Controlling Anger

Cease from anger, and forsake wrath: fret not thyself in any wise to do evil. Psalms 37:8

> *He who forgives ends the quarrel. - Proverb*

He that is void of wisdom despiseth his neighbour: but a man of understanding holdeth his peace. Proverbs 11:12

He that is slow to wrath is of great understanding: but he that is hasty of spirit exalteth folly. Proverbs 14:29

A wrathful man stirreth up strife: but he that is slow to anger appeaseth strife. Proverbs 15:18

He that is slow to anger is better than the mighty; and he that ruleth his spirit than he that taketh a city. Proverbs 16:32

Even a fool, when he holdeth his peace, is counted wise: and he that shutteth his lips is esteemed a man of understanding. Proverbs 17:28

The discretion of a man deferreth his anger; and it is his glory to pass over a transgression. Proverbs 19:11

Scornful men bring a city into a snare: but wise men turn away wrath.
Proverbs 29:8

It is better to avoid strife than to appear justified.

A fool uttereth all his mind: but a wise man keepeth it in till afterwards.
Proverbs 29:11

Be not hasty in thy spirit to be angry: for anger resteth in the bosom of fools. Ecclesiastes 7:9

Dearly beloved, avenge not yourselves, but rather give place unto wrath: for it is written, Vengeance is mine; I will repay, saith the Lord. Therefore if thine enemy hunger, feed him; if he thirst, give him drink: for in so doing thou shalt heap coals of fire on his head. Be not overcome of evil, but overcome evil with good. Romans 12:19-21

Let all bitterness, and wrath, and anger, and clamour, and evil speaking, be put away from you, with all malice: And be ye kind one to another, tenderhearted, forgiving one another, even as God for Christ's sake hath forgiven you. Ephesians 4:31-32

But now ye also put off all these; anger, wrath, malice, blasphemy, filthy communication out of your mouth. Colossians 3:8

Wherefore, my beloved brethren, let every man be swift to hear, slow to speak, slow to wrath: For the wrath of man worketh not the righteousness of God. James 1:19-20

A leader is one who leads others to leadership.

Overcoming an Envious Heart

Envious is the feeling of displeasure produced by witnessing or hearing of the advantage or prosperity of others. Envy thou not the oppressor, and choose none of his ways. Proverbs 3:31

Let not thine heart envy sinners: but be thou in the fear of the Lord all the day long. Proverbs 23:17

Be not thou envious against evil men, neither desire to be with them. Proverbs 24:1

Fret not thyself because of evil men, neither be thou envious at the wicked; Proverbs 24:19

Let us walk honestly, as in the day; not in rioting and drunkenness, not in chambering and wantonness, not in strife and envying. Romans 13:13

Let us not be desirous of vain glory, provoking one another, envying one another. Galatians 5:26

For where envying and strife is, there is confusion and every evil work. James 3:16

Wherefore laying aside all malice, and all guile, and hypocrisies, and envies, and all evil speakings, 1 Peter 2:1

A sound heart is the life of the flesh: but envy the rottenness of the bones. Proverbs 14:30

Wrath is cruel, and anger is outrageous; but who is able to stand before envy? Proverbs 27:4

Building Your Self-Confidence through Christ

Blessed shalt thou be when thou comest in, and blessed shalt thou be when thou goest out. Deuteronomy 28:6

And the Lord shall make thee the head, and not the tail; and thou shalt be above only, and thou shalt not be beneath; if that thou hearken unto the commandments of the Lord thy God, which I command thee this day, to observe and to do them. Deuteronomy 28:13

But Jesus beheld them, and said unto them, With men this is impossible; but with God all things are possible. Matthew 19:26

For with God nothing shall be impossible. Luke 1:37

71

Moreover whom he did predestinate, them he also called: and whom he called, them he also justified: and whom he justified, them he also glorified. Romans 8:30

Now thanks be unto God, which always causeth us to triumph in Christ, and maketh manifest the savour of his knowledge by us in every place.
2 Corinthians 2:14

I can do all things through Christ which strengtheneth me.
Philippians 4:13

Ye also, as lively stones, are built up a spiritual house, an holy priesthood, to offer up spiritual sacrifices, acceptable to God by Jesus Christ.
1 Peter 2:5

Ye are of God, little children, and have overcome them: because greater is he that is in you, than he that is in the world. 1 John 4:4

Building Your Self-Image through God's Word

And God said, Let us make man in our image, after our likeness: and let them have dominion over the fish of the sea, and over the fowl of the air, and over the cattle, and over all the earth, and over every creeping thing that creepeth upon the earth. So God created man in his own image, in the image of God created he him; male and female created he them.
Genesis 1:26-27

And they fell upon their faces, and said, O God, the God of the spirits of all flesh, shall one man sin, and wilt thou be wroth with all the congregation? Numbers 16:22

Let the Lord, the God of the spirits of all flesh, set a man over the congregation. Numbers 27:16

Out of the mouth of babes and sucklings hast thou ordained strength because of thine enemies, that thou mightest still the enemy and the avenger. When I consider thy heavens, the work of thy fingers, the moon and the stars, which thou hast ordained; What is man, that thou art mindful of him? and the son of man, that thou visitest him? For thou hast made him a little lower than the angels, and hast crowned him with glory and honour. Thou madest him to have dominion over the works of thy hands; thou hast put all things under his feet. Psalms 8:2-6

I have said, Ye are gods; and all of you are children of the most High.
Psalms 82:6

The burden of the word of the Lord for Israel, saith the Lord, which stretcheth forth the heavens, and layeth the foundation of the earth, and formeth the spirit of man within him. Zechariah 12:1

Therefore if any man be in Christ, he is a new creature: old things are passed away; behold, all things are become new. 2 Corinthians 5:17

Now then we are ambassadors for Christ, as though God did beseech you by us: we pray you in Christ's stead, be ye reconciled to God.
2 Corinthians 5:20

The eyes of your understanding being enlightened; that ye may know what is the hope of his calling, and what the riches of the glory of his inheritance in the saints. Ephesians 1:18

And you hath he quickened, who were dead in trespasses and sins.
Ephesians 2:1

Even when we were dead in sins, hath quickened us together with Christ, by grace ye are saved; And hath raised us up together, and made us sit together in heavenly places in Christ Jesus. Ephesians 2:5-6

For we are his workmanship, created in Christ Jesus unto good works, which God hath before ordained that we should walk in them.
Ephesians 2:10

Now therefore ye are no more strangers and foreigners, but fellow citizens with the saints, and of the household of God. Ephesians 2:19

I can do all things through Christ which strengtheneth me.
Philippians 4:13

Lie not one to another, seeing that ye have put off the old man with his deeds; And have put on the new man, which is renewed in knowledge after the image of him that created him. Colossians 3:9-10

Furthermore we have had fathers of our flesh which corrected us, and we gave them reverence: shall we not much rather be in subjection unto the Father of spirits, and live? Hebrews 12:9

But whoso looketh into the perfect law of liberty, and continueth therein, he being not a forgetful hearer, but a doer of the work, this man shall be blessed in his deed. James 1:25

Herein is our love made perfect, that we may have boldness in the day of judgment: because as he is, so are we in this world. 1 John 4:17

73

HOW TO HAVE CHURCH OR MINISTRY GROWTH

Be a Vessel of Power

But ye shall receive power, after that the Holy Ghost is come upon you: and ye shall be witnesses unto me both in Jerusalem, and in all Judaea, and in Samaria, and unto the uttermost part of the earth. Acts 1:8

And such as do wickedly against the covenant shall he corrupt by flatteries: but the people that do know their God shall be strong, and do exploits. Daniel 11:32

And he said unto them, Go ye into all the world, and preach the gospel to every creature. He that believeth and is baptized shall be saved; but he that believeth not shall be damned. And these signs shall follow them that believe; In my name shall they cast out devils; they shall speak with new tongues; They shall take up serpents; and if they drink any deadly thing, it shall not hurt them; they shall lay hands on the sick, and they shall recover. Matthew 16:15-18

Remain Humble

But it shall not be so among you: but whosoever will be great among you, let him be your minister; And whosoever will be chief among you, let him be your servant. Matthew 20:26-27

And whosoever shall exalt himself shall be abased; and he that shall humble himself shall be exalted. Matthew 23:12

He hath put down the mighty from their seats, and exalted them of low degree. Luke 1:52

But when thou art bidden, go and sit down in the lowest room; that when he that bade thee cometh, he may say unto thee, Friend, go up higher: then shalt thou have worship in the presence of them that sit at meat with thee. Luke 14:10

And there was also a strife among them, which of them should be accounted the greatest. And he said unto them, The kings of the Gentiles exercise lordship over them; and they that exercise authority upon them are called benefactors. But ye shall not be so: but he that is greatest among you, let him be as the younger; and he that is chief, as he that doth serve. For whether is greater, he that sitteth at meat, or he that serveth? is not he that sitteth at meat? but I am among you as he that serveth.

Luke 22:24-27

He must increase, but I must decrease. John 3:30

Be of the same mind one toward another. Mind not high things, but condescend to men of low estate. Be not wise in your own conceits.

Romans 12:16

But by the grace of God I am what I am: and his grace which was bestowed upon me was not in vain; but I laboured more abundantly than they all: yet not I, but the grace of God which was with me.

1 Corinthians 15:10

With all lowliness and meekness, with longsuffering, forbearing one another in love. Ephesians 4:2

I know both how to be abased, and I know how to abound: every where and in all things I am instructed both to be full and to be hungry, both to abound and to suffer need. Philippians 4:12

Let the brother of low degree rejoice in that he is exalted: But the rich, in that he is made low: because as the flower of the grass he shall pass away. James 1:9-10

Love Everyone

And thou shalt love the Lord thy God with all thy heart, and with all thy soul, and with all thy mind, and with all thy strength: this is the first commandment. And the second is like, namely this, Thou shalt love thy neighbour as thyself. There is none other commandment greater than these. Mark 12:30-31

This is my commandment, That ye love one another, as I have loved you. Greater love hath no man than this, that a man lay down his life for his friends. John 15:12-13

The purest form of leadership is influence through inspiration.

Be kindly affectioned one to another with brotherly love; in honour preferring one another. Romans 12:10

Seeing ye have purified your souls in obeying the truth through the Spirit unto unfeigned love of the brethren, see that ye love one another with a pure heart fervently. 1 Peter 1:22

He that loveth his brother abideth in the light, and there is none occasion of stumbling in him. 1 John 2:10

We know that we have passed from death unto life, because we love the brethren. He that loveth not his brother abideth in death. 1 John 3:14

My little children, let us not love in word, neither in tongue; but in deed and in truth. And hereby we know that we are of the truth, and shall assure our hearts before him. 1 John 3:18-19

Beloved, let us love one another: for love is of God; and every one that loveth is born of God, and knoweth God. He that loveth not knoweth not God; for God is love. 1 John 4:7-8

Beloved, if God so loved us, we ought also to love one another. No man hath seen God at any time. If we love one another, God dwelleth in us, and his love is perfected in us. 1 John 4:11-12

If a man say, I love God, and hateth his brother, he is a liar: for he that loveth not his brother whom he hath seen, how can he love God whom he hath not seen? And this commandment have we from him, That he who loveth God love his brother also. 1 John 4:20-21

Preaching the Gospel

To the World

For the gifts and calling of God are without repentance. Romans 11:29

I will speak of thy testimonies also before kings, and will not be ashamed. Psalms 119:46

Ask of me, and I shall give thee the heathen for thine inheritance, and the uttermost parts of the earth for thy possession. Psalms 2:8

And it shall come to pass in the last days, that the mountain of the Lord's house shall be established in the top of the mountains, and shall be exalted above the hills; and all nations shall flow unto it. And many people shall go and say, Come ye, and let us go up to the mountain of the Lord, to the house of the God of Jacob; and he will teach us of his ways, and we will walk in his paths: for out of Zion shall go forth the law, and the word of the Lord from Jerusalem. Isaiah 2:2-3

Behold, I have given him for a witness to the people, a leader and commander to the people. Behold, thou shalt call a nation that thou knowest not, and nations that knew not thee shall run unto thee because of the Lord thy God, and for the Holy One of Israel; for he hath glorified thee. Isaiah 55:4-5

And as ye go, preach, saying, The kingdom of heaven is at hand. Heal the sick, cleanse the lepers, raise the dead, cast out devils: freely ye have received, freely give. Matthew 10:7-8

And this gospel of the kingdom shall be preached in all the world for a witness unto all nations; and then shall the end come. Matthew 24:14

And Jesus came and spake unto them, saying, All power is given unto me in heaven and in earth. Go ye therefore, and teach all nations, baptizing them in the name of the Father, and of the Son, and of the Holy

Ghost: Teaching them to observe all things whatsoever I have commanded you: and, lo, I am with you alway, even unto the end of the world. Amen.
Matthew 28:18-20

And he said unto them, Go ye into all the world, and preach the gospel to every creature. He that believeth and is baptized shall be saved; but he that believeth not shall be damned. And these signs shall follow them that believe; In my name shall they cast out devils; they shall speak with new tongues; They shall take up serpents; and if they drink any deadly thing, it shall not hurt them; they shall lay hands on the sick, and they shall recover. So then after the Lord had spoken unto them, he was received up into heaven, and sat on the right hand of God. And they went forth, and preached everywhere, the Lord working with them, and confirming the word with signs following. Amen. Mark 16:15-20

The Spirit of the Lord is upon me, because he hath anointed me to preach the gospel to the poor; he hath sent me to heal the brokenhearted, to preach deliverance to the captives, and recovering of sight to the blind, to set at liberty them that are bruised, To preach the acceptable year of the Lord. Luke 4:18-19

Therefore said he unto them, The harvest truly is great, but the labourers are few: pray ye therefore the Lord of the harvest, that he would send forth labourers into his harvest. Luke 10:2

And the lord said unto the servant, Go out into the highways and hedges, and compel them to come in, that my house may be filled. Luke 14:23

And that repentance and remission of sins should be preached in his name among all nations, beginning at Jerusalem. And ye are witnesses of these things. Luke 24:47-48

And I, if I be lifted up from the earth, will draw all men unto me.
John 12:32

But ye shall receive power, after that the Holy Ghost is come upon you: and ye shall be witnesses unto me both in Jerusalem, and in all Judaea, and in Samaria, and unto the uttermost part of the earth. Acts 1:8

And when they found them not, they drew Jason and certain brethren unto the rulers of the city, crying, These that have turned the world upside down are come hither also. Acts 17:6

Real qualities of leadership are to be found in those who are willing to suffer for the sake of objectives great enough to demand their whole-hearted obedience.

For whosoever shall call upon the name of the Lord shall be saved. How then shall they call on him in whom they have not believed? and how shall they believe in him of whom they have not heard? and how shall they hear without a preacher? And how shall they preach, except they be sent? as it is written, How beautiful are the feet of them that preach the gospel of peace, and bring glad tidings of good things! But they have not all obeyed the gospel. For Esaias saith, Lord, who hath believed our report? Romans 10:13-16

But I say, Have they not heard? Yes verily, their sound went into all the earth, and their words unto the ends of the world. Romans 10:18

And ye became followers of us, and of the Lord, having received the word in much affliction, with joy of the Holy Ghost: So that ye were ensamples to all that believe in Macedonia and Achaia. For from you sounded out the word of the Lord not only in Macedonia and Achaia, but also in every place your faith to God-ward is spread abroad; so that we need not to speak any thing. 1 Thessalonians 1:6-8

Thou therefore, my son, be strong in the grace that is in Christ Jesus. And the things that thou hast heard of me among many witnesses, the same commit thou to faithful men, who shall be able to teach others also.
2 Timothy 2:1-2

Preach the word; be instant in season, out of season; reprove, rebuke, exhort with all longsuffering and doctrine. 2 Timothy 4:2

But sanctify the Lord God in your hearts: and be ready always to give an answer to every man that asketh you a reason of the hope that is in you with meekness and fear: Having a good conscience; that, whereas they speak evil of you, as of evildoers, they may be ashamed that falsely accuse your good conversation in Christ. 1 Peter 3:15-16

Use Words of Simplicity and Humility

For Christ sent me not to baptize, but to preach the gospel: not with wisdom of words, lest the cross of Christ should be made of none effect.
1 Corinthians 1:17

And I, brethren, when I came to you, came not with excellency of speech or of wisdom, declaring unto you the testimony of God. For I determined not to know any thing among you, save Jesus Christ, and him crucified. And I was with you in weakness, and in fear, and in much trembling. And my speech and my preaching was not with enticing words of man's wisdom, but in demonstration of the Spirit and of power: That your faith should not stand in the wisdom of men, but in the power of

81

God. Howbeit we speak wisdom among them that are perfect: yet not the wisdom of this world, nor of the princes of this world, that come to nought: But we speak the wisdom of God in a mystery, even the hidden wisdom, which God ordained before the world unto our glory: Which none of the princes of this world knew: for had they known it, they would not have crucified the Lord of glory. 1 Corinthians 2:1-8

Now we have received, not the spirit of the world, but the spirit which is of God; that we might know the things that are freely given to us of God. Which things also we speak, not in the words which man's wisdom teacheth, but which the Holy Ghost teacheth; comparing spiritual things with spiritual. 1 Corinthians 2:12-13

For the kingdom of God is not in word, but in power. 1 Corinthians 4:20

Not that we are sufficient of ourselves to think any thing as of ourselves; but our sufficiency is of God; Who also hath made us able ministers of the new testament; not of the letter, but of the spirit: for the letter killeth, but the spirit giveth life. 2 Corinthians 3:5-6

Seeing then that we have such hope, we use great plainness of speech:
2 Corinthians 3:12

The wise in heart shall be called prudent: and the sweetness of the lips increaseth learning. Proverbs 16:21

The wise in heart shall be called prudent, understanding and knowing; and winsome speech increases learning [in both speaker and listener].
Proverbs 16:21 AMP Version

Preach the Gospel with Pure Motives

Even as I please all men in all things, not seeking mine own profit, but the profit of many, that they may be saved. 1 Corinthians 10:33

For we are not as many, which corrupt the word of God: but as of sincerity, but as of God, in the sight of God speak we in Christ.
2 Corinthians 2:17

But have renounced the hidden things of dishonesty, not walking in craftiness, nor handling the word of God deceitfully; but by manifestation of the truth commending ourselves to every man's conscience in the sight of God. 2 Corinthians 4:2

But of these who seemed to be somewhat, (whatsoever they were, it maketh no matter to me: God accepteth no man's person:) for they who seemed to be somewhat in conference added nothing to me:
Galatians 2:6

Cursed be he that doeth the work of the Lord deceitfully, and cursed be he that keepeth back his sword from blood. Jeremiah 48:10

How To's in Ministry

How to Handle a Successful Ministry

Lord, thou hast heard the desire of the humble: thou wilt prepare their heart, thou wilt cause thine ear to hear. Psalms 10:17

The humble shall see this, and be glad: and your heart shall live that seek God. Psalms 69:32

Lord, my heart is not haughty, nor mine eyes lofty: neither do I exercise myself in great matters, or in things too high for me. Surely I have behaved and quieted myself, as a child that is weaned of his mother: my soul is even as a weaned child. Psalms 131:1-2

Though the Lord be high, yet hath he respect unto the lowly: but the proud he knoweth afar off. Psalms 138:6

The Lord lifteth up the meek: he casteth the wicked down to the ground. Psalms 147:6

For the Lord taketh pleasure in his people: he will beautify the meek with salvation. Psalms 149:4

The fear of the Lord is the instruction of wisdom; and before honour is humility. Proverbs 15:33

For all those things hath mine hand made, and those things have been, saith the Lord: but to this man will I look, even to him that is poor and of a contrite spirit, and trembleth at my word. Isaiah 66:2

He hath shewed thee, O man, what is good; and what doth the Lord require of thee, but to do justly, and to love mercy, and to walk humbly with thy God? Micah 6:8

Blessed are the poor in spirit: for theirs is the kingdom of heaven. Matthew 5:3

But it shall not be so among you: but whosoever will be great among you, let him be your minister; And whosoever will be chief among you, let him be your servant. Matthew 20:26-27

And whosoever shall exalt himself shall be abased; and he that shall humble himself shall be exalted. Matthew 23:12

He hath put down the mighty from their seats, and exalted them of low degree. Luke 1:52

But when thou art bidden, go and sit down in the lowest room; that when he that bade thee cometh, he may say unto thee, Friend, go up higher: then shalt thou have worship in the presence of them that sit at meat with thee. Luke 14:10

And the publican, standing afar off, would not lift up so much as his eyes unto heaven, but smote upon his breast, saying, God be merciful to me a sinner. I tell you, this man went down to his house justified rather than the other: for every one that exalteth himself shall be abased; and he that humbleth himself shall be exalted. Luke 18:13-14

And there was also a strife among them, which of them should be accounted the greatest. And he said unto them, The kings of the Gentiles exercise lordship over them; and they that exercise authority upon them are called benefactors. But ye shall not be so: but he that is greatest among you, let him be as the younger; and he that is chief, as he that doth serve. For whether is greater, he that sitteth at meat, or he that serveth? is not he that sitteth at meat? but I am among you as he that serveth.
Luke 22:24-27

He must increase, but I must decrease. John 3:30

Be of the same mind one toward another. Mind not high things, but condescend to men of low estate. Be not wise in your own conceits.
Romans 12:16

But by the grace of God I am what I am: and his grace which was bestowed upon me was not in vain; but I laboured more abundantly than they all: yet not I, but the grace of God which was with me.
1 Corinthians 15:10

With all lowliness and meekness, with longsuffering, forbearing one another in love. Ephesians 4:2

I know both how to be abased, and I know how to abound: every where and in all things I am instructed both to be full and to be hungry, both to abound and to suffer need. Philippians 4:12

Leadership is born out of character and determination.

Let the brother of low degree rejoice in that he is exalted: But the rich, in that he is made low: because as the flower of the grass he shall pass away. James 1:9-10

Humble yourselves in the sight of the Lord, and he shall lift you up.
James 4:10

Likewise, ye younger, submit yourselves unto the elder. Yea, all of you be subject one to another, and be clothed with humility: for God resisteth the proud, and giveth grace to the humble. Humble yourselves therefore under the mighty hand of God, that he may exalt you in due time.
1 Peter 5:5-6

How to Persevere in a Struggling Ministry

Definition of perseverance - persistance; continued efforts; to stick to a task or purpose, no matter how hard or troublesome.

Know ye not that they which run in a race run all, but one receiveth the prize? So run, that ye may obtain. 1 Corinthians 9:24

The righteous also shall hold on his way, and he that hath clean hands shall be stronger and stronger. Job 17:9

I had fainted, unless I had believed to see the goodness of the Lord in the land of the living. Wait on the Lord: be of good courage, and he shall strengthen thine heart: wait, I say, on the Lord. Psalms 27:13-14

The Lord will perfect that which concerneth me: thy mercy, O Lord, endureth for ever: forsake not the works of thine own hands.
Psalms 138:8

But the path of the just is as the shining light, that shineth more and more unto the perfect day. Proverbs 4:18

For a dream cometh through the multitude of business. Ecclesiastes 5:3

Whatsoever thy hand findeth to do, do it with thy might; for there is no work, nor device, nor knowledge, nor wisdom, in the grave, whither thou goest. Ecclesiastes 9:10

He giveth power to the faint; and to them that have no might he increaseth strength. Even the youths shall faint and be weary, and the young men shall utterly fall: But they that wait upon the Lord shall renew their strength; they shall mount up with wings as eagles; they shall run, and not be weary; and they shall walk, and not faint. Isaiah 40:29-31

Ask, and it shall be given you; seek, and ye shall find; knock, and it shall be opened unto you: Matthew 7:7

Wherefore seeing we also are compassed about with so great a cloud of witnesses, let us lay aside every weight, and the sin which doth so easily beset us, and let us run with patience the race that is set before us.
Hebrews 12:1

Therefore, my beloved brethren, be ye stedfast, unmoveable, always abounding in the work of the Lord, forasmuch as ye know that your labour is not in vain in the Lord. 1 Corinthians 15:58

And let us not be weary in well doing: for in due season we shall reap, if we faint not. Galatians 6:9

I press toward the mark for the prize of the high calling of God in Christ Jesus. Philippians 3:14

Thou therefore endure hardness, as a good soldier of Jesus Christ.
2 Timothy 2:3

Now the just shall love by faith: but if any man draw back, my soul shall have no pleasure in him. Hebrews 10:38

And whatsoever ye do, do it heartily, as to the Lord, and not unto men.
Colossians 3:23

And so, after he had patiently endured, he obtained the promise.
Hebrews 6:15

I have fought a good fight, I have finished my course, I have kept the faith: Henceforth there is laid up for me a crown of righteousness, which the Lord, the righteous judge, shall give me at that day: and not to me only, but unto all them also that love his appearing. 2 Timothy 4:7-8

Let us hold fast the profession of our faith without wavering; for he is faithful that promised. Hebrews 10:23

Cast not away therefore your confidence, which hath great recompence of reward. For ye have need of patience, that, after ye have done the will of God, ye might receive the promise. Hebrews 10:35-36

Wherefore take unto you the whole armour of God, that ye may be able to withstand in the evil day, and having done all, to stand. Stand therefore, having your loins girt about with truth, and having on the breastplate of righteousness. Ephesians 6:13-14

Therefore, my brethren dearly beloved and longed for, my joy and crown, so stand fast in the Lord, my dearly beloved. Philippians 4:1

Rooted and built up in him, and stablished in the faith, as ye have been taught, abounding therein with thanksgiving. Colossians 2:7

Prove all things; hold fast that which is good. 1 Thessalonians 5:21

Watch ye, stand fast in the faith, quit you like men, be strong.
1 Corinthians 16:13

Of the Jews five times received I forty stripes save one. Thrice was I beaten with rods, once was I stoned, thrice I suffered shipwreck, a night and a day I have been in the deep; In journeyings often, in perils of waters, in perils of robbers, in perils by mine own countrymen, in perils by the heathen, in perils in the city, in perils in the wilderness, in perils in the sea, in perils among false brethren; In weariness and painfulness, in watchings often, in hunger and thirst, in fastings often, in cold and nakedness. 2 Corinthians 11:24-27

We are troubled on every side, yet not distressed; we are perplexed, but not in despair; Persecuted, but not forsaken; cast down, but not destroyed.
2 Corinthians 4:8-9

For which cause we faint not; but though our outward man perish, yet the inward man is renewed day by day. For our light affliction, which is but for a moment, worketh for us a far more exceeding and eternal weight of glory. 2 Corinthians 4:16-17

And we desire that every one of you do shew the same diligence to the full assurance of hope unto the end. Hebrews 6:11

How to Qualify Potential Associate Ministers and Staff

Wherefore, brethren, look ye out among you seven men of honest report, full of the Holy Ghost and wisdom, whom we may appoint over this business. Acts 6:3

Not slothful in business; fervent in spirit; serving the Lord; Romans 12:11

This is a true saying, If a man desire the office of a bishop, he desireth a good work. A bishop then must be blameless, the husband of one wife, vigilant, sober, of good behaviour, given to hospitality, apt to teach; Not given to wine, no striker, not greedy of filthy lucre; but patient, not a brawler, not covetous; One that ruleth well his own house, having his children in subjection with all gravity; For if a man know not how to rule his own house, how shall he take care of the church of God? Not a novice, lest being lifted up with pride he fall into the condemnation of the devil. Moreover he must have a good report of them which are without; lest he fall into reproach and the snare of the devil. Likewise must the deacons be grave, not doubletongued, not given to much wine, not greedy of filthy lucre; Holding the mystery of the faith in a pure conscience. And let these also first be proved; then let them use the office of a deacon, being found blameless. Even so must their wives be grave, not slanderers, sober, faithful in all things. Let the deacons be the husbands of one wife, ruling their children and their own houses well. For they that have used the office of a deacon well purchase to themselves a good degree, and great boldness in the faith which is in Christ Jesus.

1 Timothy 3:1-13

If a man therefore purge himself from these, he shall be a vessel unto honour, sanctified, and meet for the master's use, and prepared unto every good work. 2 Timothy 2:21

For this cause left I thee in Crete, that thou shouldest set in order the things that are wanting, and ordain elders in every city, as I had appointed thee: If any be blameless, the husband of one wife, having faithful children not accused of riot or unruly. For a bishop must be blameless, as the steward of God; not selfwilled, not soon angry, not given to wine, no striker, not given to filthy lucre; But a lover of hospitality, a lover of good men, sober, just, holy, temperate; Holding fast the faithful word as he hath been taught, that he may be able by sound doctrine both to exhort and to convince the gainsayers. Titus 1:5-9

The aged women likewise, that they be in behaviour as becometh holiness, not false accusers, not given to much wine, teachers of good things; That they may teach the young women to be sober, to love their husbands, to love their children,To be discreet, chaste, keepers at home, good, obedient to their own husbands, that the word of God be not blasphemed. Young men likewise exhort to be sober minded. In all things shewing thyself a pattern of good works: in doctrine shewing uncorruptness, gravity, sincerity, Titus 2:3-7

The hand of the diligent shall bear rule: but the slothful shall be under tribute. Proverbs 12:24

Seest thou a man diligent in his business? he shall stand before kings; he shall not stand before mean men. Proverbs 22:29

And unto one he gave five talents, to another two, and to another one; to every man according to his several ability; and straightway took his journey. Then he that had received the five talents went and traded with the same, and made them other five talents. And likewise he that had received two, he also gained other two. But he that had received one went and digged in the earth, and hid his lord's money. After a long time the lord of those servants cometh, and reckoneth with them. And so he that

---

If you can inspire, you can mobilize.

---

had received five talents came and brought other five talents, saying, Lord, thou deliveredst unto me five talents: behold, I have gained beside them five talents more. His lord said unto him, Well done, thou good and faithful servant: thou hast been faithful over a few things, I will make thee ruler over many things: enter thou into the joy of thy lord. He also that had received two talents came and said, Lord, thou deliveredst unto me two talents: behold, I have gained two other talents beside them. His lord said unto him, Well done, good and faithful servant; thou hast been faithful over a few things, I will make thee ruler over many things: enter thou into the joy of thy lord. Then he which had received the one talent came and said, Lord, I knew thee that thou art an hard man, reaping where thou hast not sown, and gathering where thou hast not strawed: And I was afraid, and went and hid thy talent in the earth: lo, there thou hast that is thine. His lord answered and said unto him, Thou wicked and slothful servant, thou knewest that I reap where I sowed not, and gather where I have not strawed: Thou oughtest therefore to have put my money to the exchangers, and then at my coming I should have received mine own with usury. Take therefore the talent from him, and give it unto him which hath ten talents. For unto every one that hath shall be given, and he shall have abundance: but from him that hath not shall be taken away even that which he hath. Matthew 25:15-29

But he that knew not, and did commit things worthy of stripes, shall be beaten with few stripes. For unto whomsoever much is given, of him shall be much required: and to whom men have committed much, of him they will ask the more. Luke 12:48

Having then gifts differing according to the grace that is given to us, whether prophecy, let us prophesy according to the proportion of faith;
Romans 12:6

Or he that exhorteth, on exhortation: he that giveth, let him do it with simplicity; he that ruleth, with diligence; he that sheweth mercy, with cheerfulness. Romans 12:8

Moreover it is required in stewards, that a man be found faithful.
1 Corinthians 4:2

And we have sent with them our brother, whom we have oftentimes proved diligent in many things, but now much more diligent, upon the great confidence which I have in you. 2 Corinthians 8:22

How to Handle Persecution from the World and the Church

He that hideth hatred with lying lips, and he that uttereth a slander, is a fool. Proverbs 10:18

Blessed are they which are persecuted for righteousness' sake: for theirs is the kingdom of heaven. **B**lessed are ye, when men shall revile you, and persecute you, and shall say all manner of evil against you falsely, for my sake. Rejoice, and be exceeding glad: for great is your reward in heaven: for so persecuted they the prophets which were before you.
Matthew 5:10-12

But I say unto you, Love your enemies, bless them that curse you, do good to them that hate you, and pray for them which despitefully use you, and persecute you; Matthew 5:44

But he shall receive an hundredfold now in this time, houses, and brethren, and sisters, and mothers, and children, and lands, with persecutions; and in the world to come eternal life. Mark 10:30

But before all these, they shall lay their hands on you, and persecute you, delivering you up to the synagogues, and into prisons, being brought before kings and rulers for my name's sake. Luke 21:12

Remember the word that I said unto you, The servant is not greater than his lord. If they have persecuted me, they will also persecute you; if they have kept my saying, they will keep yours also. John 15:20

Who shall separate us from the love of Christ? shall tribulation, or distress, or persecution, or famine, or nakedness, or peril, or sword?
Romans 8:35

Bless them which persecute you: bless, and curse not. Romans 12:14

And labour, working with our own hands: being reviled, we bless; being persecuted, we suffer it: 1 Corinthians 4:12

Persecuted, but not forsaken; cast down, but not destroyed;
2 Corinthians 4:9

Therefore I take pleasure in infirmities, in reproaches, in necessities, in persecutions, in distresses for Christ's sake: for when I am weak, then am I strong. 2 Corinthians 12:10

But as then he that was born after the flesh persecuted him that was born after the Spirit, even so it is now. Galatians 4:29

So that we ourselves glory in you in the churches of God for your patience and faith in all your persecutions and tribulations that ye endure:
2 Thessalonians 1:4

Persecutions, afflictions, which came unto me at Antioch, at Iconium, at Lystra; what persecutions I endured: but out of them all the Lord delivered me. 2 Timothy 3:11

Yea, and all that will live godly in Christ Jesus shall suffer persecution.
2 Timothy 3:12

HINDRANCES

Pleasing God vs. Pleasing Man

1. Pleasing God

When a man's ways please the Lord, he maketh even his enemies to be at peace with him. Proverbs 16:7

And he that sent me is with me: the Father hath not left me alone; for I do always those things that please him. John 8:29

God forbid: yea, let God be true, but every man a liar; as it is written, That thou mightest be justified in thy sayings, and mightest overcome when thou art judged. Romans 3:4

So then they that are in the flesh cannot please God. Romans 8:8

But he is a Jew, which is one inwardly; and circumcision is that of the heart, in the spirit, and not in the letter; whose praise is not of men, but of God. Romans 2:29

Furthermore then we beseech you, brethren, and exhort you by the Lord Jesus, that as ye have received of us how ye ought to walk and to please God, so ye would abound more and more. 1 Thessalonians 4:1

No man that warreth entangleth himself with the affairs of this life; that he may please him who hath chosen him to be a soldier. 2 Timothy 2:4

But without faith it is impossible to please him: for he that cometh to God must believe that he is, and that he is a rewarder of them that diligently seek him. Hebrews 11:6

2. Pleasing Man

For they loved the praise of men more than the praise of God. John 12:43

93

Even as I please all men in all things, not seeking mine own profit, but the profit of many, that they may be saved. 1 Corinthians 10:33

For do I now persuade men, or God? or do I seek to please men? for if I yet pleased men, I should not be the servant of Christ. Galatians 1:10

Fear of Man

In God I will praise his word, in God I have put my trust; I will not fear what flesh can do unto me. Psalms 56:4

The Lord is on my side; I will not fear: what can man do unto me?
Psalms 118:6

The fear of man bringeth a snare: but whoso putteth his trust in the Lord shall be safe. Proverbs 29:25

So that we may boldly say, The Lord is my helper, and I will not fear what man shall do unto me. Hebrews 13:6

And fear not them which kill the body, but are not able to kill the soul: but rather fear him which is able to destroy both soul and body in hell.
Matthew 10:28

And who is he that will harm you, if ye be followers of that which is good? But and if ye suffer for righteousness' sake, happy are ye: and be not afraid of their terror, neither be troubled; 1 Peter 3:13-14

Trusting in Man or an Organization

Yea, mine own familiar friend, in whom I trusted, which did eat of my bread, hath lifted up his heel against me. Psalms 41:9

It is better to trust in the Lord than to put confidence in man. It is better to trust in the Lord than to put confidence in princes. Psalms 118:8-9

Put not your trust in princes, nor in the son of man, in whom there is no help. Psalms 146:3

Thus saith the Lord; Cursed be the man that trusteth in man, and maketh flesh his arm, and whose heart departeth from the Lord. Jeremiah 17:5

Trust ye not in a friend, put ye not confidence in a guide: keep the doors of thy mouth from her that lieth in thy bosom. Micah 7:5

True leaders learn from others, but they are not made by nor become others.

94

Flattery

Kolakia - an effort to give pleasure, but with motives of self-interest,to praise too much or without really meaning it, as in order to win favor.

He that speaketh flattery to his friends, even the eyes of his children shall fail. Job 17:5

They speak vanity every one with his neighbour: with flattering lips and with a double heart do they speak. The Lord shall cut off all flattering lips, and the tongue that speaketh proud things. Psalms 12:2-3

He that goeth about as a talebearer revealeth secrets: therefore meddle not with him that flattereth with his lips. Proverbs 20:19

A lying tongue hateth those that are afflicted by it; and a flattering mouth worketh ruin. Proverbs 26:28

He that rebuketh a man afterwards shall find more favour than he that flattereth with the tongue. Proverbs 28:23

A man that flattereth his neighbour spreadeth a net for his feet.
Proverbs 29:5

For there is no faithfulness in their mouth; their inward part is very wickedness; their throat is an open sepulchre; they flatter with their tongue.
Psalms 5:9

For he flattereth himself in his own eyes, until his iniquity be found to be hateful. Psalms 36:2

Nevertheless they did flatter him with their mouth, and they lied unto him with their tongues. Psalms 78:36

To deliver thee from the strange woman, even from the stranger which flattereth with her words. Proverbs 2:16

To keep thee from the evil woman, from the flattery of the tongue of a strange woman. Proverbs 6:24

That they may keep thee from the strange woman, from the stranger which flattereth with her words. Proverbs 7:5

For there shall be no more any vain vision nor flattering divination within the house of Israel. Ezekiel 12:24

For neither at any time used we flattering words, as ye know, nor a cloke of covetousness; God is witness. 1 Thessalonians 2:5

WHAT MAKES A CHURCH OR MINISTRY FAIL

Not Flowing in the Holy Spirit

For the Holy Ghost shall teach you in the same hour what ye ought to say. Luke 12:12

But this spake he of the Spirit, which they that believe on him should receive: for the Holy Ghost was not yet given; because that Jesus was not yet glorified. John 7:39

But the Comforter, which is the Holy Ghost, whom the Father will send in my name, he shall teach you all things, and bring all things to your remembrance, whatsoever I have said unto you. John 14:26

Howbeit when he, the Spirit of truth, is come, he will guide you into all truth: for he shall not speak of himself; but whatsoever he shall hear, that shall he speak: and he will shew you things to come. John 16:13

For as many as are led by the Spirit of God, they are the sons of God.
Romans 8:14

The Spirit itself beareth witness with our spirit, that we are the children of God. Romans 8:16

But God hath revealed them unto us by his Spirit: for the Spirit searcheth all things, yea, the deep things of God. For what man knoweth the things of a man, save the spirit of man which is in him? even so the things of God knoweth no man, but the Spirit of God. 1 Corinthians 2:10-11

Which things also we speak, not in the words which man's wisdom teacheth, but which the Holy Ghost teacheth; comparing spiritual things with spiritual. 1 Corinthians 2:13

But if ye be led of the Spirit, ye are not under the law. Galatians 5:18

Not Continuously Praying

Watch and pray, that ye enter not into temptation: the spirit indeed is willing, but the flesh is weak. Matthew 26:41

And he spake a parable unto them to this end, that men ought always to pray, and not to faint. Luke 18:1

Watch ye therefore, and pray always, that ye may be accounted worthy to escape all these things that shall come to pass, and to stand before the Son of man. Luke 21:36

And said unto them, Why sleep ye? rise and pray, lest ye enter into temptation. Luke 22:46

Continue in prayer, and watch in the same with thanksgiving;
Colossians 4:2

Pray without ceasing. 1 Thessalonians 5:17

But the end of all things is at hand: be ye therefore sober, and watch unto prayer. 1 Peter 4:7

Living in Sin

But if ye will not do so, behold, ye have sinned against the Lord: and be sure your sin will find you out. Numbers 32:23

He that covereth his sins shall not prosper: but whoso confesseth and forsaketh them shall have mercy. Proverbs 28:13

For God shall bring every work into judgment, with every secret thing, whether it be good, or whether it be evil. Ecclesiastes 12:14

For there is nothing hid, which shall not be manifested; neither was any thing kept secret, but that it should come abroad. Mark 4:22

For nothing is secret, that shall not be made manifest; neither any thing hid, that shall not be known and come abroad. Luke 8:17

For there is nothing covered, that shall not be revealed; neither hid, that shall not be known. Therefore whatsoever ye have spoken in darkness shall be heard in the light; and that which ye have spoken in the ear in closets shall be proclaimed upon the housetops. Luke 12:2-3

True success is the fulfillment of original purpose.

In the day when God shall judge the secrets of men by Jesus Christ according to my gospel. Romans 2:16

Being Prideful

Pride goeth before destruction, and an haughty spirit before a fall. Better it is to be of an humble spirit with the lowly, than to divide the spoil with the proud. Proverbs 16:18-19

Before destruction the heart of man is haughty, and before honour is humility. Proverbs 18:12

A man's pride shall bring him low: but honour shall uphold the humble in spirit. Proverbs 29:23

Wherefore let him that thinketh he standeth take heed lest he fall.
1 Corinthians 10:12

Not Controling Your Sexual Desires

Now the works of the flesh are manifest, which are these; Adultery, fornication, uncleanness, lasciviousness, Envyings, murders, drunkenness, revellings, and such like: of the which I tell you before, as I have also told you in time past, that they which do such things shall not inherit the kingdom of God. Galatians 5:19,21

Marriage is honourable in all, and the bed undefiled: but whoremongers and adulterers God will judge. Hebrews 13:4

Even as Sodom and Gomorrha, and the cities about them in like manner, giving themselves over to fornication, and going after strange flesh, are set forth for an example, suffering the vengeance of eternal fire. Jude 1:7

Thou shalt not commit adultery. Exodus 20:14

But I say unto you, That whosoever looketh on a woman to lust after her hath committed adultery with her already in his heart. Matthew 5:28

For by means of a whorish woman a man is brought to a piece of bread: and the adulteress will hunt for the precious life. Proverbs 6:26

But whoso committeth adultery with a woman lacketh understanding: he that doeth it destroyeth his own soul. Proverbs 6:32

Know ye not that the unrighteous shall not inherit the kingdom of God? Be not deceived: neither fornicators, nor idolaters, nor adulterers, nor effeminate, nor abusers of themselves with mankind. 1 Corinthians 6:9

Marriage is honourable in all, and the bed undefiled: but whoremongers and adulterers God will judge. Hebrews 13:4

Judging Members by Their Money, Race or Association

Ye shall do no unrighteousness in judgment: thou shalt not respect the person of the poor, nor honour the person of the mighty: but in righteousness shalt thou judge thy neighbour. Leviticus 19:15

Wherefore now let the fear of the Lord be upon you; take heed and do it: for there is no iniquity with the Lord our God, nor respect of persons, nor taking of gifts. 2 Chronicles 19:7

How much less to him that accepteth not the persons of princes, nor regardeth the rich more than the poor? for they all are the work of his hands. Job 34:19

To have respect of persons is not good: for for a piece of bread that man will transgress. Proverbs 28:21

These things also belong to the wise. It is not good to have respect of persons in judgment. Proverbs 24:23

I returned, and saw under the sun, that the race is not to the swift, nor the battle to the strong, neither yet bread to the wise, nor yet riches to men of understanding, nor yet favour to men of skill; but time and chance happeneth to them all. Ecclesiastes 9:11

And they shall teach no more every man his neighbour, and every man his brother, saying, Know the Lord: for they shall all know me, from the least of them unto the greatest of them, saith the Lord; for I will forgive their iniquity, and I will remember their sin no more. Jeremiah 31:34

Judge not, and ye shall not be judged: condemn not, and ye shall not be condemned: forgive, and ye shall be forgiven. Luke 6:37

And they shall come from the east, and from the west, and from the north, and from the south, and shall sit down in the kingdom of God. And, behold, there are last which shall be first, and there are first which shall be last. Luke 13:29-30

And the lord commended the unjust steward, because he had done wisely: for the children of this world are in their generation wiser than the children of light. Luke 16:8

Judge not according to the appearance, but judge righteous judgment.
John 7:24

Even the righteousness of God which is by faith of Jesus Christ unto all and upon all them that believe: for there is no difference. Romans 3:22

If then ye have judgments of things pertaining to this life, set them to judge who are least esteemed in the church. 1 Corinthians 6:4

But unto every one of us is given grace according to the measure of the gift of Christ. Ephesians 4:7

My brethren, have not the faith of our Lord Jesus Christ, the Lord of glory, with respect of persons. For if there come unto your assembly a man with a gold ring, in goodly apparel, and there come in also a poor man in vile raiment; And ye have respect to him that weareth the gay clothing, and say unto him, Sit thou here in a good place; and say to the poor, Stand thou there, or sit here under my footstool: Are ye not then partial in yourselves, and are become judges of evil thoughts? Hearken, my beloved brethren, Hath not God chosen the poor of this world rich in faith, and heirs of the kingdom which he hath promised to them that love him? But ye have despised the poor. Do not rich men oppress you, and draw you before the judgment seats? Do not they blaspheme that worthy name by the which ye are called? If ye fulfil the royal law according to the scripture, Thou shalt love thy neighbour as thyself, ye do well: But if ye have respect to persons, ye commit sin, and are convinced of the law as transgressors. James 2:1-9

Not Confronting Sin in Your Staff and Church

And have no fellowship with the unfruitful works of darkness, but rather reprove them. Ephesians 5:11

Them that sin rebuke before all, that others also may fear.
1 Timothy 5:20

All scripture is given by inspiration of God, and is profitable for doctrine, for reproof, for correction, for instruction in righteousness.
2 Timothy 3:16

This witness is true. Wherefore rebuke them sharply, that they may be sound in the faith. Titus 1:13

He that saith unto the wicked, Thou art righteous; him shall the people curse, nations shall abhor him: But to them that rebuke him shall be delight, and a good blessing shall come upon them. Proverbs 24:24-25

These things speak, and exhort, and rebuke with all authority. Let no man despise thee. Titus 2:15

When thou with rebukes dost correct man for iniquity, thou makest his beauty to consume away like a moth: surely every man is vanity. Selah.
Psalms 39:11

When with rebukes You correct and chasten man for sin, You waste his beauty like a moth and what is dear to him consumes away; surely every man is a mere breath. Selah [pause, and think calmly of that]!
Psalms 39:11 AMP

And I myself also am persuaded of you, my brethren, that ye also are full of goodness, filled with all knowledge, able also to admonish one another. Romans 15:14

Open rebuke is better than secret love. Proverbs 27:5

He that rebuketh a man afterwards shall find more favour than he that flattereth with the tongue. Proverbs 28:23

It is better to hear the rebuke of the wise, than for a man to hear the song of fools. Ecclesiastes 7:5

Reprove not a scorner, lest he hate thee: rebuke a wise man, and he will love thee. Proverbs 9:8

As an earring of gold, and an ornament of fine gold, so is a wise reprover upon an obedient ear. Proverbs 25:12

1. Make Sure Your Life is in Order Before Confronting Anyone

And having in a readiness to revenge all disobedience, when your obedience is fulfilled. 2 Corinthians 10:6

And why beholdest thou the mote that is in thy brother's eye, but considerest not the beam that is in thine own eye? Or how wilt thou say to thy brother, Let me pull out the mote out of thine eye; and, behold, a beam is in thine own eye? Thou hypocrite, first cast out the beam out of thine own eye; and then shalt thou see clearly to cast out the mote out of thy brother's eye. Matthew 7:3-5

2. Always Confront Sin in the Spirit of Love

God is love; and he that dwelleth in love dwelleth in God, and God in him. 1 John 4:16

> **The leader should not be motivated by, or greedy for money.**

A wicked messenger falleth into mischief: but a faithful ambassador is health. Proverbs 13:17

Rebuke not an elder, but intreat him as a father; and the younger men as brethren; The elder women as mothers; the younger as sisters, with all purity. 1 Timothy 5:1-2

There is no fear in love; but perfect love casteth out fear: because fear hath torment. He that feareth is not made perfect in love. 1 John 4:18

3. Examples of Godly Confrontation

But the Lord said unto me, Say not, I am a child: for thou shalt go to all that I shall send thee, and whatsoever I command thee thou shalt speak. Be not afraid of their faces: for I am with thee to deliver thee, saith the Lord. Then the Lord put forth his hand, and touched my mouth. And the Lord said unto me, Behold, I have put my words in thy mouth. See, I have this day set thee over the nations and over the kingdoms, to root out, and to pull down, and to destroy, and to throw down, to build, and to plant. Jeremiah 1:7-10

And they come to Jerusalem: and Jesus went into the temple, and began to cast out them that sold and bought in the temple, and overthrew the tables of the moneychangers, and the seats of them that sold doves; And would not suffer that any man should carry any vessel through the temple. And he taught, saying unto them, Is it not written, My house shall be called of all nations the house of prayer? but ye have made it a den of thieves. Mark 11:15-17

Why do ye not understand my speech? even because ye cannot hear my word. Ye are of your father the devil, and the lusts of your father ye will do. He was a murderer from the beginning, and abode not in the truth, because there is no truth in him. When he speaketh a lie, he speaketh of his own: for he is a liar, and the father of it. And because I tell you the truth, ye believe me not. John 8:43-45

But when I saw that they walked not uprightly according to the truth of the gospel, I said unto Peter before them all, If thou, being a Jew, livest after the manner of Gentiles, and not as do the Jews, why compellest thou the Gentiles to live as do the Jews? Galatians 2:14

Wherefore comfort yourselves together, and edify one another, even as also ye do. And we beseech you, brethren, to know them which labour among you, and are over you in the Lord, and admonish you; And to esteem them very highly in love for their work's sake. And be at peace among yourselves. Now we exhort you, brethren, warn them that are unruly, comfort the feebleminded, support the weak, be patient toward all men. 1 Thessalonians 5:11-14

For even when we were with you, this we commanded you, that if any would not work, neither should he eat. For we hear that there are some which walk among you disorderly, working not at all, but are busybodies. Now them that are such we command and exhort by our Lord Jesus Christ, that with quietness they work, and eat their own bread.
2 Thessalonians 3:10-12

And if any man obey not our word by this epistle, note that man, and have no company with him, that he may be ashamed. Yet count him not as an enemy, but admonish him as a brother.
2 Thessalonians 3:14-15

Beloved, when I gave all diligence to write unto you of the common salvation, it was needful for me to write unto you, and exhort you that ye should earnestly contend for the faith which was once delivered unto the saints. Jude 1:3

Allowing False Brothers/Teachers to Minister at Your Church or Be Members of Your Staff

For such are false apostles, deceitful workers, transforming themselves into the apostles of Christ. And no marvel; for Satan himself is transformed into an angel of light. Therefore it is no great thing if his ministers also be transformed as the ministers of righteousness; whose end shall be according to their works. 2 Corinthians 11:13-15

1. Recognizing False Brother and Teachers

a. They claim to have power but they are powerless

Whoso boasteth himself of a false gift is like clouds and wind without rain. Proverbs 25:14

These are spots in your feasts of charity, when they feast with you, feeding themselves without fear: clouds they are without water, carried about of winds; trees whose fruit withereth, without fruit, twice dead, plucked up by the roots;12 Raging waves of the sea, foaming out their own shame; wandering stars, to whom is reserved the blackness of darkness for ever. Jude 1:12-13

b. They will deny Christ

Who is a liar but he that denieth that Jesus is the Christ? He is antichrist, that denieth the Father and the Son. Whosoever denieth the Son, the same hath not the Father: (but) he hat acknowledgeth the Son hath the Father also. 1 John 2:22-23

For there are certain men crept in unawares, who were before of old ordained to this condemnation, ungodly men, turning the grace of our God into lasciviousness, and denying the only Lord God, and our Lord Jesus Christ. Jude 1:4

c. Check out their lifestyles

Ye shall know them by their fruits. Do men gather grapes of thorns, or figs of thistles? Matthew 7:16

Wherefore by their fruits ye shall know them. Matthew 7:20

Whosoever transgresseth, and abideth not in the doctrine of Christ, hath not God. He that abideth in the doctrine of Christ, he hath both the Father and the Son. 2 John 1:9

d. They teach unsound doctrine

But there were false prophets also among the people, even as there shall be false teachers among you, who privily shall bring in damnable heresies, even denying the Lord that bought them, and bring upon themselves swift destruction. 2 Peter 2:1

Now I beseech you, brethren, mark them which cause divisions and offences contrary to the doctrine which ye have learned; and avoid them. For they that are such serve not our Lord Jesus Christ, but their own belly; and by good words and fair speeches deceive the hearts of the simple. Romans 16:17-18

I marvel that ye are so soon removed from him that called you into the grace of Christ unto another gospel. Which is not another; but there be some that trouble you, and would pervert the gospel of Christ. But though we, or an angel from heaven, preach any other gospel unto you than that which we have preached unto you, let him be accursed. As we said before, so say I now again, If any man preach any other gospel unto you than that ye have received, let him be accursed.

Galatians 1:6-9

105

For the time will come when they will not endure sound doctrine; but after their own lusts shall they heap to themselves teachers, having itching ears; And they shall turn away their ears from the truth, and shall be turned unto fables. 2 Timothy 4:3-4

Holding fast the faithful word as he hath been taught, that he may be able by sound doctrine both to exhort and to convince the gainsayers. For there are many unruly and vain talkers and deceivers, specially they of the circumcision. Whose mouths must be stopped, who subvert whole houses, teaching things which they ought not, for filthy lucre's sake. Titus 1:9-11

If there come any unto you, and bring not this doctrine, receive him not into your house, neither bid him God speed: For he that biddeth him God speed is partaker of his evil deeds. 2 John 1:10-11

e. They promote religion, traditions, and rituals rather than Christ

But he answered and said unto them, Why do ye also transgress the commandment of God by your tradition? Matthew 15:3

And honour not his father or his mother, he shall be free. Thus have ye made the commandment of God of none effect by your tradition.
Matthew 15:6

For laying aside the commandment of God, ye hold the tradition of men, as the washing of pots and cups: and many other such like things ye do. And he said unto them, Full well ye reject the commandment of God, that ye may keep your own tradition. Mark 7:8-9

Making the word of God of none effect through your tradition, which ye have delivered: and many such like things do ye. Mark 7:13

Beware lest any man spoil you through philosophy and vain deceit, after the tradition of men, after the rudiments of the world, and not after Christ.
Colossians 2:8

Forasmuch as ye know that ye were not redeemed with corruptible things, as silver and gold, from your vain conversation received by tradition from your fathers; 1 Peter 1:18

f. They are smooth talkers that speak deceptive words

Let no man deceive you with vain words: for because of these things cometh the wrath of God upon the children of disobedience.
Ephesians 5:6

And this I say, lest any man should beguile you with enticing words.
Colossians 2:4

Neither give heed to fables and endless genealogies, which minister questions, rather than godly edifying which is in faith: so do.
1 Timothy 1:3-4

2. Test and Confront False Brothers and Teachers

Who is a liar but he that denieth that Jesus is the Christ? He is antichrist, that denieth the Father and the Son. Whosoever denieth the Son, the same hath not the Father: (but) he that acknowledgeth the Son hath the Father also. 1 John 2:22-23

Beloved, believe not every spirit, but try the spirits whether they are of God: because many false prophets are gone out into the world.
1 John 4:1

Hereby know ye the Spirit of God: Every spirit that confesseth that Jesus Christ is come in the flesh is of God: And every spirit that confesseth not that Jesus Christ is come in the flesh is not of God: and this is that spirit of antichrist, whereof ye have heard that it should come; and even now already is it in the world. 1 John 4:2-3

We are of God: he that knoweth God heareth us; he that is not of God heareth not us. Hereby know we the spirit of truth, and the spirit of error.
1 John 4:6

For many deceivers are entered into the world, who confess not that Jesus Christ is come in the flesh. This is a deceiver and an antichrist.
2 John 1:7

THE ROOT CAUSE FOR MINISTRY CONFLICTS AND CHURCH SPLITS

Strife

A froward man soweth strife: and a whisperer separateth chief friends.
Proverbs 16:28

Better is a dry morsel, and quietness therewith, than an house full of sacrifices with strife. Proverbs 17:1

He loveth transgression that loveth strife: and he that exalteth his gate seeketh destruction. Proverbs 17:19

It is an honour for a man to cease from strife: but every fool will be meddling. Proverbs 20:3

He that passeth by, and meddleth with strife belonging not to him, is like one that taketh a dog by the ears. Proverbs 26:17

He that is of a proud heart stirreth up strife: but he that putteth his trust in the Lord shall be made fat. Proverbs 28:25

An angry man stirreth up strife, and a furious man aboundeth in transgression. Proverbs 29:22

Let us walk honestly, as in the day; not in rioting and drunkenness, not in chambering and wantonness, not in strife and envying. Romans 13:13

Let nothing be done through strife or vainglory; but in lowliness of mind let each esteem other better than themselves. Philippians 2:3

1. Causes of Strife

Hatred stirreth up strifes: but love covereth all sins. Proverbs 10:12

The beginning of strife is as when one letteth out water: therefore leave off contention, before it be meddled with. Proverbs 17:14

A fool's lips enter into contention, and his mouth calleth for strokes.
Proverbs 18:6

Surely the churning of milk bringeth forth butter, and the wringing of the nose bringeth forth blood: so the forcing of wrath bringeth forth strife.
Proverbs 30:33

But foolish and unlearned questions avoid, knowing that they do gender strifes. 2 Timothy 2:23

For where envying and strife is, there is confusion and every evil work.
James 3:16

2. Stopping Strife

Cast out the scorner, and contention shall go out; yea, strife and reproach shall cease. Proverbs 22:10

Where no wood is, there the fire goeth out: so where there is no tale-bearer, the strife ceaseth. Proverbs 26:20

A wrathful man stirreth up strife: but he that is slow to anger appeaseth strife. Proverbs 15:18

In thee, O Lord, do I put my trust: let me never be put to confusion.
Psalms 71:1

For God is not the author of confusion, but of peace, as in all churches of the saints. 1 Corinthians 14:33

Contention

Only by pride cometh contention: but with the well advised is wisdom.
Proverbs 13:10

The beginning of strife is as when one letteth out water: therefore leave off contention, before it be meddled with. Proverbs 17:14

A fool's lips enter into contention, and his mouth calleth for strokes.
Proverbs 18:6

Cast out the scorner, and contention shall go out; yea, strife and reproach shall cease. Proverbs 22:10

Effectiveness is not doing things right, but doing the right things.

But avoid foolish questions, and genealogies, and contentions, and strivings about the law; for they are unprofitable and vain. Titus 3:9

1. A Contentious Woman

A foolish son is the calamity of his father: and the contentions of a wife are a continual dropping. Proverbs 19:13

It is better to dwell in the wilderness, than with a contentious and an angry woman. Proverbs 21:19

A continual dropping in a very rainy day and a contentious woman are alike. Whosoever hideth her hideth the wind, and the ointment of his right hand, which bewrayeth itself. Proverbs 27:15-16

A continual dripping on a day of violent showers and a contentious woman are alike. Whoever attempts to restrain a contentious woman might as well try to stop the wind; his right hand encounters oil [and she slips through his fingers]. Proverbs 27:15-16 AMP Version

It is better to dwell in the corner of the housetop, than with a brawling woman and in a wide house. Proverbs 25:24

2. A Contentious Man

As coals are to burning coals, and wood to fire; so is a contentious man to kindle strife. Proverbs 26:21

A wrathful man stirreth up strife: but he that is slow to anger appeaseth strife. Proverbs 15:18

An angry man stirreth up strife, and a furious man aboundeth in transgression. Proverbs 29:22

Gossip

Thou shalt not go up and down as a talebearer among thy people: neither shalt thou stand against the blood of thy neighbour: I am the Lord.
Leviticus 19:16

He that backbiteth not with his tongue, nor doeth evil to his neighbour, nor taketh up a reproach against his neighbour. Psalms 15:3

Keep thy tongue from evil, and thy lips from speaking guile.
Psalms 34:13

Thy tongue deviseth mischiefs; like a sharp rasor, working deceitfully.
Psalms 52:2

A talebearer revealeth secrets: but he that is of a faithful spirit concealeth the matter. Proverbs 11:13

A froward man soweth strife: and a whisperer separateth chief friends.
Proverbs 16:28

He that covereth a transgression seeketh love; but he that repeateth a matter separateth very friends. Proverbs 17:9

The words of a talebearer are as wounds, and they go down into the innermost parts of the belly. Proverbs 26:22

The words of a whisperer or slanderer are as dainty morsels or words of sport [to some, but to others are as deadly wound], and they go down into the innermost parts of the body [or of the victim's nature].
Proverbs 26:22 AMP Version

He that goeth about as a talebearer revealeth secrets: therefore meddle not with him that flattereth with his lips. Proverbs 20:19

Debate thy cause with thy neighbour himself; and discover not a secret to another: Lest he that heareth it put thee to shame, and thine infamy turn not away. Proverbs 25:9-10

The north wind driveth away rain: so doth an angry countenance a back-biting tongue. Proverbs 25:23

Where no wood is, there the fire goeth out: so where there is no tale-bearer, the strife ceaseth. As coals are to burning coals, and wood to fire; so is a contentious man to kindle strife. The words of a talebearer are as wounds, and they go down into the innermost parts of the belly.
Proverbs 26:20-22

But I say unto you, That every idle word that men shall speak, they shall give account thereof in the day of judgment. Matthew 12:36

And withal they learn to be idle, wandering about from house to house; and not only idle, but tattlers also and busybodies, speaking things which they ought not. 1 Timothy 5:13

And that ye study to be quiet, and to do your own business, and to work with your own hands, as we commanded you.
1 Thessalonians 4:11

Slander

Thou shalt be hid from the scourge of the tongue: neither shalt thou be afraid of destruction when it cometh. Job 5:21

112

Thou shalt hide them in the secret of thy presence from the pride of man: thou shalt keep them secretly in a pavilion from the strife of tongues.
Psalms 31:20

He shall send from heaven, and save from the reproach of him that would swallow me up. Selah. God shall send forth his mercy and his truth.
Psalms 57:3

He that hideth hatred with lying lips, and he that uttereth a slander, is a fool. Proverbs 10:18

A froward man soweth strife: and a whisperer separateth chief friends.
Proverbs 16:28

Hearken unto me, ye that know righteousness, the people in whose heart is my law; fear ye not the reproach of men, neither be ye afraid of their revilings. Isaiah 51:7

Blessed are ye, when men shall revile you, and persecute you, and shall say all manner of evil against you falsely, for my sake. Rejoice, and be exceeding glad: for great is your reward in heaven: for so persecuted they the prophets which were before you. Matthew 5:11-12

But if ye bite and devour one another, take heed that ye be not consumed one of another. Galatians 5:15

If ye be reproached for the name of Christ, happy are ye; for the spirit of glory and of God resteth upon you: on their part he is evil spoken of, but on your part he is glorified. 1 Peter 4:14

Envy

Definition of envy - the feeling of displeaure produced by witnessing or hearing of the advantage or prosperity of others.

Envy thou not the oppressor, and choose none of his ways.
Proverbs 3:31

Let not thine heart envy sinners: but be thou in the fear of the Lord all the day long. Proverbs 23:17

Be not thou envious against evil men, neither desire to be with them.
Proverbs 24:1

Fret not thyself because of evil men, neither be thou envious at the wicked;
Proverbs 24:19

Let us walk honestly, as in the day; not in rioting and drunkenness, not in chambering and wantonness, not in strife and envying. Romans 13:13

Let us not be desirous of vain glory, provoking one another, envying one another. Galatians 5:26

For where envying and strife is, there is confusion and every evil work. James 3:16

Wherefore laying aside all malice, and all guile, and hypocrisies, and envies, and all evil speakings, 1 Peter 2:1

A sound heart is the life of the flesh: but envy the rottenness of the bones. Proverbs 14:30

Wrath is cruel, and anger is outrageous; but who is able to stand before envy? Proverbs 27:4

Lying

Let the lying lips be put to silence; which speak grievous things proudly and contemptuously against the righteous. Psalms 31:18

These six things doth the Lord hate: yea, seven are an abomination unto him: **A** proud look, a lying tongue, and hands that shed innocent blood, **An** heart that deviseth wicked imaginations, feet that be swift in running to mischief, **A** false witness that speaketh lies, and he that soweth discord among brethren. Proverbs 6:16-19

He that hideth hatred with lying lips, and he that uttereth a slander, is a fool. Proverbs 10:18

The lip of truth shall be established for ever: but a lying tongue is but for a moment. Proverbs 12:19

Lying lips are abomination to the Lord: but they that deal truly are his delight. Proverbs 12:22

A righteous man hateth lying: but a wicked man is loathsome, and cometh to shame. Proverbs 13:5

A faithful witness will not lie: but a false witness will utter lies. Proverbs 14:5

A wicked doer giveth heed to false lips; and a liar giveth ear to a naughty tongue. Proverbs 17:4

The desire of a man is his kindness: and a poor man is better than a liar. Proverbs 19:22

> **Real leadership power comes from an honorable character.**

The getting of treasures by a lying tongue is a vanity tossed to and fro of them that seek death. Proverbs 21:6

A lying tongue hateth those that are afflicted by it; and a flattering mouth worketh ruin. Proverbs 26:28

Add thou not unto his words, lest he reprove thee, and thou be found a liar. Proverbs 30:6

Ye are of your father the devil, and the lusts of your father ye will do. He was a murderer from the beginning, and abode not in the truth, because there is no truth in him. When he speaketh a lie, he speaketh of his own: for he is a liar, and the father of it. John 8:44

Wherefore putting away lying, speak every man truth with his neighbour: for we are members one of another. Ephesians 4:25

Lie not one to another, seeing that ye have put off the old man with his deeds. Colossians 3:9

But if ye have bitter envying and strife in your hearts, glory not, and lie not against the truth. James 3:14

Who is a liar but he that denieth that Jesus is the Christ? He is antichrist, that denieth the Father and the Son. 1 John 2:22

If a man say, I love God, and hateth his brother, he is a liar: for he that loveth not his brother whom he hath seen, how can he love God whom he hath not seen? 1 John 4:20

But the fearful, and unbelieving, and the abominable, and murderers, and whoremongers, and sorcerers, and idolaters, and all liars shall have their part in the lake which burneth with fire and brimstone: which is the second death. Revelation 21:8

Judgmental Attitudes

Judge not, that ye be not judged. For with what judgment ye judge, ye shall be judged: and with what measure ye mete, it shall be measured to you again. And why beholdest thou the mote that is in thy brother's eye, but considerest not the beam that is in thine own eye? Or how wilt thou say to thy brother, Let me pull out the mote out of thine eye; and, behold, a beam is in thine own eye? Thou hypocrite, first cast out the beam out of thine own eye; and then shalt thou see clearly to cast out the mote out of thy brother's eye. Matthew 7:1-5

Judge not, and ye shall not be judged: condemn not, and ye shall not be condemned: forgive, and ye shall be forgiven. Luke 6:37

And thinkest thou this, O man, that judgest them which do such things, and doest the same, that thou shalt escape the judgment of God?

Romans 2:3

But why dost thou judge thy brother? or why dost thou set at nought thy brother? for we shall all stand before the judgment seat of Christ.

Romans 14:10

SPIRITUAL DISCERNMENT

Spiritual Eyes and Ears

Open thou mine eyes, that I may behold wondrous things out of thy law.
Psalms 119:18

Make me to understand the way of thy precepts: so shall I talk of thy wondrous works. Psalms 119:27

Give me understanding, and I shall keep thy law; yea, I shall observe it with my whole heart. Psalms 119:34

The earth, O Lord, is full of thy mercy: teach me thy statutes.
Psalms 119:64

Thy hands have made me and fashioned me: give me understanding, that I may learn thy commandments. Psalms 119:73

Turn you at my reproof: behold, I will pour out my spirit unto you, I will make known my words unto you. Proverbs 1:23

And in that day shall the deaf hear the words of the book, and the eyes of the blind shall see out of obscurity, and out of darkness. Isaiah 29:18

They also that erred in spirit shall come to understanding, and they that murmured shall learn doctrine. Isaiah 29:24

And I will bring the blind by a way that they knew not; I will lead them in paths that they have not known: I will make darkness light before them, and crooked things straight. These things will I do unto them, and not forsake them. Isaiah 42:16

He answered and said unto them, Because it is given unto you to know the mysteries of the kingdom of heaven, but to them it is not given.
Matthew 13:11

But blessed are your eyes, for they see: and your ears, for they hear. For verily I say unto you, That many prophets and righteous men have desired to see those things which ye see, and have not seen them; and to hear those things which ye hear, and have not heard them.

Matthew 13:16-17

That the God of our Lord Jesus Christ, the Father of glory, may give unto you the spirit of wisdom and revelation in the knowledge of him. The eyes of your understanding being enlightened; that ye may know what is the hope of his calling, and what the riches of the glory of his inheritance in the saints. Ephesians 1:17-18

He that hath an ear, let him hear what the Spirit saith unto the churches; To him that overcometh will I give to eat of the tree of life, which is in the midst of the paradise of God. Revelation 2:7

Spiritual Blindness and Deafness

For whosoever hath, to him shall be given, and he shall have more abundance: but whosoever hath not, from him shall be taken away even that he hath. Therefore speak I to them in parables: because they seeing see not; and hearing they hear not, neither do they understand. And in them is fulfilled the prophecy of Esaias, which saith, By hearing ye shall hear, and shall not understand; and seeing ye shall see, and shall not perceive: For this people's heart is waxed gross, and their ears are dull of hearing, and their eyes they have closed; lest at any time they should see with their eyes, and hear with their ears, and should understand with their heart, and should be converted, and I should heal them.

Matthew 13:12-15

Let them alone: they be blind leaders of the blind. And if the blind lead the blind, both shall fall into the ditch. Mark 15:14

And he said unto them, Unto you it is given to know the mystery of the kingdom of God: but unto them that are without, all these things are done in parables: That seeing they may see, and not perceive; and hearing they may hear, and not understand; lest at any time they should be converted, and their sins should be forgiven them. Mark 4:11-12

Good leaders employ others, great leaders deploy themselves and others.

For I would not, brethren, that ye should be ignorant of this mystery, lest ye should be wise in your own conceits; that blindness in part is happened to Israel, until the fulness of the Gentiles be come in.

Romans 11:25

But their minds were blinded: for until this day remaineth the same vail untaken away in the reading of the old testament; which vail is done away in Christ. 2 Corinthians 3:14

In whom the god of this world hath blinded the minds of them which believe not, lest the light of the glorious gospel of Christ, who is the image of God, should shine unto them. 2 Corinthians 4:4

Having the understanding darkened, being alienated from the life of God through the ignorance that is in them, because of the blindness of their heart. Ephesians 4:18

Ever learning, and never able to come to the knowledge of the truth.

2 Timothy 3:7

Of whom we have many things to say, and hard to be uttered, seeing ye are dull of hearing. Hebrews 5:11

Concerning this we have much to say which is hard to explain, since you have become dull in your [spiritual] hearing and sluggish, even slothful [in achieving spiritual insight]. Hebrews 5:11 AMP Version

But he that hateth his brother is in darkness, and walketh in darkness, and knoweth not whither he goeth, because that darkness hath blinded his eyes. 1 John 2:11

Discernment

But the natural man receiveth not the things of the Spirit of God: for they are foolishness unto him: neither can he know them, because they are spiritually discerned. 1 Corinthians 2:14

To another the working of miracles; to another prophecy; to another discerning of spirits; to another divers kinds of tongues; to another the interpretation of tongues: 1 Corinthians 12:10

Lest satan should get an advantage of us: for we are not ignorant of his devices. 2 Corinthians 2:11

Discerning Good and Evil

Give therefore thy servant an understanding heart to judge thy people, that I may discern between good and bad: for who is able to judge this thy so great a people? 1 Kings 3:9

119

And they shall teach my people the difference between the holy and profane, and cause them to discern between the unclean and the clean.
Ezekiel 44:23

Then shall ye return, and discern between the righteous and the wicked, between him that serveth God and him that serveth him not.
Malachi 3:18

But strong meat belongeth to them that are of full age, even those who by reason of use have their senses exercised to discern both good and evil. Hebrews 5:14

Discernment from God's Word

My son, let not them depart from thine eyes: keep sound wisdom and discretion: So shall they be life unto thy soul, and grace to thy neck. Then shalt thou walk in thy way safely, and thy foot shall not stumble. When thou liest down, thou shalt not be afraid: yea, thou shalt lie down, and thy sleep shall be sweet. Proverbs 3:21-24

For the word of God is quick, and powerful, and sharper than any twoedged sword, piercing even to the dividing asunder of soul and spirit, and of the joints and marrow, and is a discerner of the thoughts and intents of the heart. Hebrews 4:12

Deception

1. Being Deceived by Others

And Jesus answered and said unto them, Take heed that no man deceive you. For many shall come in my name, saying, I am Christ; and shall deceive many. Matthew 24:4-5

Frowardness is in his heart, he deviseth mischief continually; he soweth discord. Proverbs 6:14

The thoughts of the righteous are right: but the counsels of the wicked are deceit. Proverbs 12:5

Deceit is in the heart of them that imagine evil: but to the counsellors of peace is joy. Proverbs 12:20

Be not a witness against thy neighbour without cause; and deceive not with thy lips. Proverbs 24:28

So is the man that deceiveth his neighbour, and saith, Am not I in sport?
Proverbs 26:19

He that hateth dissembleth with his lips, and layeth up deceit within him;
Proverbs 26:24

And many false prophets shall rise, and shall deceive many.
Matthew 24:11

For there shall arise false Christs, and false prophets, and shall shew great signs and wonders; insomuch that, if it were possible, they shall deceive the very elect. Matthew 24:24

> *satan has a false gospel, a false repentance, a false dedication, a false faith, a false everything. Weak Christians, not well read in the scriptures, will easily fall prey to modern magicians.*
> *- Vance Havner*

And Jesus answering them began to say, Take heed lest any man deceive you: For many shall come in my name, saying, I am Christ; and shall deceive many. Mark 13:5-6

And he said, Take heed that ye be not deceived: for many shall come in my name, saying, I am Christ; and the time draweth near: go ye not therefore after them. Luke 21:8

For they that are such serve not our Lord Jesus Christ, but their own belly; and by good words and fair speeches deceive the hearts of the simple. Romans 16:18

Be not deceived: evil communications corrupt good manners.
1 Corinthians 15:33

Know ye not that the unrighteous shall not inherit the kingdom of God? Be not deceived: neither fornicators, nor idolaters, nor adulterers, nor effeminate, nor abusers of themselves with mankind. 1 Corinthians 6:9

That we henceforth be no more children, tossed to and fro, and carried about with every wind of doctrine, by the sleight of men, and cunning craftiness, whereby they lie in wait to deceive. Ephesians 4:14

Let no man deceive you with vain words: for because of these things cometh the wrath of God upon the children of disobedience.
Ephesians 5:6

Let no man deceive you by any means: for that day shall not come, except there come a falling away first, and that man of sin be revealed, the son of perdition. 2 Thessalonians 2:3

But evil men and seducers shall wax worse and worse, deceiving, and being deceived. 2 Timothy 3:13

For there are many unruly and vain talkers and deceivers, specially they of the circumcision. Titus 1:10

Little children, let no man deceive you: he that doeth righteousness is righteous, even as he is righteous. 1 John 3:7

For many deceivers are entered into the world, who confess not that Jesus Christ is come in the flesh. This is a deceiver and an antichrist.
2 John 1:7

Wine is a mocker, strong drink is raging: and whosoever is deceived thereby is not wise. Proverbs 20:1

Be not a witness against thy neighbour without cause; and deceive not with thy lips. Proverbs 24:28

2. Self-Deception

Take heed to yourselves, that your heart be not deceived, and ye turn aside, and serve other gods, and worship them. Deuteronomy 11:16

Thus saith the Lord; Deceive not yourselves, saying, The Chaldeans shall surely depart from us: for they shall not depart. Jeremiah 37:9

Let no man deceive himself. If any man among you seemeth to be wise in this world, let him become a fool, that he may be wise.
1 Corinthians 3:18

For if a man think himself to be something, when he is nothing, he deceiveth himself. Galatians 6:3

But be ye doers of the word, and not hearers only, deceiving your own selves. James 1:22

> *We are challenged these days, but not changed, convicted, but not converted. We hear, but do not and thereby we deceive ourselves. - Vance Havner*

If any man among you seem to be religious, and bridleth not his tongue, but deceiveth his own heart, this man's religion is vain. James 1:26

And shall receive the reward of unrighteousness, as they that count it pleasure to riot in the day time. Spots they are and blemishes, sporting themselves with their own deceivings while they feast with you.
2 Peter 2:13

True character is made in secret and is displayed openly.

If we say that we have fellowship with him, and walk in darkness, we lie, and do not the truth. 1 John 1:6

If we say that we have no sin, we deceive ourselves, and the truth is not in us. 1 John 1:8

He that committeth sin is of the devil; for the devil sinneth from the beginning. For this purpose the Son of God was manifested, that he might destroy the works of the devil. Whosoever is born of God doth not commit sin; for his seed remaineth in him: and he cannot sin, because he is born of God. In this the children of God are manifest, and the children of the devil: whosoever doeth not righteousness is not of God, neither he that loveth not his brother. 1 John 3:8-10

Be not deceived; God is not mocked: for whatsoever a man soweth, that shall he also reap. Galatians 6:7

> *There is one thing worse than not coming to church, and that is to come and do nothing about the message one hears. James tells us that hearing without doing means self-deception. - Vance Havner*

3. Deceived by Darkness

And the great dragon was cast out, that old serpent, called the Devil, and Satan, which deceiveth the whole world: he was cast out into the earth, and his angels were cast out with him. Revelation 12:9

And deceiveth them that dwell on the earth by the means of those miracles which he had power to do in the sight of the beast; saying to them that dwell on the earth, that they should make an image to the beast, which had the wound by a sword, and did live. Revelation 13:14

And the light of a candle shall shine no more at all in thee; and the voice of the bridegroom and of the bride shall be heard no more at all in thee: for thy merchants were the great men of the earth; for by thy sorceries were all nations deceived. Revelation 18:23

And the beast was taken, and with him the false prophet that wrought miracles before him, with which he deceived them that had received the mark of the beast, and them that worshipped his image. These both were cast alive into a lake of fire burning with brimstone. Revelation 19:20

And cast him into the bottomless pit, and shut him up, and set a seal upon him, that he should deceive the nations no more, till the thousand years should be fulfilled: and after that he must be loosed a little season.
Revelation 20:3

And shall go out to deceive the nations which are in the four quarters of the earth, Gog and Magog, to gather them together to battle: the number of whom is as the sand of the sea. Revelation 20:8

And the devil that deceived them was cast into the lake of fire and brimstone, where the beast and the false prophet are, and shall be tormented day and night for ever and ever. Revelation 20:10

The Strategies of satan (the devil)

1. satan's most infamous strategy is lying.

He was a murderer from the beginning, and abode not in the truth, because there is no truth in him. When he speaketh a lie, he speaketh of his own: for he is a liar, and the father of it. John 8:44

2. satan seeks to steal from, kill, and destroy anybody that will let him.

The thief cometh not, but for to steal, and to kill, and to destroy:
John 10:10

Be sober, be vigilant; because your adversary the devil, as a roaring lion, walketh about, seeking whom he may devour. 1 Peter 5:8

3. satan is the inventor of sin, and he is constantly tempting mankind to sin against God.

He that committeth sin is of the devil; for the devil sinneth from the beginning. For this purpose the Son of God was manifested, that he might destroy the works of the devil. 1 John 3:8

4. satan tries to steal and choke the Word of God out of the heart of man.

He also that received seed among the thorns is he that heareth the word; and the care of this world, and the deceitfulness of riches, choke the word, and he becometh unfruitful. Matthew 13:22

For all that is in the world, the lust of the flesh, and the lust of the eyes, and the pride of life, is not of the Father, but is of the world.
1 John 2:16

Those by the way side are they that hear; then cometh the devil, and taketh away the word out of their hearts, lest they should believe and be saved. Luke 8:12

5. satan will try to put evil, vile, crazy, doubtful, and fearful thoughts into your mind.

Casting down imaginations, and every high thing that exalteth itself against the knowledge of God, and bringing into captivity every thought to the obedience of Christ. 2 Corinthians 10:5

6. satan tries to deceive believers and unbelievers into doctrines of devils, false religions, cults, and the occult, by using false christs, false teachers, false prophets, gurus, and the like.

And Jesus answered and said unto them, Take heed that no man deceive you. For many shall come in my name, saying, I am Christ; and shall deceive many. Matthew 24:4-5

And many false prophets shall rise, and shall deceive many.
Matthew 24:11

For there shall arise false Christs, and false prophets, and shall shew great signs and wonders; insomuch that, if it were possible, they shall deceive the very elect. Matthew 24:24

And Jesus answering them began to say, Take heed lest any man deceive you: For many shall come in my name, saying, I am Christ; and shall deceive many. Mark 13:5-6

And he said, Take heed that ye be not deceived: for many shall come in my name, saying, I am Christ; and the time draweth near: go ye not therefore after them. Luke 21:8

For such are false apostles, deceitful workers, transforming themselves into the apostles of Christ. And no marvel; for Satan himself is transformed into an angel of light. Therefore it is no great thing if his ministers also be transformed as the ministers of righteousness; whose end shall be according to their works. 2 Corinthians 11:13-15

I marvel that ye are so soon removed from him that called you into the grace of Christ unto another gospel: Which is not another; but there be some that trouble you, and would pervert the gospel of Christ. But though we, or an angel from heaven, preach any other gospel unto you than that which we have preached unto you, let him be accursed. As we said before, so say I now again, If any man preach any other gospel unto you than that ye have received, let him be accursed. Galatians 1:6-9

That we henceforth be no more children, tossed to and fro, and carried about with every wind of doctrine, by the sleight of men, and cunning craftiness, whereby they lie in wait to deceive. Ephesians 4:14

Let no man deceive you with vain words: for because of these things cometh the wrath of God upon the children of disobedience.

Ephesians 5:6

And this I say, lest any man should beguile you with enticing words.

Colossians 2:4

Little children, let no man deceive you: he that doeth righteousness is righteous, even as he is righteous. 1 John 3:7

7. satan and his forces work overtime to lure, trick and trap mankind with various sinful temptations.

Put on the whole armour of God, that ye may be able to stand against the wiles of the devil. Ephesians 6:11

Definition of *wiles*: A craft, deceit, or cunning device, clever trick used to fool or lure someone.

8. satan tries to condemn believers of their past life-styles and present walk with Christ.

For the accuser of our brethren is cast down, which accused them before our God day and night. Revelation 12:10

9. satan tries to convince sinners and believers that God is angry with them and that He condemns them for their sins.

I am come that they might have life, and that they might have it more abundantly. John 10:10

For God sent not his Son into the world to condemn the world; but that the world through him might be saved. John 3:17

Verily, verily, I say unto you, He that heareth my word, and believeth on him that sent me, hath everlasting life, and shall not come into condemnation; but is passed from death unto life. John 5:24

There is therefore now no condemnation to them which are in Christ Jesus, who walk not after the flesh, but after the Spirit. Romans 8:1

She said, No man, Lord. And Jesus said unto her, Neither do I condemn thee: go, and sin no more. John 8:11

For if our heart condemn us, God is greater than our heart, and knoweth all things. 1 John 3:20

> **Good leaders employ others, great leaders deploy themselves and others.**

Beloved, if our heart condemn us not, then have we confidence toward God. 1 John 3:21

10. satan uses mind-control to prevent people from hearing and accepting the Gospel of Christ.

But if our gospel be hid, it is hid to them that are lost: In whom the god of this world hath blinded the minds of them which believe not, lest the light of the glorious gospel of Christ, who is the image of God, should shine unto them. 2 Corinthians 4:3-4

11. satan tries to control human life-styles.

Wherein in time past ye walked according to the course of this world, according to the prince of the power of the air, the spirit that now worketh in the children of disobedience. Ephesians 2:2

12. satan and his forces try to delay believers' prayers from being answered on time.

But the prince of the kingdom of Persia withstood me one and twenty days: but, lo, Michael, one of the chief princes, came to help me; and I remained there with the kings of Persia. Daniel 10:13

Then said he, Knowest thou wherefore I come unto thee? and now will I return to fight with the prince of Persia: and when I am gone forth, lo, the prince of Grecia shall come. Daniel 10:20

13. satan and his evil forces try to prevent people—and leaders especially—from hearing and receiving the Gospel of Jesus Christ.

But Elymas the sorcerer (for so is his name by interpretation) withstood them, seeking to turn away the deputy from the faith. Then Saul, (who also is called Paul,) filled with the Holy Ghost, set his eyes on him, And said, O full of all subtlety and all mischief, thou child of the devil, thou enemy of all righteousness, wilt thou not cease to pervert the right ways of the Lord? And now, behold, the hand of the Lord is upon thee, and thou shalt be blind, not seeing the sun for a season. And immediately there fell on him a mist and a darkness; and he went about seeking some to lead him by the hand. Acts 13:8-11

14. satan and his forces are highly organized and they are in constant spiritual warfare with God's army around the world.

And if Satan cast out Satan, he is divided against himself; how shall then his kingdom stand? Matthew 12:26

127

For we wrestle not against flesh and blood, but against principalities, against powers, against the rulers of the darkness of this world, against spiritual wickedness in high places. Ephesians 6:12

15. Any sickness, death, tragedy, temptation, natural disaster, or situation contrary to the Word of God can always be–in some way– traced directly to satan and his evil forces.

satan is never happier than when he has convinced people that he is nonexistent. The very popular modern denial of the existence of a personal devil is one of satan's major triumphs. We have a real enemy on our hands and we shall greatly weaken our position by blissfully disregarding his presence and power. - Vance Havner

Laying On of Hands

1. Miracles of Jesus through the Laying On of Hands

And Jesus put forth his hand, and touched him, saying, I will; be thou clean. And immediately his leprosy was cleansed. Matthew 8:3

And he touched her hand, and the fever left her: and she arose, and ministered unto them. Matthew 8:15

While he spake these things unto them, behold, there came a certain ruler, and worshipped him, saying, My daughter is even now dead: but come and lay thy hand upon her, and she shall live. Matthew 9:18

And besought him greatly, saying, My little daughter lieth at the point of death: I pray thee, come and lay thy hands on her, that she may be healed; and she shall live. Mark 5:23

2. Spiritual Gifts Given through the Laying On of Hands

Then laid they their hands on them, and they received the Holy Ghost. And when Simon saw that through laying on of the apostles' hands the Holy Ghost was given, he offered them money, Acts 8:17-18

And Ananias went his way, and entered into the house; and putting his hands on him said, Brother Saul, the Lord, even Jesus, that appeared unto thee in the way as thou camest, hath sent me, that thou mightest receive thy sight, and be filled with the Holy Ghost. Acts 9:17

He said unto them, Have ye received the Holy Ghost since ye believed? And they said unto him, We have not so much as heard whether there be any Holy Ghost. And he said unto them, Unto what then were ye baptized? And they said, Unto John's baptism. Then said Paul, John verily baptized with the baptism of repentance, saying unto the people, that they should believe on him which should come after him, that is, on Christ Jesus. When they heard this, they were baptized in the name of the Lord Jesus. And when Paul had laid his hands upon them, the Holy Ghost came on them; and they spake with tongues, and prophesied.

Acts 19:2-6

For I long to see you, that I may impart unto you some spiritual gift, to the end ye may be established; Romans 1:11

Neglect not the gift that is in thee, which was given thee by prophecy, with the laying on of the hands of the presbytery. 1 Timothy 4:14

Wherefore I put thee in remembrance that thou stir up the gift of God, which is in thee by the putting on of my hands. 2 Timothy 1:6

Of the doctrine of baptisms, and of laying on of hands, and of resurrection of the dead, and of eternal judgment. Hebrews 6:2

3. Blessings through the Laying On of Hands

And Joseph took them both, Ephraim in his right hand toward Israel's left hand, and Manasseh in his left hand toward Israel's right hand, and brought them near unto him. And Israel stretched out his right hand, and laid it upon Ephraim's head, who was the younger, and his left hand upon Manasseh's head, guiding his hands wittingly; for Manasseh was the firstborn. Genesis 48:13-14

And when Joseph saw that his father laid his right hand upon the head of Ephraim, it displeased him: and he held up his father's hand, to remove it from Ephraim's head unto Manasseh's head. And Joseph said unto his father, Not so, my father: for this is the firstborn; put thy right hand upon his head. And his father refused, and said, I know it, my son, I know it: he also shall become a people, and he also shall be great: but truly his younger brother shall be greater than he, and his seed shall become a multitude of nations. And he blessed them that day, saying, In thee shall Israel bless, saying, God make thee as Ephraim and as Manasseh: and he set Ephraim before Manasseh. Genesis 48:17-20

4. Miracles of the Disciples through the Laying On of Hands

Long time therefore abode they speaking boldly in the Lord, which gave testimony unto the word of his grace, and granted signs and wonders to be done by their hands. Acts 14:3

129

They shall take up serpents; and if they drink any deadly thing, it shall not hurt them; they shall lay hands on the sick, and they shall recover.

Mark 16:18

And God wrought special miracles by the hands of Paul: Acts 19:11

5. Transference of Spirits

And the Lord said unto Moses, Gather unto me seventy men of the elders of Israel, whom thou knowest to be the elders of the people, and officers over them; and bring them unto the tabernacle of the congregation, that they may stand there with thee. And I will come down and talk with thee there: and I will take of the spirit which is upon thee, and will put it upon them; and they shall bear the burden of the people with thee, that thou bear it not thyself alone. Numbers 11:16-17

And the Lord came down in a cloud, and spake unto him, and took of the spirit that was upon him, and gave it unto the seventy elders: and it came to pass, that, when the spirit rested upon them, they prophesied, and did not cease. Numbers 11:25

And the Lord said unto Moses, Take thee Joshua the son of Nun, a man in whom is the spirit, and lay thine hand upon him; And set him before Eleazar the priest, and before all the congregation; and give him a charge in their sight. And thou shalt put some of thine honour upon him, that all the congregation of the children of Israel may be obedient.

Numbers 27:18-20

Warning! Be careful about who you lay your hands upon, also be cautious about letting any one at random lay their hands upon you.

Lay hands suddenly on no man, neither be partaker of other men's sins: keep thyself pure. 1 Timothy 5:22

False Prophets

Then the Lord said unto me, The prophets prophesy lies in my name: I sent them not, neither have I commanded them, neither spake unto them: they prophesy unto you a false vision and divination, and a thing of nought, and the deceit of their heart. Therefore thus saith the Lord concerning the prophets that prophesy in my name, and I sent them not, yet they say,

Leaders are more concerned with expressing themselves, than with proving themselves.

Sword and famine shall not be in this land; By sword and famine shall those prophets be consumed. Jeremiah 14:14-15

For both prophet and priest are profane; yea, in my house have I found their wickedness, saith the Lord. Wherefore their way shall be unto them as slippery ways in the darkness: they shall be driven on, and fall therein: for I will bring evil upon them, even the year of their visitation, saith the Lord. And I have seen folly in the prophets of Samaria; they prophesied in Baal, and caused my people Israel to err. I have seen also in the prophets of Jerusalem an horrible thing: they commit adultery, and walk in lies: they strengthen also the hands of evildoers, that none doth return from his wickedness: they are all of them unto me as Sodom, and the inhabitants thereof as Gomorrah. Therefore thus saith the Lord of hosts concerning the prophets; Behold, I will feed them with wormwood, and make them drink the water of gall: for from the prophets of Jerusalem is profaneness gone forth into all the land. Thus saith the Lord of hosts, Hearken not unto the words of the prophets that prophesy unto you: they make you vain: they speak a vision of their own heart, and not out of the mouth of the Lord. Jeremiah 23:11-16

I have not sent these prophets, yet they ran: I have not spoken to them, yet they prophesied. Jeremiah 23:21

I have heard what the prophets said, that prophesy lies in my name, saying, I have dreamed, I have dreamed. How long shall this be in the heart of the prophets that prophesy lies? yea, they are prophets of the deceit of their own heart; Which think to cause my people to forget my name by their dreams which they tell every man to his neighbour, as their fathers have forgotten my name for Baal. The prophet that hath a dream, let him tell a dream; and he that hath my word, let him speak my word faithfully. What is the chaff to the wheat? saith the Lord. Is not my word like as a fire? saith the Lord; and like a hammer that breaketh the rock in pieces?
Jeremiah 23:25-29

> *In the Old Testament, prophets were stoned if their prophecies were not true. In the New Testament prophecies are examined in light of the Word of God, accepted if they are true, and ignored if they are false.*

Behold, I am against the prophets, saith the Lord, that use their tongues, and say, He saith. Behold, I am against them that prophesy false dreams, saith the Lord, and do tell them, and cause my people to err by their lies, and by their lightness; yet I sent them not, nor commanded them: therefore they shall not profit this people at all, saith the Lord.
Jeremiah 23:31-32

But if they be prophets, and if the word of the Lord be with them, let them now make intercession to the Lord of hosts, that the vessels which are left in the house of the Lord, and in the house of the king of Judah, and at Jerusalem, go not to Babylon. Jeremiah 27:18

The prophets that have been before me and before thee of old prophesied both against many countries, and against great kingdoms, of war, and of evil, and of pestilence. The prophet which prophesieth of peace, when the word of the prophet shall come to pass, then shall the prophet be known, that the Lord hath truly sent him. Jeremiah 28:8-9

For thus saith the Lord of hosts, the God of Israel; Let not your prophets and your diviners, that be in the midst of you, deceive you, neither hearken to your dreams which ye cause to be dreamed. For they prophesy falsely unto you in my name: I have not sent them, saith the Lord.
Jeremiah 29:8-9

A prophecy spoken to you and for you should always confirm what God has already been speaking to your spirit.

Son of man, prophesy against the prophets of Israel that prophesy, and say thou unto them that prophesy out of their own hearts, Hear ye the word of the Lord; Thus saith the Lord God; Woe unto the foolish prophets, that follow their own spirit, and have seen nothing! O Israel, thy prophets are like the foxes in the deserts. Ye have not gone up into the gaps, neither made up the hedge for the house of Israel to stand in the battle in the day of the Lord. They have seen vanity and lying divination, saying, The Lord saith: and the Lord hath not sent them: and they have made others to hope that they would confirm the word. Have ye not seen a vain vision, and have ye not spoken a lying divination, whereas ye say, The Lord saith it; albeit I have not spoken? Therefore thus saith the Lord God; Because ye have spoken vanity, and seen lies, therefore, behold, I am against you, saith the Lord God. And mine hand shall be upon the prophets that see vanity, and that divine lies: they shall not be in the assembly of my people, neither shall they be written in the writing of the house of Israel, neither shall they enter into the land of Israel; and ye shall know that I am the Lord God. Ezekiel 13:2-9

When a person starts prophesying over you and you know that it is a false prophecy–contrary to God's Word or coming from their flesh or from the devil–stop them immediately. Tell them, in the spirit of love and boldness, that their prophecy is false and that you will not receive it. It's better for them to be confronted with truth and publicly embarrassed than for you to be cursed and deceived.

And it shall come to pass, that when any shall yet prophesy, then his father and his mother that begat him shall say unto him, Thou shalt not live; for thou speakest lies in the name of the Lord: and his father and his mother that begat him shall thrust him through when he prophesieth. And it shall come to pass in that day, that the prophets shall be ashamed every one of his vision, when he hath prophesied; neither shall they wear a rough garment to deceive: But he shall say, I am no prophet, I am an husbandman; for man taught me to keep cattle from my youth.

Zechariah 13:3-5

And if the prophet be deceived when he hath spoken a thing, I the Lord have deceived that prophet, and I will stretch out my hand upon him, and will destroy him from the midst of my people Israel. And they shall bear the punishment of their iniquity: the punishment of the prophet shall be even as the punishment of him that seeketh unto him; Ezekiel 14:9-10

Beware of false prophets, which come to you in sheep's clothing, but inwardly they are ravening wolves. Matthew 7:15

Judging Prophecy

Beloved, believe not every spirit, but try the spirits whether they are of God: because many false prophets are gone out into the world.

1 John 4:1

The simple believeth every word: but the prudent man looketh well to his going. Proverbs 14:15

The word of God is the measuring rod by which we judge every prophetic utterance. - Rick Godwin

133

THE MINISTER IN COUNSELLING

Wisdom

The fear of the Lord is the beginning of wisdom: a good understanding have all they that do his commandments: his praise endureth for ever.
Psalms 111:10

Wisdom crieth without; she uttereth her voice in the streets.
Proverbs 1:20

1. How to Obtain Wisdom

If any of you lack wisdom, let him ask of God, that giveth to all men liberally, and upbraideth not; and it shall be given him. James 1:5

> *If you lack knowledge, go to school. If you lack wisdom, get on your knees! Knowledge is not wisdom. Wisdom is proper use of knowledge. - Vance Havner*

2. Wisdom Comes From God

For the Lord giveth wisdom: out of his mouth cometh knowledge and understanding. He layeth up sound wisdom for the righteous: he is a buckler to them that walk uprightly. Proverbs 2:6-7

For God giveth to a man that is good in his sight wisdom, and knowledge, and joy: but to the sinner he giveth travail, to gather and to heap up, that he may give to him that is good before God. This also is vanity and vexation of spirit. Ecclesiastes 2:26

There is no wisdom nor understanding nor counsel against the Lord.
Proverbs 21:30

Wherein he hath abounded toward us in all wisdom and prudence.
Ephesians 1:8

That the God of our Lord Jesus Christ, the Father of glory, may give unto you the spirit of wisdom and revelation in the knowledge of him.
Ephesians 1:17

To the intent that now unto the principalities and powers in heavenly places might be known by the church the manifold wisdom of God.
Ephesians 3:10

In whom are hid all the treasures of wisdom and knowledge.
Colossians 2:3

But unto them which are called, both Jews and Greeks, Christ the power of God, and the wisdom of God. 1 Corinthians 1:24

But of him are ye in Christ Jesus, who of God is made unto us wisdom, and righteousness, and sanctification, and redemption. 1 Corinthians 1:30

3. True Wisdom

But the wisdom that is from above is first pure, then peaceable, gentle, and easy to be entreated, full of mercy and good fruits, without partiality, and without hypocrisy. James 3:17

4. Pursue Wisdom

So that thou incline thine ear unto wisdom, and apply thine heart to understanding. Proverbs 2:2

Happy is the man that findeth wisdom, and the man that getteth understanding. Proverbs 3:13

My son, let not them depart from thine eyes: keep sound wisdom and discretion. Proverbs 3:21

Get wisdom, get understanding: forget it not; neither decline from the words of my mouth. Proverbs 4:5

Wisdom is the principal thing; therefore get wisdom: and with all thy getting get understanding. Proverbs 4:7

So shall the knowledge of wisdom be unto thy soul: when thou hast found it, then there shall be a reward, and thy expectation shall not be cut off. Proverbs 24:14

> True success is the fulfillment of original purpose.

5. Wisdom Enters the Heart

Who hath put wisdom in the inward parts? or who hath given understanding to the heart? Job 38:36

Behold, thou desirest truth in the inward parts: and in the hidden part thou shalt make me to know wisdom. Psalms 51:6

When wisdom entereth into thine heart, and knowledge is pleasant unto thy soul. Proverbs 2:10

Wisdom resteth in the heart of him that hath understanding: but that which is in the midst of fools is made known. Proverbs 14:33

How much better is it to get wisdom than gold! and to get understanding rather to be chosen than silver! Proverbs 16:16

I applied mine heart to know, and to search, and to seek out wisdom, and the reason of things, and to know the wickedness of folly, even of foolishness and madness. Ecclesiastes 7:25

Let the word of Christ dwell in you richly in all wisdom; teaching and admonishing one another in psalms and hymns and spiritual songs, singing with grace in your hearts to the Lord. Colossians 3:16

6. Wisdom is Valuable

For wisdom is better than rubies; and all the things that may be desired are not to be compared to it. I wisdom dwell with prudence, and find out knowledge of witty inventions. Proverbs 8:11-12

7. Wisdom is Found in Counsel

Counsel is mine, and sound wisdom: I am understanding; I have strength.
Proverbs 8:14

Only by pride cometh contention: but with the well advised is wisdom.
Proverbs 13:10

8. The Benefits of Wisdom

with the ancient is wisdom; and in length of days understanding. With him is wisdom and strength, he hath counsel and understanding.
Job 12:12-13

Thou through thy commandments hast made me wiser than mine enemies: for they are ever with me. Psalms 119:98

Give instruction to a wise man, and he will be yet wiser: teach a just man, and he will increase in learning. Proverbs 9:9

Wisdom is good with an inheritance: and by it there is profit to them that see the sun. For wisdom is a defence, and money is a defence: but the excellency of knowledge is, that wisdom giveth life to them that have it. Ecclesiastes 7:11-12

Wisdom strengtheneth the wise more than ten mighty men which are in the city. Ecclesiastes 7:19

Then said I, Wisdom is better than strength: nevertheless the poor man's wisdom is despised, and his words are not heard. Ecclesiastes 9:16

Happy is the man that findeth wisdom, and the man that getteth understanding. Proverbs 3:13

If the iron be blunt, and he do not whet the edge, then must he put to more strength: but wisdom is profitable to direct. Ecclesiastes 10:10

O the depth of the riches both of the wisdom and knowledge of God! how unsearchable are his judgments, and his ways past finding out! Romans 11:33

And that from a child thou hast known the holy scriptures, which are able to make thee wise unto salvation through faith which is in Christ Jesus. 2 Timothy 3:15

The fear of the Lord is the beginning of wisdom: and the knowledge of the holy is understanding. Proverbs 9:10

9. Wisdom in Action

Who is a wise man and endued with knowledge among you? let him shew out of a good conversation his works with meekness of wisdom. James 3:13

Walk in wisdom toward them that are without, redeeming the time. Colossians 4:5

The wisdom of the prudent is to understand his way: but the folly of fools is deceit. Proverbs 14:8

Knowledge

1. God is the Source of Knowledge

The eyes of the Lord preserve knowledge, and he overthroweth the words of the transgressor. Proverbs 22:12

For God giveth to a man that is good in his sight wisdom, and knowledge, and joy: but to the sinner he giveth travail, to gather and to heap up, that he may give to him that is good before God. This also is vanity and vexation of spirit. Ecclesiastes 2:26

And the Lord hath given me knowledge of it, and I know it: then thou shewedst me their doings. Jeremiah 11:18

That in every thing ye are enriched by him, in all utterance, and in all knowledge; 1 Corinthians 1:5

For to one is given by the Spirit the word of wisdom; to another the word of knowledge by the same Spirit; 1 Corinthians 12:8

For God, who commanded the light to shine out of darkness, hath shined in our hearts, to give the light of the knowledge of the glory of God in the face of Jesus Christ. 2 Corinthians 4:6

In whom are hid all the treasures of wisdom and knowledge.
Colossians 2:3

2. Pursue Knowledge

The fear of the Lord is the beginning of knowledge: but fools despise wisdom and instruction. Proverbs 1:7

Then shalt thou understand the fear of the Lord, and find the knowledge of God. For the Lord giveth wisdom: out of his mouth cometh knowledge and understanding. Proverbs 2:5-6

Wise men lay up knowledge: but the mouth of the foolish is near destruction. Proverbs 10:14

Also, that the soul be without knowledge, it is not good; and he that hasteth with his feet sinneth. Proverbs 19:2

And I myself also am persuaded of you, my brethren, that ye also are full of goodness, filled with all knowledge, able also to admonish one another. Romans 15:14

> *Head-knowledge is useful, but unless it is sanctified by the Holy Spirit it can be the most dangerous thing in the world. - Vance Havner*

And beside this, giving all diligence, add to your faith virtue; and to virtue knowledge; And to knowledge temperance; and to temperance patience; and to patience godliness. 2 Peter 1:5-6

139

3. The Benefits of Obtaining Knowledge

When wisdom entereth into thine heart, and knowledge is pleasant unto thy soul; Proverbs 2:10

And by knowledge shall the chambers be filled with all precious and pleasant riches. Proverbs 24:4

Fortune favors the prepared mind. - Louis Pasteur

A wise man is strong; yea, a man of knowledge increaseth strength.
Proverbs 24:5

So shall the knowledge of wisdom be unto thy soul: when thou hast found it, then there shall be a reward, and thy expectation shall not be cut off. Proverbs 24:14

For wisdom is a defence, and money is a defence: but the excellency of knowledge is, that wisdom giveth life to them that have it.
Ecclesiastes 7:12

And wisdom and knowledge shall be the stability of thy times, and strength of salvation: the fear of the Lord is his treasure. Isaiah 33:6

4. The Consequences of Lacking Knowledge

Therefore my people are gone into captivity, because they have no knowledge: and their honourable men are famished, and their multitude dried up with thirst. Isaiah 5:13

My people are destroyed for lack of knowledge: because thou hast rejected knowledge, I will also reject thee, that thou shalt be no priest to me: seeing thou hast forgotten the law of thy God, I will also forget thy children. Hosea 4:6

And even as they did not like to retain God in their knowledge, God gave them over to a reprobate mind, to do those things which are not convenient; Romans 1:28

Awake to righteousness, and sin not; for some have not the knowledge of God: I speak this to your shame. 1 Corinthians 15:34

5. Knowledge from God's Word

Teach me good judgment and knowledge: for I have believed thy commandments. Psalms 119:66

> **Leaders are individuals who have declared independence from the expectations of others.**

Receive my instruction, and not silver; and knowledge rather than choice gold. Proverbs 8:10

Cease, my son, to hear the instruction that causeth to err from the words of knowledge. Proverbs 19:27

Yea doubtless, and I count all things but loss for the excellency of the knowledge of Christ Jesus my Lord: for whom I have suffered the loss of all things, and do count them but dung, that I may win Christ.
Philippians 3:8

Bow down thine ear, and hear the words of the wise, and apply thine heart unto my knowledge. Proverbs 22:17

Have not I written to thee excellent things in counsels and knowledge.
Proverbs 22:20

Apply thine heart unto instruction, and thine ears to the words of knowledge. Proverbs 23:12

Whereby, when ye read, ye may understand my knowledge in the mystery of Christ. Ephesians 3:4

And this I pray, that your love may abound yet more and more in knowledge and in all judgment; Philippians 1:9

For if we sin wilfully after that we have received the knowledge of the truth, there remaineth no more sacrifice for sins. Hebrews 10:26

But grow in grace, and in the knowledge of our Lord and Saviour Jesus Christ. To him be glory both now and for ever. Amen. 2 Peter 3:18

Understanding

Discretion shall preserve thee, understanding shall keep thee.
Proverbs 2:11

Good understanding giveth favour: but the way of transgressors is hard.
Proverbs 13:15

Understanding is a wellspring of life unto him that hath it: but the instruction of fools is folly. Proverbs 16:22

Through wisdom is an house builded; and by understanding it is established. Proverbs 24:3

With thy wisdom and with thine understanding thou hast gotten thee riches, and hast gotten gold and silver into thy treasures. Ezekiel 28:4

1. Godly Understanding

But there is a spirit in man: and the inspiration of the Almighty giveth them understanding. Job 32:8

Who hath put wisdom in the inward parts? or who hath given understanding to the heart? Job 38:36

For the Lord giveth wisdom: out of his mouth cometh knowledge and understanding. Proverbs 2:6

The fear of the Lord is the beginning of wisdom: and the knowledge of the holy is understanding. Proverbs 9:10

There is no wisdom nor understanding nor counsel against the Lord.
Proverbs 21:30

Then opened he their understanding, that they might understand the scriptures. Luke 24:25

The eyes of your understanding being enlightened; that ye may know what is the hope of his calling, and what the riches of the glory of his inheritance in the saints. Ephesians 1:18

If a great man says something that seems illogical, don't laugh; try to understand it. - The Talmud

Consider what I say; and the Lord give thee understanding in all things.
2 Timothy 2:7

And we know that the Son of God is come, and hath given us an understanding, that we may know him that is true, and we are in him that is true, even in his Son Jesus Christ. This is the true God, and eternal life.
1 John 5:20

2. Obtaining Understanding

The fear of the Lord is the beginning of wisdom: a good understanding have all they that do his commandments: his praise endureth for ever.
Psalms 111:10

Through thy precepts I get understanding: therefore I hate every false way. Psalms 119:104

The entrance of thy words giveth light; it giveth understanding unto the simple. Psalms 119:130

So that thou incline thine ear unto wisdom, and apply thine heart to understanding. Proverbs 2:2

Let not mercy and truth forsake thee: bind them about thy neck; write them upon the table of thine heart: So shalt thou find favour and good understanding in the sight of God and man. Trust in the Lord with all thine heart; and lean not unto thine own understanding. Proverbs 3:3-5

Hear, ye children, the instruction of a father, and attend to know understanding. Proverbs 4:1

Get wisdom, get understanding: forget it not; neither decline from the words of my mouth. Proverbs 4:5

Happy is the man that findeth wisdom, and the man that getteth understanding. Proverbs 3:13

Wisdom is the principal thing; therefore get wisdom: and with all thy getting get understanding. Proverbs 4:7

My son, attend unto my wisdom, and bow thine ear to my understanding. Proverbs 5:1

Doth not wisdom cry? and understanding put forth her voice?
Proverbs 8:1

Counsel is mine, and sound wisdom: I am understanding; I have strength.
Proverbs 8:14

How much better is it to get wisdom than gold! and to get understanding rather to be chosen than silver! Proverbs 16:16

He that getteth wisdom loveth his own soul: he that keepeth understanding shall find good. Proverbs 19:8

Wherefore be ye not unwise, but understanding what the will of the Lord is. Ephesians 5:17

For this cause we also, since the day we heard it, do not cease to pray for you, and to desire that ye might be filled with the knowledge of his will in all wisdom and spiritual understanding. Colossians 1:9

Curses

Definition of Curse: A curse (from God) is righteous judgement against disobedience. To curse is to pray against, or wish evil against a person or thing.

And I will bless them that bless thee, and curse him that curseth thee: and in thee shall all families of the earth be blessed. Genesis 12:3

How shall I curse, whom God hath not cursed? or how shall I defy, whom the Lord hath not defied? Numbers 23:8

Whoso curseth his father or his mother, his lamp shall be put out in obscure darkness. Proverbs 20:20

He that giveth unto the poor shall not lack: but he that hideth his eyes shall have many a curse. Proverbs 28:27

Thus saith the Lord; Cursed be the man that trusteth in man, and maketh flesh his arm, and whose heart departeth from the Lord. Jeremiah 17:5

And Peter calling to remembrance saith unto him, Master, behold, the fig tree which thou cursedst is withered away. Mark 11:21

1. Curses Activated by Disobedience to God's Word

And a curse, if ye will not obey the commandments of the Lord your God, but turn aside out of the way which I command you this day, to go after other gods, which ye have not known. Deuteronomy 11:28

The curse of the Lord is in the house of the wicked: but he blesseth the habitation of the just. Proverbs 3:33

And say thou unto them, Thus saith the Lord God of Israel; Cursed be the man that obeyeth not the words of this covenant. Jeremiah 11:3

2. Curses Activated by Words

Therewith bless we God, even the Father; and therewith curse we men, which are made after the similitude of God. Out of the same mouth proceedeth blessing and cursing. My brethren, these things ought not so to be. James 3:9-10

Death and life are in the power of the tongue: and they that love it shall eat the fruit thereof. Proverbs 18:21

3. How to Break Curses

Christ hath redeemed us from the curse of the law, being made a curse for us: for it is written, Cursed is every one that hangeth on a tree:
Galatians 3:13

a. Obey God's Word

Behold, I set before you this day a blessing and a curse; A blessing, if ye obey the commandments of the Lord your God, which I command you this day. Deuteronomy 11:26-27

Until you are willing to die for what you are living for, you cannot become a true leader.

I call heaven and earth to record this day against you, that I have set before you life and death, blessing and cursing: therefore choose life, that both thou and thy seed may live. Deuteronomy 30:19

The curse of the Lord is in the house of the wicked: but he blesseth the habitation of the just. Proverbs 3:33

b. Pray blessings on your enemies

But I say unto you, Love your enemies, bless them that curse you, do good to them that hate you, and pray for them which despitefully use you, and persecute you. Matthew 5:44

Bless them that curse you, and pray for them which despitefully use you. Luke 6:28

Bless them which persecute you: bless, and curse not. Romans 12:14

Generational (Hereditary) Sins

Thou shalt not bow down thyself to them, nor serve them: for I the Lord thy God am a jealous God, visiting the iniquity of the fathers upon the children unto the third and fourth generation of them that hate me.

Exodus 20:5

The Lord is longsuffering, and of great mercy, forgiving iniquity and transgression, and by no means clearing the guilty, visiting the iniquity of the fathers upon the children unto the third and fourth generation.

Numbers 14:18

Thou shalt not bow down thyself unto them, nor serve them: for I the Lord thy God am a jealous God, visiting the iniquity of the fathers upon the children unto the third and fourth generation of them that hate me, And shewing mercy unto thousands of them that love me and keep my commandments. Deuteronomy 5:9-10

He that speaketh flattery to his friends, even the eyes of his children shall fail. Job 17:5

In those days they shall say no more, The fathers have eaten a sour grape, and the children's teeth are set on edge. Jeremiah 31:29

What mean ye, that ye use this proverb concerning the land of Israel, saying, The fathers have eaten sour grapes, and the children's teeth are set on edge? Ezekiel 18:2

But if a man be just, and do that which is lawful and right, Hath walked in my statutes, and hath kept my judgments, to deal truly; he is just, he shall surely live, saith the Lord God. Ezekiel 18:5,9

145

If he beget a son that is a robber, a shedder of blood, and that doeth the like to any one of these things, Hath given forth upon usury, and hath taken increase: shall he then live? he shall not live: he hath done all these abominations; he shall surely die; his blood shall be upon him.

Ezekiel 18:10,13

Now, lo, if he beget a son, that seeth all his father's sins which he hath done, and considereth, and doeth not such like, That hath taken off his hand from the poor, that hath not received usury nor increase, hath executed my judgments, hath walked in my statutes; he shall not die for the iniquity of his father, he shall surely live. As for his father, because he cruelly oppressed, spoiled his brother by violence, and did that which is not good among his people, lo, even he shall die in his iniquity.

Ezekiel 18:14,17-18

Yet say ye, Why? doth not the son bear the iniquity of the father? When the son hath done that which is lawful and right, and hath kept all my statutes, and hath done them, he shall surely live. The soul that sinneth, it shall die. The son shall not bear the iniquity of the father, neither shall the father bear the iniquity of the son: the righteousness of the righteous shall be upon him, and the wickedness of the wicked shall be upon him.

Ezekiel 18:19-20

Casting Out devils/demons

1. Examples of Jesus Casting Out devils

And his fame went throughout all Syria: and they brought unto him all sick people that were taken with divers diseases and torments, and those which were possessed with devils, and those which were lunatic, and those that had the palsy; and he healed them. Matthew 4:24

When the even was come, they brought unto him many that were possessed with devils: and he cast out the spirits with his word, and healed all that were sick. Matthew 8:16

As they went out, behold, they brought to him a dumb man possessed with a devil. And when the devil was cast out, the dumb spake: and the multitudes marvelled, saying, It was never so seen in Israel.

Matthew 9:32-33

Then was brought unto him one possessed with a devil, blind, and dumb: and he healed him, insomuch that the blind and dumb both spake and saw. Matthew 12:22

146

And, behold, a woman of Canaan came out of the same coasts, and cried unto him, saying, Have mercy on me, O Lord, thou Son of David; my daughter is grievously vexed with a devil. Matthew 15:22

Then Jesus answered and said unto her, O woman, great is thy faith: be it unto thee even as thou wilt. And her daughter was made whole from that very hour. Matthew 15:28

And Jesus rebuked the devil; and he departed out of him: and the child was cured from that very hour. Matthew 17:18

And when he was come out of the ship, immediately there met him out of the tombs a man with an unclean spirit, Who had his dwelling among the tombs; and no man could bind him, no, not with chains: Because that he had been often bound with fetters and chains, and the chains had been plucked asunder by him, and the fetters broken in pieces: neither could any man tame him. And always, night and day, he was in the mountains, and in the tombs, crying, and cutting himself with stones. But when he saw Jesus afar off, he ran and worshipped him, And cried with a loud voice, and said, What have I to do with thee, Jesus, thou Son of the most high God? I adjure thee by God, that thou torment me not. For he said unto him, Come out of the man, thou unclean spirit. And he asked him, What is thy name? And he answered, saying, My name is Legion: for we are many. And he besought him much that he would not send them away out of the country. Now there was there nigh unto the mountains a great herd of swine feeding. And all the devils besought him, saying, Send us into the swine, that we may enter into them. And forthwith Jesus gave them leave. And the unclean spirits went out, and entered into the swine: and the herd ran violently down a steep place into the sea, (they were about two thousand;) and were choked in the sea. And they that fed the swine fled, and told it in the city, and in the country. And they went out to see what it was that was done. And they come to Jesus, and see him that was possessed with the devil, and had the legion, sitting, and clothed, and in his right mind: and they were afraid. Mark 5:2-15

And at even, when the sun did set, they brought unto him all that were diseased, and them that were possessed with devils. And all the city was gathered together at the door. And he healed many that were sick of divers diseases, and cast out many devils; and suffered not the devils to speak, because they knew him. Mark 1:32-34

And he preached in their synagogues throughout all Galilee, and cast out devils. Mark 1:39

The woman was a Greek, a Syrophenician by nation; and she besought him that he would cast forth the devil out of her daughter. Mark 7:26

147

And he said unto her, For this saying go thy way; the devil is gone out of thy daughter. And when she was come to her house, she found the devil gone out, and her daughter laid upon the bed. Mark 7:29-30

Now when Jesus was risen early the first day of the week, he appeared first to Mary Magdalene, out of whom he had cast seven devils.

Mark 16:9

And in the synagogue there was a man, which had a spirit of an unclean devil, and cried out with a loud voice, Saying, Let us alone; what have we to do with thee, thou Jesus of Nazareth? art thou come to destroy us? I know thee who thou art; the Holy One of God. And Jesus rebuked him, saying, Hold thy peace, and come out of him. And when the devil had thrown him in the midst, he came out of him, and hurt him not.

Luke 4:33-35

And devils also came out of many, crying out, and saying, Thou art Christ the Son of God. And he rebuking them suffered them not to speak: for they knew that he was Christ. Luke 4:41

And certain women, which had been healed of evil spirits and infirmities, Mary called Magdalene, out of whom went seven devils. Luke 8:2

And as he was yet a coming, the devil threw him down, and tare him. And Jesus rebuked the unclean spirit, and healed the child, and delivered him again to his father. Luke 9:42

And he was casting out a devil, and it was dumb. And it came to pass, when the devil was gone out, the dumb spake; and the people wondered.

Luke 11:14

How God anointed Jesus of Nazareth with the Holy Ghost and with power: who went about doing good, and healing all that were oppressed of the devil; for God was with him. Acts 10:38

2. Disciples Casting Out devils

Heal the sick, cleanse the lepers, raise the dead, cast out devils: freely ye have received, freely give. Matthew 10:8

And he ordained twelve, that they should be with him, and that he might send them forth to preach, And to have power to heal sicknesses, and to cast out devils. Mark 3:14-15

If you are ready for criticism, you're ready for leadership.

And they went out, and preached that men should repent. And they cast out many devils, and anointed with oil many that were sick, and healed them. Mark 6:12-13

Then he called his twelve disciples together, and gave them power and authority over all devils, and to cure diseases. Luke 9:1

And the seventy returned again with joy, saying, Lord, even the devils are subject unto us through thy name. Luke 10:17

3. You Can Cast Out devils

And these signs shall follow them that believe; In my name shall they cast out devils; they shall speak with new tongues. Mark 16:17

Behold, I give unto you power to tread on serpents and scorpions, and over all the power of the enemy: and nothing shall by any means hurt you. Luke 10:19

Verily, verily, I say unto you, He that believeth on me, the works that I do shall he do also; and greater works than these shall he do; because I go unto my Father. John 14:12

4. Before Casting Out devils

And having in a readiness to revenge all disobedience, when your obedience is fulfilled. 2 Corinthians 10:6

Submit yourselves therefore to God. Resist the devil, and he will flee from you. James 4:7

Howbeit this kind goeth not out but by prayer and fasting. Matthew 17:21

Submit yourselves therefore to God. Resist the devil, and he will flee from you. James 4:7

> *You have to say "yes" to God first before you can effectively say "no" to the devil. - Vance Havner*

5. Keys to Remember When Casting Out devils

a. satan is subject to the Lord Jesus Christ

Yet Michael the archangel, when contending with the devil he disputed about the body of Moses, durst not bring against him a railing accusation, but said, The Lord rebuke thee. Jude 1:9

149

Then he answered and spake unto me, saying, This is the word of the Lord unto Zerubbabel, saying, Not by might, nor by power, but by my spirit, saith the Lord of hosts. Zechariah 4:6

b. After you cast the devil out of someone, advise them to receive Christ and to study and obey God's Word.

When the unclean spirit is gone out of a man, he walketh through dry places, seeking rest, and findeth none. Then he saith, I will return into my house from whence I came out; and when he is come, he findeth it empty, swept, and garnished. Then goeth he, and taketh with himself seven other spirits more wicked than himself, and they enter in and dwell there: and the last state of that man is worse than the first. Even so shall it be also unto this wicked generation.
Matthew 12:43-45

When the unclean spirit is gone out of a man, he walketh through dry places, seeking rest; and finding none, he saith, I will return unto my house whence I came out. And when he cometh, he findeth it swept and garnished. Then goeth he, and taketh to him seven other spirits more wicked than himself; and they enter in, and dwell there: and the last state of that man is worse than the first. Luke 11:24-26

Afterward Jesus findeth him in the temple, and said unto him, Behold, thou art made whole: sin no more, lest a worse thing come unto thee. John 5:14

Having therefore these promises, dearly beloved, let us cleanse ourselves from all filthiness of the flesh and spirit, perfecting holiness in the fear of God. 2 Corinthians 7:1

SALVATION

The Plan of Salvation

1. How to Obtain Eternal Life through Jesus Christ

That if thou shalt confess with thy mouth the Lord Jesus, and shalt believe in thine heart that God hath raised him from the dead, thou shalt be saved. Romans 10:9

2. How to be Saved

a. Admit that you have sinned and confess (to God) and repent.

b. Confess (speak aloud) that Jesus Christ is Lord – the Son of God.

c. Believe in your heart (inner most being, spirit, the real you) that God raised Jesus Christ from the dead.

d. After completing the above three steps (according to the Word of God), you are now saved and have eternal life through Jesus Christ.

For with the heart man believeth unto righteousness; and with the mouth confession is made unto salvation. Romans 10:10

3. How to Know You are Really Saved

a. Read what God's Word says about your salvation.

For whosoever shall call upon the name of the Lord shall be saved.
Romans 10:1

Verily, verily, I say unto you, He that heareth my word, and believeth on him that sent me, hath everlasting life, and shall not come into condemnation; but is passed from death unto life. John 5:24

And I give unto them eternal life; and they shall never perish, neither shall any man pluck them out of my hand. John 10:28

These things have I written unto you that believe on the name of the Son of God; that ye may know that ye have eternal life, and that ye may believe on the name of the Son of God. 1 John 5:13

And we know that the Son of God is come, and hath given us an understanding, that we may know him that is true, and we are in him that is true, even in his Son Jesus Christ. This is the true God, and eternal life. 1 John 5:20

For with the heart man believeth unto righteousness; and with the mouth confession is made unto salvation. Romans 10:10

b. The devil might try to play with your mind and tell you that "you are not saved."

He was a murderer from the beginning, and abode not in the truth, because there is no truth in him. When he speaketh a lie, he speaketh of his own: for he is a liar, and the father of it. John 8:44

c. You will obey God's Word.

If ye know that he is righteous, ye know that every one that doeth righteousness is born of him. 1 John 2:29

Whosoever abideth in him sinneth not: whosoever sinneth hath not seen him, neither known him. 1 John 3:6

Whosoever is born of God doth not commit sin; for his seed remaineth in him: and he cannot sin, because he is born of God. 1 John 3:9

We know that whosoever is born of God sinneth not; but he that is begotten of God keepeth himself, and that wicked one toucheth him not. 1 John 5:18

4. Now That You are Saved

a. Receive the baptism of the Holy Spirit.

b. Find a Bible-believing church that is on fire and alive. (Read the book of Acts)

c. Pray and read God's Word everyday of your life.

d. Obtain a Bible that you can understand. (i.e. The Living Bible, The New International Version, or the Amplified Bible)

True leaders are inwardly directed, self assured, and, as a result, truly charismatic.

---

e. Know your inheritance in Jesus Christ.

f. Obey the Word of God.

g. Don't be deceived.

h. Know and use your authority in Jesus Christ over satan.

i. Tell others what God has done for you.

Saved by Grace

Even when we were dead in sins, hath quickened us together with Christ, by grace ye are saved. Ephesians 2:5

For by grace are ye saved through faith; and that not of yourselves: it is the gift of God. Ephesians 2:8

For the grace of God that bringeth salvation hath appeared to all men.
Titus 2:11

That being justified by his grace, we should be made heirs according to the hope of eternal life. Titus 3:7

Who hath saved us, and called us with an holy calling, not according to our works, but according to his own purpose and grace, which was given us in Christ Jesus before the world began. 2 Timothy 1:9

1. Respecting the Grace of God

We then, as workers together with him, beseech you also that ye receive not the grace of God in vain. 2 Corinthians 6:1

I do not frustrate the grace of God: for if righteousness come by the law, then Christ is dead in vain. Galatians 2:21

What shall we say then? Shall we continue in sin, that grace may abound?
Romans 6:1

Sanctification

And ye shall keep my statutes, and do them: I am the Lord which sanctify you. Leviticus 20:8

That I should be the minister of Jesus Christ to the Gentiles, ministering the gospel of God, that the offering up of the Gentiles might be acceptable, being sanctified by the Holy Ghost. Romans 15:16

153

And the very God of peace sanctify you wholly; and I pray God your whole spirit and soul and body be preserved blameless unto the coming of our Lord Jesus Christ. 1 Thessalonians 5:23

But we are bound to give thanks alway to God for you, brethren beloved of the Lord, because God hath from the beginning chosen you to salvation through sanctification of the Spirit and belief of the truth:
2 Thessalonians 2:13

For both he that sanctifieth and they who are sanctified are all of one: for which cause he is not ashamed to call them brethren. Hebrews 2:11

For both He Who sanctifies–making men holy–and those who are sanctified all have one [Father]. For this reason He is not ashamed to call them brethren. Hebrews 2:11 AMP

Elect according to the foreknowledge of God the Father, through sanctification of the Spirit, unto obedience and sprinkling of the blood of Jesus Christ: Grace unto you, and peace, be multiplied. 1 Peter 1:2

Jude, the servant of Jesus Christ, and brother of James, to them that are sanctified by God the Father, and preserved in Jesus Christ, and called:
Jude 1:1

1. Sanctified by the Word of God

Sanctify them through thy truth: thy word is truth. John 17:17

That he might sanctify and cleanse it with the washing of water by the word. Ephesians 5:26

2. Sanctified through Jesus Christ

Unto the church of God which is at Corinth, to them that are sanctified in Christ Jesus, called to be saints, with all that in every place call upon the name of Jesus Christ our Lord, both theirs and ours: 1 Corinthians 1:2

But of him are ye in Christ Jesus, who of God is made unto us wisdom, and righteousness, and sanctification, and redemption: 1 Corinthians 1:30

And such were some of you: but ye are washed, but ye are sanctified, but ye are justified in the name of the Lord Jesus, and by the Spirit of our God. 1 Corinthians 6:11

By the which will we are sanctified through the offering of the body of Jesus Christ once for all. Hebrews 10:10

For by one offering he hath perfected for ever them that are sanctified.
Hebrews 10:14

Wherefore Jesus also, that he might sanctify the people with his own blood, suffered without the gate. Hebrews 13:12

To open their eyes, and to turn them from darkness to light, and from the power of Satan unto God, that they may receive forgiveness of sins, and inheritance among them which are sanctified by faith that is in me.

Acts 26:18

3. Set Apart from the Sins of the World

For this is the will of God, even your sanctification, that ye should abstain from fornication: 1 Thessalonians 4:3

That every one of you should know how to possess his vessel in sanctification and honour; 1 Thessalonians 4:4

If a man therefore purge himself from these, he shall be a vessel unto honour, sanctified, and meet for the master's use, and prepared unto every good work. 2 Timothy 2:21

And now, brethren, I commend you to God, and to the word of his grace, which is able to build you up, and to give you an inheritance among all them which are sanctified. Acts 20:32

Righteousness

1. Righteousness through Jesus Christ

Even the righteousness of God which is by faith of Jesus Christ unto all and upon all them that believe: for there is no difference: For all have sinned, and come short of the glory of God; Romans 3:22-23

For if by one man's offence death reigned by one; much more they which receive abundance of grace and of the gift of righteousness shall reign in life by one, Jesus Christ. Therefore as by the offence of one judgment came upon all men to condemnation; even so by the righteousness of one the free gift came upon all men unto justification of life.

Romans 5:17-18

> *This is the mystery of the riches of divine grace for sinners; for by a wonderful exchange our sins are now not ours but Christ's, and Christ's righteousness is not Christ's but ours. - Martin Luther*

Moreover the law entered, that the offence might abound. But where sin abounded, grace did much more abound: That as sin hath reigned unto death, even so might grace reign through righteousness unto eternal life by Jesus Christ our Lord. Romans 5:20-21

And if Christ be in you, the body is dead because of sin; but the Spirit is life because of righteousness. Romans 8:10

But of him are ye in Christ Jesus, who of God is made unto us wisdom, and righteousness, and sanctification, and redemption: 1 Corinthians 1:30

For he hath made him to be sin for us, who knew no sin; that we might be made the righteousness of God in him. 2 Corinthians 5:21

And that ye put on the new man, which after God is created in righteousness and true holiness. Ephesians 4:24

Being filled with the fruits of righteousness, which are by Jesus Christ, unto the glory and praise of God. Philippians 1:11

Who his own self bare our sins in his own body on the tree, that we, being dead to sins, should live unto righteousness: by whose stripes ye were healed. 1 Peter 2:24

2. Believing Unto Righteousness

For what saith the scripture? Abraham believed God, and it was counted unto him for righteousness. Romans 4:3

For with the heart man believeth unto righteousness; and with the mouth confession is made unto salvation. Romans 10:10

3. The Word of God is Our Instruction for Righteous Living

All scripture is given by inspiration of God, and is profitable for doctrine, for reproof, for correction, for instruction in righteousness:
2 Timothy 3:16

For every one that useth milk is unskillful in the word of righteousness: for he is a babe. Hebrews 5:13

4. Man-Made Righteousness

For I bear them record that they have a zeal of God, but not according to knowledge. For they being ignorant of God's righteousness, and going about to establish their own righteousness, have not submitted themselves unto the righteousness of God. Romans 10:2-3

The greatest display of leadership is service.

And be found in him, not having mine own righteousness, which is of the law, but that which is through the faith of Christ, the righteousness which is of God by faith: Philippians 3:9

Justification

And by him all that believe are justified from all things, from which ye could not be justified by the law of Moses. Acts 13:39

Being justified freely by his grace through the redemption that is in Christ Jesus: Romans 3:24

To declare, I say, at this time his righteousness: that he might be just, and the justifier of him which believeth in Jesus. Romans 3:26

But to him that worketh not, but believeth on him that justifieth the ungodly, his faith is counted for righteousness. Romans 4:5

Therefore being justified by faith, we have peace with God through our Lord Jesus Christ: Romans 5:1

Who was delivered for our offences, and was raised again for our justification. Romans 4:25

Much more then, being now justified by his blood, we shall be saved from wrath through him. Romans 5:9

Therefore as by the offence of one judgment came upon all men to condemnation; even so by the righteousness of one the free gift came upon all men unto justification of life. Romans 5:18

And such were some of you: but ye are washed, but ye are sanctified, but ye are justified in the name of the Lord Jesus, and by the Spirit of our God. 1 Corinthians 6:11

Wherefore the law was our schoolmaster to bring us unto Christ, that we might be justified by faith. Galatians 3:24

And without controversy great is the mystery of godliness: God was manifest in the flesh, justified in the Spirit, seen of angels, preached unto the Gentiles, believed on in the world, received up into glory.
1 Timothy 3:16

That being justified by his grace, we should be made heirs according to the hope of eternal life. Titus 3:7

For not the hearers of the law are just before God, but the doers of the law shall be justified. Romans 2:13

Remaining in the Kingdom of God

Blessed are the pure in heart: for they shall see God. Matthew 5:8

And ye shall be hated of all men for my name's sake: but he that endureth to the end shall be saved. Matthew 10:22

But he that shall endure unto the end, the same shall be saved.
Matthew 24:13

He that hath an ear, let him hear what the Spirit saith unto the churches; To him that overcometh will I give to eat of the tree of life, which is in the midst of the paradise of God. Revelation 2:7

He that hath an ear, let him hear what the Spirit saith unto the churches; He that overcometh shall not be hurt of the second death.
Revelation 2:11

He that hath an ear, let him hear what the Spirit saith unto the churches; To him that overcometh will I give to eat of the hidden manna, and will give him a white stone, and in the stone a new name written, which no man knoweth saving he that receiveth it. Revelation 2:17

And he that overcometh, and keepeth my works unto the end, to him will I give power over the nations. Revelation 2:26

He that overcometh, the same shall be clothed in white raiment; and I will not blot out his name out of the book of life, but I will confess his name before my Father, and before his angels. Revelation 3:5

Him that overcometh will I make a pillar in the temple of my God, and he shall go no more out: and I will write upon him the name of my God, and the name of the city of my God, which is new Jerusalem, which cometh down out of heaven from my God: and I will write upon him my new name. Revelation 3:12

To him that overcometh will I grant to sit with me in my throne, even as I also overcame, and am set down with my Father in his throne.
Revelation 3:21

He that overcometh shall inherit all things; and I will be his God, and he shall be my son. Revelation 21:7

Backslider

Definition of backslider: A Christian that no longer walks in fellowship with God nor obeys His Word

As a dog returneth to his vomit, so a fool returneth to his folly.
Proverbs 26:11

158

The backslider in heart shall be filled with his own ways: and a good man shall be satisfied from himself. Proverbs 14:14

Thine own wickedness shall correct thee, and thy backslidings shall reprove thee: know therefore and see that it is an evil thing and bitter, that thou hast forsaken the Lord thy God, and that my fear is not in thee, saith the Lord God of hosts. Jeremiah 2:19

Go and proclaim these words toward the north, and say, Return, thou backsliding Israel, saith the Lord; and I will not cause mine anger to fall upon you: for I am merciful, saith the Lord, and I will not keep anger for ever. Jeremiah 3:12

Turn, O backsliding children, saith the Lord; for I am married unto you: and I will take you one of a city, and two of a family, and I will bring you to Zion. Jeremiah 3:14

Return, ye backsliding children, and I will heal your backslidings. Behold, we come unto thee; for thou art the Lord our God. Jeremiah 3:22

O Israel, return unto the Lord thy God; for thou hast fallen by thine iniquity. Hosea 14:1

But now, after that ye have known God, or rather are known of God, how turn ye again to the weak and beggarly elements, whereunto ye desire again to be in bondage? Galatians 4:9

Having damnation, because they have cast off their first faith.
1 Timothy 5:12

Compromising Christian

Definition of Compromising Christian: Luke warm, Uncommitted

They profess that they know God; but in works they deny him, being abominable, and disobedient, and unto every good work reprobate.
Titus 1:16

What shall we say then? Shall we continue in sin, that grace may abound?
Romans 6:1

Salt is good: but if the salt have lost his saltness, wherewith will ye season it? Have salt in yourselves, and have peace one with another.
Mark 9:50

And that, knowing the time, that now it is high time to awake out of sleep: for now is our salvation nearer than when we believed. The night is far spent, the day is at hand: let us therefore cast off the works of darkness, and let us put on the armour of light. Let us walk honestly, as in the day; not in rioting and drunkenness, not in chambering and wantonness, not in strife and envying. But put ye on the Lord Jesus Christ, and make not provision for the flesh, to fulfil the lusts thereof.

Romans 13:11-14

A whole new generation of Christians has come up believing that it is possible to "accept" Christ without forsaking the world.
- A. W. Tozer

But I keep under my body, and bring it into subjection: lest that by any means, when I have preached to others, I myself should be a castaway.

1 Corinthians 9:27

Now this I say, brethren, that flesh and blood cannot inherit the kingdom of God; neither doth corruption inherit incorruption. 1 Corinthians 15:50

We then, as workers together with him, beseech you also that ye receive not the grace of God in vain. For he saith, I have heard thee in a time accepted, and in the day of salvation have I succoured thee: behold, now is the accepted time; behold, now is the day of salvation.

2 Corinthians 6:1-2

I do not frustrate the grace of God: for if righteousness come by the law, then Christ is dead in vain. Galatians 2:21

Set your affection on things above, not on things on the earth.

Colossians 3:2

Now the Spirit speaketh expressly, that in the latter times some shall depart from the faith, giving heed to seducing spirits, and doctrines of devils. 1 Timothy 4:1

We are not here to learn how to live in the dark but to walk in the light. We are not here to get along with evil but to overcome it with good. - Vance Havner

Teaching us that, denying ungodliness and worldly lusts, we should live soberly, righteously, and godly, in this present world; Looking for that blessed hope, and the glorious appearing of the great God and our Saviour Jesus Christ. Titus 2:12-13

Ye have not yet resisted unto blood, striving against sin. Hebrews 12:4

When people have confidence in your leadership, your work will prosper.

You have not yet struggled and fought agonizingly against sin, nor have you yet resisted and withstood to the point of pouring out your [own] blood. Hebrews 12:4 AMP

Pure religion and undefiled before God and the Father is this, To visit the fatherless and widows in their affliction, and to keep himself unspotted from the world. James 1:27

For if after they have escaped the pollutions of the world through the knowledge of the Lord and Saviour Jesus Christ, they are again entangled therein, and overcome, the latter end is worse with them than the beginning. For it had been better for them not to have known the way of righteousness, than, after they have known it, to turn from the holy commandment delivered unto them. But it is happened unto them according to the true proverb, The dog is turned to his own vomit again; and the sow that was washed to her wallowing in the mire. 2 Peter 2:20-22

Christians are not just nice people. They're new creatures. If you are what you have always been you are not a Christian. A Christian is something new; old things have passed away and all things are become new. - Vance Havner

Love not the world, neither the things that are in the world. If any man love the world, the love of the Father is not in him. For all that is in the world, the lust of the flesh, and the lust of the eyes, and the pride of life, is not of the Father, but is of the world. And the world passeth away, and the lust thereof: but he that doeth the will of God abideth for ever.
1 John 2:15-17

Is your lifestyle taking the people around you to heaven or hell?

Then shall the kingdom of heaven be likened unto ten virgins, which took their lamps, and went forth to meet the bridegroom. And five of them were wise, and five were foolish. They that were foolish took their lamps, and took no oil with them: But the wise took oil in their vessels with their lamps. While the bridegroom tarried, they all slumbered and slept. And at midnight there was a cry made, Behold, the bridegroom cometh; go ye out to meet him. Then all those virgins arose, and trimmed their lamps. And the foolish said unto the wise, Give us of your oil; for our lamps are gone out. But the wise answered, saying, Not so; lest there be not enough for us and you: but go ye rather to them that sell, and buy for yourselves. And while they went to buy, the bridegroom came; and they that were ready went in with him to the marriage: and the door was shut. Afterward came also the other virgins, saying, Lord, Lord, open to us. But he answered and said, Verily I say unto you, I know you not.

Watch therefore, for ye know neither the day nor the hour wherein the Son of man cometh. Matthew 25:1-13

A Warning for the Backslider or Compromising Christian

I know thy works, that thou art neither cold nor hot: I would thou wert cold or hot. So then because thou art lukewarm, and neither cold nor hot, I will spue thee out of my mouth. Because thou sayest, I am rich, and increased with goods, and have need of nothing; and knowest not that thou art wretched, and miserable, and poor, and blind, and naked.
Revelation 3:15-17

Enter ye in at the strait gate: for wide is the gate, and broad is the way, that leadeth to destruction, and many there be which go in thereat: Because strait is the gate, and narrow is the way, which leadeth unto life, and few there be that find it. Matthew 7:13-14

*Life is too short and hell is too hot to play
games with your eternal future.*

Not every one that saith unto me, Lord, Lord, shall enter into the kingdom of heaven; but he that doeth the will of my Father which is in heaven. Many will say to me in that day, Lord, Lord, have we not prophesied in thy name? and in thy name have cast out devils? and in thy name done many wonderful works? And then will I profess unto them, I never knew you: depart from me, ye that work iniquity. Matthew 7:21-23

Strive to enter in at the strait gate: for many, I say unto you, will seek to enter in, and shall not be able. When once the master of the house is risen up, and hath shut to the door, and ye begin to stand without, and to knock at the door, saying, Lord, Lord, open unto us; and he shall answer and say unto you, I know you not whence ye are: Then shall ye begin to say, We have eaten and drunk in thy presence, and thou hast taught in our streets. But he shall say, I tell you, I know you not whence ye are; depart from me, all ye workers of iniquity. There shall be weeping and gnashing of teeth, when ye shall see Abraham, and Isaac, and Jacob, and all the prophets, in the kingdom of God, and you yourselves thrust out.
Luke 13:24-28

For it is impossible for those who were once enlightened, and have tasted of the heavenly gift, and were made partakers of the Holy Ghost, And have tasted the good word of God, and the powers of the world to come, If they shall fall away, to renew them again unto repentance; seeing they crucify to themselves the Son of God afresh, and put him to an open shame. Hebrews 6:4-6

For it is impossible [to restore and bring again to repentance] those who have been once for all enlightened, who have consciously tasted the heavenly gift, and have become sharers of the Holy Spirit. And have felt how good the Word of God is and the mighty powers of the age and world to come. If they then deviate from the faith and turn away from their allegiance; [it is impossible] to bring them back to repentance, for (because, while, as long as) they nail up on the cross the Son of God afresh, as far as they are concerned, and are holding [him] up to contempt and shame and public disgrace. Hebrews 6:4-6 AMP

For if we sin wilfully after that we have received the knowledge of the truth, there remaineth no more sacrifice for sins, But a certain fearful looking for of judgment and fiery indignation, which shall devour the adversaries. He that despised Moses' law died without mercy under two or three witnesses: Of how much sorer punishment, suppose ye, shall he be thought worthy, who hath trodden under foot the Son of God, and hath counted the blood of the covenant, wherewith he was sanctified, an unholy thing, and hath done despite unto the Spirit of grace? For we know him that hath said, Vengeance belongeth unto me, I will recompense, saith the Lord. And again, The Lord shall judge his people. It is a fearful thing to fall into the hands of the living God. Hebrews 10:26-31

For if we go on deliberately and willingly sinning after once acquiring the knowledge of the Truth, there is no longer any sacrifice left to atone for [our] sins—no further offering to which to look forward. There is nothing left for us then but a kind of awful and fearful prospect and expectation of divine judgment and the fury of burning wrath and indignation which will consume those who put themselves in opposition to God. Any person who has violated and [thus] rejected and set at naught the Law of Moses is put to death without pity or mercy on the evidence of two or three witnesses. How much worse (sterner and heavier) punishment do you suppose he will be judged to deserve who has spurned and [thus] trampled under foot the Son of God, and who has considered the covenant blood by which he was consecrated common and unhallowed, thus profaning it and insulting and outraging the (Holy) Spirit [Who imparts] grace—the unmerited favor and blessing of God? For we know Him Who said, Vengeance is Mine—retribution and the meting out of full justice rest with Me; I will repay—I will exact the compensation, says the Lord. And again, The Lord will judge and determine and solve and settle the cause and the cases of His people. Is a fearful (formidable and terrible) thing to incur the divine penalties and be cast into the hands of the living God! Hebrews 10:26-31 AMP

Nevertheless I have somewhat against thee, because thou hast left thy first love. Remember therefore from whence thou art fallen, and repent,

163

and do the first works; or else I will come unto thee quickly, and will remove thy candlestick out of his place, except thou repent.

Revelation 2:4-5

LOVE

God is love; and he that dwelleth in love dwelleth in God, and God in him. 1 John 4:16

Ther1e is no fear in love; but perfect love casteth out fear: because fear hath torment. He that feareth is not made perfect in love. 1 John 4:18

Characteristics of Love

Charity suffereth long, and is kind; charity envieth not; charity vaunteth not itself, is not puffed up, Doth not behave itself unseemly, seekteh not her own, is not easily provoked, thinketh no evil; Rejoiceth not in iniquity, but rejoiceth in the truth; Beareth all things, believeth all things, hopeth all things, endureth all things. Charity never faileth.

1 Corinthians 13:4-8a

1. **Love is patient.**
2. **Love is kind.**
3. **Love does not envy.**
4. **Love does not boast.**
5. **Love is not proud.**
6. **Love is not rude.**
7. **Love is not self-seeking.**
8. **Love is not easily angered.**
9. **Love keeps no record of wrongs.**
10. **Love does not delight in evil but rejoices with the truth.**
11. **Love always protects.**
12. **Love always trusts.**
13. **Love always hopes.**
14. **Love always perseveres.**
15. **Love never fails.**

Though I speak with the tongues of men and of angels, and have not charity (love), I am become as sounding brass, or a tinkling cymbal. And though I have the gift of prophecy, and understand all mysteries, and all knowledge; and though I have all faith, so that I could remove mountains, and have not charity (love), I am nothing. And though I bestow all my goods to feed the poor, and though I give my body to be burned, and have not charity (love), it profiteth me nothing.

1 Corinthians 13:1-3

And now abideth faith, hope, charity, these three; but the greatest of these is charity. 1 Corinthians 13:13

God's Love

The Lord openeth the eyes of the blind: the Lord raiseth them that are bowed down: the Lord loveth the righteous. Psalms 146:8

For as a young man marrieth a virgin, so shall thy sons marry thee: and as the bridegroom rejoiceth over the bride, so shall thy God rejoice over thee. Isaiah 62:5

The Lord hath appeared of old unto me, saying, Yea, I have loved thee with an everlasting love: therefore with lovingkindness have I drawn thee. Jeremiah 31:3

I will heal their backsliding, I will love them freely: for mine anger is turned away from him. Hosea 14:4

For God so loved the world, that he gave his only begotten Son, that whosoever believeth in him should not perish, but have everlasting life.

John 3:16

For the Father himself loveth you, because ye have loved me, and have believed that I came out from God. John 16:27

And the glory which thou gavest me I have given them; that they may be one, even as we are one: I in them, and thou in me, that they may be made perfect in one; and that the world may know that thou hast sent me, and hast loved them, as thou hast loved me. John 17:22-23

And I have declared unto them thy name, and will declare it: that the love wherewith thou hast loved me may be in them, and I in them.

John 17:26

> **True leaders are not annoyed by people's failures, they are challenged by them.**

But God commendeth his love toward us, in that, while we were yet sinners, Christ died for us. Romans 5:8

But God, who is rich in mercy, for his great love wherewith he loved us, Even when we were dead in sins, hath quickened us together with Christ, by grace ye are saved. And hath raised us up together, and made us sit together in heavenly places in Christ Jesus: That in the ages to come he might shew the exceeding riches of his grace in his kindness toward us through Christ Jesus. Ephesians 2:4-7

And to know the love of Christ, which passeth knowledge, that ye might be filled with all the fulness of God. Ephesians 3:19

Now our Lord Jesus Christ himself, and God, even our Father, which hath loved us, and hath given us everlasting consolation and good hope through grace, Comfort your hearts, and stablish you in every good word and work 2 Thessalonians 2:16-17

Behold, what manner of love the Father hath bestowed upon us, that we should be called the sons of God: therefore the world knoweth us not, because it knew him not. 1 John 3:1

Beloved, let us love one another: for love is of God; and every one that loveth is born of God, and knoweth God. He that loveth not knoweth not God; for God is love. In this was manifested the love of God toward us, because that God sent his only begotten Son into the world, that we might live through him. Herein is love, not that we loved God, but that he loved us, and sent his Son to be the propitiation for our sins. Beloved, if God so loved us, we ought also to love one another. 1 John 4:7-11

And we have known and believed the love that God hath to us. God is love; and he that dwelleth in love dwelleth in God, and God in him.
1 John 4:16

We love him, because he first loved us. 1 John 4:19

Loving God

But as it is written, Eye hath not seen, nor ear heard, neither have entered into the heart of man, the things which God hath prepared for them that love him. 1 Corinthians 2:9

Know therefore that the Lord thy God, he is God, the faithful God, which keepeth covenant and mercy with them that love him and keep his commandments to a thousand generations. Deuteronomy 7:9

167

Delight thyself also in the Lord; and he shall give thee the desires of thine heart. Psalms 37:4

Whom have I in heaven but thee? and there is none upon earth that I desire beside thee. Psalms 73:25

Because he hath set his love upon me, therefore will I deliver him: I will set him on high, because he hath known my name. Psalms 91:14

The Lord preserveth all them that love him: but all the wicked will he destroy. Psalms 145:20

I love them that love me; and those that seek me early shall find me.
Proverbs 8:17

That I may cause those that love me to inherit substance; and I will fill their treasures. Proverbs 8:21

He that hath my commandments, and keepeth them, he it is that loveth me: and he that loveth me shall be loved of my Father, and I will love him, and will manifest myself to him. John 14:21

Grace be with all them that love our Lord Jesus Christ in sincerity. Amen.
Ephesians 6:24

Loving Others

Behold, how good and how pleasant it is for brethren to dwell together in unity! Psalms 133:1

But I say unto you, Love your enemies, bless them that curse you, do good to them that hate you, and pray for them which despitefully use you, and persecute you. Matthew 5:44

Therefore all things whatsoever ye would that men should do to you, do ye even so to them: for this is the law and the prophets. Matthew 7:12

And thou shalt love the Lord thy God with all thy heart, and with all thy soul, and with all thy mind, and with all thy strength: this is the first commandment. And the second is like, namely this, Thou shalt love thy neighbour as thyself. There is none other commandment greater than these. Mark 12:30-31

This is my commandment, That ye love one another, as I have loved you. Greater love hath no man than this, that a man lay down his life for his friends. John 15:12-13

Be kindly affectioned one to another with brotherly love; in honour preferring one another. Romans 12:10

Love worketh no ill to his neighbour: therefore love is the fulfilling of the law. Romans 13:10

Finally, brethren, farewell. Be perfect, be of good comfort, be of one mind, live in peace; and the God of love and peace shall be with you.
2 Corinthians 13:11

Seeing ye have purified your souls in obeying the truth through the Spirit unto unfeigned love of the brethren, see that ye love one another with a pure heart fervently. 1 Peter 1:22

Finally, be ye all of one mind, having compassion one of another, love as brethren, be pitiful, be courteous: Not rendering evil for evil, or railing for railing: but contrariwise blessing; knowing that ye are thereunto called, that ye should inherit a blessing. 1 Peter 3:8-9

He that loveth his brother abideth in the light, and there is none occasion of stumbling in him. 1 John 2:10

We know that we have passed from death unto life, because we love the brethren. He that loveth not his brother abideth in death. 1 John 3:14

My little children, let us not love in word, neither in tongue; but in deed and in truth. And hereby we know that we are of the truth, and shall assure our hearts before him. 1 John 3:18-19

Beloved, let us love one another: for love is of God; and every one that loveth is born of God, and knoweth God. He that loveth not knoweth not God; for God is love. 1 John 4:7-8

Beloved, if God so loved us, we ought also to love one another. No man hath seen God at any time. If we love one another, God dwelleth in us, and his love is perfected in us. 1 John 4:11-12

If a man say, I love God, and hateth his brother, he is a liar: for he that loveth not his brother whom he hath seen, how can he love God whom he hath not seen? And this commandment have we from him, That he who loveth God love his brother also. 1 John 4:20-21

And now I beseech thee, lady, not as though I wrote a new commandment unto thee, but that which we had from the beginning, that we love one another. 2 John 1:5

169

MATURING IN CHRIST

Forgiveness

Thou shalt not avenge, nor bear any grudge against the children of thy people, but thou shalt love thy neighbour as thyself: I am the Lord.
Leviticus 19:18

Therefore if thou bring thy gift to the altar, and there rememberest that thy brother hath ought against thee; Leave there thy gift before the altar, and go thy way; first be reconciled to thy brother, and then come and offer thy gift. Matthew 5:23-24

But I say unto you, Love your enemies, bless them that curse you, do good to them that hate you, and pray for them which despitefully use you, and persecute you. Matthew 5:44

And forgive us our debts, as we forgive our debtors. Matthew 6:12

For if ye forgive men their trespasses, your heavenly Father will also forgive you: But if ye forgive not men their trespasses, neither will your Father forgive your trespasses. Matthew 6:14-15

> *"I can forgive, but I cannot forget," is only another way of saying, "I cannot forgive." - Henry Ward Beecher*

Then came Peter to him, and said, Lord, how oft shall my brother sin against me, and I forgive him? till seven times? Jesus saith unto him, I say not unto thee, Until seven times: but, Until seventy times seven.
Matthew 18:21-22

Judge not, and ye shall not be judged: condemn not, and ye shall not be condemned: forgive, and ye shall be forgiven. Luke 6:37

Whose soever sins ye remit, they are remitted unto them; and whose soever sins ye retain, they are retained. John 20:23

To whom ye forgive any thing, I forgive also: for if I forgave any thing, to whom I forgave it, for your sakes forgave I it in the person of Christ;

171

Lest satan should get an advantage of us: for we are not ignorant of his devices. 2 Corinthians 2:10-11

Let all bitterness, and wrath, and anger, and clamour, and evil speaking, be put away from you, with all malice: And be ye kind one to another, tenderhearted, forgiving one another, even as God for Christ's sake hath forgiven you. Ephesians 4:31-32

Grudge not one against another, brethren, lest ye be condemned: behold, the judge standeth before the door. James 5:9

Use hospitality one to another without grudging. 1 Peter 4:9

Forbearing one another, and forgiving one another, if any man have a quarrel against any: even as Christ forgave you, so also do ye.
Colossians 3:13

*Forgiving your offenders sets you free
more than it does anyone else.*

Patience

Wait on the Lord: be of good courage, and he shall strengthen thine heart: wait, I say, on the Lord. Psalms 27:14

Rest in the Lord, and wait patiently for him: fret not thyself because of him who prospereth in his way, because of the man who bringeth wicked devices to pass. Cease from anger, and forsake wrath: fret not thyself in any wise to do evil. For evildoers shall be cut off: but those that wait upon the Lord, they shall inherit the earth. Psalms 37:7-9

Wait on the Lord, and keep his way, and he shall exalt thee to inherit the land: when the wicked are cut off, thou shalt see it. Psalms 37:34

I waited patiently for the Lord; and he inclined unto me, and heard my cry. Psalms 40:1

Better is the end of a thing than the beginning thereof: and the patient in spirit is better than the proud in spirit. Ecclesiastes 7:8

These wait all upon thee; that thou mayest give them their meat in due season. Psalms 104:27

*Impatience and doubt are thieves of the perfect will
of God and His greatest blessings.*

**True leadership brings followers into leadership
and makes itself increasingly unnecessary.**

Say not thou, I will recompense evil; but wait on the Lord, and he shall save thee. Proverbs 20:22

And it shall be said in that day, Lo, this is our God; we have waited for him, and he will save us: this is the Lord; we have waited for him, we will be glad and rejoice in his salvation. Isaiah 25:9

It is good that a man should both hope and quietly wait for the salvation of the Lord. Lamentations 3:26

In your patience possess ye your souls. Luke 21:19

To them who by patient continuance in well doing seek for glory and honour and immortality, eternal life. Romans 2:7

But if we hope for that we see not, then do we with patience wait for it.
Romans 8:25

Strengthened with all might, according to his glorious power, unto all patience and longsuffering with joyfulness. Colossians 1:11

Now we exhort you, brethren, warn them that are unruly, comfort the feebleminded, support the weak, be patient toward all men.
1 Thessalonians 5:14

Just as faith without works is dead, so is faith without patience.

And the Lord direct your hearts into the love of God, and into the patient waiting for Christ. 2 Thessalonians 3:5

Wherefore seeing we also are compassed about with so great a cloud of witnesses, let us lay aside every weight, and the sin which doth so easily beset us, and let us run with patience the race that is set before us,
Hebrews 12:1

Be patient therefore, brethren, unto the coming of the Lord. Behold, the husbandman waiteth for the precious fruit of the earth, and hath long patience for it, until he receive the early and latter rain. Be ye also patient; stablish your hearts: for the coming of the Lord draweth nigh.
James 5:7-8

Take, my brethren, the prophets, who have spoken in the name of the Lord, for an example of suffering affliction, and of patience. James 5:10

Whereby are given unto us exceeding great and precious promises: that by these ye might be partakers of the divine nature, having escaped the corruption that is in the world through lust. 2 Peter 1:4

173

And to knowledge temperance; and to temperance patience; and to patience godliness. 2 Peter 1:6

The Lord is not slack concerning his promise, as some men count slackness; but is longsuffering to us-ward, not willing that any should perish, but that all should come to repentance. 2 Peter 3:9

Because thou hast kept the word of my patience, I also will keep thee from the hour of temptation, which shall come upon all the world, to try them that dwell upon the earth. Revelation 3:10

Here is the patience of the saints: here are they that keep the commandments of God, and the faith of Jesus. Revelation 14:12

1. Remaining Patient in Tribulations

And not only so, but we glory in tribulations also: knowing that tribulation worketh patience; And patience, experience; and experience, hope. And hope maketh not ashamed; because the love of God is shed abroad in our hearts by the Holy Ghost which is given unto us. Romans 5:3-5

Rejoicing in hope; patient in tribulation; continuing instant in prayer.
Romans 12:12

Some experiences may not contribute ot happiness, but all can be made to contribute to the development of patience.

Knowing this, that the trying of your faith worketh patience. But let patience have her perfect work, that ye may be perfect and entire, wanting nothing. James 1:3-4

Living in Holiness

For I am the Lord your God: ye shall therefore sanctify yourselves, and ye shall be holy; for I am holy: neither shall ye defile yourselves with any manner of creeping thing that creepeth upon the earth. For I am the Lord that bringeth you up out of the land of Egypt, to be your God: ye shall therefore be holy, for I am holy. Leviticus 11:44-45

There is none holy as the Lord: for there is none beside thee: neither is there any rock like our God. Isaiah 2:2

That he would grant unto us, that we being delivered out of the hand of our enemies might serve him without fear, In holiness and righteousness before him, all the days of our life. Luke 1:74-75

I speak after the manner of men because of the infirmity of your flesh: for as ye have yielded your members servants to uncleanness and to iniquity unto iniquity; even so now yield your members servants to righteousness unto holiness. Romans 6:19

The essence of true holiness consists in conformity to the nature and will of God. - Samuel Lucas

But now being made free from sin, and become servants to God, ye have your fruit unto holiness, and the end everlasting life. Romans 6:22

I beseech you therefore, brethren, by the mercies of God, that ye present your bodies a living sacrifice, holy, acceptable unto God, which is your reasonable service. Romans 12:1

Having therefore these promises, dearly beloved, let us cleanse ourselves from all filthiness of the flesh and spirit, perfecting holiness in the fear of God. 2 Corinthians 7:1

According as he hath chosen us in him before the foundation of the world, that we should be holy and without blame before him in love:
Ephesians 1:4

And that ye put on the new man, which after God is created in righteousness and true holiness. Ephesians 4:24

That he might present it to himself a glorious church, not having spot, or wrinkle, or any such thing; but that it should be holy and without blemish. Ephesians 5:27

To the end he may stablish your hearts unblameable in holiness before God, even our Father, at the coming of our Lord Jesus Christ with all his saints. 1 Thessalonians 3:13

For God hath not called us unto uncleanness, but unto holiness.
1 Thessalonians 4:7

The aged women likewise, that they be in behaviour as becometh holiness, not false accusers, not given to much wine, teachers of good things;
Titus 2:3

For they verily for a few days chastened us after their own pleasure; but he for our profit, that we might be partakers of his holiness.
Hebrews 12:10

Follow peace with all men, and holiness, without which no man shall see the Lord: Hebrews 12:14

175

But as he which hath called you is holy, so be ye holy in all manner of conversation; Because it is written, Be ye holy; for I am holy.

1 Peter 1:15-16

A man ought to live so that everybody knows he is a Christian.... and most of all, his family ought to know. - D. L. Moody

Fruitful Living

Bring forth therefore fruits meet for repentance. Matthew 3:8

And now also the axe is laid unto the root of the trees: therefore every tree which bringeth not forth good fruit is hewn down, and cast into the fire. Matthew 3:10

Ye shall know them by their fruits. Do men gather grapes of thorns, or figs of thistles? Even so every good tree bringeth forth good fruit; but a corrupt tree bringeth forth evil fruit. A good tree cannot bring forth evil fruit, neither can a corrupt tree bring forth good fruit. Every tree that bringeth not forth good fruit is hewn down, and cast into the fire. Wherefore by their fruits ye shall know them. Matthew 7:16-20

And all the people were amazed, and said, Is not this the son of David?

Matthew 12:23

Faith makes a Christian.

Life proves a Christian.

Trials confirm a Christian.

Death crowns a Christian.

- Anonymous

Either make the tree good, and his fruit good; or else make the tree corrupt, and his fruit corrupt: for the tree is known by his fruit.

Matthew 12:33

I am the true vine, and my Father is the husbandman. Every branch in me that beareth not fruit he taketh away: and every branch that beareth fruit, he purgeth it, that it may bring forth more fruit. Now ye are clean through the word which I have spoken unto you. Abide in me, and I in you. As the branch cannot bear fruit of itself, except it abide in the vine; no more can ye, except ye abide in me. I am the vine, ye are the branches: He that abideth in me, and I in him, the same bringeth forth much fruit: for without me ye can do nothing. John 15:1-5

You are a successful leader when your followers can lead others.

Herein is my Father glorified, that ye bear much fruit; so shall ye be my disciples. John 15:8

Ye have not chosen me, but I have chosen you, and ordained you, that ye should go and bring forth fruit, and that your fruit should remain: that whatsoever ye shall ask of the Father in my name, he may give it you.
John 15:16

But now being made free from sin, and become servants to God, ye have your fruit unto holiness, and the end everlasting life. Romans 6:22

Therefore, as ye abound in every thing, in faith, and utterance, and knowledge, and in all diligence, and in your love to us, see that ye abound in this grace also. 2 Corinthians 8:7

But if I live in the flesh, this is the fruit of my labour: yet what I shall choose I wot not. Philippians 1:22

Which is come unto you, as it is in all the world; and bringeth forth fruit, as it doth also in you, since the day ye heard of it, and knew the grace of God in truth. Colossians 1:6

That ye might walk worthy of the Lord unto all pleasing, being fruitful in every good work, and increasing in the knowledge of God.
Colossians 1:10

Now no chastening for the present seemeth to be joyous, but grievous: nevertheless afterward it yieldeth the peaceable fruit of righteousness unto them which are exercised thereby. Hebrews 12:11

For if these things be in you, and abound, they make you that ye shall neither be barren nor unfruitful in the knowledge of our Lord Jesus Christ.
2 Peter 1:8

Peacemaker

Hatred stirreth up strifes: but love covereth all sins. Proverbs 10:12

A soft answer turneth away wrath: but grievous words stir up anger.
Proverbs 15:1

A wrathful man stirreth up strife: but he that is slow to anger appeaseth strife. Proverbs 15:18

He that covereth a transgression seeketh love; but he that repeateth a matter separateth very friends. Proverbs 17:9

A gift in secret pacifieth anger: and a reward in the bosom strong wrath.
Proverbs 21:14

177

By long forbearing is a prince persuaded, and a soft tongue breaketh the bone. Proverbs 25:15

By long forbearing and calmness of spirit a judge or ruler is persuaded, and soft speech breaks down the most bonelike resistance.

Proverbs 25:15 AMP

Scornful men bring a city into a snare: but wise men turn away wrath.

Proverbs 29:8

If the spirit of the ruler rise up against thee, leave not thy place; for yielding pacifieth great offences. Ecclesiastes 10:4

Blessed are the peacemakers: for they shall be called the children of God. Matthew 5:9

If it be possible, as much as lieth in you, live peaceably with all men.

Romans 12:18

And to esteem them very highly in love for their work's sake. And be at peace among yourselves. 1 Thessalonians 5:13

Follow peace with all men, and holiness, without which no man shall see the Lord. Hebrews 12:14

Let him eschew evil, and do good; let him seek peace, and ensue it.

1 Peter 3:11

And the fruit of righteousness is sown in peace of them that make peace.

James 3:18

Overcoming Covetousness

Thou shalt not covet thy neighbour's house, thou shalt not covet thy neighbour's wife, nor his manservant, nor his maidservant, nor his ox, nor his ass, nor any thing that is thy neighbour's. Exodus 20:17

Incline my heart unto thy testimonies, and not to covetousness.

Psalms 119:36

And he said unto them, Take heed, and beware of covetousness: for a man's life consisteth not in the abundance of the things which he possesseth. And he spake a parable unto them, saying, The ground of a certain rich man brought forth plentifully: And he thought within himself, saying, What shall I do, because I have no room where to bestow all my fruits and my goods. And I will say to my soul, Soul, thou hast much goods laid up for many years; take thine ease, eat, drink, and be merry. But God said unto him, Thou fool, this night thy soul shall be required of thee: then whose shall those things be, which thou hast provided? So is he that layeth up treasure for himself, and is not rich toward God.

Luke 12:15-21

Let your conversation be without covetousness; and be content with such things as ye have: for he hath said, I will never leave thee, nor forsake thee. Hebrews 13:5

The prince that wanteth understanding is also a great oppressor: but he that hateth covetousness shall prolong his days. Proverbs 28:16

1. The Consequences of Covetousness

Nor thieves, nor covetous, nor drunkards, nor revilers, nor extortioners, shall inherit the kingdom of God. 1 Corinthians 6:10

For this ye know, that no whoremonger, nor unclean person, nor covetous man, who is an idolater, hath any inheritance in the kingdom of Christ and of God. Ephesians 5:5

COMMITTING TO CHRIST

Seeking God

If my people, which are called by my name, shall humble themselves, and pray, and seek my face, and turn from their wicked ways; then will I hear from heaven, and will forgive their sin, and will heal their land.
2 Chronicles 7:14

I would seek unto God, and unto God would I commit my cause. Job 5:8

And they that know thy name will put their trust in thee: for thou, Lord, hast not forsaken them that seek thee. Psalms 9:10

When thou saidst, Seek ye my face; my heart said unto thee, Thy face, Lord, will I seek. Psalms 27:8

God looked down from heaven upon the children of men, to see if there were any that did understand, that did seek God. Psalms 53:2

The humble shall see this, and be glad: and your heart shall live that seek God. Psalms 69:32

> *Jesus Christ is the first and last, author and finisher, beginning and end, alpha and omega, and by Him all other things hold together. He must be first or nothing. God never comes next!*
> *- Vance Havner*

But it is good for me to draw near to God: I have put my trust in the Lord God, that I may declare all thy works. Psalms 73:28

And I set my face unto the Lord God, to seek by prayer and supplication, with fasting, and sackcloth, and ashes. Daniel 9:3

For thus saith the Lord unto the house of Israel, Seek ye me, and ye shall live. Amos 5:4

Seek him that maketh the seven stars and Orion, and turneth the shadow of death into the morning, and maketh the day dark with night: that calleth for the waters of the sea, and poureth them out upon the face of the earth: The Lord is his name. Amos 5:8

Seek ye the Lord, all ye meek of the earth, which have wrought his judgment; seek righteousness, seek meekness: it may be ye shall be hid in the day of the Lord's anger. Zephaniah 2:3

Yea, many people and strong nations shall come to seek the Lord of hosts in Jerusalem, and to pray before the Lord. Zechariah 8:22

But seek ye first the kingdom of God, and his righteousness; and all these things shall be added unto you. Matthew 6:33

Ask, and it shall be given you; seek, and ye shall find; knock, and it shall be opened unto you: For every one that asketh receiveth; and he that seeketh findeth; and to him that knocketh it shall be opened.
Matthew 7:7-8

And I say unto you, Ask, and it shall be given you; seek, and ye shall find; knock, and it shall be opened unto you. For every one that asketh receiveth; and he that seeketh findeth; and to him that knocketh it shall be opened. Luke 11:9-10

And seek not ye what ye shall eat, or what ye shall drink, neither be ye of doubtful mind. For all these things do the nations of the world seek after: and your Father knoweth that ye have need of these things. But rather seek ye the kingdom of God; and all these things shall be added unto you. Luke 12:29-31

But the hour cometh, and now is, when the true worshippers shall worship the Father in spirit and in truth: for the Father seeketh such to worship him. John 4:23

That they should seek the Lord, if haply they might feel after him, and find him, though he be not far from every one of us. Acts 17:27

If ye then be risen with Christ, seek those things which are above, where Christ sitteth on the right hand of God. Colossians 3:1

For the law made nothing perfect, but the bringing in of a better hope did; by the which we draw nigh unto God. Hebrews 7:19

Draw nigh to God, and he will draw nigh to you. Cleanse your hands, ye sinners; and purify your hearts, ye double minded. James 4:8

The purpose for leadership is not the maintenance of followers, but the production of leaders.

---

1. Seek after God with Your Whole Being (Spirit, Soul and Body)

But if from thence thou shalt seek the Lord thy God, thou shalt find him, if thou seek him with all thy heart and with all thy soul.
Deuteronomy 4:29

Now set your heart and your soul to seek the Lord your God.
1 Chronicles 22:19

And they entered into a covenant to seek the Lord God of their fathers with all their heart and with all their soul. 2 Chronicles 15:12

Blessed are they that keep his testimonies, and that seek him with the whole heart. Psalms 119:2

And ye shall seek me, and find me, when ye shall search for me with all your heart. Jeremiah 29:13

2. Seek God Early in the Morning

O God, thou art my God; early will I seek thee: my soul thirsteth for thee, my flesh longeth for thee in a dry and thirsty land, where no water is. Psalms 63:1

With my soul have I desired thee in the night; yea, with my spirit within me will I seek thee early: for when thy judgments are in the earth, the inhabitants of the world will learn righteousness. Isaiah 26:9

I will go and return to my place, till they acknowledge their offence, and seek my face: in their affliction they will seek me early. Hosea 5:15

> *Whatever is your best time in the day, give that to communion with God. - Hudson Taylor*

I love them that love me; and those that seek me early shall find me.
Proverbs 8:17

3. Seek God Continuously

Therefore came I forth to meet thee, diligently to seek thy face, and I have found thee. Proverbs 7:15

Glory ye in his holy name: let the heart of them rejoice that seek the Lord. Seek the Lord and his strength, seek his face continually.
1 Chronicles 16:10-11

Seek the Lord, and his strength: seek his face evermore. Psalms 105:4

Seek ye the Lord while he may be found, call ye upon him while he is near. Isaiah 55:6

Yet they seek me daily, and delight to know my ways, as a nation that did righteousness, and forsook not the ordinance of their God: they ask of me the ordinances of justice; they take delight in approaching to God.
Isaiah 58:2

But without faith it is impossible to please him: for he that cometh to God must believe that he is, and that he is a rewarder of them that diligently seek him. Hebrews 11:6

4. The Results of Continuously Seeking God

The meek shall eat and be satisfied: they shall praise the Lord that seek him: your heart shall live for ever. Psalms 22:26

The young lions do lack, and suffer hunger: but they that seek the Lord shall not want any good thing. Psalms 34:10

Evil men understand not judgment: but they that seek the Lord understand all things. Proverbs 28:5

The Lord is good unto them that wait for him, to the soul that seeketh him. Lamentations 3:25

5. The Consequences of Not Seeking God

And he did evil, because he prepared not his heart to seek the Lord.
2 Chronicles 12:14

Obeying the Word of God

O that there were such an heart in them, that they would fear me, and keep all my commandments always, that it might be well with them, and with their children for ever! Deuteronomy 5:29

And thou shalt do that which is right and good in the sight of the Lord: that it may be well with thee, and that thou mayest go in and possess the good land which the Lord sware unto thy fathers. Deuteronomy 6:18

Wherefore it shall come to pass, if ye hearken to these judgments, and keep, and do them, that the Lord thy God shall keep unto thee the covenant and the mercy which he sware unto thy fathers. Deuteronomy 7:12

Keep therefore the words of this covenant, and do them, that ye may prosper in all that ye do. Deuteronomy 29:9

See, I have set before thee this day life and good, and death and evil; In that I command thee this day to love the Lord thy God, to walk in his ways, and to keep his commandments and his statutes and his judgments, that thou mayest live and multiply: and the Lord thy God shall bless thee in the land whither thou goest to possess it. Deuteronomy 30:15-16

If they obey and serve him, they shall spend their days in prosperity, and their years in pleasures. Job 36:11

Blessed are they that keep judgment, and he that doeth righteousness at all times. Psalms 106:3

So shall I keep thy law continually for ever and ever. Psalms 119:44

I made haste, and delayed not to keep thy commandments. Psalms 119:60

I have refrained my feet from every evil way, that I might keep thy word.
Psalms 119:101

Thy testimonies are wonderful: therefore doth my soul keep them.
Psalms 119:129

Wherewithal shall a young man cleanse his way? by taking heed thereto according to thy word. Psalms 119:9

My son, keep thy father's commandment, and forsake not the law of thy mother: **B**ind them continually upon thine heart, and tie them about thy neck. **W**hen thou goest, it shall lead thee; when thou sleepest, it shall keep thee; and when thou awakest, it shall talk with thee.
Proverbs 6:20-22

Whoso despiseth the word shall be destroyed: but he that feareth the commandment shall be rewarded. Proverbs 13:13

Whosoever therefore shall break one of these least commandments, and shall teach men so, he shall be called the least in the kingdom of heaven: but whosoever shall do and teach them, the same shall be called great in the kingdom of heaven. Matthew 5:19

Not every one that saith unto me, Lord, Lord, shall enter into the kingdom of heaven; but he that doeth the will of my Father which is in heaven.
Matthew 7:21

For whosoever shall do the will of my Father which is in heaven, the same is my brother, and sister, and mother. Matthew 12:50

But Jesus said, Suffer little children, and forbid them not, to come unto me: for of such is the kingdom of heaven. Matthew 19:14

Verily, verily, I say unto you, He that heareth my word, and believeth on him that sent me, hath everlasting life, and shall not come into condemnation; but is passed from death unto life. John 5:24

Verily, verily, I say unto you, If a man keep my saying, he shall never see death. John 8:51

If ye know these things, happy are ye if ye do them. John 13:17

If ye love me, keep my commandments. John 14:15

He that hath my commandments, and keepeth them, he it is that loveth me: and he that loveth me shall be loved of my Father, and I will love him, and will manifest myself to him. John 14:21

Jesus answered and said unto him, If a man love me, he will keep my words: and my Father will love him, and we will come unto him, and make our abode with him. He that loveth me not keepeth not my sayings: and the word which ye hear is not mine, but the Father's which sent me. John 14:23-24

If ye keep my commandments, ye shall abide in my love; even as I have kept my Father's commandments, and abide in his love. John 15:10

Ye are my friends, if ye do whatsoever I command you. John 15:14

Let every soul be subject unto the higher powers. For there is no power but of God: the powers that be are ordained of God. Romans 13:1

Those things, which ye have both learned, and received, and heard, and seen in me, do: and the God of peace shall be with you. Philippians 4:9

Believing and confessing Jesus Christ as Lord and Savior is the prerequisite for salvation, but obedience to God's Word and a loving heart is the proof of salvation.

And being made perfect, he became the author of eternal salvation unto all them that obey him. Hebrews 5:9

And hereby we do know that we know him, if we keep his commandments. He that saith, I know him, and keepeth not his commandments, is a liar, and the truth is not in him. But whoso keepeth his word, in him verily is the love of God perfected: hereby know we that we are in him. He that saith he abideth in him ought himself also so to walk, even as he walked. 1 John 2:3-6

And the world passeth away, and the lust thereof: but he that doeth the will of God abideth for ever. 1 John 2:17

A good leader knows how to love people just as they are.

And whatsoever we ask, we receive of him, because we keep his commandments and do those things that are pleasing in his sight. 1 John 3:22

1. True Obedience

But he said, Yea rather, blessed are they that hear the word of God, and keep it. Luke 11:28

For not the hearers of the law are just before God, but the doers of the law shall be justified. Romans 2:13

Therefore whosoever heareth these sayings of mine, and doeth them, I will liken him unto a wise man, which built his house upon a rock: And the rain descended, and the floods came, and the winds blew, and beat upon that house; and it fell not: for it was founded upon a rock.
Matthew 7:24-25

But whoso looketh into the perfect law of liberty, and continueth therein, he being not a forgetful hearer, but a doer of the work, this man shall be blessed in his deed. James 1:25

We have not learned the commandments until we have learned to do them. - Vance Havner

Submitting to the Correction of God

Behold, happy is the man whom God correcteth: therefore despise not thou the chastening of the Almighty: For he maketh sore, and bindeth up: he woundeth, and his hands make whole. Job 5:17-18

Blessed is the man whom thou chastenest, O Lord, and teachest him out of thy law; That thou mayest give him rest from the days of adversity, until the pit be digged for the wicked. Psalms 94:12-13

My son, despise not the chastening of the Lord; neither be weary of his correction. For whom the Lord loveth he correcteth; even as a father the son in whom he delighteth. Proverbs 3:11-12

But when we are judged, we are chastened of the Lord, that we should not be condemned with the world. 1 Corinthians 11:32

And ye have forgotten the exhortation which speaketh unto you as unto children, My son, despise not thou the chastening of the Lord, nor faint when thou art rebuked of him: For whom the Lord loveth he chasteneth, and scourgeth every son whom he receiveth. If ye endure chastening, God dealeth with you as with sons; for what son is he whom the father chasteneth not? But if ye be without chastisement, whereof all are partakers, then are ye bastards, and not sons. Furthermore we have had fathers of our flesh which corrected us, and we gave them reverence: shall we not much rather be in subjection unto the Father of spirits, and live? For they verily for a few days chastened us after their own pleasure; but he for our profit, that we might be partakers of his holiness. Now no chastening for the present seemeth to be joyous, but grievous: nevertheless afterward it yieldeth the peaceable fruit of righteousness unto them which are exercised thereby. Hebrews 12:5-11

As many as I love, I rebuke and chasten: be zealous therefore, and repent. Revelation 3:19

Dying to Self

He that findeth his life shall lose it: and he that loseth his life for my sake shall find it. Matthew 10:39

For whosoever will save his life shall lose it; but whosoever shall lose his life for my sake and the gospel's, the same shall save it. Mark 8:35

And he said to them all, If any man will come after me, let him deny himself, and take up his cross daily, and follow me. For whosoever will save his life shall lose it: but whosoever will lose his life for my sake, the same shall save it. For what is a man advantaged, if he gain the whole world, and lose himself, or be cast away? Luke 9:23-25

Whosoever shall seek to save his life shall lose it; and whosoever shall lose his life shall preserve it. Luke 17:33

The man who is prepared to die is prepared to live.
- Vance Havner

He that loveth his life shall lose it; and he that hateth his life in this world shall keep it unto life eternal. John 12:25

Likewise reckon ye also yourselves to be dead indeed unto sin, but alive unto God through Jesus Christ our Lord. Let not sin therefore reign in your mortal body, that ye should obey it in the lusts thereof.
Romans 6:11-12

All things are lawful for me, but all things are not expedient: all things are lawful for me, but all things edify not. 1 Corinthians 10:23

For the love of Christ constraineth us; because we thus judge, that if one died for all, then were all dead: And that he died for all, that they which live should not henceforth live unto themselves, but unto him which died for them, and rose again. Wherefore henceforth know we no man after the flesh: yea, though we have known Christ after the flesh, yet now henceforth know we him no more. Therefore if any man be in Christ, he is a new creature: old things are passed away; behold, all things are become new. 2 Corinthians 5:14-17

> *In this day of self-exaltation the Bible teaches self-execution. Not that we execute ourselves but that we submit to the death of self by the hand of God. Paul witnessed his own execution, but there came forth a new Paul: "I live, yet not I, but Christ liveth in me." - Vance Havner*

For though he was crucified through weakness, yet he liveth by the power of God. For we also are weak in him, but we shall live with him by the power of God toward you. 2 Corinthians 13:4

I am crucified with Christ: nevertheless I live; yet not I, but Christ liveth in me: and the life which I now live in the flesh I live by the faith of the Son of God, who loved me, and gave himself for me. Galatians 2:20

That ye put off concerning the former conversation the old man, which is corrupt according to the deceitful lusts; And be renewed in the spirit of your mind; And that ye put on the new man, which after God is created in righteousness and true holiness. Ephesians 4:22-24

> *We are always trying to "find ourselves" when that is exactly what we need to lose. - Vance Havner*

But what things were gain to me, those I counted loss for Christ.
Philippians 3:7

Following Christ and Carrying Your Cross

And he that taketh not his cross, and followeth after me, is not worthy of me. Matthew 10:38

Then said Jesus unto his disciples, If any man will come after me, let him deny himself, and take up his cross, and follow me. Matthew 16:24

And when he had called the people unto him with his disciples also, he said unto them, Whosoever will come after me, let him deny himself, and take up his cross, and follow me. Mark 8:34

Then Jesus beholding him loved him, and said unto him, One thing thou lackest: go thy way, sell whatsoever thou hast, and give to the poor, and thou shalt have treasure in heaven: and come, take up the cross, and follow me. Mark 10:21

But God forbid that I should glory, save in the cross of our Lord Jesus Christ, by whom the world is crucified unto me, and I unto the world. Galatians 6:14

And he said to them all, If any man will come after me, let him deny himself, and take up his cross daily, and follow me. Luke 9:23

And whosoever doth not bear his cross, and come after me, cannot be my disciple. Luke 14:27

Salvation is free. The gift of God is eternal life. It is not cheap for it cost God his Son and the Son His life, but it is free. However, when we become believers we become disciples and that will cost everything we have. - Vance Havner

Being a True Representative of God

1. Living the Life of Christ Before God and Man

The just man walketh in his integrity: his children are blessed after him. Proverbs 20:7

Let your light so shine before men, that they may see your good works, and glorify your Father which is in heaven. Matthew 5:16

Thou therefore which teachest another, teachest thou not thyself? thou that preachest a man should not steal, dost thou steal? Thou that sayest a man should not commit adultery, dost thou commit adultery? thou that abhorrest idols, dost thou commit sacrilege? Thou that makest thy boast of the law, through breaking the law dishonourest thou God? For the name of God is blasphemed among the Gentiles through you, as it is written. Romans 2:21-24

But I keep under my body, and bring it into subjection: lest that by any means, when I have preached to others, I myself should be a castaway. 1 Corinthians 9:27

Where one reads the Bible, a hundred
read you and me. - D. L. Moody

Teaching us that, denying ungodliness and worldly lusts, we should live soberly, righteously, and godly, in this present world. Titus 2:12

One is not qualified to give orders until he can receive them.

They profess that they know God; but in works they deny him, being abominable, and disobedient, and unto every good work reprobate.
Titus 1:16

A righteous man falling down before the wicked is as a troubled fountain, and a corrupt spring. Proverbs 25:26

Like a muddied fountain and a polluted spring is a righteous man who yields, falls down and compromises his integrity before the wicked.
Proverbs 25:26 AMP

He that saith, I know him, and keepeth not his commandments, is a liar, and the truth is not in him. 1 John 2:4

Giving no offence in any thing, that the ministry be not blamed: But in all things approving ourselves as the ministers of God, in much patience, in afflictions, in necessities, in distresses, In stripes, in imprisonments, in tumults, in labours, in watchings, in fastings; By pureness, by knowledge, by longsuffering, by kindness, by the Holy Ghost, by love unfeigned, By the word of truth, by the power of God, by the armour of righteousness on the right hand and on the left, By honour and dishonour, by evil report and good report: as deceivers, and yet true; As unknown, and yet well known; as dying, and, behold, we live; as chastened, and not killed; As sorrowful, yet alway rejoicing; as poor, yet making many rich; as having nothing, and yet possessing all things.
2 Corinthians 6:3-10

Avoiding this, that no man should blame us in this abundance which is administered by us: Providing for honest things, not only in the sight of the Lord, but also in the sight of men. 2 Corinthians 8:20-21

2. Being a True Representative of God is

a. Knowing the Word of God when sharing with unbelievers

Then will I teach transgressors thy ways; and sinners shall be converted unto thee. Psalms 51:13

The heart of the righteous studieth to answer. Proverbs 15:28

The fruit of the righteous is a tree of life; and he that winneth souls is wise. Proverbs 11:30

That I might make thee know the certainty of the words of truth; that thou mightest answer the words of truth to them that send unto thee?
Proverbs 22:21

Study to shew thyself approved unto God, a workman that needeth not to be ashamed, rightly dividing the word of truth. 2 Timothy 2:15

That the communication of thy faith may become effectual by the acknowledging of every good thing which is in you in Christ Jesus.
Philemon 1:6

But sanctify the Lord God in your hearts: and be ready always to give an answer to every man that asketh you a reason of the hope that is in you with meekness and fear: Having a good conscience; that, whereas they speak evil of you, as of evildoers, they may be ashamed that falsely accuse your good conversation in Christ. 1 Peter 3:15-16

Holding fast the faithful word as he hath been taught, that he may be able by sound doctrine both to exhort and to convince the gainsayers. Titus 1:9

You and I are human post offices. We are daily giving out messages of some sort to the world. They do not come from us, but through us we do not create, we convey. And they come either from hell or from heaven. - Vance Havner

And moreover, because the preacher was wise, he still taught the people knowledge; yea, he gave good heed, and sought out, and set in order many proverbs. The preacher sought to find out acceptable words: and that which was written was upright, even words of truth. The words of the wise are as goads, and as nails fastened by the masters of assemblies, which are given from one shepherd.
Ecclesiastes 12:9-11

b. Loving everyone from your heart

We know that we have passed from death unto life, because we love the brethren. He that loveth not his brother abideth in death.
1 John 3:14

By this shall all men know that ye are my disciples, if ye have love one to another. John 13:35

c. Never denying Jesus Christ

Whosoever therefore shall confess me before men, him will I confess also before my Father which is in heaven. But whosoever shall deny me before men, him will I also deny before my Father which is in heaven. Matthew 10:32-33

Also I say unto you, Whosoever shall confess me before men, him shall the Son of man also confess before the angels of God: But he that denieth me before men shall be denied before the angels of God.
Luke 12:8-9

If we suffer, we shall also reign with him: if we deny him, he also will deny us. 2 Timothy 2:12

I know thy works: behold, I have set before thee an open door, and no man can shut it: for thou hast a little strength, and hast kept my word, and hast not denied my name. Revelation 3:8

d. Being a vessel for God's power to flow through

But ye shall receive power, after that the Holy Ghost is come upon you: and ye shall be witnesses unto me both in Jerusalem, and in all Judaea, and in Samaria, and unto the uttermost part of the earth.
Acts 1:8

And such as do wickedly against the covenant shall he corrupt by flatteries: but the people that do know their God shall be strong, and do exploits. Daniel 11:32

Verily, verily, I say unto you, He that believeth on me, the works that I do shall he do also; and greater works than these shall he do; because I go unto my Father. John 14:12

And he said unto them, Go ye into all the world, and preach the gospel to every creature. He that believeth and is baptized shall be saved; but he that believeth not shall be damned. And these signs shall follow them that believe; In my name shall they cast out devils; they shall speak with new tongues; They shall take up serpents; and if they drink any deadly thing, it shall not hurt them; they shall lay hands on the sick, and they shall recover. Mark 16:15-18

Fasting

Is it such a fast that I have chosen? a day for a man to afflict his soul? is it to bow down his head as a bulrush, and to spread sackcloth and ashes under him? wilt thou call this a fast, and an acceptable day to the Lord? Is not this the fast that I have chosen? to loose the bands of wickedness, to undo the heavy burdens, and to let the oppressed go free, and that ye break every yoke? Isaiah 58:5-6

But as for me, when they were sick, my clothing was sackcloth: I humbled my soul with fasting; and my prayer returned into mine own bosom.
Psalms 35:13

And I set my face unto the Lord God, to seek by prayer and supplication, with fasting, and sackcloth, and ashes: Daniel 9:3

And when he had fasted forty days and forty nights, he was afterward an hungered. Matthew 4:2

Fasting is the attitude of, "Lord, empty me of self." Prayer is the insistent cry of one's soul, "Lord, fill me with thyself." - H. H. Leavitt

1. Fasting Gives You Power Over satan

When Jesus saw that the people came running together, he rebuked the foul spirit, saying unto him, Thou dumb and deaf spirit, I charge thee, come out of him, and enter no more into him. And the spirit cried, and rent him sore, and came out of him: and he was as one dead; insomuch that many said, He is dead. But Jesus took him by the hand, and lifted him up; and he arose. And when he was come into the house, his disciples asked him privately, Why could not we cast him out? And he said unto them, This kind can come forth by nothing, but by prayer and fasting. Mark 9:25-29

2. Fasting with Pure Motives

Moreover when ye fast, be not, as the hypocrites, of a sad countenance: for they disfigure their faces, that they may appear unto men to fast. Verily I say unto you, They have their reward. But thou, when thou fastest, anoint thine head, and wash thy face; That thou appear not unto men to fast, but unto thy Father which is in secret: and thy Father, which seeth in secret, shall reward thee openly. Matthew 6:16-18

The Pharisee stood and prayed thus with himself, God, I thank thee, that I am not as other men are, extortioners, unjust, adulterers, or even as this publican. I fast twice in the week, I give tithes of all that I possess. And the publican, standing afar off, would not lift up so much as his eyes unto heaven, but smote upon his breast, saying, God be merciful to me a sinner. Luke 18:11-13

OVERCOMING SIN

Sin

All unrighteousness is sin: and there is a sin not unto death. 1 John 5:17

Jesus answered them, Verily, verily, I say unto you, Whosoever committeth sin is the servant of sin. John 8:34

These six things doth the Lord hate: yea, seven are an abomination unto him. A proud look, a lying tongue, and hands that shed innocent blood. An heart that deviseth wicked imaginations, feet that be swift in running to mischief, A false witness that speaketh lies, and he that soweth discord among brethren. Proverbs 6:16-19

Now the works of the flesh are manifest, which are these; Adultery, fornication, uncleanness, lasciviousness, Idolatry, witchcraft, hatred, variance, emulations, wrath, strife, seditions, heresies, envyings, murders, drunkenness, revellings, and such like: of the which I tell you before, as I have also told you in time past, that they which do such things shall not inherit the kingdom of God. Galatians 5:19-21

He that committeth sin is of the devil; for the devil sinneth from the beginning. For this purpose the Son of God was manifested, that he might destroy the works of the devil. Whosoever is born of God doth not commit sin; for his seed remaineth in him: and he cannot sin, because he is born of God. In this the children of God are manifest, and the children of the devil: whosoever doeth not righteousness is not of God, neither he that loveth not his brother. 1 John 3:8-10

Whosoever abideth in him sinneth not: whosoever sinneth hath not seen him, neither known him. 1 John 3:6

Whosoever is born of God doth not commit sin; for his seed remaineth in him: and he cannot sin, because he is born of God. 1 John 3:9

We know that whosoever is born of God sinneth not; but he that is begotten of God keepeth himself, and that wicked one toucheth him not.
1 John 5:18

There is a way that seemeth right unto a man, but the end thereof are the ways of death. Proverbs 16:25

The Bible will keep you from sin, or sin will keep you from the Bible - D. L. Moody

And he that doubteth is damned if he eat, because he eateth not of faith: for whatsoever is not of faith is sin. Romans 14:23

But the man who has doubts–misgivings, an uneasy conscience-about eating, and then eats [perhaps because of you], stands condemned [before God], because he is not true to his convictions and he does not act from faith. For whatever does not originate and proceed from faith is sin–that is, whatever is done without a conviction of its approval by God is sinful. Romans 14:23 AMP

What Should I Do When I Sin?

1. Repent

Definition of repent - to change one's mind or purpose with regard to sin, a sorrow for sin.

Or despisest thou the riches of his goodness and forbearance and longsuffering; not knowing that the goodness of God leadeth thee to repentance? Romans 2:4

The Lord is not slack concerning his promise, as some men count slackness; but is longsuffering to us-ward, not willing that any should perish, but that all should come to repentance. 2 Peter 3:9

I tell you, Nay: but, except ye repent, ye shall all likewise perish.
Luke 13:3

Therefore I will judge you, O house of Israel, every one according to his ways, saith the Lord God. Repent, and turn yourselves from all your transgressions; so iniquity shall not be your ruin. Ezekiel 18:30

For godly sorrow worketh repentance to salvation not to be repented of: but the sorrow of the world worketh death. 2 Corinthians 7:10

Say unto them, As I live, saith the Lord God, I have no pleasure in the death of the wicked; but that the wicked turn from his way and live: turn ye, turn ye from your evil ways; for why will ye die, O house of Israel?
Ezekiel 33:11

> **Authority does not make you a leader;**
> **it gives you the opportunity to be one.**

And saying, The time is fulfilled, and the kingdom of God is at hand: repent ye, and believe the gospel. Mark 1:15

And saying, Repent ye: for the kingdom of heaven is at hand.
Matthew 3:2

Repent ye therefore, and be converted, that your sins may be blotted out, when the times of refreshing shall come from the presence of the Lord.
Acts 3:19

From that time Jesus began to preach, and to say, Repent: for the kingdom of heaven is at hand. Matthew 4:17

I say unto you, that likewise joy shall be in heaven over one sinner that repenteth, more than over ninety and nine just persons, which need no repentance. Luke 15:7

> *True repentance has a double aspect; it looks upon things past with a weeping eye, and upon the future with a watchful eye. - Robert Smith*

When Jesus heard it, he saith unto them, They that are whole have no need of the physician, but they that are sick: I came not to call the righteous, but sinners to repentance. Mark 2:17

And the times of this ignorance God winked at; but now commandeth all men every where to repent. Acts 17:30

I came not to call the righteous, but sinners to repentance. Luke 5:32

Likewise, I say unto you, there is joy in the presence of the angels of God over one sinner that repenteth. Luke 15:10

Him hath God exalted with his right hand to be a Prince and a Saviour, for to give repentance to Israel, and forgiveness of sins. Acts 5:31

a. Proof of Repentance

I thought on my ways, and turned my feet unto thy testimonies.
Psalms 119:59

> *True repentance is proceeded by a passionate commitment to obey God's Word.*

But shewed first unto them of Damascus, and at Jerusalem, and throughout all the coasts of Judaea, and then to the Gentiles, that they should repent and turn to God, and do works meet for repentance. Acts 26:20

They profess that they know God; but in works they deny him, being abominable, and disobedient, and unto every good work reprobate. Titus 1:16

Bring forth therefore fruits meet for repentance. Matthew 3:8

2. Confess the Sin

He that covereth his sins shall not prosper: but whoso confesseth and forsaketh them shall have mercy. Proverbs 28:13

And it shall be, when he shall be guilty in one of these things, that he shall confess that he hath sinned in that thing. Leviticus 5:5

If we confess our sins, he is faithful and just to forgive us our sins, and to cleanse us from all unrighteousness. 1 John 1:9

And the seed of Israel separated themselves from all strangers, and stood and confessed their sins, and the iniquities of their fathers. Nehemiah 9:2

Before you were even born God knew every sin that you would commit throughout your lifetime, therefore it is useless to run and hide from God. When you sin, run to God, repent, confess the sin, and humbly receive God's merciful forgiveness through the shed blood of his son Jesus Christ.

I acknowledged my sin unto thee, and mine iniquity have I not hid. I said, I will confess my transgressions unto the Lord; and thou forgavest the iniquity of my sin. Selah. Psalms 32:5

And were baptized of him in Jordan, confessing their sins. Matthew 3:6

And many that believed came, and confessed, and shewed their deeds. Acts 19:18

Confess your faults one to another, and pray one for another, that ye may be healed. The effectual fervent prayer of a righteous man availeth much. James 5:16

3. Stop Sinning

Ye have not yet resisted unto blood, striving against sin. Hebrews 12:4

You have not yet struggled and fought agonizingly against sin, nor have you yet resisted and withstood to the point of pouring out your [own] blood. Hebrews 12:4 AMP

If iniquity be in thine hand, put it far away, and let not wickedness dwell in thy tabernacles. Job 11:14

The night is far spent, the day is at hand: let us therefore cast off the works of darkness, and let us put on the armour of light. Romans 13:12

Wherefore, O king, let my counsel be acceptable unto thee, and break off thy sins by righteousness, and thine iniquities by shewing mercy to the poor; if it may be a lengthening of thy tranquillity. Daniel 4:27

She said, No man, Lord. And Jesus said unto her, Neither do I condemn thee: go, and sin no more. John 8:11

Mortify therefore your members which are upon the earth; fornication, uncleanness, inordinate affection, evil concupiscence, and covetousness, which is idolatry. Colossians 3:5

Lie not one to another, seeing that ye have put off the old man with his deeds. Colossians 3:9

Let all bitterness, and wrath, and anger, and clamour, and evil speaking, be put away from you, with all malice. Ephesians 4:31

> *Blunders we shall make and failures will shame our faces and dampen our eyes. But if we can manage not to remember what we ought to forget and not to forget what we ought to remember, then forgetting the things behind and stirring up our minds by way of remembrance, we shall press on for the prize. - Vance Havner*

Neither filthiness, nor foolish talking, nor jesting, which are not convenient: but rather giving of thanks. For this ye know, that no whoremonger, nor unclean person, nor covetous man, who is an idolater, hath any inheritance in the kingdom of Christ and of God. Ephesians 5:4-5

Nevertheless the foundation of God standeth sure, having this seal, The Lord knoweth them that are his. And, Let every one that nameth the name of Christ depart from iniquity. 2 Timothy 2:19

Wherefore lay apart all filthiness and superfluity of naughtiness, and receive with meekness the engrafted word, which is able to save your souls. James 1:21

Deliverance from Sin

And she shall bring forth a son, and thou shalt call his name Jesus: for he shall save his people from their sins. Matthew 1:21

The next day John seeth Jesus coming unto him, and saith, Behold the Lamb of God, which taketh away the sin of the world. John 1:29

199

For he hath made him to be sin for us, who knew no sin; that we might be made the righteousness of God in him. 2 Corinthians 5:21

For when we were yet without strength, in due time Christ died for the ungodly. Romans 5:6

But God commendeth his love toward us, in that, while we were yet sinners, Christ died for us. Romans 5:8

For the law of the Spirit of life in Christ Jesus hath made me free from the law of sin and death. Romans 8:2

> *Prayer will make a man cease from sin, or sin will entice a man to cease from prayer. - John Bunyan*

To wit, that God was in Christ, reconciling the world unto himself, not imputing their trespasses unto them; and hath committed unto us the word of reconciliation. 2 Corinthians 5:19

Who gave himself for our sins, that he might deliver us from this present evil world, according to the will of God and our Father. Galatians 1:4

And, having made peace through the blood of his cross, by him to reconcile all things unto himself; by him, I say, whether they be things in earth, or things in heaven. Colossians 1:20

Secret Sins

But if ye will not do so, behold, ye have sinned against the Lord: and be sure your sin will find you out. Numbers 32:23

He that covereth his sins shall not prosper: but whoso confesseth and forsaketh them shall have mercy. Proverbs 28:13

For God shall bring every work into judgment, with every secret thing, whether it be good, or whether it be evil. Ecclesiastes 12:14

For there is nothing hid, which shall not be manifested; neither was any thing kept secret, but that it should come abroad. Mark 4:22

For nothing is secret, that shall not be made manifest; neither any thing hid, that shall not be known and come abroad. Luke 8:17

For there is nothing covered, that shall not be revealed; neither hid, that shall not be known. Therefore whatsoever ye have spoken in darkness

---

You should be motivated by your love for people, not by your desire to be great.

shall be heard in the light; and that which ye have spoken in the ear in closets shall be proclaimed upon the housetops. Luke 12:2-3

In the day when God shall judge the secrets of men by Jesus Christ according to my gospel. Romans 2:16

1. The Pleasure of Sin is Only Temporary

Choosing rather to suffer affliction with the people of God, than to enjoy the pleasures of sin for a season. Hebrews 11:25

Deliberate and Willful Sin

What shall we say then? Shall we continue in sin, that grace may abound?
Romans 6:1

For if we sin wilfully after that we have received the knowledge of the truth, there remaineth no more sacrifice for sins, But a certain fearful looking for of judgment and fiery indignation, which shall devour the adversaries. He that despised Moses' law died without mercy under two or three witnesses: Of how much sorer punishment, suppose ye, shall he be thought worthy, who hath trodden under foot the Son of God, and hath counted the blood of the covenant, wherewith he was sanctified, an unholy thing, and hath done despite unto the Spirit of grace? For we know him that hath said, Vengeance belongeth unto me, I will recompense, saith the Lord. And again, The Lord shall judge his people. It is a fearful thing to fall into the hands of the living God. Hebrews 10:26-31

> *We are not to tolerate evil but abhor it. The mood of the age is to put up with evil, allow it, and then move easily to play with it and finally practice it. - Vance Havner*

For if we go on deliberately and willingly sinning after once acquiring the knowledge of the Truth, there is no longer any sacrifice left to atone for [our] sins–no further offering to which to look forward. There is nothing left for us then but a kind of awful and fearful prospect and expectation of divine judgment and the fury of burning wrath and indignation which will consume those who put themselves in opposition to God. Any person who has violated and [thus] rejected and set at naught the Law of Moses is put to death without pity or mercy on the evidence of two or three witnesses. How much worse (sterner and heavier) punishment do you suppose he will be judged to deserve who has spurned and [thus] trampled under foot the Son of God, and who has considered the covenant blood by which he was consecrated common and unhallowed, thus profaning it and insulting and outraging the (Holy) Spirit [Who

201

imparts] grace–he unmerited favor and blessing of God? For we know Him Who said, Vengeance is Mine–retribution and the meting out of full justice rest with Me; I will repay–I will exact the compensation, says the Lord. And again, The Lord will judge and determine and solve and settle the cause and the cases of His people. Is a fearful (formidable and terrible) thing to incur the divine penalties and be cast into the hands of the living God! Hebrews 10:26-31 AMP

Sowing Sin and Reaping its Consequences

But he that doeth wrong shall receive for the wrong which he hath done: and there is no respect of persons. Colossians 3:25

Even as I have seen, they that plow iniquity, and sow wickedness, reap the same. Job 4:8

Evil pursueth sinners: but to the righteous good shall be repayed.
Proverbs 13:21

Whoso rewardeth evil for good, evil shall not depart from his house.
Proverbs 17:13

He that soweth iniquity shall reap vanity: and the rod of his anger shall fail. Proverbs 22:8

Whoso diggeth a pit shall fall therein: and he that rolleth a stone, it will return upon him. Proverbs 26:27

Whoso causeth the righteous to go astray in an evil way, he shall fall himself into his own pit: but the upright shall have good things in possession. Proverbs 28:10

He that diggeth a pit shall fall into it; and whoso breaketh an hedge, a serpent shall bite him. Ecclesiastes 10:8

For they have sown the wind, and they shall reap the whirlwind: it hath no stalk: the bud shall yield no meal: if so be it yield, the strangers shall swallow it up. Hosea 8:7

Ye have plowed wickedness, ye have reaped iniquity; ye have eaten the fruit of lies: because thou didst trust in thy way, in the multitude of thy mighty men. Hosea 10:13

For the wages of sin is death; but the gift of God is eternal life through Jesus Christ our Lord. Romans 6:23

Be not deceived; God is not mocked: for whatsoever a man soweth, that shall he also reap. For he that soweth to his flesh shall of the flesh reap corruption; but he that soweth to the Spirit shall of the Spirit reap life everlasting. Galatians 6:7-8

A sinful lifestyle is spiritual insanity.

Sin Gives satan Entrance into Your Life

Be ye angry, and sin not: let not the sun go down upon your wrath: Neither give place to the devil. Ephesians 4:26-27

Hereafter I will not talk much with you: for the prince of this world cometh, and hath nothing in me. John 14:30

Afterward Jesus findeth him in the temple, and said unto him, Behold, thou art made whole: sin no more, lest a worse thing come unto thee.
John 5:14

To whom ye forgive any thing, I forgive also: for if I forgave any thing, to whom I forgave it, for your sakes forgave I it in the person of Christ; Lest satan should get an advantage of us: for we are not ignorant of his devices. 2 Corinthians 2:10-11

Not a novice, lest being lifted up with pride he fall into the condemnation of the devil. Moreover he must have a good report of them which are without; lest he fall into reproach and the snare of the devil.
1 Timothy 3:6-7

And that they may recover themselves out of the snare of the devil, who are taken captive by him at his will. 2 Timothy 2:26

But I have a few things against thee, because thou hast there them that hold the doctrine of Balaam, who taught Balac to cast a stumblingblock before the children of Israel, to eat things sacrificed unto idols, and to commit fornication. Revelation 2:14

Then came Peter to him, and said, Lord, how oft shall my brother sin against me, and I forgive him? till seven times? Jesus saith unto him, I say not unto thee, Until seven times: but, Until seventy times seven. Therefore is the kingdom of heaven likened unto a certain king, which would take account of his servants. Then his lord, after that he had called him, said unto him, O thou wicked servant, I forgave thee all that debt, because thou desiredst me: Shouldest not thou also have had compassion on thy fellowservant, even as I had pity on thee? And his lord was wroth, and delivered him to the tormentors, till he should pay all that was due unto him. So likewise shall my heavenly Father do also unto you, if ye from your hearts forgive not every one his brother their trespasses. Matthew 18:21-23,32-35

The Hardships of a Life of Sin

Correction is grievous unto him that forsaketh the way: and he that hateth reproof shall die. Proverbs 15:10

For the wages of sin is death; but the gift of God is eternal life through Jesus Christ our Lord. Romans 6:23

The wicked man travaileth with pain all his days, and the number of years is hidden to the oppressor. Job 15:20

But the transgressors shall be destroyed together: the end of the wicked shall be cut off. Psalms 37:38

Fools because of their transgression, and because of their iniquities, are afflicted. Psalms 107:17

Thorns and snares are in the way of the froward: he that doth keep his soul shall be far from them. Proverbs 22:5

But the wicked shall be cut off from the earth, and the transgressors shall be rooted out of it. Proverbs 2:22

Good understanding giveth favour: but the way of transgressors is hard.
Proverbs 13:15

In the transgression of an evil man there is a snare: but the righteous doth sing and rejoice. Proverbs 29:6

RECEIVING GOD'S FORGIVENESS FOR YOUR SINS

Sins Cleansed by the Blood of Jesus

But now in Christ Jesus ye who sometimes were far off are made nigh by the blood of Christ. Ephesians 2:13

In whom we have redemption through his blood, even the forgiveness of sins. Colossians 1:14

For this is my blood of the new testament, which is shed for many for the remission of sins. Matthew 26:28

Neither by the blood of goats and calves, but by his own blood he entered in once into the holy place, having obtained eternal redemption for us. Hebrews 9:12

And almost all things are by the law purged with blood; and without shedding of blood is no remission. Hebrews 9:22

And from Jesus Christ, who is the faithful witness, and the first begotten of the dead, and the prince of the kings of the earth. Unto him that loved us, and washed us from our sins in his own blood. Revelation 1:5

God Will Forgive Your Sins

For if ye turn again unto the Lord, your brethren and your children shall find compassion before them that lead them captive, so that they shall come again into this land: for the Lord your God is gracious and merciful, and will not turn away his face from you, if ye return unto him.
2 Chronicles 30:9

Blessed is he whose transgression is forgiven, whose sin is covered. Blessed is the man unto whom the Lord imputeth not iniquity, and in whose spirit there is no guile. Psalms 32:1-2

I acknowledged my sin unto thee, and mine iniquity have I not hid. I said, I will confess my transgressions unto the Lord; and thou forgavest the iniquity of my sin. Selah. Psalms 32:5

For thou, Lord, art good, and ready to forgive; and plenteous in mercy unto all them that call upon thee. Psalms 86:5

And the inhabitant shall not say, I am sick: the people that dwell therein shall be forgiven their iniquity. Isaiah 33:24

I have blotted out, as a thick cloud, thy transgressions, and, as a cloud, thy sins: return unto me; for I have redeemed thee. Isaiah 44:22

The forgiveness of God is the foundation of every bridge from a hopeless past to a courageous present. - George Adam Smith

Who is a God like unto thee, that pardoneth iniquity, and passeth by the transgression of the remnant of his heritage? he retaineth not his anger for ever, because he delighteth in mercy. He will turn again, he will have compassion upon us; he will subdue our iniquities; and thou wilt cast all their sins into the depths of the sea. Micah 7:18-19

And forgive us our debts, as we forgive our debtors. Matthew 6:12

For if ye forgive men their trespasses, your heavenly Father will also forgive you: But if ye forgive not men their trespasses, neither will your Father forgive your trespasses. Matthew 6:14-15

In whom we have redemption through his blood, the forgiveness of sins, according to the riches of his grace. Ephesians 1:7

For I will be merciful to their unrighteousness, and their sins and their iniquities will I remember no more. Hebrews 8:12

But this man, after he had offered one sacrifice for sins for ever, sat down on the right hand of God. Hebrews 10:12

And their sins and iniquities will I remember no more. Now where remission of these is, there is no more offering for sin. Hebrews 10:17-18

If we confess our sins, he is faithful and just to forgive us our sins, and to cleanse us from all unrighteousness. 1 John 1:9

My little children, these things write I unto you, that ye sin not. And if any man sin, we have an advocate with the Father, Jesus Christ the righteous: And he is the propitiation for our sins: and not for ours only, but also for the sins of the whole world. 1 John 2:1-2

A true leader hates the things God hates.

God Will Not Remember Your Sins

Remember not the sins of my youth, nor my transgressions: according to thy mercy remember thou me for thy goodness' sake, O Lord. Psalms 25:7

O remember not against us former iniquities: let thy tender mercies speedily prevent us: for we are brought very low. Psalms 79:8

And they shall teach no more every man his neighbour, and every man his brother, saying, Know the Lord: for they shall all know me, from the least of them unto the greatest of them, saith the Lord; for I will forgive their iniquity, and I will remember their sin no more. Jeremiah 31:34

He will turn again, he will have compassion upon us; he will subdue our iniquities; and thou wilt cast all their sins into the depths of the sea.
Micah 7:19

This is the covenant that I will make with them after those days, saith the Lord, I will put my laws into their hearts, and in their minds will I write them; And their sins and iniquities will I remember no more.
Hebrews 10:16-17

God Will Blot Out Your Sins

Have mercy upon me, O God, according to thy lovingkindness: according unto the multitude of thy tender mercies blot out my transgressions.
Psalms 51:1

Hide thy face from my sins, and blot out all mine iniquities. Psalms 51:9

I, even I, am he that blotteth out thy transgressions for mine own sake, and will not remember thy sins. Isaiah 43:25

I have blotted out, as a thick cloud, thy transgressions, and, as a cloud, thy sins: return unto me; for I have redeemed thee. Isaiah 44:22

Repent ye therefore, and be converted, that your sins may be blotted out, when the times of refreshing shall come from the presence of the Lord.
Acts 3:19

Overcoming Guilt

Brethren, I count not myself to have apprehended: but this one thing I do, forgetting those things which are behind, and reaching forth unto those things which are before, Philippians 3:13

For if ye turn again unto the Lord, your brethren and your children shall find compassion before them that lead them captive, so that they shall

come again into this land: for the Lord your God is gracious and merciful, and will not turn away his face from you, if ye return unto him.
2 Chronicles 30:9

As far as the east is from the west, so far hath he removed our transgressions from us. Psalms 103:12

> *Memory can become a tyrant instead of a treasure chest. From the mistakes of the past, let us learn whatever lessons they teach, then forget them, even as God remembers our sins no more. Let precious memories be benedictions but not bonds. - Vance Havner*

Let the wicked forsake his way, and the unrighteous man his thoughts: and let him return unto the Lord, and he will have mercy upon him; and to our God, for he will abundantly pardon. Isaiah 55:7

And they shall teach no more every man his neighbour, and every man his brother, saying, Know the Lord: for they shall all know me, from the least of them unto the greatest of them, saith the Lord; for I will forgive their iniquity, and I will remember their sin no more. Jeremiah 31:34

And I will cleanse them from all their iniquity, whereby they have sinned against me; and I will pardon all their iniquities, whereby they have sinned, and whereby they have transgressed against me. Jeremiah 33:8

For God sent not his Son into the world to condemn the world; but that the world through him might be saved. He that believeth on him is not condemned: but he that believeth not is condemned already, because he hath not believed in the name of the only begotten Son of God.
John 3:17-18

Therefore if any man be in Christ, he is a new creature: old things are passed away; behold, all things are become new. 2 Corinthians 5:17

For I will be merciful to their unrighteousness, and their sins and their iniquities will I remember no more. Hebrews 8:12

Let us draw near with a true heart in full assurance of faith, having our hearts sprinkled from an evil conscience, and our bodies washed with pure water. Hebrews 10:22

But if we walk in the light, as he is in the light, we have fellowship one with another, and the blood of Jesus Christ his Son cleanseth us from all sin. 1 John 1:7

If we confess our sins, he is faithful and just to forgive us our sins, and to cleanse us from all unrighteousness. 1 John 1:9

I write unto you, little children, because your sins are forgiven you for his name's sake. 1 John 2:12

For if our heart condemn us, God is greater than our heart, and knoweth all things. 1 John 3:20

> *Sometimes, we want to fly before we walk; we want to be perfect before we start toward perfection. It is not a mark of godliness to be forever condemning oneself in morbid self-accusation. - Vance Havner*

Overcoming Condemnation

For God sent not his Son into the world to condemn the world; but that the world through him might be saved. John 3:17

Verily, verily, I say unto you, He that heareth my word, and believeth on him that sent me, hath everlasting life, and shall not come into condemnation; but is passed from death unto life. John 5:24

There is therefore now no condemnation to them which are in Christ Jesus, who walk not after the flesh, but after the Spirit. Romans 8:1

For if our heart condemn us, God is greater than our heart, and knoweth all things. Beloved, if our heart condemn us not, then have we confidence toward God. 1 John 3:20-21

> *The voice of sin may be loud, but the voice of forgiveness is louder. - D. L. Moody*

1. You Are Condemned When You

a. Reject Christ

He that believeth on him is not condemned: but he that believeth not is condemned already, because he hath not believed in the name of the only begotten Son of God. And this is the condemnation, that light is come into the world, and men loved darkness rather than light, because their deeds were evil. John 3:18-19

b. Willfully sin

Hast thou faith? have it to thyself before God. Happy is he that condemneth not himself in that thing which he alloweth.Romans 14:22

Knowing that he that is such is subverted, and sinneth, being condemned of himself. Titus 3:11

.

DEVELOPING THE WHOLE MAN

The Spirit

God is the Creator of Human Spirits

And God said, Let us make man in our image, after our likeness: and let them have dominion over the fish of the sea, and over the fowl of the air, and over the cattle, and over all the earth, and over every creeping thing that creepeth upon the earth. So God created man in his own image, in the image of God created he him; male and female created he them.

Genesis 1:26-27

Let the Lord, the God of the spirits of all flesh, set a man over the congregation. Numbers 27:16

The burden of the word of the Lord for Israel, saith the Lord, which stretcheth forth the heavens, and layeth the foundation of the earth, and formeth the spirit of man within him. Zechariah 12:1

Furthermore we have had fathers of our flesh which corrected us, and we gave them reverence: shall we not much rather be in subjection to the Father of spirits, and live? Hebrews 12:9

"O God, the God of the spirits of all flesh" Numbers 16:22

God Has Ultimate Control Over Human Spirits

There is no man that hath power over the spirit to retain the spirit; neither hath he power in the day of death: and there is no discharge in that war; neither shall wickedness deliver those that are given to it.

Ecclesiastes 8:8

Then shall the dust return to the earth as it was: and the spirit shall return unto God who gave it. Ecclesiastes 12:7

211

The Body is the Temporary Container for the Human Spirit

For as the body without the spirit is dead, so faith without works is dead also. James 2:26

Know ye not that ye are the temple of God, and that the Spirit of God dwelleth in you? If any man defile the temple of God, him shall God destroy; for the temple of God is holy, which temple ye are.
1 Corinthians 3:16-17

What? know ye not that your body is the temple of the Holy Ghost which is in you, which ye have of God, and ye are not your own? For ye are bought with a price: therefore glorify God in your body, and in your spirit, which are God's. 1 Corinthians 6:19-20

And the very God of peace sanctify you wholly; and I pray God your whole spirit and soul and body be preserved blameless unto the coming of our Lord Jesus Christ. 1 Thessalonians 5:23

The Life of the Human Spirit

He that hath the Son hath life; and he that hath not the Son of God hath not life. 1 John 5:12

It is the spirit that quickeneth; the flesh profiteth nothing: the words that I speak unto you, they are spirit, and they are life. John 6:63

For the law of the Spirit of life in Christ Jesus hath made me free from the law of sin and death. Romans 8:2

And so it is written, The first man Adam was made a living soul; the last Adam was made a quickening spirit. 1 Corinthians 15:45

God Communicates with Your Spirit

The Spirit itself beareth witness with our spirit, that we are the children of God: Romans 8:16

God is a Spirit: and they that worship him must worship him in spirit and in truth. John 4:24

True leadership cannot be divorced from the basic qualities that produce good sound character.

The Spirit of Man

But there is a spirit in man: and the inspiration of the Almighty giveth them understanding. Job 32:8

The spirit of a man will sustain his infirmity; but a wounded spirit who can bear? Proverbs 18:14

The spirit of man is the candle of the Lord, searching all the inward parts of the belly. Proverbs 20:27

To the general assembly and church of the firstborn, which are written in heaven, and to God the Judge of all, and to the spirits of just men made perfect, Hebrews 12:23

By which also he went and preached unto the spirits in prison;
1 Peter 3:19

Renewed (Born Again) Spirit

But he that is joined unto the Lord is one spirit. 1 Corinthians 6:17

Create in me a clean heart, O God; and renew a right spirit within me.
Psalms 51:10

A new heart also will I give you, and a new spirit will I put within you: and I will take away the stony heart out of your flesh, and I will give you an heart of flesh. And I will put my spirit within you, and cause you to walk in my statutes, and ye shall keep my judgments, and do them.
Ezekiel 36:26-27

Jesus answered and said unto his, Verily, verily, I say unto thee, Except a man be born again, he cannot see the kingdom of God. Nicodemus saith unto him, How can a man be born when he is old? can he enter the second time into his mother's womb, and be born? Jesus answered, Verily, verily, I say unto thee, Except a man be born of water and of the Spirit, he cannot enter into the kingdom of God. That which is born of the flesh is flesh; and that which is born of the Spirit is spirit. Marvel not that I said unto thee, Ye must be born again. John 3:3-7

God doesn't have any grandchildren. - E. Stanley Jones

Food (God's Word) for the Spirit

But he answered and said, It is written, Man shall not live by bread alone, but by every word that proceedeth out of the mouth of God. Matthew 4:4

And Jesus answered him, saying, It is written, That man shall not live by bread alone, but by every word of God. Luke 4:4

But he said unto them, I have meat to eat that ye know not of. John 4:32

Labour not for the meat which perisheth, but for that meat which endureth unto everlasting life, which the Son of man shall give unto you: for him hath God the Father sealed. John 6:27

Then Jesus said unto them, Verily, verily, I say unto you, Moses gave you not that bread from heaven; but my Father giveth you the true bread from heaven. For the bread of God is he which cometh down from heaven, and giveth life unto the world. Then said they unto him, Lord, evermore give us this bread. And Jesus said unto them, I am the bread of life: he that cometh to me shall never hunger; and he that believeth on me shall never thirst. John 6:32-35

I am the living bread which came down from heaven: if any man eat of this bread, he shall live for ever: and the bread that I will give is my flesh, which I will give for the life of the world. John 6:51

This is that bread which came down from heaven: not as your fathers did eat manna, and are dead: he that eateth of this bread shall live for ever.
John 6:58

So when they had dined, Jesus saith to Simon Peter, Simon, son of Jonas, lovest thou me more than these? He saith unto him, Yea, Lord; thou knowest that I love thee. He saith unto him, Feed my lambs. He saith to him again the second time, Simon, son of Jonas, lovest thou me? He saith unto him, Yea, Lord; thou knowest that I love thee. He saith unto him, Feed my sheep. John 21:15-16

And I, brethren, could not speak unto you as unto spiritual, but as unto carnal, even as unto babes in Christ. I have fed you with milk, and not with meat: for hitherto ye were not able to bear it, neither yet now are ye able. For ye are yet carnal: for whereas there is among you envying, and strife, and divisions, are ye not carnal, and walk as men?
1 Corinthians 3:1-3

And did all eat the same spiritual meat; And did all drink the same spiritual drink: for they drank of that spiritual Rock that followed them: and that Rock was Christ. 1 Corinthians 10:3-4

For when for the time ye ought to be teachers, ye have need that one teach you again which be the first principles of the oracles of God; and are become such as have need of milk, and not of strong meat. For every one that useth milk is unskilful in the word of righteousness: for he is a babe. **B**ut strong meat belongeth to them that are of full age, even those who by reason of use have their senses exercised to discern both good and evil. Hebrews 5:12-14

As newborn babes, desire the sincere milk of the word, that ye may grow thereby. 1 Peter 2:2

The Word of God Planted in the Heart of Man

I delight to do thy will, O my God: yea, thy law is within my heart.
Psalms 40:8

I have not hid thy righteousness within my heart; I have declared thy faithfulness and thy salvation. Psalms 40:10

Thy word have I hid in mine heart, that I might not sin against thee.
Psalms 119:11

Incline my heart unto thy testimonies, and not to covetousness.
Psalms 119:36

Let my heart be sound in thy statutes; that I be not ashamed.
Psalms 119:80

My son, forget not my law; but let thine heart keep my commandments.
Proverbs 3:1

He taught me also, and said unto me, Let thine heart retain my words: keep my commandments, and live. Proverbs 4:4

My son, attend to my words; incline thine ear unto my sayings. **L**et them not depart from thine eyes; keep them in the midst of thine heart. **F**or they are life unto those that find them, and health to all their flesh. **K**eep thy heart with all diligence; for out of it are the issues of life.
Proverbs 4:20-23

My son, keep thy father's commandment, and forsake not the law of thy mother: **B**ind them continually upon thine heart, and tie them about thy neck. Proverbs 6:20-21

My son, keep my words, and lay up my commandments with thee. **K**eep my commandments, and live; and my law as the apple of thine eye. **B**ind them upon thy fingers, write them upon the table of thine heart.
Proverbs 7:1-3

He that soweth iniquity shall reap vanity: and the rod of his anger shall fail. Proverbs 22:8

Bow down thine ear, and hear the words of the wise, and apply thine heart unto my knowledge. Proverbs 22:17

But this shall be the covenant that I will make with the house of Israel; After those days, saith the Lord, I will put my law in their inward parts, and write it in their hearts; and will be their God, and they shall be my people. Jeremiah 31:33

But what saith it? The word is nigh thee, even in thy mouth, and in thy heart: that is, the word of faith, which we preach. Romans 10:8

This is the covenant that I will make with them after those days, saith the Lord, I will put my laws into their hearts, and in their minds will I write them. Hebrews 10:16

Ye are our epistle written in our hearts, known and read of all men: Forasmuch as ye are manifestly declared to be the epistle of Christ ministered by us, written not with ink, but with the Spirit of the living God; not in tables of stone, but in fleshy tables of the heart.

2 Corinthians 3:2-3

God's Word Discerns the Heart

Yea, a sword shall pierce through thy own soul also, that the thoughts of many hearts may be revealed. Luke 2:35

For the word of God is quick, and powerful, and sharper than any twoedged sword, piercing even to the dividing asunder of soul and spirit, and of the joints and marrow, and is a discerner of the thoughts and intents of the heart. Hebrews 4:12

I have read many books, but the Bible reads me. - Anonymous

Thoughts and Words Originate in the Heart of Man

For as he thinketh in his heart, so is he: Eat and drink, saith he to thee; but his heart is not with thee. Proverbs 23:7

What we love usually manages to get into our conversation. What is down in the well of the heart will come up in the bucket of the speech. - Vance Havner

---

The character of a leader should be one that commands respect from all, even his enemies.

But those things which proceed out of the mouth come forth from the heart; and they defile the man. Matthew 15:18

A good man out of the good treasure of his heart bringeth forth that which is good; and an evil man out of the evil treasure of his heart bringeth forth that which is evil: for of the abundance of the heart his mouth speaketh. Luke 6:45

Living and Walking in the Spiritual Realm

That the righteousness of the law might be fulfilled in us, who walk not after the flesh, but after the Spirit. For they that are after the flesh do mind the things of the flesh; but they that are after the Spirit the things of the Spirit. Romans 8:4-5

But ye are not in the flesh, but in the Spirit, if so be that the Spirit of God dwell in you. Now if any man have not the Spirit of Christ, he is none of his. And if Christ be in you, the body is dead because of sin; but the Spirit is life because of righteousness. But if the Spirit of him that raised up Jesus from the dead dwell in you, he that raised up Christ from the dead shall also quicken your mortal bodies by his Spirit that dwelleth in you. Romans 8:9-11

For if ye live after the flesh, ye shall die: but if ye through the Spirit do mortify the deeds of the body, ye shall live. Romans 8:13

This I say then, Walk in the Spirit, and ye shall not fulfil the lust of the flesh. Galatians 5:16

But if ye be led of the Spirit, ye are not under the law. Galatians 5:18

If we live in the Spirit, let us also walk in the Spirit. Galatians 5:25

For this cause was the gospel preached also to them that are dead, that they might be judged according to men in the flesh, but live according to God in the spirit.1 Peter 4:6

Fruit of the Spirit

But the fruit of the Spirit is love, joy, peace, longsuffering, gentleness, goodness, faith, Meekness, temperance: against such there is no law.
Galatians 5:22-23

For the fruit of the Spirit is in all goodness and righteousness and truth.
Ephesians 5:9

Being filled with the fruits of righteousness, which are by Jesus Christ, unto the glory and praise of God. Philippians 1:11

The Mind

Renewing Your Mind

That ye be not soon shaken in mind, or be troubled, neither by spirit, nor by word, nor by letter as from us, as that the day of Christ is at hand.
2 Thessalonians 2:2

For God hath not given us the spirit of fear; but of power, and of love, and of a sound mind. 2 Timothy 1:7

Young men likewise exhort to be sober minded. Titus 2:6

Wherefore gird up the loins of your mind, be sober, and hope to the end for the grace that is to be brought unto you at the revelation of Jesus Christ. 1 Peter 1:13

He hath delivered my soul in peace from the battle that was against me: for there were many with me. Psalms 55:18

Focusing Your Mind on the Word of God

The law of the Lord is perfect, converting the soul: the testimony of the Lord is sure, making wise the simple. Psalms 19:7

When wisdom entereth into thine heart, and knowledge is pleasant unto thy soul. Proverbs 2:10

My son, let not them depart from thine eyes: keep sound wisdom and discretion: So shall they be life unto thy soul, and grace to thy neck.
Proverbs 3:21-22

Thus saith the Lord, Stand ye in the ways, and see, and ask for the old paths, where is the good way, and walk therein, and ye shall find rest for your souls. But they said, We will not walk therein. Jeremiah 6:16

And be not conformed to this world: but be ye transformed by the renewing of your mind, that ye may prove what is that good, and acceptable, and perfect, will of God. Romans 12:2

And be renewed in the spirit of your mind. Ephesians 4:23

This is the covenant that I will make with them after those days, saith the Lord, I will put my laws into their hearts, and in their minds will I write them. Hebrews 10:16

Wherefore lay apart all filthiness and superfluity of naughtiness, and receive with meekness the engrafted word, which is able to save your souls. James 1:21

This second epistle, beloved, I now write unto you; in both which I stir up your pure minds by way of remembrance: That ye may be mindful of the words which were spoken before by the holy prophets, and of the commandment of us the apostles of the Lord and Saviour. 2 Peter 3:1-2

For the word of God is quick, and powerful, and sharper than any twoedged sword, piercing even to the dividing asunder of soul and spirit, and of the joints and marrow, and is a discerner of the thoughts and intents of the heart. Hebrews 4:12

Focusing Your Mind on Jesus

Thou wilt keep him in perfect peace, whose mind is stayed on thee: because he trusteth in thee. Isaiah 26:3

Jesus said unto him, Thou shalt love the Lord thy God with all thy heart, and with all thy soul, and with all thy mind. Matthew 22:37

For who hath known the mind of the Lord, that he may instruct him? But we have the mind of Christ. 1 Corinthians 2:16

And the peace of God, which passeth all understanding, shall keep your hearts and minds through Christ Jesus. Philippians 4:7

Controlling Imaginations and Thoughts

I hate vain thoughts: but thy law do I love. Psalms 119:113

The thoughts of the righteous are right: but the counsels of the wicked are deceit. Proverbs 12:5

Commit thy works unto the Lord, and thy thoughts shall be established.
Proverbs 16:3

The thought of foolishness is sin: and the scorner is an abomination to men. Proverbs 24:9

For the weapons of our warfare are not carnal, but mighty through God to the pulling down of strong holds; Casting down imaginations, and every high thing that exalteth itself against the knowledge of God, and bringing into captivity every thought to the obedience of Christ.
2 Corinthians 10:4-5

219

For to be carnally minded is death; but to be spiritually minded is life and peace. Because the carnal mind is enmity against God: for it is not subject to the law of God, neither indeed can be. Romans 8:6-7

Finally, brethren, whatsoever things are true, whatsoever things are honest, whatsoever things are just, whatsoever things are pure, whatsoever things are lovely, whatsoever things are of good report; if there be any virtue, and if there be any praise, think on these things. Philippians 4:8

Television, Movies and Music

1. Would Jesus listen to this music, or watch this TV program or movie?

Then spake Jesus again unto them, saying, I am the light of the world: he that followeth me shall not walk in darkness, but shall have the light of life. John 8:12

I am come a light into the world, that whosoever believeth on me should not abide in darkness. John 12:46

2. Through your TV and music, what kind of people or evil spirits are you inviting into your home?

I wrote unto you in an epistle not to company with fornicators: Yet not altogether with the fornicators of this world, or with the covetous, or extortioners, or with idolaters; for then must ye needs go out of the world. But now I have written unto you not to keep company, if any man that is called a brother be a fornicator, or covetous, or an idolater, or a railer, or a drunkard, or an extortioner; with such an one no not to eat.
1 Corinthians 5:9-11

Be ye not unequally yoked together with unbelievers: for what fellowship hath righteousness with unrighteousness? and what communion hath light with darkness? And what concord hath Christ with Belial? or what part hath he that believeth with an infidel? 2 Corinthians 6:14-15

And have no fellowship with the unfruitful works of darkness, but rather reprove them. Ephesians 5:11

3. Is it contrary to God's Word?

The thought of foolishness is sin: and the scorner is an abomination to men. Proverbs 24:9

**No true leader can expect to live a
normal life as other people do.**

Cease, my son, to hear the instruction that causeth to err from the words of knowledge. Proverbs 19:27

Casting down imaginations, and every high thing that exalteth itself against the knowledge of God, and bringing into captivity every thought to the obedience of Christ. 2 Corinthians 10:5

4. Is the TV program or music bringing you closer to Christ?

Ye adulterers and adulteresses, know ye not that the friendship of the world is enmity with God? whosoever therefore will be a friend of the world is the enemy of God. James 4:4

All things are lawful unto me, but all things are not expedient: all things are lawful for me, but I will not be brought under the power of any.
1 Corinthians 6:12

All things are lawful for me, but all things are not expedient: all things are lawful for me, but all things edify not. 1 Corinthians 10:23

Wherefore seeing we also are compassed about with so great a cloud of witnesses, let us lay aside every weight, and the sin which doth so easily beset us, and let us run with patience the race that is set before us.
Hebrews 12:1

5. Is it causing you to compromise and sin?

Ye cannot drink the cup of the Lord, and the cup of devils: ye cannot be partakers of the Lord's table, and of the table of devils.
1 Corinthians 10:21

And if thine eye offend thee, pluck it out, and cast it from thee: it is better for thee to enter into life with one eye, rather than having two eyes to be cast into hell fire. Matthew 18:9

6. What are you putting in your heart (through your eyes and ears)?

I will set no wicked thing before mine eyes: I hate the work of them that turn aside; it shall not cleave to me. Psalms 101:3

Turn away mine eyes from beholding vanity; and quicken thou me in thy way. Psalms 119:37

Thine eyes shall behold strange women, and thine heart shall utter perverse things. Proverbs 23:33

A wicked doer giveth heed to false lips; and a liar giveth ear to a naughty tongue. Proverbs 17:4

And he said unto them, Take heed what ye hear. Mark 4:24

Be not deceived: evil communications corrupt good manners.
1 Corinthians 15:33

Abstain from all appearance of evil. 1 Thessalonians 5:22

Being filled with all unrighteousness, fornication, wickedness, covetousness, maliciousness; full of envy, murder, debate, deceit, malignity; whisperers, **B**ackbiters, haters of God, despiteful, proud, boasters, inventors of evil things, disobedient to parents, without understanding, covenantbreakers, without natural affection, implacable, unmerciful: **W**ho knowing the judgment of God, that they which commit such things are worthy of death, not only do the same, but have pleasure in them that do them. Romans 1:29-32

Until they were filled–permeated and saturated–with every kind of unrighteousness, iniquity, grasping and covetous greed, [and] malice. [They were] full of envy and jealousy, murder, strife, deceit and treachery, ill will and cruel ways. [They were] secret backbiters and gossipers, Slanderers, hateful to and hating God, full of insolence, arrogance [and] boasting; inventors of new forms of evil, disobedient and undutiful to parents. [They were] without understanding, conscienceless and faithless, heartless and loveless [and] merciless. Though they are fully aware of God's righteous decree that those who do such things deserve to die, they not only do them themselves but approve and applaud others who practice them. Romans 1:29-32 AMP

7. Are you wasting time?

Redeeming the time, because the days are evil. Ephesians 5:16

Walk in wisdom toward them that are without, redeeming the time.
Colossians 4:5

And if ye call on the Father, who without respect of persons judgeth according to every man's work, pass the time of your sojourning here in fear. 1 Peter 1:17

8. How do you qualify good TV programs, movies, and music?

If ye then be risen with Christ, seek those things which are above, where Christ sitteth on the right hand of God. Colossians 3:1

Finally, brethren, whatsoever things are true, whatsoever things are honest, whatsoever things are just, whatsoever things are pure, whatsoever things are lovely, whatsoever things are of good report; if there be any virtue, and if there be any praise, think on these things. Philippians 4:8

Every good gift and every perfect gift is from above, and cometh down from the Father of lights, with whom is no variableness, neither shadow of turning. James 1:17

Controlling Lust

Lust not after her beauty in thine heart; neither let her take thee with her eyelids. Proverbs 6:25

But I say unto you, That whosoever looketh on a woman to lust after her hath committed adultery with her already in his heart. Matthew 5:28

And the cares of this world, and the deceitfulness of riches, and the lusts of other things entering in, choke the word, and it becometh unfruitful.
Mark 4:19

Ye are of your father the devil, and the lusts of your father ye will do. He was a murderer from the beginning, and abode not in the truth, because there is no truth in him. When he speaketh a lie, he speaketh of his own: for he is a liar, and the father of it. John 8:44

Wherefore God also gave them up to uncleanness through the lusts of their own hearts, to dishonour their own bodies between themselves.
Romans 1:24

Let not sin therefore reign in your mortal body, that ye should obey it in the lusts thereof. Romans 6:12

But put ye on the Lord Jesus Christ, and make not provision for the flesh, to fulfil the lusts thereof. Romans 13:14

Now these things were our examples, to the intent we should not lust after evil things, as they also lusted. 1 Corinthians 10:6

This I say then, Walk in the Spirit, and ye shall not fulfill the lust of the flesh. For the flesh lusteth against the Spirit, and the Spirit against the flesh: and these are contrary the one to the other: so that ye cannot do the things that ye would. Galatians 5:16-17

And they that are Christ's have crucified the flesh with the affections and lusts. Galatians 5:24

Wherein in time past ye walked according to the course of this world, according to the prince of the power of the air, the spirit that now worketh in the children of disobedience: Among whom also we all had our conversation in times past in the lusts of our flesh, fulfilling the desires of the flesh and of the mind; and were by nature the children of wrath, even as others. But God, who is rich in mercy, for his great love wherewith he loved us, Even when we were dead in sins, hath quickened us together with Christ, (by grace ye are saved;) And hath raised us up together, and made us sit together in heavenly places in Christ Jesus. Ephesians 2:2-6

That ye put off concerning the former conversation the old man, which is corrupt according to the deceitful lusts. Ephesians 4:22

Flee also youthful lusts: but follow righteousness, faith, charity, peace, with them that call on the Lord out of a pure heart. 2 Timothy 2:22

Teaching us that, denying ungodliness and worldly lusts, we should live soberly, righteously, and godly, in this present world. Titus 2:12

Let no man say when he is tempted, I am tempted of God: for God cannot be tempted with evil, neither tempteth he any man: But every man is tempted, when he is drawn away of his own lust, and enticed. Then when lust hath conceived, it bringeth forth sin: and sin, when it is finished, bringeth forth death. James 1:13-15

From whence come wars and fightings among you? come they not hence, even of your lusts that war in your members? Ye lust, and have not: ye kill, and desire to have, and cannot obtain: ye fight and war, yet ye have not, because ye ask not. Ye ask, and receive not, because ye ask amiss, that ye may consume it upon your lusts. James 4:1-3

As obedient children, not fashioning yourselves according to the former lusts in your ignorance. 1 Peter 1:14

Dearly beloved, I beseech you as strangers and pilgrims, abstain from fleshly lusts, which war against the soul. 1 Peter 2:11

That he no longer should live the rest of his time in the flesh to the lusts of men, but to the will of God. 1 Peter 4:2

Whereby are given unto us exceeding great and precious promises: that by these ye might be partakers of the divine nature, having escaped the corruption that is in the world through lust. 2 Peter 1:4

For all that is in the world, the lust of the flesh, and the lust of the eyes, and the pride of life, is not of the Father, but is of the world. And the world passeth away, and the lust thereof: but he that doeth the will of God abideth for ever. 1 John 2:16-17

A leader should be above reproach.

The Body

The Temple of the Holy Spirit

Know ye not that ye are the temple of God, and that the Spirit of God dwelleth in you? If any man defile the temple of God, him shall God destroy; for the temple of God is holy, which temple ye are.

1 Corinthians 3:16-17

What? know ye not that your body is the temple of the Holy Ghost which is in you, which ye have of God, and ye are not your own? For ye are bought with a price: therefore glorify God in your body, and in your spirit, which are God's. 1 Corinthians 6:19-20

Whether therefore ye eat, or drink, or whatsoever ye do, do all to the glory of God. 1 Corinthians 10:31

For bodily exercise profiteth little: but godliness is profitable unto all things, having promise of the life that now is, and of that which is to come. 1 Timothy 4:8

Beloved, I wish above all things that thou mayest prosper and be in health, even as thy soul prospereth. 3 John 1:2

Sex Before Marriage

But that we write unto them, that they abstain from pollutions of idols, and from fornication, and from things strangled, and from blood.

Acts 15:20

That ye abstain from meats offered to idols, and from blood, and from things strangled, and from fornication: from which if ye keep yourselves, ye shall do well. Fare ye well. Acts 15:29

As touching the Gentiles which believe, we have written and concluded that they observe no such thing, save only that they keep themselves from things offered to idols, and from blood, and from strangled, and from fornication. Acts 21:25

But now I have written unto you not to keep company, if any man that is called a brother be a fornicator, or covetous, or an idolater, or a railer, or a drunkard, or an extortioner; with such an one no not to eat.

1 Corinthians 5:11

Know ye not that your bodies are the members of Christ? shall I then take the members of Christ, and make them the members of an harlot?

225

God forbid. What? know ye not that he which is joined to an harlot is one body? for two, saith he, shall be one flesh. 1 Corinthians 6:15-16

Flee fornication. Every sin that a man doeth is without the body; but he that commiteth fornication sinneth against his own body. What? know ye not that your body is the temple of the Holy Ghost which is in you, which ye have of God, and ye are not your own? For ye are bought with a price: therefore glorify God in your body, and in your spirit, which are God's. 1 Corinthians 6:18-20

Now concerning the things whereof ye wrote unto me: It is good for a man not to touch a woman. Nevertheless, to avoid fornication, let every man have his own wife, and let every woman have her own husband.
1 Corinthians 7:1-2

Neither let us commit fornication, as some of them committed, and fell in one day three and twenty thousand. 1 Corinthians 10:8

But fornication, and all uncleanness, or covetousness, let it not be once named among you, as becometh saints. Ephesians 5:3

For this is the will of God, even your sanctification, that ye should abstain from fornication: 1 Thessalonians 4:3

1. Sex is Only for Married Couples

Let the husband render unto the wife due benevolence: and likewise also the wife unto the husband. The wife hath not power of her own body, but the husband: and likewise also the husband hath not power of his own body, but the wife. Defraud ye not one the other, except it be with consent for a time, that ye may give yourselves to fasting and prayer; and come together again, that Satan tempt you not for your incontinency.
1 Corinthians 7:3-5

The Consequences of Fornication

Now the works of the flesh are manifest, which are these; Adultery, fornication, uncleanness, lasciviousness, Envyings, murders, drunkenness, revellings, and such like: of the which I tell you before, as I have also told you in time past, that they which do such things shall not inherit the kingdom of God. Galatians 5:19,21

Marriage is honourable in all, and the bed undefiled: but whoremongers and adulterers God will judge. Hebrews 13:4

Even as Sodom and Gomorrha, and the cities about them in like manner, giving themselves over to fornication, and going after strange flesh, are set forth for an example, suffering the vengeance of eternal fire. Jude 1:7

Adultery

Thou shalt not commit adultery. Exodus 20:14

And the man that committeth adultery with another man's wife, even he that committeth adultery with his neighbour's wife, the adulterer and the adulteress shall surely be put to death. Leviticus 20:10

Neither shalt thou commit adultery. Deuteronomy 5:18

Such is the way of an adulterous woman; she eateth, and wipeth her mouth, and saith, I have done no wickedness. Proverbs 30:20

But I say unto you, That whosoever looketh on a woman to lust after her hath committed adultery with her already in his heart. Matthew 5:28

The Consequences of Adultery

For by means of a whorish woman a man is brought to a piece of bread: and the adulteress will hunt for the precious life. Proverbs 6:26

But whoso committeth adultery with a woman lacketh understanding: he that doeth it destroyeth his own soul. Proverbs 6:32

Know ye not that the unrighteous shall not inherit the kingdom of God? Be not deceived: neither fornicators, nor idolaters, nor adulterers, nor effeminate, nor abusers of themselves with mankind. 1 Corinthians 6:9

Marriage is honourable in all, and the bed undefiled: but whoremongers and adulterers God will judge. Hebrews 13:4

Homosexuality and Lesbianism

Thou shalt not lie with mankind, as with womankind: it is abomination.
Leviticus 18:22

If a man also lie with mankind, as he lieth with a woman, both of them have committed an abomination: they shall surely be put to death; their blood shall be upon them. Leviticus 20:13

Wherefore God also gave them up to uncleanness through the lusts of their own hearts, to dishonour their own bodies between themselves.
Romans 1:24

For this cause God gave them up unto vile affections: for even their women did change the natural use into that which is against nature: And likewise also the men, leaving the natural use of the woman, burned in their lust one toward another; men with men working that which is unseemly, and receiving in themselves that recompence of their error which was meet. And even as they did not like to retain God in their knowledge, God gave them over to a reprobate mind, to do those things which are not convenient. Romans 1:26-28

Without understanding, covenantbreakers, without natural affection, implacable, unmerciful. Romans 1:31

Mortify therefore your members which are upon the earth; fornication, uncleanness, inordinate affection, evil concupiscence, and covetousness, which is idolatry. Colossians 3:5

Without natural affection, trucebreakers, false accusers, incontinent, fierce, despisers of those that are good. 2 Timothy 3:3

> *God hates sin, but He loves the sinner. In order for mankind to enter heaven, God requires three things: acceptance of Jesus Christ as their Lord and Savior, true repentance, and obedience to his Commandments.*

Gluttony

When thou sittest to eat with a ruler, consider diligently what is before thee: And put a knife to thy throat, if thou be a man given to appetite. Be not desirous of his dainties: for they are deceitful meat. Proverbs 23:1-3

Be not among winebibbers; among riotous eaters of flesh: For the drunkard and the glutton shall come to poverty: and drowsiness shall clothe a man with rags. Proverbs 23:20-21

Hast thou found honey? eat so much as is sufficient for thee, lest thou be filled therewith, and vomit it. Proverbs 25:16

He that hath no rule over his own spirit is like a city that is broken down, and without walls. Proverbs 25:28

Blessed art thou, O land, when thy king is the son of nobles, and thy princes eat in due season, for strength, and not for drunkenness!
Ecclesiastes 10:17

Whose end is destruction, whose God is their belly, and whose glory is in their shame, who mind earthly things. Philippians 3:19

**True leaders cultivate character
with the fertilizer of self discipline.**

For the time past of our life may suffice us to have wrought the will of the Gentiles, when we walked in lasciviousness, lusts, excess of wine, revellings, banquetings, and abominable idolatries. 1 Peter 4:3

Biblical Diet

And God said, Behold, I have given you every herb bearing seed, which is upon the face of all the earth, and every tree, in the which is the fruit of a tree yielding seed; to you it shall be for meat. Genesis 1:29

Ye shall keep my statutes. Thou shalt not let thy cattle gender with a diverse kind: thou shalt not sow thy field with mingled seed: neither shall a garment mingled of linen and woollen come upon thee.
Leviticus 19:19

Take thou also unto thee wheat, and barley, and beans, and lentiles, and millet, and fitches, and put them in one vessel, and make thee bread thereof, according to the number of the days that thou shalt lie upon thy side, three hundred and ninety days shalt thou eat thereof. Ezekiel 4:9

And by the river upon the bank thereof, on this side and on that side, shall grow all trees for meat, whose leaf shall not fade, neither shall the fruit thereof be consumed: it shall bring forth new fruit according to his months, because their waters they issued out of the sanctuary: and the fruit thereof shall be for meat, and the leaf thereof for medicine.
Ezekiel 47:12

Prove thy servants, I beseech thee, ten days; and let them give us pulse to eat, and water to drink. Then let our countenances be looked upon before thee, and the countenance of the children that eat of the portion of the king's meat: and as thou seest, deal with thy servants. So he consented to them in this matter, and proved them ten days. And at the end of ten days their countenances appeared fairer and fatter in flesh than all the children which did eat the portion of the king's meat. Thus Melzar took away the portion of their meat, and the wine that they should drink; and gave them pulse. Daniel 1:12-16

Give the devil no place in your life; not
even in the food that you eat.

Healing

1. Provisions for Healing

But he was wounded for our transgressions, he was bruised for our iniquities: the chastisement of our peace was upon him; and with his stripes we are healed. Isaiah 53:5

Who his own self bare our sins in his own body on the tree, that we, being dead to sins, should live unto righteousness: by whose stripes ye were healed. 1 Peter 2:24

2. Preventive Medicine

And said, If thou wilt diligently hearken to the voice of the Lord thy God, and wilt do that which is right in his sight, and wilt give ear to his commandments, and keep all his statutes, I will put none of these diseases upon thee, which I have brought upon the Egyptians: for I am the Lord that healeth thee. Exodus 15:26

Thou shalt therefore keep the commandments, and the statutes, and the judgments, which I command thee this day, to do them. Wherefore it shall come to pass, if ye hearken to these judgments, and keep, and do them, that the Lord thy God shall keep unto thee the covenant and the mercy which he sware unto thy fathers: And he will love thee, and bless thee, and multiply thee: he will also bless the fruit of thy womb, and the fruit of thy land, thy corn, and thy wine, and thine oil, the increase of thy kine, and the flocks of thy sheep, in the land which he sware unto thy fathers to give thee. Thou shalt be blessed above all people: there shall not be male or female barren among you, or among your cattle. And the Lord will take away from thee all sickness, and will put none of the evil diseases of Egypt, which thou knowest, upon thee; but will lay them upon all them that hate thee. Deuteronomy 7:11-15

Trust in the Lord with all thine heart; and lean not unto thine own understanding. In all thy ways acknowledge him, and he shall direct thy paths. Be not wise in thine own eyes: fear the Lord, and depart from evil. It shall be health to thy navel, and marrow to thy bones. Proverbs 3:5-8

> *Jesus is the Divine Physician and pharmacist and His prescriptions are never out of balance. - Vance Havner*

3. God's Promises for Healing

And ye shall serve the Lord your God, and he shall bless thy bread, and thy water; and I will take sickness away from the midst of thee.
Exodus 23:25

Behold, thou hast instructed many, and thou hast strengthened the weak hands. Thy words have upholden him that was falling, and thou hast strengthened the feeble knees. Job 4:3-4

O Lord my God, I cried unto thee, and thou hast healed me. Psalms 30:2

He keepeth all his bones: not one of them is broken. Psalms 34:20

The Lord will strengthen him upon the bed of languishing: thou wilt make all his bed in his sickness. Psalms 41:3

Why art thou cast down, O my soul? and why art thou disquieted within me? hope thou in God: for I shall yet praise him, who is the health of my countenance, and my God. Psalms 42:11

Surely he shall deliver thee from the snare of the fowler, and from the noisome pestilence. Psalms 91:3

There shall no evil befall thee, neither shall any plague come nigh thy dwelling. Psalms 91:10

Who forgiveth all thine iniquities; who healeth all thy diseases. Who redeemeth thy life from destruction; who crowneth thee with lovingkindness and tender mercies; Who satisfieth thy mouth with good things; so that thy youth is renewed like the eagle's. Psalms 103:3-5

He sent his word, and healed them, and delivered them from their destructions. Psalms 107:20

The Lord upholdeth all that fall, and raiseth up all those that be bowed down. Psalms 145:14

The Lord openeth the eyes of the blind: the Lord raiseth them that are bowed down: the Lord loveth the righteous. Psalms 146:8

He healeth the broken in heart, and bindeth up their wounds.
Psalms 147:3

My son, attend to my words; incline thine ear unto my sayings. Let them not depart from thine eyes; keep them in the midst of thine heart. For they are life unto those that find them, and health to all their flesh.
Proverbs 4:20-22

For by me thy days shall be multiplied, and the years of thy life shall be increased. Proverbs 9:11

A sound heart is the life of the flesh: but envy the rottenness of the bones.
Proverbs 14:30

Pleasant words are as an honeycomb, sweet to the soul, and health to the bones. Proverbs 16:24

Strengthen ye the weak hands, and confirm the feeble knees. Isaiah 35:3

He giveth power to the faint; and to them that have no might he increaseth strength. Isaiah 40:29

And the Lord shall guide thee continually, and satisfy thy soul in drought, and make fat thy bones: and thou shalt be like a watered garden, and like a spring of water, whose waters fail not. Isaiah 58:11

And when ye see this, your heart shall rejoice, and your bones shall flourish like an herb: and the hand of the Lord shall be known toward his servants, and his indignation toward his enemies. Isaiah 66:14

Heal me, O Lord, and I shall be healed; save me, and I shall be saved: for thou art my praise. Jeremiah 17:14

For I will restore health unto thee, and I will heal thee of thy wounds, saith the Lord; because they called thee an Outcast, saying, This is Zion, whom no man seeketh after. Jeremiah 30:17

Behold, I will bring it health and cure, and I will cure them, and will reveal unto them the abundance of peace and truth. Jeremiah 33:6

For I will cleanse their blood that I have not cleansed: for the Lord dwelleth in Zion. Joel 3:21

And they that were vexed with unclean spirits: and they were healed. And the whole multitude sought to touch him: for there went virtue out of him, and healed them all. Luke 6:18-19

Christ hath redeemed us from the curse of the law, being made a curse for us: for it is written, Cursed is every one that hangeth on a tree:
Galatians 3:13

Wherefore lift up the hands which hang down, and the feeble knees; And make straight paths for your feet, lest that which is lame be turned out of the way; but let it rather be healed. Hebrews 12:12-13

Beloved, I wish above all things that thou mayest prosper and be in health, even as thy soul prospereth. 3 John 1:2

4. Praying for Healing

Is any among you afflicted? let him pray. Is any merry? let him sing psalms. Is any sick among you? let him call for the elders of the church; and let them pray over him, anointing him with oil in the name of the Lord: And the prayer of faith shall save the sick, and the Lord shall raise him up; and if he have committed sins, they shall be forgiven him. Con-

> **The man who is impatient with weakness
> will be defective in his leadership.**

fess your faults one to another, and pray one for another, that ye may be healed. The effectual fervent prayer of a righteous man availeth much.

James 5:13-16

Living a Long and Satisfied Life

Ye shall walk in all the ways which the Lord your God hath commanded you, that ye may live, and that it may be well with you, and that ye may prolong your days in the land which ye shall possess. Deuteronomy 5:33

That thou mightest fear the Lord thy God, to keep all his statutes and his commandments, which I command thee, thou, and thy son, and thy son's son, all the days of thy life; and that thy days may be prolonged.

Deuteronomy 6:2

Thou shalt come to thy grave in a full age, like as a shock of corn cometh in in his season. Job 5:26

Cast me not off in the time of old age; forsake me not when my strength faileth. Psalms 71:9

O God, thou hast taught me from my youth: and hitherto have I declared thy wondrous works. Now also when I am old and greyheaded, O God, forsake me not; until I have shewed thy strength unto this generation, and thy power to every one that is to come. Psalms 71:17-18

The days of our years are threescore years and ten; and if by reason of strength they be fourscore years, yet is their strength labour and sorrow; for it is soon cut off, and we fly away. Psalms 90:10

So teach us to number our days, that we may apply our hearts unto wisdom. Psalms 90:12

With long life will I satisfy him, and shew him my salvation.

Psalms 91:16

The righteous shall flourish like the palm tree: he shall grow like a cedar in Lebanon. Those that be planted in the house of the Lord shall flourish in the courts of our God. They shall still bring forth fruit in old age; they shall be fat and flourishing; To shew that the Lord is upright: he is my rock, and there is no unrighteousness in him. Psalms 92:12-15

Who satisfieth thy mouth with good things; so that thy youth is renewed like the eagle's. Psalms 103:5

My son, forget not my law; but let thine heart keep my commandments: For length of days, and long life, and peace, shall they add to thee.

Proverbs 3:1-2

For by me thy days shall be multiplied, and the years of thy life shall be increased. Proverbs 9:11

The fear of the Lord prolongeth days: but the years of the wicked shall be shortened. Proverbs 10:27

Children's children are the crown of old men; and the glory of children are their fathers. Proverbs 17:6

The glory of young men is their strength: and the beauty of old men is the grey head. Proverbs 20:29

And even to your old age I am he; and even to hoar hairs will I carry you: I have made, and I will bear; even I will carry, and will deliver you.
Isaiah 46:4

For which cause we faint not; but though our outward man perish, yet the inward man is renewed day by day. For our light affliction, which is but for a moment, worketh for us a far more exceeding and eternal weight of glory; While we look not at the things which are seen, but at the things which are not seen: for the things which are seen are temporal; but the things which are not seen are eternal. 2 Corinthians 4:16-18

HOLY SPIRIT

Respecting the Holy Spirit

Wherefore I say unto you, All manner of sin and blasphemy shall be forgiven unto men: but the blasphemy against the Holy Ghost shall not be forgiven unto men. And whosoever speaketh a word against the Son of man, it shall be forgiven him: but whosoever speaketh against the Holy Ghost, it shall not be forgiven him, neither in this world, neither in the world to come. Matthew 12:31-32

And grieve not the holy Spirit of God, whereby ye are sealed unto the day of redemption. Ephesians 4:30

Quench not the Spirit. 1 Thessalonians 5:19

Of how much sorer punishment, suppose ye, shall he be thought worthy, who hath trodden under foot the Son of God, and hath counted the blood of the covenant, wherewith he was sanctified, an unholy thing, and hath done despite unto the Spirit of grace? Hebrews 10:29

> *The first step toward establishing a relationship with the Holy Spirit is to respect and acknowledge Him as God and not as an "it."*

Receiving the Baptism of the Holy Spirit

If ye then, being evil, know how to give good gifts unto your children: how much more shall your heavenly Father give the Holy Spirit to them that ask him? Luke 11:13

And when he had said this, he breathed on them, and saith unto them, Receive ye the Holy Ghost. John 20:22

And be not drunk with wine, wherein is excess; but be filled with the Spirit. Ephesians 5:18

But ye, beloved, building up yourselves on your most holy faith, praying in the Holy Ghost. Jude 1:20

235

Wherefore, brethren, covet to prophesy, and forbid not to speak with tongues. 1 Corinthians 14:39

The Benefits of Praying in the Holy Spirit

Likewise the Spirit also helpeth our infirmities: for we know not what we should pray for as we ought: but the Spirit itself maketh intercession for us with groanings which cannot be uttered. And he that searcheth the hearts knoweth what is the mind of the Spirit, because he maketh intercession for the saints according to the will of God. Romans 8:26-27

For he that speaketh in an unknown tongue speaketh not unto men, but unto God: for no man understandeth him; howbeit in the spirit he speaketh mysteries. 1 Corinthians 14:2

For if I pray in an unknown tongue, my spirit prayeth, but my understanding is unfruitful. What is it then? I will pray with the spirit, and I will pray with the understanding also: I will sing with the spirit, and I will sing with the understanding also. 1 Corinthians 14:14-15

> *Praying in the Spirit guarantees perfect prayer that is directed by the Holy Spirit; untouched by doubt and fear of the mind; and impossible for the devil to understand or hinder.*

Praying always with all prayer and supplication in the Spirit, and watching thereunto with all perseverance and supplication for all saints.
Ephesians 6:18

Examples of Believers Being Filled with the Holy Spirit

And they were all filled with the Holy Ghost, and began to speak with other tongues, as the Spirit gave them utterance. Acts 2:4

Now when the apostles which were at Jerusalem heard that Samaria had received the word of God, they sent unto them Peter and John: Who, when they were come down, prayed for them, that they might receive the Holy Ghost: For as yet he was fallen upon none of them: only they were baptized in the name of the Lord Jesus. Then laid they their hands on them, and they received the Holy Ghost. Acts 8:14-17

And Ananias went his way, and entered into the house; and putting his hands on him said, Brother Saul, the Lord, even Jesus, that appeared

---

A good leader does not depend on people's opinions to confirm God's will for his life.

---

unto thee in the way as thou camest, hath sent me, that thou mightest receive thy sight, and be filled with the Holy Ghost. Acts 9:17

While Peter yet spake these words, the Holy Ghost fell on all them which heard the word. And they of the circumcision which believed were astonished, as many as came with Peter, because that on the Gentiles also was poured out the gift of the Holy Ghost. For they heard them speak with tongues, and magnify God. Then answered Peter, Can any man forbid water, that these should not be baptized, which have received the Holy Ghost as well as we? Acts 10:44-47

And God, which knoweth the hearts, bare them witness, giving them the Holy Ghost, even as he did unto us; And put no difference between us and them, purifying their hearts by faith. Acts 15:8-9

He said unto them, Have ye received the Holy Ghost since ye believed? And they said unto him, We have not so much as heard whether there be any Holy Ghost. And he said unto them, Unto what then were ye baptized? And they said, Unto John's baptism. Then said Paul, John verily baptized with the baptism of repentance, saying unto the people, that they should believe on him which should come after him, that is, on Christ Jesus. When they heard this, they were baptized in the name of the Lord Jesus. And when Paul had laid his hands upon them, the Holy Ghost came on them; and they spake with tongues, and prophesied.
Acts 19:2-6

The Holy Spirit is the Teacher, Leader, Guide and Counselor

For the Holy Ghost shall teach you in the same hour what ye ought to say. Luke 12:12

But this spake he of the Spirit, which they that believe on him should receive: for the Holy Ghost was not yet given; because that Jesus was not yet glorified. John 7:39

But the Comforter, which is the Holy Ghost, whom the Father will send in my name, he shall teach you all things, and bring all things to your remembrance, whatsoever I have said unto you. John 14:26

Howbeit when he, the Spirit of truth, is come, he will guide you into all truth: for he shall not speak of himself; but whatsoever he shall hear, that shall he speak: and he will shew you things to come. John 16:13

For as many as are led by the Spirit of God, they are the sons of God.
Romans 8:14

The Spirit itself beareth witness with our spirit, that we are the children of God. Romans 8:16

But God hath revealed them unto us by his Spirit: for the Spirit searcheth all things, yea, the deep things of God. For what man knoweth the things of a man, save the spirit of man which is in him? even so the things of God knoweth no man, but the Spirit of God. 1 Corinthians 2:10-11

Which things also we speak, not in the words which man's wisdom teacheth, but which the Holy Ghost teacheth; comparing spiritual things with spiritual. 1 Corinthians 2:13

But if ye be led of the Spirit, ye are not under the law. Galatians 5:18

The Holy Spirit Living Inside the Believer

And I will put my spirit within you, and cause you to walk in my statutes, and ye shall keep my judgments, and do them. Ezekiel 36:27

Even the Spirit of truth; whom the world cannot receive, because it seeth him not, neither knoweth him: but ye know him; for he dwelleth with you, and shall be in you. John 14:17

Know ye not that ye are the temple of God, and that the Spirit of God dwelleth in you? 1 Corinthians 3:16

What? know ye not that your body is the temple of the Holy Ghost which is in you, which ye have of God, and ye are not your own?
1 Corinthians 6:19

And because ye are sons, God hath sent forth the Spirit of his Son into your hearts, crying, Abba, Father. Galatians 4:6

That he would grant you, according to the riches of his glory, to be strengthened with might by his Spirit in the inner man. Ephesians 3:16

That good thing which was committed unto thee keep by the Holy Ghost which dwelleth in us. 2 Timothy 1:14

> If you have been born of the Holy Spirit, you will not have to serve God ...it will become the natural thing to do. - D. L. Moody

And he that keepeth his commandments dwelleth in him, and he in him. And hereby we know that he abideth in us, by the Spirit which he hath given us. 1 John 3:24

Hereby know we that we dwell in him, and he in us, because he hath given us of his Spirit. 1 John 4:13

Sealed by the Holy Spirit

Who hath also sealed us, and given the earnest of the Spirit in our hearts.
2 Corinthians 1:22

In whom ye also trusted, after that ye heard the word of truth, the gospel of your salvation: in whom also after that ye believed, ye were sealed with that holy Spirit of promise, Ephesians 1:13

And grieve not the holy Spirit of God, whereby ye are sealed unto the day of redemption. Ephesians 4:30

The Power of the Holy Spirit

But ye shall receive power, after that the Holy Ghost is come upon you: and ye shall be witnesses unto me both in Jerusalem, and in all Judaea, and in Samaria, and unto the uttermost part of the earth. Acts 1:8

And it shall come to pass in the last days, saith God, I will pour out of my Spirit upon all flesh: and your sons and your daughters shall prophesy, and your young men shall see visions, and your old men shall dream dreams: And on my servants and on my handmaidens I will pour out in those days of my Spirit; and they shall prophesy. Acts 2:17-18

And when they were come up out of the water, the Spirit of the Lord caught away Philip, that the eunuch saw him no more: and he went on his way rejoicing. Acts 8:39

But if the Spirit of him that raised up Jesus from the dead dwell in you, he that raised up Christ from the dead shall also quicken your mortal bodies by his Spirit that dwelleth in you. Romans 8:11

> *To be "fervent in spirit" is to be "boiling in spirit," and to boil we must be near the Fire. - Vance Havner*

And my speech and my preaching was not with enticing words of man's wisdom, but in demonstration of the Spirit and of power.
1 Corinthians 2:4

And such were some of you: but ye are washed, but ye are sanctified, but ye are justified in the name of the Lord Jesus, and by the Spirit of our God. 1 Corinthians 6:11

For our gospel came not unto you in word only, but also in power, and in the Holy Ghost, and in much assurance; as ye know what manner of men we were among you for your sake. 1 Thessalonians 1:5

239

God also bearing them witness, both with signs and wonders, and with divers miracles, and gifts of the Holy Ghost, according to his own will?
Hebrews 2:4

Jesus Christ is the same yesterday, and today, and forever. Hebrews 13:8

Never let a person or man-made doctrine talk you out of the power of God. The gods of the pagans are dead and powerless but the God of Israel heals, delivers and manifests His glory in Sovereign miracles through His Son Jesus Christ.

The Gifts of the Holy Spirit

Now there are diversities of gifts, but the same Spirit. And there are differences of administrations, but the same Lord. And there are diversities of operations, but it is the same God which worketh all in all. But the manifestation of the Spirit is given to every man to profit withal. For to one is given by the Spirit the word of wisdom; to another the word of knowledge by the same Spirit; To another faith by the same Spirit; to another the gifts of healing by the same Spirit; To another the working of miracles; to another prophecy; to another discerning of spirits; to another divers kinds of tongues; to another the interpretation of tongues: But all these worketh that one and the selfsame Spirit, dividing to every man severally as he will. 1 Corinthians 12:4-11

PRAYER

Let us therefore come boldly unto the throne of grace, that we may obtain mercy, and find grace to help in time of need. Hebrews 4:16

Having therefore, brethren, boldness to enter into the holiest by the blood of Jesus. Hebrews 10:19

If ye then, being evil, know how to give good gifts unto your children, how much more shall your Father which is in heaven give good things to them that ask him? Matthew 7:11

Ask, and it shall be given you; seek, and ye shall find; knock, and it shall be opened unto you: For every one that asketh receiveth; and he that seeketh findeth; and to him that knocketh it shall be opened. Or what man is there of you, whom if his son ask bread, will he give him a stone? Or if he ask a fish, will he give him a serpent? If ye then, being evil, know how to give good gifts unto your children, how much more shall your Father which is in heaven give good things to them that ask him?

Matthew 7:7-11

Prayer moves the hand which moves the world. - John A. Wallace

Praying in the Name of Jesus

Again I say unto you, That if two of you shall agree on earth as touching any thing that they shall ask, it shall be done for them of my Father which is in heaven. For where two or three are gathered together in my name, there am I in the midst of them. Matthew 18:19-20

And whatsoever ye shall ask in my name, that will I do, that the Father may be glorified in the Son. If ye shall ask any thing in my name, I will do it. John 14:13-14

Ye have not chosen me, but I have chosen you, and ordained you, that ye should go and bring forth fruit, and that your fruit should remain: that whatsoever ye shall ask of the Father in my name, he may give it you.

John 15:16

And in that day ye shall ask me nothing. Verily, verily, I say unto you, Whatsoever ye shall ask the Father in my name, he will give it you. Hitherto have ye asked nothing in my name: ask, and ye shall receive, that your joy may be full. John 16:23-24

At that day ye shall ask in my name: and I say not unto you, that I will pray the Father for you. John 16:26

Is any sick among you? let him call for the elders of the church; and let them pray over him, anointing him with oil in the name of the Lord.
James 5:14

The Lord's Prayer

After this manner therefore pray ye: Our Father which art in heaven, Hallowed be thy name. Thy kingdom come. Thy will be done in earth, as it is in heaven. Give us this day our daily bread. And forgive us our debts, as we forgive our debtors. And lead us not into temptation, but deliver us from evil: For thine is the kingdom, and the power, and the glory, for ever. Amen. Matthew 6:9-13

God Hears Your Prayers

Am I a God at hand, saith the Lord, and not a God afar off?
Jeremiah 23:23

But know that the Lord hath set apart him that is godly for himself: the Lord will hear when I call unto him. Psalms 4:3

My voice shalt thou hear in the morning, O Lord; in the morning will I direct my prayer unto thee, and will look up. Psalms 5:3

I waited patiently for the Lord; and he inclined unto me, and heard my cry. Psalms 40:1

Evening, and morning, and at noon, will I pray, and cry aloud: and he shall hear my voice. Psalms 55:17

The Lord is far from the wicked: but he heareth the prayer of the righteous. Proverbs 15:29

The eyes of the Lord are upon the righteous, and his ears are open unto their cry. Psalms 34:15

Failure is a temporary detour and should never become a permanent address.

Therefore I will look unto the Lord; I will wait for the God of my salvation: my God will hear me. Micah 7:7

And this is the confidence that we have in him, that, if we ask any thing according to his will, he heareth us: And if we know that he hear us, whatsoever we ask, we know that we have the petitions that we desired of him. 1 John 5:14-15

Hindrances to Prayer

If I regard iniquity in my heart, the Lord will not hear me. Psalms 66:18

Whoso stoppeth his ears at the cry of the poor, he also shall cry himself, but shall not be heard. Proverbs 21:13

He that turneth away his ear from hearing the law, even his prayer shall be abomination. Proverbs 28:9

Behold, the Lord's hand is not shortened, that it cannot save; neither his ear heavy, that it cannot hear: But your iniquities have separated between you and your God, and your sins have hid his face from you, that he will not hear. Isaiah 59:1-2

Then shall they cry unto the Lord, but he will not hear them: he will even hide his face from them at that time, as they have behaved themselves ill in their doings. Micah 3:4

Ye lust, and have not: ye kill, and desire to have, and cannot obtain: ye fight and war, yet ye have not, because ye ask not. Ye ask, and receive not, because ye ask amiss, that ye may consume it upon your lusts.
James 4:2-3

Likewise, ye husbands, dwell with them according to knowledge, giving honour unto the wife, as unto the weaker vessel, and as being heirs together of the grace of life; that your prayers be not hindered. 1 Peter 3:7

For the eyes of the Lord are over the righteous, and his ears are open unto their prayers: but the face of the Lord is against them that do evil. 1 Peter 3:12

Praying with the Right Attitude and Motives

And when thou prayest, thou shalt not be as the hypocrites are: for they love to pray standing in the synagogues and in the corners of the streets, that they may be seen of men. Verily I say unto you, They have their reward. But thou, when thou prayest, enter into thy closet, and when thou hast shut thy door, pray to thy Father which is in secret; and thy

Father which seeth in secret shall reward thee openly. **But** when ye pray, use not vain repetitions, as the heathen do: for they think that they shall be heard for their much speaking. **Be** not ye therefore like unto them: for your Father knoweth what things ye have need of, before ye ask him.

Matthew 6:5-8

Praying only when you are in trouble or when you need something; being thankful only when you get your way; and ignoring God when things are going great, is a terrible way to treat God!

For if ye forgive men their trespasses, your heavenly Father will also forgive you: **But** if ye forgive not men their trespasses, neither will your Father forgive your trespasses. **Moreover** when ye fast, be not, as the hypocrites, of a sad countenance: for they disfigure their faces, that they may appear unto men to fast. Verily I say unto you, They have their reward. **But** thou, when thou fastest, anoint thine head, and wash thy face; **That** thou appear not unto men to fast, but unto thy Father which is in secret: and thy Father, which seeth in secret, shall reward thee openly.

Matthew 6:14-18

And when ye stand praying, forgive, if ye have ought against any: that your Father also which is in heaven may forgive you your trespasses.

Mark 11:25

Different Kinds of Prayer

I cried to thee, O Lord; and unto the Lord I made supplication.

Psalms 30:8

I will offer to thee the sacrifice of thanksgiving, and will call upon the name of the Lord. Psalms 116:17

And I set my face unto the Lord God, to seek by prayer and supplication, with fasting, and sackcloth, and ashes. Daniel 9:3

Praying always with all prayer and supplication in the Spirit, and watching thereunto with all perseverance and supplication for all saints.

Ephesians 6:18

I exhort therefore, that, first of all, supplications, prayers, intercessions, and giving of thanks, be made for all men. 1 Timothy 2:1

The measure of any Christian is his prayer life. - Vance Havner

Prayer of Agreement

How should one chase a thousand, and two put ten thousand to flight.
Deuteronomy 32:30

This is the third time I am coming to you. In the mouth of two or three witnesses shall every word be established. 2 Corinthians 13:1

Verily I say unto you, Whatsoever ye shall bind on earth shall be bound in heaven: and whatsoever ye shall loose on earth shall be loosed in heaven. Again I say unto you, That if two of you shall agree on earth as touching any thing that they shall ask, it shall be done for them of my Father which is in heaven. Matthew 18:18-19

Praying in Faith

Jesus answered and said unto them, Verily I say unto you, If ye have faith, and doubt not, ye shall not only do this which is done to the fig tree, but also if ye shall say unto this mountain, Be thou removed, and be thou cast into the sea; it shall be done. And all things, whatsoever ye shall ask in prayer, believing, ye shall receive. Matthew 21:21-22

Jesus said unto him, If thou canst believe, all things are possible to him that believeth. And straightway the father of the child cried out, and said with tears, Lord, I believe; help thou mine unbelief. Mark 9:23-24

Therefore I say unto you, What things soever ye desire, when ye pray, believe that ye receive them, and ye shall have them. Mark 11:24

And the prayer of faith shall save the sick, and the Lord shall raise him up; and if he have committed sins, they shall be forgiven him James 5:15

Waiting on God in Prayer

But they that wait upon the Lord shall renew their strength; they shall mount up with wings as eagles; they shall run, and not be weary; and they shall walk, and not faint. Isaiah 40:31

Call unto me, and I will answer thee, and shew thee great and mighty things, which thou knowest not. Jeremiah 33:3

Praying in the Holy Spirit

Likewise the Spirit also helpeth our infirmities: for we know not what we should pray for as we ought: but the Spirit itself maketh intercession for us with groanings which cannot be uttered. And he that searcheth the hearts knoweth what is the mind of the Spirit, because he maketh intercession for the saints according to the will of God. Romans 8:26-27

Praying in the Spirit guarantees perfect prayer that is directed by the Holy Spirit; untouched by doubt and fear of the mind; and impossible for the devil to understand or hinder.

For if I pray in an unknown tongue, my spirit prayeth, but my understanding is unfruitful. What is it then? I will pray with the spirit, and I will pray with the understanding also: I will sing with the spirit, and I will sing with the understanding also. 1 Corinthians 14:14-15

But ye, beloved, building up yourselves on your most holy faith, praying in the Holy Ghost. Jude 1:20

Intercessory Prayer

And he saw that there was no man, and wondered that there was no intercessor: therefore his arm brought salvation unto him; and his righteousness, it sustained him. Isaiah 59:16

And I sought for a man among them, that should make up the hedge, and stand in the gap before me for the land, that I should not destroy it: but I found none. Ezekiel 22:30

But I have prayed for thee, that thy faith fail not: and when thou art converted, strengthen thy brethren. Luke 22:32

At that day ye shall ask in my name: and I say not unto you, that I will pray the Father for you. John 16:26

I pray for them: I pray not for the world, but for them which thou hast given me; for they are thine. John 17:9

Neither pray I for these alone, but for them also which shall believe on me through their word. John 17:20

Brethren, my heart's desire and prayer to God for Israel is, that they might be saved. Romans 10:1

Now I beseech you, brethren, for the Lord Jesus Christ's sake, and for the love of the Spirit, that ye strive together with me in your prayers to God for me. Romans 15:30

Leaders see the world while others see the village.

For this cause we also, since the day we heard it, do not cease to pray for you, and to desire that ye might be filled with the knowledge of his will in all wisdom and spiritual understanding. Colossians 1:9

Withal praying also for us, that God would open unto us a door of utterance, to speak the mystery of Christ, for which I am also in bonds.
Colossians 4:3

Wherefore also we pray always for you, that our God would count you worthy of this calling, and fulfil all the good pleasure of his goodness, and the work of faith with power. 2 Thessalonians 1:11

Finally, brethren, pray for us, that the word of the Lord may have free course, and be glorified, even as it is with you: And that we may be delivered from unreasonable and wicked men: for all men have not faith.
2 Thessalonians 3:1-2

Confess your faults one to another, and pray one for another, that ye may be healed. The effectual fervent prayer of a righteous man availeth much.
James 5:16

Examples of Prayer Warriors

And she was a widow of about fourscore and four years, which departed not from the temple, but served God with fastings and prayers night and day. Luke 2:37

And it came to pass in those days, that he went out into a mountain to pray, and continued all night in prayer to God. Luke 6:12

And suddenly there came a sound from heaven as of a rushing mighty wind, and it filled all the house where they were sitting. And there appeared unto them cloven tongues like as of fire, and it sat upon each of them. And they were all filled with the Holy Ghost, and began to speak with other tongues, as the Spirit gave them utterance. Acts 2:2-4

Praying Continuously

Watch and pray, that ye enter not into temptation: the spirit indeed is willing, but the flesh is weak. Matthew 26:41

And he spake a parable unto them to this end, that men ought always to pray, and not to faint. Luke 18:1

Watch ye therefore, and pray always, that ye may be accounted worthy to escape all these things that shall come to pass, and to stand before the Son of man. Luke 21:36

And said unto them, Why sleep ye? rise and pray, lest ye enter into temptation. Luke 22:46

Continue in prayer, and watch in the same with thanksgiving;
Colossians 4:2

Pray without ceasing. 1 Thessalonians 5:17

But the end of all things is at hand: be ye therefore sober, and watch unto prayer. 1 Peter 4:7

To be a Christian without prayer is no more possible than to be alive without breathing. - Martin Luther

THE BELIEVER'S AUTHORITY

The Superior Power and Authority of Christ

For it is written, As I live, saith the Lord, every knee shall bow to me, and every tongue shall confess to God. Romans 14:11

And Jesus came and spake unto them, saying, All power is given unto me in heaven and in earth. Go ye therefore, and teach all nations, baptizing them in the name of the Father, and of the Son, and of the Holy Ghost: Matthew 28:18-19

And what is the exceeding greatness of his power to usward who believe, according to the working of his mighty power, Which he wrought in Christ, when he raised him from the dead, and set him at his own right hand in the heavenly places, Far above all principality, and power, and might, and dominion, and every name that is named, not only in this world, but also in that which is to come: And hath put all things under his feet, and gave him to be the head over all things to the church, Which is his body, the fulness of him that filleth all in all. Ephesians 1:19-23

Who is the image of the invisible God, the firstborn of every creature: For by him were all things created, that are in heaven, and that are in earth, visible and invisible, whether they be thrones, or dominions, or principalities, or powers: all things were created by him, and for him: And he is before all things, and by him all things consist. And he is the head of the body, the church: who is the beginning, the firstborn from the dead; that in all things he might have the preeminence.

Colossians 1:15-18

And ye are complete in him, which is the head of all principality and power: Colossians 2:10

And having spoiled principalities and powers, he made a shew of them openly, triumphing over them in it. Colossians 2:15

Let every soul be subject unto the higher powers. For there is no power but of God: the powers that be are ordained of God. Romans 13:1

249

I am he that liveth, and was dead; and, behold, I am alive for evermore, Amen; and have the keys of hell and of death. Revelation 1:18

But this man, after he had offered one sacrifice for sins for ever, sat down on the right hand of God; From henceforth expecting till his enemies be made his footstool. Hebrews 10:12-13

He that committeth sin is of the devil; for the devil sinneth from the beginning. For this purpose the Son of God was manifested, that he might destroy the works of the devil. 1 John 3:8

You Have Power Over the devil and his demons

And when he had called unto him his twelve disciples, he gave them power against unclean spirits, to cast them out, and to heal all manner of sickness and all manner of disease. Matthew 10:1

Behold, I give unto you power to tread on serpents and scorpions, and over all the power of the enemy: and nothing shall by any means hurt you. Notwithstanding in this rejoice not, that the spirits are subject unto you; but rather rejoice, because your names are written in heaven.
Luke 10:19-20

And when all things shall be subdued unto him, then shall the Son also himself be subject unto him that put all things under him, that God may be all in all. 1 Corinthians 15:28

For God hath not given us the spirit of fear; but of power, and of love, and of a sound mind. 2 Timothy 1:7

Forasmuch then as the children are partakers of flesh and blood, he also himself likewise took part of the same; that through death he might destroy him that had the power of death, that is, the devil; And deliver them who through fear of death were all their lifetime subject to bondage.
Hebrews 2:14-15

Submit yourselves therefore to God. Resist the devil, and he will flee from you. James 4:7

Who is gone into heaven, and is on the right hand of God; angels and authorities and powers being made subject unto him. 1 Peter 3:22

If you are going to be an effective leader, you must be prepared.

Thou shalt bring down the noise of strangers, as the heat in a dry place; even the heat with the shadow of a cloud: the branch of the terrible ones shall be brought low. And he will destroy in this mountain the face of the covering cast over all people, and the veil that is spread over all nations.
Isaiah 25:5,7

For the terrible one is brought to nought, and the scorner is consumed, and all that watch for iniquity are cut off: Isaiah 29:20

No weapon that is formed against thee shall prosper; and every tongue that shall rise against thee in judgment thou shalt condemn. This is the heritage of the servants of the Lord, and their righteousness is of me, saith the Lord. Isaiah 54:17

I am he that liveth, and was dead; and, behold, I am alive for evermore, Amen; and have the keys of hell and of death. Revelation 1:18

Spiritual Warfare

1. The Armor for the Spiritual Realm

   a. Loins girt about with truth

   b. Breastplate of righteousness

   c. Feet shod with the preparation of the gospel of peace

   d. Shield of faith

   e. Helmet of salvation

   f. Sword of the Spirit, which is the Word of God

Finally, my brethren, be strong in the Lord, and in the power of his might. Put on the whole armour of God, that ye may be able to stand against the wiles of the devil. For we wrestle not against flesh and blood, but against principalities, against powers, against the rulers of the darkness of this world, against spiritual wickedness in high places. Wherefore take unto you the whole armour of God, that ye may be able to withstand in the evil day, and having done all, to stand. Stand therefore, having your loins girt about with truth, and having on the breastplate of righteousness; And your feet shod with the preparation of the gospel of peace; Above all, taking the shield of faith, wherewith ye shall be able to quench all the fiery darts of the wicked. And take the helmet of salvation, and the sword of the Spirit, which is the word of God: Ephesians 6:10-17

251

The Weapons of the Spiritual Realm

1. The Name of Jesus

And the seventy returned again with joy, saying, Lord, even the devils are subject unto us through thy name. Luke 10:17

Wherefore God also hath highly exalted him, and given him a name which is above every name: That at the name of Jesus every knee should bow, of things in heaven, and things in earth, and things under the earth;
Philippians 2:9-10

2. The Blood of Jesus

And they (Christians) overcame him (devil) by the blood of the Lamb, and by the word of their testimony; and they loved not their lives unto the death. Revelation 12:11

3. The Sword of the Spirit (The Word of God)

Yea, a sword shall pierce through thy own soul also, that the thoughts of many hearts may be revealed. Luke 2:35

And take the helmet of salvation, and the sword of the Spirit, which is the word of God. Ephesians 6:17

And then shall that Wicked be revealed, whom the Lord shall consume with the spirit of his mouth, and shall destroy with the brightness of his coming. 2 Thessalonians 2:8

For the word of God is quick, and powerful, and sharper than any twoedged sword, piercing even to the dividing asunder of soul and spirit, and of the joints and marrow, and is a discerner of the thoughts and intents of the heart. Hebrews 4:12

And he had in his right hand seven stars: and out of his mouth went a sharp twoedged sword: and his countenance was as the sun shineth in his strength. Revelation 1:16

> *The devil is a spiritual being and the spoken Word of God is the sword of the Spirit. Nothing else cuts, controls, binds, hinders, and defeats the devil and his demons more than a Christian confessing God's Word in faith.*

And to the angel of the church in Pergamos write; These things saith he which hath the sharp sword with two edges. Revelation 2:12

Repent; or else I will come unto thee quickly, and will fight against them with the sword of my mouth. Revelation 2:16

And out of his mouth goeth a sharp sword, that with it he should smite the nations: and he shall rule them with a rod of iron: and he treadeth the winepress of the fierceness and wrath of Almighty God. Revelation 19:15

"Submit yourselves therefore to God. Resist the devil, and he will flee from you." James 4:7

You have to say "yes" to God first before you can effectively say "no" to the devil. - Vance Havner

Binding and Loosing

Verily I say unto you, Whatsoever ye shall bind on earth shall be bound in heaven: and whatsoever ye shall loose on earth shall be loosed in heaven. Matthew 18:18

Or else how can one enter into a strong man's house, and spoil his goods, except he first bind the strong man? and then he will spoil his house.
Matthew 12:29

God's End-Time Army

Ye are of God, little children, and have overcome them: because greater is he that is in you, than he that is in the world. 1 John 4:4

Neither shall one thrust another; they shall walk every one in his path: and when they fall upon the sword, they shall not be wounded. They shall run to and fro in the city; they shall run upon the wall, they shall climb up upon the houses; they shall enter in at the windows like a thief. The earth shall quake before them; the heavens shall tremble: the sun and the moon shall be dark, and the stars shall withdraw their shining: And the Lord shall utter his voice before his army: for his camp is very great: for he is strong that executeth his word: for the day of the Lord is great and very terrible; and who can abide it? Joel 2:7-11

Spiritual Enemies

For though we walk in the flesh, we do not war after the flesh: For the weapons of our warfare are not carnal, but mighty through God to the pulling down of strong holds; Casting down imaginations, and every high thing that exalteth itself against the knowledge of God, and bringing into captivity every thought to the obedience of Christ;
2 Corinthians 10:3-5

253

For we wrestle not against flesh and blood, but against principalities, against powers, against the rulers of the darkness of this world, against spiritual wickedness in high places. Ephesians 6:12

Attacking the Enemy

And they blessed Rebekah, and said unto her, Thou art our sister, be thou the mother of thousands of millions, and let thy seed possess the gate of those which hate them. Genesis 24:60

And I say also unto thee, That thou art Peter, and upon this rock I will build my church; and the gates of hell shall not prevail against it.
Matthew 16:18

And I tell you, you are Peter [petros, masculine, a large piece of rock], and on this rock [petr a, feminine, a huge rock like Gibraltar] I will build My church, and the gates of Hades (the powers of the infernal region shall not overpower it–or be strong to its detriment, or hold out against it. Matthew 16:18 AMP

And from the days of John the Baptist until now the kingdom of heaven suffereth violence, and the violent take it by force. Matthew 11:12

And from the days of John the Baptist until the present time the kingdom of heaven has endured violent assault, and violent men seize it by force [as a precious prize]–a share in the heavenly kingdom is sought for with most ardent zeal and intense exertion. Matthew 11:12 AMP

And ye shall chase your enemies, and they shall fall before you by the sword. And five of you shall chase an hundred, and an hundred of you shall put ten thousand to flight: and your enemies shall fall before you by the sword. For I will have respect unto you, and make you fruitful, and multiply you, and establish my covenant with you. Leviticus 26:7-9

How should one chase a thousand, and two put ten thousand to flight, except their Rock had sold them, and the Lord had shut them up?
Deuteronomy 32:30

Quenched the violence of fire, escaped the edge of the sword, out of weakness were made strong, waxed valiant in fight, turned to flight the armies of the aliens. Hebrews 11:34

One man of you shall chase a thousand: for the Lord your God, he it is that fighteth for you, as he hath promised you. Joshua 23:10

A thousand shall fall at thy side, and ten thousand at thy right hand; but it shall not come nigh thee. Psalms 91:7

THE BELIEVER'S PLACE AND IDENTITY IN JESUS CHRIST

In Christ

But he that is joined unto the Lord is one spirit. 1 Corinthians 6:17

Abide in me, and I in you. As the branch cannot bear fruit of itself, except it abide in the vine; no more can ye, except ye abide in me.
John 15:4

If ye abide in me, and my words abide in you, ye shall ask what ye will, and it shall be done unto you. John 15:7

For who hath known the mind of the Lord, that he may instruct him? But we have the mind of Christ. 1 Corinthians 2:16

Being justified freely by his grace through the redemption that is in Christ Jesus. Romans 3:24

There is therefore now no condemnation to them which are in Christ Jesus, who walk not after the flesh, but after the Spirit. For the law of the Spirit of life in Christ Jesus hath made me free from the law of sin and death. Romans 8:1-2

Nor height, nor depth, nor any other creature, shall be able to separate us from the love of God, which is in Christ Jesus our Lord. Romans 8:39

So we, being many, are one body in Christ, and every one members one of another. Romans 12:5

Unto the church of God which is at Corinth, to them that are sanctified in Christ Jesus, called to be saints, with all that in every place call upon the name of Jesus Christ our Lord, both theirs and ours. 1 Corinthians 1:2

But of him are ye in Christ Jesus, who of God is made unto us wisdom, and righteousness, and sanctification, and redemption. 1 Corinthians 1:30

We are fools for Christ's sake, but ye are wise in Christ; we are weak, but ye are strong; ye are honourable, but we are despised. 1 Corinthians 4:10

For though ye have ten thousand instructors in Christ, yet have ye not many fathers: for in Christ Jesus I have begotten you through the gospel. 1 Corinthians 4:15

For as in Adam all die, even so in Christ shall all be made alive. 1 Corinthians 15:22

I protest by your rejoicing which I have in Christ Jesus our Lord, I die daily. 1 Corinthians 15:31

Now he which stablisheth us with you in Christ, and hath anointed us, is God; 2 Corinthians 1:21

Now thanks be unto God, which always causeth us to triumph in Christ, and maketh manifest the savour of his knowledge by us in every place. 2 Corinthians 2:14

But their minds were blinded: for until this day remaineth the same vail untaken away in the reading of the old testament; which vail is done away in Christ. 2 Corinthians 3:14

Therefore if any man be in Christ, he is a new creature: old things are passed away; behold, all things are become new. 2 Corinthians 5:17

To wit, that God was in Christ, reconciling the world unto himself, not imputing their trespasses unto them; and hath committed unto us the word of reconciliation. 2 Corinthians 5:19

And that because of false brethren unawares brought in, who came in privily to spy out our liberty which we have in Christ Jesus, that they might bring us into bondage: Galatians 2:4

And this I say, that the covenant, that was confirmed before of God in Christ, the law, which was four hundred and thirty years after, cannot disannul, that it should make the promise of none effect. Galatians 3:17

For ye are all the children of God by faith in Christ Jesus. Galatians 3:26

There is neither Jew nor Greek, there is neither bond nor free, there is neither male nor female: for ye are all one in Christ Jesus. Galatians 3:28

For in Jesus Christ neither circumcision availeth anything, nor uncircumcision; but faith which worketh by love. Galatians 5:6

A good leader remains optimistic.

For in Christ Jesus neither circumcision availeth anything, nor uncircumcision, but a new creature. Galatians 6:15

Blessed be the God and Father of our Lord Jesus Christ, who hath blessed us with all spiritual blessings in heavenly places in Christ. Ephesians 1:3

That in the dispensation of the fulness of times he might gather together in one all things in Christ, both which are in heaven, and which are on earth; even in him. Ephesians 1:10

That we should be to the praise of his glory, who first trusted in Christ.
Ephesians 1:12

Which he wrought in Christ, when he raised him from the dead, and set him at his own right hand in the heavenly places. Ephesians 1:20

And hath raised us up together, and made us sit together in heavenly places in Christ Jesus. Ephesians 2:6

For we are his workmanship, created in Christ Jesus unto good works, which God hath before ordained that we should walk in them.
Ephesians 2:10

But now in Christ Jesus ye who sometimes were far off are made nigh by the blood of Christ. Ephesians 2:13

That the Gentiles should be fellowheirs, and of the same body, and partakers of his promise in Christ by the gospel. Ephesians 3:6

If there be therefore any consolation in Christ, if any comfort of love, if any fellowship of the Spirit, if any bowels and mercies. Philippians 2:1

Let this mind be in you, which was also in Christ Jesus. Philippians 2:5

For we are the circumcision, which worship God in the spirit, and rejoice in Christ Jesus, and have no confidence in the flesh. Philippians 3:3

Brethren, I count not myself to have apprehended: but this one thing I do, forgetting those things which are behind, and reaching forth unto those things which are before, **I** press toward the mark for the prize of the high calling of God in Christ Jesus. Philippians 3:13-14

Since we heard of your faith in Christ Jesus, and of the love which ye have to all the saints. Colossians 1:4

Whom we preach, warning every man, and teaching every man in all wisdom; that we may present every man perfect in Christ Jesus.
Colossians 1:20

For though I be absent in the flesh, yet am I with you in the spirit, joying and beholding your order, and the stedfastness of your faith in Christ.
Colossians 2:5

For the Lord himself shall descend from heaven with a shout, with the voice of the archangel, and with the trump of God: and the dead in Christ shall rise first: 1 Thessalonians 4:16

In every thing give thanks: for this is the will of God in Christ Jesus concerning you. 1 Thessalonians 5:18

And the grace of our Lord was exceeding abundant with faith and love which is in Christ Jesus. 1 Timothy 1:14

For they that have used the office of a deacon well purchase to themselves a good degree, and great boldness in the faith which is in Christ Jesus. 1 Timothy 3:13

Who hath saved us, and called us with an holy calling, not according to our works, but according to his own purpose and grace, which was given us in Christ Jesus before the world began. 2 Timothy 1:9

Hold fast the form of sound words, which thou hast heard of me, in faith and love which is in Christ Jesus. 2 Timothy 1:13

Thou therefore, my son, be strong in the grace that is in Christ Jesus.
2 Timothy 2:1

Therefore I endure all things for the elect's sakes, that they may also obtain the salvation which is in Christ Jesus with eternal glory.
2 Timothy 2:10

Yea, and all that will live godly in Christ Jesus shall suffer persecution.
2 Timothy 3:12

And that from a child thou hast known the holy scriptures, which are able to make thee wise unto salvation through faith which is in Christ Jesus. 2 Timothy 3:15

That the communication of thy faith may become effectual by the acknowledging of every good thing which is in you in Christ Jesus.
Philemon 1:6

Wherefore, though I might be much bold in Christ to enjoin thee that which is convenient. Philemon 1:8

Having a good conscience; that, whereas they speak evil of you, as of evildoers, they may be ashamed that falsely accuse your good conversation in Christ. 1 Peter 3:16

For if these things be in you, and abound, they make you that ye shall neither be barren nor unfruitful in the knowledge of our Lord Jesus Christ.
2 Peter 1:8

Whosoever transgresseth, and abideth not in the doctrine of Christ, hath not God. He that abideth in the doctrine of Christ, he hath both the Father and the Son. 2 John 1:9

By Christ

Even the righteousness of God which is by faith of Jesus Christ unto all and upon all them that believe: for there is no difference. Romans 3:22

But not as the offence, so also is the free gift. For if through the offence of one many be dead, much more the grace of God, and the gift by grace, which is by one man, Jesus Christ, hath abounded unto many.
Romans 5:15

For if by one man's offence death reigned by one; much more they which receive abundance of grace and of the gift of righteousness shall reign in life by one, Jesus Christ. Therefore as by the offence of one judgment came upon all men to condemnation; even so by the righteousness of one the free gift came upon all men unto justification of life. For as by one man's disobedience many were made sinners, so by the obedience of one shall many be made righteous. Romans 5:17-19

Wherefore, my brethren, ye also are become dead to the law by the body of Christ; that ye should be married to another, even to him who is raised from the dead, that we should bring forth fruit unto God. Romans 7:4

I thank my God always on your behalf, for the grace of God which is given you by Jesus Christ. 1 Corinthians 1:4

For as the sufferings of Christ abound in us, so our consolation also aboundeth by Christ. 2 Corinthians 1:5

And all things are of God, who hath reconciled us to himself by Jesus Christ, and hath given to us the ministry of reconciliation.
2 Corinthians 5:18

Knowing that a man is not justified by the works of the law, but by the faith of Jesus Christ, even we have believed in Jesus Christ, that we might be justified by the faith of Christ, and not by the works of the law: for by the works of the law shall no flesh be justified. But if, while we seek to be justified by Christ, we ourselves also are found sinners, is therefore Christ the minister of sin? God forbid. Galatians 2:16-17

259

Having predestinated us unto the adoption of children by Jesus Christ to himself, according to the good pleasure of his will. Ephesians 1:5

Unto him be glory in the church by Christ Jesus throughout all ages, world without end. Amen. Ephesians 3:21

Being filled with the fruits of righteousness, which are by Jesus Christ, unto the glory and praise of God. Philippians 1:11

But my God shall supply all your need according to his riches in glory by Christ Jesus. Philippians 4:19

Blessed be the God and Father of our Lord Jesus Christ, which according to his abundant mercy hath begotten us again unto a lively hope by the resurrection of Jesus Christ from the dead. 1 Peter 1:3

Ye also, as lively stones, are built up a spiritual house, an holy priesthood, to offer up spiritual sacrifices, acceptable to God by Jesus Christ.
1 Peter 2:5

But the God of all grace, who hath called us unto his eternal glory by Christ Jesus, after that ye have suffered a while, make you perfect, stablish, strengthen, settle you. 1 Peter 5:10

In Him

In him was life; and the life was the light of men. John 1:4

But to us there is but one God, the Father, of whom are all things, and we in him; and one Lord Jesus Christ, by whom are all things, and we by him. 1 Corinthians 8:6

For all the promises of God in him are yea, and in him Amen, unto the glory of God by us. 2 Corinthians 1:20

For he hath made him to be sin for us, who knew no sin; that we might be made the righteousness of God in him. 2 Corinthians 5:21

For though he was crucified through weakness, yet he liveth by the power of God. For we also are weak in him, but we shall live with him by the power of God toward you. 2 Corinthians 13:4

According as he hath chosen us in him before the foundation of the world, that we should be holy and without blame before him in love.
Ephesians. 1:4

Success without a successor is failure.

That in the dispensation of the fulness of times he might gather together in one all things in Christ, both which are in heaven, and which are on earth; even in him. Ephesians 1:10

And be found in him, not having mine own righteousness, which is of the law, but that which is through the faith of Christ, the righteousness which is of God by faith. Philippians 3:9

For it pleased the Father that in him should all fulness dwell.
Colossians 1:19

As ye have therefore received Christ Jesus the Lord, so walk ye in him. Rooted and built up in him, and stablished in the faith, as ye have been taught, abounding therein with thanksgiving. Colossians 2:6-7

For in him dwelleth all the fulness of the Godhead bodily. And ye are complete in him, which is the head of all principality and power.
Colossians 2:9-10

That the name of our Lord Jesus Christ may be glorified in you, and ye in him, according to the grace of our God and the Lord Jesus Christ.
2 Thessalonians 1:12

And again, I will put my trust in him. And again, Behold I and the children which God hath given me. Hebrews 2:13

Now the just shall live by faith: but if any man draw back, my soul shall have no pleasure in him. Hebrews 10:38

This then is the message which we have heard of him, and declare unto you, that God is light, and in him is no darkness at all. 1 John 1:5

But the anointing which ye have received of him abideth in you, and ye need not that any man teach you: but as the same anointing teacheth you of all things, and is truth, and is no lie, and even as it hath taught you, ye shall abide in him. And now, little children, abide in him; that, when he shall appear, we may have confidence, and not be ashamed before him at his coming. 1 John 2:27-28

And every man that hath this hope in him purifieth himself, even as he is pure. 1 John 3:3

Whosoever abideth in him sinneth not: whosoever sinneth hath not seen him, neither known him. 1 John 3:5-6

Hereby know we that we dwell in him, and he in us, because he hath given us of his Spirit. 1 John 4:13

And this is the confidence that we have in him, that, if we ask any thing according to his will, he heareth us. 1 John 5:14

And we know that the Son of God is come, and hath given us an understanding, that we may know him that is true, and we are in him that is true, even in his Son Jesus Christ. This is the true God, and eternal life.
1 John 5:20

By Him

That in every thing ye are enriched by him, in all utterance, and in all knowledge; 1 Corinthians 1:5

But to us there is but one God, the Father, of whom are all things, and we in him; and one Lord Jesus Christ, by whom are all things, and we by him. 1 Corinthians 8:6

For by him were all things created, that are in heaven, and that are in earth, visible and invisible, whether they be thrones, or dominions, or principalities, or powers: all things were created by him, and for him: And he is before all things, and by him all things consist.
Colossians 1:16-17

And, having made peace through the blood of his cross, by him to reconcile all things unto himself; by him, I say, whether they be things in earth, or things in heaven. Colossians 1:20

And whatsoever ye do in word or deed, do all in the name of the Lord Jesus, giving thanks to God and the Father by him. Colossians 3:17

Wherefore he is able also to save them to the uttermost that come unto God by him, seeing he ever liveth to make intercession for them.
Hebrews 7:25

By him therefore let us offer the sacrifice of praise to God continually, that is, the fruit of our lips giving thanks to his name. Hebrews 13:15

Who by him do believe in God, that raised him up from the dead, and gave him glory; that your faith and hope might be in God. 1 Peter 1:21

Through Christ

Therefore being justified by faith, we have peace with God through our Lord Jesus Christ. Romans 5:1

And not only so, but we also joy in God through our Lord Jesus Christ, by whom we have now received the atonement. Romans 5:11

Likewise reckon ye also yourselves to be dead indeed unto sin, but alive unto God through Jesus Christ our Lord. Romans 6:11

For the wages of sin is death; but the gift of God is eternal life through Jesus Christ our Lord. Romans 6:23

But thanks be to God, which giveth us the victory through our Lord Jesus Christ. 1 Corinthians 15:57

And such trust have we through Christ to God-ward. 2 Corinthians 3:4

Christ hath redeemed us from the curse of the law, being made a curse for us: for it is written, Cursed is every one that hangeth on a tree: That the blessing of Abraham might come on the Gentiles through Jesus Christ; that we might receive the promise of the Spirit through faith.
Galatians 3:13-14

Wherefore thou art no more a servant, but a son; and if a son, then an heir of God through Christ. Galatians 4:7

That in the ages to come he might shew the exceeding riches of his grace in his kindness toward us through Christ Jesus. Ephesians 2:7

Be careful for nothing; but in every thing by prayer and supplication with thanksgiving let your requests be made known unto God.
Philippians 4:6

And the peace of God, which passeth all understanding, shall keep your hearts and minds through Christ Jesus. Philippians 4:7

I can do all things through Christ which strengtheneth me.
Philippians 4:13

By the which will we are sanctified through the offering of the body of Jesus Christ once for all. Hebrews 10:10

Now the God of peace, that brought again from the dead our Lord Jesus, that great shepherd of the sheep, through the blood of the everlasting covenant, Make you perfect in every good work to do his will, working in you that which is wellpleasing in his sight, through Jesus Christ; to whom be glory for ever and ever. Amen. Hebrews 13:20-21

Of Christ

For we are unto God a sweet savour of Christ, in them that are saved, and in them that perish. 2 Corinthians 2:15

Not as though I had already attained, either were already perfect: but I follow after, if that I may apprehend that for which also I am apprehended of Christ Jesus. Philippians 3:12

Which are a shadow of things to come; but the body is of Christ.
Colossians 2:17

Knowing that of the Lord ye shall receive the reward of the inheritance: for ye serve the Lord Christ. Colossians 3:24

With Christ

Now if we be dead with Christ, we believe that we shall also live with him. Romans 6:8

I am crucified with Christ: nevertheless I live; yet not I, but Christ liveth in me: and the life which I now live in the flesh I live by the faith of the Son of God, who loved me, and gave himself for me. Galatians 2:20

Even when we were dead in sins, hath quickened us together with Christ, by grace ye are saved. Ephesians 2:5

Wherefore if ye be dead with Christ from the rudiments of the world, why, as though living in the world, are ye subject to ordinances.
Colossians 2:20

If ye then be risen with Christ, seek those things which are above, where Christ sitteth on the right hand of God. Colossians 3:1

For ye are dead, and your life is hid with Christ in God. Colossians 3:3

By Himself

Who being the brightness of his glory, and the express image of his person, and upholding all things by the word of his power, when he had by himself purged our sins, sat down on the right hand of the Majesty on high. Hebrews 1:3

For then must he often have suffered since the foundation of the world: but now once in the end of the world hath he appeared to put away sin by the sacrifice of himself. Hebrews 9:26

Great leaders love knowledge; they always want to know.

By Whom

By whom also we have access by faith into this grace wherein we stand, and rejoice in hope of the glory of God. Romans 5:2

And not only so, but we also joy in God through our Lord Jesus Christ, by whom we have now received the atonement. Romans 5:11

But God forbid that I should glory, save in the cross of our Lord Jesus Christ, by whom the world is crucified unto me, and I unto the world.
Galatians 6:14

From Whom

From whom the whole body fitly joined together and compacted by that which every joint supplieth, according to the effectual working in the measure of every part, maketh increase of the body unto the edifying of itself in love. Ephesians 4:16

And not holding the Head, from which all the body by joints and bands having nourishment ministered, and knit together, increaseth with the increase of God. Colossians 2:19

In Whom

Who delivered us from so great a death, and doth deliver: in whom we trust that he will yet deliver us. 2 Corinthians 1:10

In whom we have redemption through his blood, the forgiveness of sins, according to the riches of his grace. Ephesians 1:7

In whom also we have obtained an inheritance, being predestinated according to the purpose of him who worketh all things after the counsel of his own will. Ephesians 1:11

In whom ye also trusted, after that ye heard the word of truth, the gospel of your salvation: in whom also after that ye believed, ye were sealed with that holy Spirit of promise. Ephesians 1:13

And are built upon the foundation of the apostles and prophets, Jesus Christ himself being the chief corner stone; In whom all the building fitly framed together groweth unto an holy temple in the Lord: In whom ye also are builded together for an habitation of God through the Spirit.
Ephesians 2:20-22

In whom we have boldness and access with confidence by the faith of him. Ephesians 3:12

265

In whom we have redemption through his blood, even the forgiveness of sins. Colossians 1:14

In whom are hid all the treasures of wisdom and knowledge.
Colossians 2:3

In whom also ye are circumcised with the circumcision made without hands, in putting off the body of the sins of the flesh by the circumcision of Christ. Colossians 2:11

Whom having not seen, ye love; in whom, though now ye see him not, yet believing, ye rejoice with joy unspeakable and full of glory.
1 Peter 1:8

Of Him

This then is the message which we have heard of him, and declare unto you, that God is light, and in him is no darkness at all. 1 John 1:5

But the anointing which ye have received of him abideth in you, and ye need not that any man teach you: but as the same anointing teacheth you of all things, and is truth, and is no lie, and even as it hath taught you, ye shall abide in him. 1 John 2:27

Through Him

For God sent not his Son into the world to condemn the world; but that the world through him might be saved. John 3:17

Much more then, being now justified by his blood, we shall be saved from wrath through him. Romans 5:9

Nay, in all these things we are more than conquerors through him that loved us. Romans 8:37

In this was manifested the love of God toward us, because that God sent his only begotten Son into the world, that we might live through him.
1 John 4:9

With Christ

Now if we be dead with Christ, we believe that we shall also live with him. Romans 6:8

I am crucified with Christ: nevertheless I live; yet not I, but Christ liveth in me: and the life which I now live in the flesh I live by the faith of the Son of God, who loved me, and gave himself for me. Galatians 2:20

Even when we were dead in sins, hath quickened us together with Christ, by grace ye are saved. Ephesians 2:5

Wherefore if ye be dead with Christ from the rudiments of the world, why, as though living in the world, are ye subject to ordinances.
Colossians 2:20

If ye then be risen with Christ, seek those things which are above, where Christ sitteth on the right hand of God. Set your affection on things above, not on things on the earth. For ye are dead, and your life is hid with Christ in God Colossians 3:1-3

With Him

Therefore we are buried with him by baptism into death: that like as Christ was raised up from the dead by the glory of the Father, even so we also should walk in newness of life. Romans 6:4

Knowing this, that our old man is crucified with him, that the body of sin might be destroyed, that henceforth we should not serve sin. Romans 6:6

He that spared not his own Son, but delivered him up for us all, how shall he not with him also freely give us all things? Romans 8:32

For though he was crucified through weakness, yet he liveth by the power of God. For we also are weak in him, but we shall live with him by the power of God toward you. 2 Corinthians 13:4

Buried with him in baptism, wherein also ye are risen with him through the faith of the operation of God, who hath raised him from the dead.
Colossians 2:12

And you, being dead in your sins and the uncircumcision of your flesh, hath he quickened together with him, having forgiven you all trespasses; Blotting out the handwriting of ordinances that was against us, which was contrary to us, and took it out of the way, nailing it to his cross; And having spoiled principalities and powers, he made a shew of them openly, triumphing over them in it. Colossians 2:13-15

When Christ, who is our life, shall appear, then shall ye also appear with him in glory. Colossians 3:4

It is a faithful saying: For if we be dead with him, we shall also live with him: If we suffer, we shall also reign with him: if we deny him, he also will deny us. 2 Timothy 2:11-12

THE NAME OF JESUS

The Different Names of Jesus

Advocate with the Father .... 1 John 2:1

Alpha and Omega .... Revelation 22:13

Almighty, The .... Revelation 1:8

Amen, The .... Revelation 3:14

Apostle, The .... Hebrews 3:1

Author and Finisher of Our Faith .... Hebrews 12:2

Beginning, The .... Colossians 1:18

Beginning and the End .... Revelation 21:6, 22:13

Beginning of the Creation of God .... Revelation 3:14

Begotten of God .... 1 John 5:18

Beloved, The .... Ephesians 1:6

Blessed Hope .... Titus 2:13

Bishop of Your Souls .... 1 Peter 2:25

Branch, The .... Isaiah 11:1, Matthew 2:23

Branch of Righteousness .... Jeremiah 33:15

Bridegroom .... Matthew 9:15

Bright and Morning Star .... Revelation 22:16

Bread of Life .... John 6:35

Captain of the Lord's Host .... Joshua 5:15

Chief Corner Stone .... 1 Peter 2:6

Chiefest Among Ten Thousand .... Song of Solomon 5:10

Christ, The .... John 1:41

Consolation .... Luke 2:25

Cornerstone .... Ephesians 2:20

Counsellor .... Isaiah 9:6

Day Spring, The .... Luke 1:78

Day Star, The .... 2 Peter 1:19

Deliverer, The .... Romans 11:26

Door, The .... John 10:9

Elect, The .... 1 Peter 2:6

269

Emmanuel .... Matthew 1:23
Eternal Life .... 1 John 5:20
Everlasting Father .... Isaiah 9:6
Faithful, The .... Revelation 3:14
Faithful Witness .... Revelation 1:5
Faithful and True .... Revelation 19:11
First Begotten .... Hebrews 1:6
First Begotten of the Dead .... Revelation 1:5
First and the Last .... Revelation 22:13
Firstborn .... Psalms 89:27
Firstborn Among Many Brethren .... Romans 8:29
Firstborn From the Dead .... Colossians 1:18
Firstborn of Every Creature .... Colossians 1:15
Firstfruit, The .... 1 Corinthians 15:23
Glorious Lord .... Isaiah 33:21
God .... John 1:1, Isaiah 9:6
God with Us .... Matthew 1:23
Good Shepherd .... John 10:11
Governor .... Matthew 2:6
Great High Priest .... Hebrews 4:14
Head of the Body .... Colossians 1:18
Head of the Church .... Ephesians 5:23
Head Over All Things .... Ephesians 1:22
Head Stone of the Corner .... Psalms 118:22
Heir of All Things .... Hebrews 1:2
High Priest .... Hebrews 3:1
Holy One of Israel .... Isaiah 41:14
Hope of Glory .... Colossians 1:27
I Am .... John 8:58
Image of the Invisible God .... Colossians 1:15
Immanuel .... Isaiah 7:14
King .... Zechariah 9:9
King Eternal .... 1 Timothy 1:17
King of Glory .... Psalms 24:7
King of Kings .... 1 Timothy 6:15
King Over All the Earth .... Zechariah 14:9
Lamb of God .... John 1:29

**A leader must have a proper
estimation of himself in Christ Jesus.**

Last Adam .... 1 Corinthians 15:45
Life, The .... John 14:6
Light of the Gentiles .... Isaiah 42:6
Light of the World .... John 8:12
Lily of the Valleys .... Song of Solomon 2:1
Living Bread .... John 6:51
Lord and Saviour .... 2 Peter 2:20
Lord of All .... Acts 10:36
Lord of Lords .... 1 Timothy 6:15
Lord Our Righteousness .... Jeremiah 23:6
Lord God Almighty .... Revelation 4:8
Love .... 1 John 4:8
Made Perfect .... Hebrews 5:9
Man .... 1 Timothy 2:5
Master .... Matthew 23:10
Messiah .... Daniel 9:25-26, John 1:41
Mighty God .... Isaiah 9:6
Most Mighty .... Psalms 45:3
Nazarene .... Matthew 2:23
Offspring of David .... Revelation 22:16
Only Begotten of the Father .... John 1:14
Only Wise God, The .... 1 Timothy 1:17
Our Lord .... Romans 8:39
Our Passover .... 1 Corinthians 5:7
Our Profession .... Hebrews 3:1
Precious .... 1 Peter 2:6
Precious Corner Stone .... Isaiah 28:16
Prince of Peace .... Isaiah 9:6
Prince of the Kings of the Earth .... Revelation 1:5
Propitiation, The .... Romans 3:25
Rabbi .... John 1:49
Redeemer .... Isaiah 41:14
Root, The .... Revelation 22:16
Root of Jesse .... Isaiah 11:10
Rose of Sharon .... Song of Solomon 2:1
Resurrection, The .... John 11:25
Righteous, The .... 1 John 2:1
Saviour .... Titus 2:13
Saviour of the World .... 1 John 4:14
Second Man, The .... 1 Corinthians 15:47
Seed of David .... Romans 1:3

Shepherd .... 1 Peter 2:25
Son of God .... Romans 1:4
Son of Man .... Acts 7:56, John 7:42
Son of Mary .... Mark 6:3
Son of the Highest .... Luke 1:32
Spiritual Rock .... 1 Corinthians 10:4
Star Out of Jacob .... Numbers 24:17
Stone, The .... Matthew 21:42, Psalms 118:22
Sun of Righteousness .... Malachi 4:2
True .... 1 John 5:20
True Vine .... John 15:1
True Witness .... Revelation 3:14
Truth, The .... John 14:6
Unspeakable Gift .... 2 Corinthians 9:15
Way, The .... John 14:6
Which Is .... Revelation 1:8
Which Was .... Revelation 1:8
Which is to Come .... Revelation 1:8
Wisdom of God .... 1 Corinthians 1:24
Wonderful .... Isaiah 9:6
Word, The .... John 1:14
Word of God, The .... Revelation 19:13

The Name Above All Names

Wherefore God also hath highly exalted him, and given him a name which is above every name: That at the name of Jesus every knee should bow, of things in heaven, and things in earth, and things under the earth; And that every tongue should confess that Jesus Christ is Lord, to the glory of God the Father. Philippians 2:9-11

Being made so much better than the angels, as he hath by inheritance obtained a more excellent name than they. Hebrews 1:4

Praying in the Name of Jesus

Again I say unto you, That if two of you shall agree on earth as touching any thing that they shall ask, it shall be done for them of my Father which is in heaven. For where two or three are gathered together in my name, there am I in the midst of them. Matthew 18:19-20

And whatsoever ye shall ask in my name, that will I do, that the Father may be glorified in the Son. If ye shall ask any thing in my name, I will do it. John 14:13-14

Ye have not chosen me, but I have chosen you, and ordained you, that ye should go and bring forth fruit, and that your fruit should remain: that whatsoever ye shall ask of the Father in my name, he may give it you.
John 15:16

And in that day ye shall ask me nothing. Verily, verily, I say unto you, Whatsoever ye shall ask the Father in my name, he will give it you. Hitherto have ye asked nothing in my name: ask, and ye shall receive, that your joy may be full. John 16:23-24

At that day ye shall ask in my name: and I say not unto you, that I will pray the Father for you. John 16:26

Is any sick among you? let him call for the elders of the church; and let them pray over him, anointing him with oil in the name of the Lord.
James 5:14

Power in the Name of Jesus

And these signs shall follow them that believe; In my name shall they cast out devils; they shall speak with new tongues; They shall take up serpents; and if they drink any deadly thing, it shall not hurt them; they shall lay hands on the sick, and they shall recover. Mark 16:17-18

And the seventy returned again with joy, saying, Lord, even the devils are subject unto us through thy name. Luke 10:17

But as many as received him, to them gave he power to become the sons of God, even to them that believe on his name. John 1:12

Then Peter said, Silver and gold have I none; but such as I have give I thee: In the name of Jesus Christ of Nazareth rise up and walk. Acts 3:6

And his name through faith in his name hath made this man strong, whom ye see and know: yea, the faith which is by him hath given him this perfect soundness in the presence of you all. Acts 3:16

And when they had set them in the midst, they asked, By what power, or by what name, have ye done this? Then Peter, filled with the Holy Ghost, said unto them, Ye rulers of the people, and elders of Israel, Be it known unto you all, and to all the people of Israel, that by the name of Jesus Christ of Nazareth, whom ye crucified, whom God raised from the dead, even by him doth this man stand here before you whole. Acts 4:7-8,10

And this did she many days. But Paul, being grieved, turned and said to the spirit, I command thee in the name of Jesus Christ to come out of her. And he came out the same hour. Acts 16:18

The name of the Lord is a strong tower: the righteous runneth into it, and is safe. Proverbs 18:10

Believing in the Name of Jesus

He that believeth on him is not condemned: but he that believeth not is condemned already, because he hath not believed in the name of the only begotten Son of God. John 3:18

But these are written, that ye might believe that Jesus is the Christ, the Son of God; and that believing ye might have life through his name.
John 20:31

And it shall come to pass, that whosoever shall call on the name of the Lord shall be saved. Acts 2:21

Then Peter said unto them, Repent, and be baptized every one of you in the name of Jesus Christ for the remission of sins, and ye shall receive the gift of the Holy Ghost. Acts 2:38

Neither is there salvation in any other: for there is none other name under heaven given among men, whereby we must be saved. Acts 4:12

To him give all the prophets witness, that through his name whosoever believeth in him shall receive remission of sins. Acts 10:43

For whosoever shall call upon the name of the Lord shall be saved.
Romans 10:13

And in his name shall the Gentiles trust. Matthew 12:21

And this is his commandment, That we should believe on the name of his Son Jesus Christ, and love one another, as he gave us commandment.
1 John 3:23

These things have I written unto you that believe on the name of the Son of God; that ye may know that ye have eternal life, and that ye may believe on the name of the Son of God. 1 John 5:13

Now when he was in Jerusalem at the passover, in the feast day, many believed in his name, when they saw the miracles which he did.
John 2:23

Great leaders are ordinary people who did extraordinary things because circumstances made demands on their potential.

Serving in the Name of Jesus

For whosoever shall give you a cup of water to drink in my name, because ye belong to Christ, verily I say unto you, he shall not lose his reward. Mark 9:41

And whatsoever ye do in word or deed, do all in the name of the Lord Jesus, giving thanks to God and the Father by him. Colossians 3:17

For God is not unrighteous to forget your work and labour of love, which ye have shewed toward his name, in that ye have ministered to the saints, and do minister. Hebrews 6:10

Suffering for the Name of Jesus

And every one that hath forsaken houses, or brethren, or sisters, or father, or mother, or wife, or children, or lands, for my name's sake, shall receive an hundredfold, and shall inherit everlasting life. Matthew 19:29

Remember the word that I said unto you, The servant is not greater than his lord. If they have persecuted me, they will also persecute you; if they have kept my saying, they will keep yours also. But all these things will they do unto you for my name's sake, because they know not him that sent me. John 15:20-21

And Jesus answered and said, Verily I say unto you, There is no man that hath left house, or brethren, or sisters, of father, or mother, or wife, or children, of lands, for my sake, and the gospel's. But he shall receive an hundredfold now in this time, houses, and brethren, and sisters, and mothers, and children, and lands, with persecutions; and in the world to come eternal life. Mark 10:29-30

And to him they agreed: and when they had called the apostles, and beaten them, they commanded that they should not speak in the name of Jesus, and let them go. And they departed from the presence of the council, rejoicing that they were counted worthy to suffer shame for his name. And daily in the temple, and in every house, they ceased not to teach and preach Jesus Christ. Acts 5:40-42

If ye be reproached for the name of Christ, happy are ye; for the spirit of glory and of God resteth upon you: on their part he is evil spoken of, but on your part he is glorified. 1 Peter 4:14

God's Word

The Integrity of God's Word

God is not a man, that he should lie; neither the son of man, that he should repent: hath he said, and shall he not do it? or hath he spoken, and shall he not make it good? Numbers 23:19

Know therefore that the Lord thy God, he is God, the faithful God, which keepeth covenant and mercy with them that love him and keep his commandments to a thousand generations. Deuteronomy 7:9

And, behold, this day I am going the way of all the earth: and ye know in all your hearts and in all your souls, that not one thing hath failed of all the good things which the Lord your God spake concerning you; all are come to pass unto you, and not one thing hath failed thereof.
Joshua 23:14

The Lord of hosts hath sworn, saying, Surely as I have thought, so shall it come to pass; and as I have purposed, so shall it stand: Isaiah 14:24

And also the Strength of Israel will not lie nor repent: for he is not a man, that he should repent. 1 Samuel 15:29

The grass withereth, the flower fadeth: but the word of our God shall stand for ever. Isaiah 40:8

Blessed be the Lord, that hath given rest unto his people Israel, according to all that he promised: there hath not failed one word of all his good promise, which he promised by the hand of Moses his servant.
1 Kings 8:56

By the word of the Lord were the heavens made; and all the host of them by the breath of his mouth. Psalms 33:6

For he spake, and it was done; he commanded, and it stood fast.
Psalms 33:9

My covenant will I not break, nor alter the thing that is gone out of my lips. Psalms 89:34

He hath remembered his covenant for ever, the word which he commanded to a thousand generations. Psalms 105:8

He hath given meat unto them that fear him: he will ever be mindful of his covenant. Psalms 111:5

All thy commandments are faithful. Psalms 119:86

For ever, O Lord, thy word is settled in heaven. Psalms 119:89

Thy word is true from the beginning: and every one of thy righteous judgments endureth for ever. Psalms 119:160

I will worship toward thy holy temple, and praise thy name for thy lovingkindness and for thy truth: for thou hast magnified thy word above all thy name. Psalms 138:2

Every word of God is pure: he is a shield unto them that put their trust in him. Proverbs 30:5

I have spoken it, I will also bring it to pass; I have purposed it, I will also do it. Isaiah 46:11

For as the rain cometh down, and the snow from heaven, and returneth not thither, but watereth the earth, and maketh it bring forth and bud, that it may give seed to the sower, and bread to the eater: So shall my word be that goeth forth out of my mouth: it shall not return unto me void, but it shall accomplish that which I please, and it shall prosper in the thing whereto I sent it. Isaiah 55:10-11

I the Lord have spoken it: it shall come to pass, and I will do it; I will not go back, neither will I spare, neither will I repent; according to thy ways, and according to thy doings, shall they judge thee, saith the Lord God.
Ezekiel 24:14

Heaven and earth shall pass away: but my words shall not pass away.
Mark 13:31

Sanctify them through thy truth: thy word is truth. John 17:17

And being fully persuaded that, what he had promised, he was able also to perform. Romans 4:21

As a leader, you cannot "drive" people; you must "lead" them.

For all the promises of God in him are yea, and in him Amen, unto the glory of God by us. 2 Corinthians 1:20

In hope of eternal life, which God, that cannot lie, promised before the world began. Titus 1:2

Hath in these last days spoken unto us by his Son, whom he hath appointed heir of all things, by whom also he made the worlds; Who being the brightness of his glory, and the express image of his person, and upholding all things by the word of his power, when he had by himself purged our sins, sat down on the right hand of the Majesty on high.
Hebrews 1:2-3

And being fully persuaded that, what he had promised, he was able also to perform. Romans 4:21

That by two immutable things, in which it was impossible for God to lie, we might have a strong consolation, who have fled for refuge to lay hold upon the hope set before us. Hebrews 6:18

Through faith we understand that the worlds were framed by the word of God, so that things which are seen were not made of things which do appear. Hebrews 11:3

Jesus Christ the same yesterday, and today, and forever. Hebrews 13:8

Being born again, not of corruptible seed, but of incorruptible, by the word of God, which liveth and abideth for ever. 1 Peter 1:23

But the word of the Lord endureth for ever. And this is the word which by the gospel is preached unto you. 1 Peter 1:25

The Lord is not slack concerning his promise, as some men count slackness; but is longsuffering to us-ward, not willing that any should perish, but that all should come to repentance. 2 Peter 3:9

> *His promises are checks to be cashed, not mere mottoes to hang on the wall! - Vance Havner*

God's Word is Spiritual Food

But he answered and said, It is written, Man shall not live by bread alone, but by every word that proceedeth out of the mouth of God. Matthew 4:4

And Jesus answered him, saying, It is written, That man shall not live by bread alone, but by every word of God. Luke 4:4

But he said unto them, I have meat to eat that ye know not of. John 4:32

Labour not for the meat which perisheth, but for that meat which endureth unto everlasting life, which the Son of man shall give unto you: for him hath God the Father sealed. John 6:27

Then Jesus said unto them, Verily, verily, I say unto you, Moses gave you not that bread from heaven; but my Father giveth you the true bread from heaven. For the bread of God is he which cometh down from heaven, and giveth life unto the world. Then said they unto him, Lord, evermore give us this bread. And Jesus said unto them, I am the bread of life: he that cometh to me shall never hunger; and he that believeth on me shall never thirst. John 6:32-35

> Hunger for God's Word is not a natural appetite. We are not born with it. It comes with the new birth when we begin with milk and should go on to meat. - Vance Havner

I am the living bread which came down from heaven: if any man eat of this bread, he shall live for ever: and the bread that I will give is my flesh, which I will give for the life of the world. John 6:51

This is that bread which came down from heaven: not as your fathers did eat manna, and are dead: he that eateth of this bread shall live for ever.
John 6:58

So when they had dined, Jesus saith to Simon Peter, Simon, son of Jonas, lovest thou me more than these? He saith unto him, Yea, Lord; thou knowest that I love thee. He saith unto him, Feed my lambs. He saith to him again the second time, Simon, son of Jonas, lovest thou me? He saith unto him, Yea, Lord; thou knowest that I love thee. He saith unto him, Feed my sheep. John 21:15-16

And I, brethren, could not speak unto you as unto spiritual, but as unto carnal, even as unto babes in Christ. I have fed you with milk, and not with meat: for hitherto ye were not able to bear it, neither yet now are ye able. For ye are yet carnal: for whereas there is among you envying, and strife, and divisions, are ye not carnal, and walk as men?
1 Corinthians 3:1-3

And did all eat the same spiritual meat; And did all drink the same spiritual drink: for they drank of that spiritual Rock that followed them: and that Rock was Christ. 1 Corinthians 10:3-4

For when for the time ye ought to be teachers, ye have need that one teach you again which be the first principles of the oracles of God; and are become such as have need of milk, and not of strong meat. For every one that useth milk is unskilful in the word of righteousness: for he is a babe. **B**ut strong meat belongeth to them that are of full age, even those who by reason of use have their senses exercised to discern both good and evil. Hebrews 5:12-14

As newborn babes, desire the sincere milk of the word, that ye may grow thereby. 1 Peter 2:2

The Word of God in the Heart

I delight to do thy will, O my God: yea, thy law is within my heart.
Psalms 40:8

I have not hid thy righteousness within my heart; I have declared thy faithfulness and thy salvation. Psalms 40:10

Thy word have I hid in mine heart, that I might not sin against thee.
Psalms 119:11

Incline my heart unto thy testimonies, and not to covetousness.
Psalms 119:36

Let my heart be sound in thy statutes; that I be not ashamed.
Psalms 119:80

My son, forget not my law; but let thine heart keep my commandments.
Proverbs 3:1

He taught me also, and said unto me, Let thine heart retain my words: keep my commandments, and live. Proverbs 4:4

> *It is not the Word hidden in the head but in the heart that keeps us from sin. - Vance Havner*

My son, attend to my words; incline thine ear unto my sayings. **L**et them not depart from thine eyes; keep them in the midst of thine heart. **F**or they are life unto those that find them, and health to all their flesh. **K**eep thy heart with all diligence; for out of it are the issues of life.
Proverbs 4:20-23

My son, keep thy father's commandment, and forsake not the law of thy mother: **B**ind them continually upon thine heart, and tie them about thy neck. Proverbs 6:20-21

My son, keep my words, and lay up my commandments with thee. **K**eep my commandments, and live; and my law as the apple of thine eye. **B**ind them upon thy fingers, write them upon the table of thine heart.
Proverbs 7:1-3

281

He that soweth iniquity shall reap vanity: and the rod of his anger shall fail. Proverbs 22:8

Bow down thine ear, and hear the words of the wise, and apply thine heart unto my knowledge. Proverbs 22:17

But this shall be the covenant that I will make with the house of Israel; After those days, saith the Lord, I will put my law in their inward parts, and write it in their hearts; and will be their God, and they shall be my people. Jeremiah 31:33

But what saith it? The word is nigh thee, even in thy mouth, and in thy heart: that is, the word of faith, which we preach. Romans 10:8

This is the covenant that I will make with them after those days, saith the Lord, I will put my laws into their hearts, and in their minds will I write them. Hebrews 10:16

Ye are our epistle written in our hearts, known and read of all men: Forasmuch as ye are manifestly declared to be the epistle of Christ ministered by us, written not with ink, but with the Spirit of the living God; not in tables of stone, but in fleshy tables of the heart.

2 Corinthians 3:2-3

1. Different Ways the Word of God is Taken Out of the Heart of Man

a. Not understanding the Word of God

When any one heareth the word of the kingdom, and understandeth it not, then cometh the wicked one, and catcheth away that which was sown in his heart. This is he which received seed by the way side. Matthew 13:19

While any one is hearing the Word of the kingdom and does not grasp and comprehend it, the evil one comes and snatches away what is sown in his heart. This is what was sown along the roadside.

Matthew 13:19 AMP

b. Tribulation and persecution

But he that received the seed into stony places, the same is he that heareth the word, and anon with joy receiveth it; Yet hath he not root in himself, but dureth for a while: for when tribulation or persecution ariseth because of the word, by and by he is offended.

Matthew 13:20-21

If you are not willing to stand alone in your vision, not many will be willing to stand with you.

As for what was sown on thin (rocky) soil, this is he who hears the Word and at once welcomes and accepts it with joy. Yet it has no real root in himself, but is temporary–inconstant, lasts but a little while and when affliction or trouble or persecution comes on account of the Word, at once he is caused to stumble–he is repelled and begins to distrust and desert Him Whom he ought to trust and obey, and he falls away. Matthew 13:20-21 AMP

c. The cares of this world and deceitfulness of riches

He also that received seed among the thorns is he that heareth the word; and the care of this world, and the deceitfulness of riches, choke the word, and he becometh unfruitful. Matthew 13:22

As for what was sown among thorns, this is he who hears the Word, but the cares of the world and the pleasure and delight and glamour and deceitfulness of riches choke and suffocate the Word and it yields no fruit. Matthew 13:22 AMP

d. satan will try to steal the Word of God

And these are they by the way side, where the word is sown; but when they have heard, Satan cometh immediately, and taketh away the word that was sown in their hearts. Mark 4:15

The ones along the path are those who have the Word sown [in their hearts], but when they hear, satan comes at once and (by force) takes away the message which is sown in them. Mark 4:15 AMP

2. A Good Heart for the Word of God

But he that received seed into the good ground is he that heareth the word, and understandeth it; which also beareth fruit, and bringeth forth, some an hundredfold, some sixty, some thirty. Matthew 13:23

And these are they which are sown on good ground; such as hear the word, and receive it, and bring forth fruit, some thirtyfold, some sixty, and some an hundred. Mark 4:20

And those that were sown on the good (well-adapted) soil are the ones who hear the Word, and receive and accept and welcome it and bear fruit, some thirty times as much as was sown, some sixty times as much, and some [even] a hundred times as much. Mark 4:20 AMP

Meditating on God's Word

Definitions for Meditating

1. To care for, to attend to, practice, to ponder, or imagine
2. To pass some time thinking in a quiet way; reflect
3. To plan or consider

This book of the law shall not depart out of thy mouth; but thou shalt meditate therein day and night, that thou mayest observe to do according to all that is written therein: for then thou shalt make thy way prosperous, and then thou shalt have good success. Joshua 1:8

But his delight is in the law of the Lord; and in his law doth he meditate day and night. Psalms 1:2

Give ear to my words, O Lord, consider my meditation. Psalms 5:1

Let the words of my mouth, and the meditation of my heart, be acceptable in thy sight, O Lord, my strength, and my redeemer. Psalms 19:14

My mouth shall speak of wisdom; and the meditation of my heart shall be of understanding. Psalms 49:3

When I remember thee upon my bed, and meditate on thee in the night watches. Psalms 63:6

I will meditate also of all thy work, and talk of thy doings. Psalms 77:12

My meditation of him shall be sweet: I will be glad in the Lord.
Psalms 104:34

I will meditate in thy precepts, and have respect unto thy ways.
Psalms 119:15

Princes also did sit and speak against me: but thy servant did meditate in thy statutes. Psalms 119:23

My hands also will I lift up unto thy commandments, which I have loved; and I will meditate in thy statutes. Psalms 119:48

God does not give the soul a vacation, He gives it a vocation.
- Vance Havner

Let the proud be ashamed; for they dealt perversely with me without a cause: but I will meditate in thy precepts. Psalms 119:78

O how love I thy law! it is my meditation all the day. Psalms 119:97

I have more understanding than all my teachers: for thy testimonies are my meditation. Psalms 119:99

Mine eyes prevent the night watches, that I might meditate in thy word. Psalms 119:148

I remember the days of old; I meditate on all thy works; I muse on the work of thy hands. Psalms 143:5

Till I come, give attendance to reading, to exhortation, to doctrine. **Meditate upon these things; give thyself wholly to them; that thy profiting may appear to all. 1 Timothy 4:13,15**

How to Obtain Promises From God's Word

1. Confess the Word of God

And take not the word of truth utterly out of my mouth; for I have hoped in thy judgments. Psalms 119:43

My tongue shall speak of thy word: for all thy commandments are righteousness. Psalms 119:172

We having the same spirit of faith, according as it is written, I believed, and therefore have I spoken; we also believe, and therefore speak.
2 Corinthians 4:13

Fight the good fight of faith, lay hold on eternal life, whereunto thou art also called, and hast professed a good profession before many witnesses.
1 Timothy 6:12

Seeing then that we have a great high priest, that is passed into the heavens, Jesus the Son of God, let us hold fast our profession. Hebrews 4:14

Let us hold fast the profession of our faith without wavering; for he is faithful that promised. Hebrews 10:23

But what saith it? The word is nigh thee, even in thy mouth, and in thy heart: that is, the word of faith, which we preach. Romans 10:8

Say unto them, As truly as I live, saith the Lord, as ye have spoken in mine ears, so will I do to you. Numbers 14:28

2. Remain Patient

But that on the good ground are they, which in an honest and good heart, having heard the word, keep it, and bring forth fruit with patience.
Luke 8:15

For whatsoever things were written aforetime were written for our learning, that we through patience and comfort of the scriptures might have hope. Romans 15:4

And let us not be weary in well doing: for in due season we shall reap, if we faint not. Galatians 6:9

For all the promises of God in him are yea, and in him Amen, unto the glory of God by us. 2 Corinthians 1:20

That ye be not slothful, but followers of them who through faith and patience inherit the promises. Hebrews 6:12

And so, after he had patiently endured, he obtained the promise.

Hebrews 6:15

Just as faith without works is dead, so is faith without patience.

Cast not away therefore your confidence, which hath great recompence of reward. For ye have need of patience, that, after ye have done the will of God, ye might receive the promise. For yet a little while, and he that shall come will come, and will not tarry. Hebrews 10:35-37

Who through faith subdued kingdoms, wrought righteousness, obtained promises, stopped the mouths of lions. Hebrews 11:33

3. Do Not Doubt the Ability of God and His Word

But let him ask in faith, nothing wavering. For he that wavereth is like a wave of the sea driven with the wind and tossed. For let not that man think that he shall receive any thing of the Lord. A double minded man is unstable in all his ways. James 1:6-8

Only it must be in faith that he asks, with no wavering—no hesitating, no doubting. For the one who wavers (hesitates, doubts) is like the billowing surge out at sea, that is blown hither and thither and tossed by the wind. For truly, let not such a person imagine that he will receive anything [he asks for] from the Lord, [For being as he is] a man of two minds—hesitating, dubious, irresolute—[he is] unstable and unreliable and uncertain about everything (he thinks, feels, decides). James 1:6-8 AMP

And Jesus answering saith unto them, Have faith in God. For verily I say unto you, That whosoever shall say unto this mountain, Be thou removed, and be thou cast into the sea; and shall not doubt in his heart, but shall

> **Effective leadership is the perfect balance of competence, vision and virtue.**

believe that those things which he saith shall come to pass; he shall have whatsoever he saith. Therefore I say unto you, What things soever ye desire, when ye pray, believe that ye receive them, and ye shall have them. Mark 11:22-24

He staggered not at the promise of God through unbelief; but was strong in faith, giving glory to God; Romans 4:20

Well; because of unbelief they were broken off, and thou standest by faith. Be not highminded, but fear: Romans 11:20

That is true. But they were broken (pruned) off because of their unbelief–their lack of real faith, and you are established through faith–because you do believe. So do not become proud and conceited, but rather stand in awe and be reverently afraid. Romans 11:20 AMP

And he did not many mighty works there because of their unbelief.
                                                                    Matthew 13:58

The Cleansing of the Word of God

Wherewithal shall a young man cleanse his way? by taking heed thereto according to thy word. Psalms 119:9

Seeing ye have purified your souls in obeying the truth through the Spirit unto unfeigned love of the brethren, see that ye love one another with a pure heart fervently. 1 Peter 1:22

Having therefore these promises, dearly beloved, let us cleanse ourselves from all filthiness of the flesh and spirit, perfecting holiness in the fear of God. 2 Corinthians 7:1

That he might sanctify and cleanse it with the washing of water by the word. Ephesians 5:26

The words of the Lord are pure words: as silver tried in a furnace of earth, purified seven times. Psalms 12:6

The statutes of the Lord are right, rejoicing the heart: the commandment of the Lord is pure, enlightening the eyes. Psalms 19:8

And now, brethren, I commend you to God, and to the word of his grace, which is able to build you up, and to give you an inheritance among all them which are sanctified. Acts 20:32

Memorizing the Word of God

And ye shall know the truth, and the truth shall make you free. John 8:32

That ye may remember, and do all my commandments, and be holy unto your God. Numbers 15:40

Beware that thou forget not the Lord thy God, in not keeping his commandments, and his judgments, and his statutes, which I command thee this day. Deuteronomy 8:11

But the mercy of the Lord is from everlasting to everlasting upon them that fear him, and his righteousness unto children's children. To such as keep his covenant, and to those that remember his commandments to do them. Psalms 103:17-18

I will delight myself in thy statutes: I will not forget thy word.
Psalms 119:16

For I am become like a bottle in the smoke; yet do I not forget thy statutes. Psalms 119:83

I will never forget thy precepts: for with them thou hast quickened me.
Psalms 119:93

I am small and despised: yet do not I forget thy precepts. Psalms 119:141

My son, forget not my law; but let thine heart keep my commandments.
Proverbs 3:1

By which also ye are saved, if ye keep in memory what I preached unto you, unless ye have believed in vain. 1 Corinthians 15:2

But whoso looketh into the perfect law of liberty, and continueth therein, he being not a forgetful hearer, but a doer of the work, this man shall be blessed in his deed. James 1:25

But, beloved, remember ye the words which were spoken before of the apostles of our Lord Jesus Christ. Jude 1:17

Guidance from God's Word

Thou shalt guide me with thy counsel, and afterward receive me to glory.
Psalms 73:24

Thy word is a lamp unto my feet, and a light unto my path. Psalms 119:105

Order my steps in thy word: and let not any iniquity have dominion over me. Psalms 119:133

I thought on my ways, and turned my feet unto thy testimonies.
Psalms 119:59

The entrance of thy words giveth light; it giveth understanding unto the simple. Psalms 119:130

All scripture is given by inspiration of God, and is profitable for doctrine, for reproof, for correction, for instruction in righteousness. That the man of God may be perfect, thoroughly furnished unto all good works.
2 Timothy 3:16-17

For whatsoever things were written aforetime were written for our learning, that we through patience and comfort of the scriptures might have hope. Romans 15:4

The Spoken Word of God

1. Is the Sword of the Spirit

Yea, a sword shall pierce through thy own soul also, that the thoughts of many hearts may be revealed. Luke 2:35

And take the helmet of salvation, and the sword of the Spirit, which is the word of God. Ephesians 6:17

For the word of God is quick, and powerful, and sharper than any twoedged sword, piercing even to the dividing asunder of soul and spirit, and of the joints and marrow, and is a discerner of the thoughts and intents of the heart. Hebrews 4:12

And then shall that Wicked be revealed, whom the Lord shall consume with the spirit of his mouth, and shall destroy with the brightness of his coming. 2 Thessalonians 2:8

And he had in his right hand seven stars: and out of his mouth went a sharp twoedged sword: and his countenance was as the sun shineth in his strength. Revelation 1:16

And to the angel of the church in Pergamos write; These things saith he which hath the sharp sword with two edges. Revelation 2:12

Repent; or else I will come unto thee quickly, and will fight against them with the sword of my mouth. Revelation 2:16

And out of his mouth goeth a sharp sword, that with it he should smite the nations: and he shall rule them with a rod of iron: and he treadeth the winepress of the fierceness and wrath of Almighty God. Revelation 19:15

2. Gives Faith to the Believer

So then faith cometh by hearing, and hearing by the word of God.
Romans 10:17

3. Convicts and Converts the Unbeliever

For whosoever shall call upon the name of the Lord shall be saved. **H**ow then shall they call on him in whom they have not believed? and how shall they believe in him of whom they have not heard? and how shall they hear without a preacher? Romans 10:13-14

Now when they heard this, they were pricked in their heart, and said unto Peter and to the rest of the apostles, Men and brethren, what shall we do? Acts 2:37

4. Angers the Sinner

When they heard that, they were cut to the heart, and took counsel to slay them. Acts 5:33

When they heard these things, they were cut to the heart, and they gnashed on him with their teeth. Acts 7:54

5. Will Cast Out demon spirits

When the even was come, they brought unto him many that were possessed with devils: and he cast out the spirits with his word, and healed all that were sick: Matthew 8:16

> *Jesus met the devil not in His own name, not in His own power, but with the Scriptures: "It is written... It is written..." If he could defeat the devil with three verses out of Deuteronomy, we ought to be able to do it with the whole Bible. - Vance Havner*

6. Puts satan to Flight

And when the tempter came to him, he said, If thou be the Son of God, command that these stones be made bread. **B**ut he answered and said, it is written, man shall not live by bread alone, but by every word that proceedeth out of the mouth of God. **T**hen the devil taketh him up into the holy city, and setteth him on a pinnacle of the temple, **A**nd saith unto him, If thou be the Son of God, cast thyself down: for it is written, He shall give his angels charge concerning thee: and in their hands they shall bear thee up, lest at any time thou dash thy foot against a stone. **J**esus said unto him, it is written again, thou shalt not tempt the Lord thy God. **A**gain, the devil taketh him up into an exceeding high mountain, and sheweth him all the kingdoms of the world, and the glory of them; **A**nd saith unto him, All these things will I give thee, if thou wilt fall down and worship me. **T**hen saith Jesus unto him, get thee hence, satan: for it is written, Thou shalt worship the Lord thy God, and him only shalt thou serve. **T**hen the devil leaveth him, and, behold, angels came and ministered unto him. Matthew 4:3-11

THE KEYS OF SUCCESS

Direction

Thou wilt shew me the path of life: in thy presence is fulness of joy; at thy right hand there are pleasures for evermore. Psalms 16:11

Shew me thy ways, O Lord; teach me thy paths. Lead me in thy truth, and teach me: for thou art the God of my salvation; on thee do I wait all the day. Psalms 25:4-5

The meek will he guide in judgment: and the meek will he teach his way. All the paths of the Lord are mercy and truth unto such as keep his covenant and his testimonies. Psalms 25:9-10

I will instruct thee and teach thee in the way which thou shalt go: I will guide thee with mine eye. Psalms 32:8

The steps of a good man are ordered by the Lord: and he delighteth in his way. Though he fall, he shall not be utterly cast down: for the Lord upholdeth him with his hand. Psalms 37:23-24

For this God is our God for ever and ever: he will be our guide even unto death. Psalms 48:14

> *Once God speaks to you, do not confer with flesh and blood any longer.*

Nevertheless I am continually with thee: thou hast holden me by my right hand. Thou shalt guide me with thy counsel, and afterward receive me to glory. Psalms 73:23-24

So he fed them according to the integrity of his heart; and guided them by the skilfulness of his hands. Psalms 78:72

For he shall give his angels charge over thee, to keep thee in all thy ways. Psalms 91:11

The Lord shall preserve thy going out and thy coming in from this time forth, and even for evermore. Psalms 121:8

The Lord will perfect that which concerneth me: thy mercy, O Lord, endureth for ever: forsake not the works of thine own hands.
Psalms 138:8

He keepeth the paths of judgment, and preserveth the way of his saints.
Proverbs 2:8

Trust in the Lord with all thine heart; and lean not unto thine own understanding. In all thy ways acknowledge him, and he shall direct thy paths.
Proverbs 3:5-6

The integrity of the upright shall guide them: but the perverseness of transgressors shall destroy them. Proverbs 11:3

Without counsel purposes are disappointed: but in the multitude of counsellers they are established. Proverbs 15:22

Commit thy works unto the Lord, and thy thoughts shall be established.
Proverbs 16:3

Blessed is the man who finds out which way God is moving and then gets going in the same direction. - Anonymous.

A man's heart deviseth his way: but the Lord directeth his steps.
Proverbs 16:9

Man's goings are of the Lord; how can a man then understand his own way? Proverbs 20:24

And many people shall go and say, Come ye, and let us go up to the mountain of the Lord, to the house of the God of Jacob; and he will teach us of his ways, and we will walk in his paths: for out of Zion shall go forth the law, and the word of the Lord from Jerusalem. Isaiah 2:3

For his God doth instruct him to discretion, and doth teach him.
Isaiah 28:26

And thine ears shall hear a word behind thee, saying, This is the way, walk ye in it, when ye turn to the right hand, and when ye turn to the left.
Isaiah 30:21

**When you have tasted possibilities, it is
very difficult to settle for impossibilities.**

And I will bring the blind by a way that they knew not; I will lead them in paths that they have not known: I will make darkness light before them, and crooked things straight. These things will I do unto them, and not forsake them. Isaiah 42:16

I will go before thee, and make the crooked places straight: I will break in pieces the gates of brass, and cut in sunder the bars of iron. Isaiah 45:2

I have raised him up in righteousness, and I will direct all his ways: he shall build my city, and he shall let go my captives, not for price nor reward, saith the Lord of hosts. Isaiah 45:13

Thus saith the Lord, thy Redeemer, the Holy One of Israel; I am the Lord thy God which teacheth thee to profit, which leadeth thee by the way that thou shouldest go. Isaiah 48:17

I have seen his ways, and will heal him: I will lead him also, and restore comforts unto him and to his mourners. Isaiah 57:18

But seek ye first the kingdom of God, and his righteousness; and all these things shall be added unto you. Matthew 6:33

And when he putteth forth his own sheep, he goeth before them, and the sheep follow him: for they know his voice. And a stranger will they not follow, but will flee from him: for they know not the voice of strangers.
John 10:4-5

My sheep hear my voice, and I know them, and they follow me:
John 10:27

Howbeit when he, the Spirit of truth, is come, he will guide you into all truth: for he shall not speak of himself; but whatsoever he shall hear, that shall he speak: and he will shew you things to come. John 16:13

This I say then, Walk in the Spirit, and ye shall not fulfil the lust of the flesh. Galatians 5:16

For it is God which worketh in you both to will and to do of his good pleasure. Philippians 2:13

If any of you lack wisdom, let him ask of God, that giveth to all men liberally, and upbraideth not; and it shall be given him. James 1:15

But ye have an unction from the Holy One, and ye know all things.
1 John 2:20

I know thy works: behold, I have set before thee an open door, and no man can shut it: for thou hast a little strength, and hast kept my word, and hast not denied my name. Revelation 3:8

Favor from God

And the child Samuel grew on, and was in favour both with the Lord, and also with men. 1 Samuel 2:26

For thou, Lord, wilt bless the righteous; with favour wilt thou compass him as with a shield. Psalms 5:12

For his anger endureth but a moment; in his favour is life: weeping may endure for a night, but joy cometh in the morning. Psalms 30:5

Lord, by thy favour thou hast made my mountain to stand strong: thou didst hide thy face, and I was troubled. Psalms 30:7

By this I know that thou favourest me, because mine enemy doth not triumph over me. Psalms 41:11

A good man sheweth favour, and lendeth: he will guide his affairs with discretion. Psalms 112:5

I entreated thy favour with my whole heart: be merciful unto me according to thy word. Psalms 119:58

For whoso findeth me findeth life, and shall obtain favour of the Lord.
Proverbs 8:35

A good man obtaineth favour of the Lord: but a man of wicked devices will he condemn. Proverbs 12:2

So shalt thou find favour and good understanding in the sight of God and man. Proverbs 3:4

And Jesus increased in wisdom and stature, and in favour with God and man. Luke 2:52

Decisions

And let the peace of God rule in your hearts, to the which also ye thankful. Colossians 3:15

1. Say "No"
   a. When it's contrary to God's Word
   b. When you have prayed and God has said "no"
   c. When you feel manipulated
   d. When you feel intimidated
   e. When you feel uneasy
   f. When you feel hesitant
   g. When you feel pushed

    h. When you feel used
    i. When you feel rushed
    j. When you feel unsure
    k. When it's an unrealistic offer
    l. When you feel condemned
    m. When you feel guilty
    n. When you feel convicted
    o. When you haven't sought godly counsel

2. Say "Yes"

    a. When it's in agreement with God's Word
    b. When you have prayed and received a confirmation from God
    c. When you feel at peace in your spirit
    d. When you have thoroughly thought out the consequences
    e. When you have sought godly counsel

Diligence

Thou hast commanded us to keep thy precepts diligently. Psalms 119:4

Therefore came I forth to meet thee, diligently to seek thy face, and I have found thee. Proverbs 7:15

He that diligently seeketh good procureth favour: but he that seeketh mischief, it shall come unto him. Proverbs 11:27

When thou sittest to eat with a ruler, consider diligently what is before thee. Proverbs 23:1

And we have sent with them our brother, whom we have oftentimes proved diligent in many things, but now much more diligent, upon the great confidence which I have in you. 2 Corinthians 8:22

Wherefore the rather, brethren, give diligence to make your calling and election sure: for if ye do these things, ye shall never fall. 2 Peter 1:10

Wherefore, beloved, seeing that ye look for such things, be diligent that ye may be found of him in peace, without spot, and blameless.

2 Peter 3:14

> *Destiny is not a matter of chance, it is a matter of choice; it is not a thing to be waited for, it is a thing to be achieved. - William Jennings Bryan*

1. Diligence in Work and Business

The hand of the diligent shall bear rule: but the slothful shall be under tribute. Proverbs 12:24

The slothful man roasteth not that which he took in hunting: but the substance of a diligent man is precious. Proverbs 12:27

The soul of the sluggard desireth, and hath nothing: but the soul of the diligent shall be made fat. Proverbs 13:4

The thoughts of the diligent tend only to plenteousness; but of every one that is hasty only to want. Proverbs 21:5

Seest thou a man diligent in his business? he shall stand before kings; he shall not stand before mean men. Proverbs 22:29

Be thou diligent to know the state of thy flocks, and look well to thy herds. For riches are not for ever: and doth the crown endure to every generation? Proverbs 27:23-24

People can be divided into three groups: Those who make things happen, those who watch things happen, and those who wonder what happenned. - John W. Newbern

Wise and Godly Counsel

A wise man will hear, and will increase learning; and a man of understanding shall attain unto wise counsels. Proverbs 1:5

But whoso hearkeneth unto me shall dwell safely, and shall be quiet from fear of evil. Proverbs 1:33

Hear, O my son, and receive my sayings; and the years of thy life shall be many. Proverbs 4:10

Hear instruction, and be wise, and refuse it not. Proverbs 8:33

He is in the way of life that keepeth instruction: but he that refuseth reproof erreth. Proverbs 10:17

Whoso loveth instruction loveth knowledge: but he that hateth reproof is brutish. Proverbs 12:1

Poverty and shame shall be to him that refuseth instruction: but he that regardeth reproof shall be honoured. Proverbs 13:18

The ear that heareth the reproof of life abideth among the wise. He that refuseth instruction despiseth his own soul: but he that heareth reproof getteth understanding. Proverbs 15:31-32

If you are willing to pay the price of fatigue, then you are willing to lead.

A reproof entereth more into a wise man than an hundred stripes into a fool. Proverbs 17:10

Hear counsel, and receive instruction, that thou mayest be wise in thy latter end. Proverbs 19:20

Buy the truth, and sell it not; also wisdom, and instruction, and understanding. Proverbs 23:23

For the commandment is a lamp; and the law is light; and reproofs of instruction are the way of life. Proverbs 6:23

Faithfulness

O love the Lord, all ye his saints: for the Lord preserveth the faithful, and plentifully rewardeth the proud doer. Psalms 31:23

Mine eyes shall be upon the faithful of the land, that they may dwell with me: he that walketh in a perfect way, he shall serve me. Psalms 101:6

A talebearer revealeth secrets: but he that is of a faithful spirit concealeth the matter. Proverbs 11:13

A wicked messenger falleth into mischief: but a faithful ambassador is health. Proverbs 13:17

Most men will proclaim every one his own goodness: but a faithful man who can find? Proverbs 20:6

Confidence in an unfaithful man in time of trouble is like a broken tooth, and a foot out of joint. Proverbs 25:19

> *The ability to accept responsibility is the measure of the man. - Roy L. Smith*

A faithful man shall abound with blessings: but he that maketh haste to be rich shall not be innocent. Proverbs 28:20

His lord said unto him, Well done, good and faithful servant; thou hast been faithful over a few things, I will make thee ruler over many things: enter thou into the joy of thy lord. Matthew 25:23

And the Lord said, Who then is that faithful and wise steward, whom his lord shall make ruler over his household, to give them their portion of meat in due season? **B**lessed is that servant, whom his lord when he cometh shall find so doing. Luke 12:42-43

If therefore ye have not been faithful in the unrighteous mammon, who will commit to your trust the true riches? And if ye have not been faithful in that which is another man's, who shall give you that which is your own? Luke 16:11-12

The greatest ability is dependability. - Vance Havner

Rejoicing in hope; patient in tribulation; continuing instant in prayer.
Romans 12:12

God is faithful, by whom ye were called unto the fellowship of his Son Jesus Christ our Lord. 1 Corinthians 1:9

Moreover it is required in stewards, that a man be found faithful.
1 Corinthians 4:2

And I thank Christ Jesus our Lord, who hath enabled me, for what he counted me faithful, putting me into the ministry. 1 Timothy 1:12

Who was faithful to him that appointed him, as also Moses was faithful in all his house. Hebrews 3:2

And Moses verily was faithful in all his house, as a servant, for a testimony of those things which were to be spoken after; But Christ as a son over his own house; whose house are we, if we hold fast the confidence and the rejoicing of the hope firm unto the end. Hebrews 3:5-6

Beloved, thou doest faithfully whatsoever thou doest to the brethren, and to strangers. 3 John 1:5

Here is the patience of the saints: here are they that keep the commandments of God, and the faith of Jesus. Revelation 14:12

Few ever die from commitment, perseverance, faith, and achievement, but many die from neglected responsibilities, impatience, doubt and unfulfilled dreams.

Overcoming Laziness

Go to the ant, thou sluggard; consider her ways, and be wise: Which having no guide, overseer, or ruler, Provideth her meat in the summer, and gathereth her food in the harvest. How long wilt thou sleep, O sluggard? when wilt thou arise out of thy sleep? Yet a little sleep, a little slumber, a little folding of the hands to sleep: So shall thy poverty come as one that travelleth, and thy want as an armed man. Proverbs 6:6-11

He becometh poor that dealeth with a slack hand: but the hand of the diligent maketh rich. Proverbs 10:4

The labour of the righteous tendeth to life: the fruit of the wicked to sin. Proverbs 10:16

The hand of the diligent shall bear rule: but the slothful shall be under tribute. Proverbs 12:24

The way of the slothful man is as an hedge of thorns: but the way of the righteous is made plain. Proverbs 15:19

Yet a little sleep, a little slumber, a little folding of the hands to sleep: So shall thy poverty come as one that travelleth; and thy want as an armed man. Proverbs 24:33-34

In the morning sow thy seed, and in the evening withhold not thine hand: for thou knowest not whether shall prosper, either this or that, or whether they both shall be alike good. Ecclesiastes 11:6

Not slothful in business; fervent in spirit; serving the Lord. Romans 12:11

Neither did we eat any man's bread for nought; but wrought with labour and travail night and day, that we might not be chargeable to any of you. 2 Thessalonians 3:8

For we hear that there are some which walk among you disorderly, working not at all, but are busybodies. Now them that are such we command and exhort by our Lord Jesus Christ, that with quietness they work, and eat their own bread. 2 Thessalonians 3:11-12

But if any provide not for his own, and specially for those of his own house, he hath denied the faith, and is worse than an infidel. 1 Timothy 5:8

And withal they learn to be idle, wandering about from house to house; and not only idle, but tattlers also and busybodies, speaking things which they ought not. 1 Timothy 5:13

For the scripture saith, Thou shalt not muzzle the ox that treadeth out the corn. And, The labourer is worthy of his reward. 1 Timothy 5:18

That ye be not slothful, but followers of them who through faith and patience inherit the promises. Hebrews 6:12

For if these things be in you, and abound, they make you that ye shall neither be barren nor unfruitful in the knowledge of our Lord Jesus Christ. 2 Peter 1:8

Work

Six days shalt thou labour, and do all thy work. Exodus 20:9

He that is despised, and hath a servant, is better than he that honoureth himself, and lacketh bread. Proverbs 12:9

Better is he who is lightly esteemed but works for his own support, than he who assumes honor for himself and lacks bread. Proverbs 12:9 AMP

He that laboureth laboureth for himself; for his mouth craveth it of him.
Proverbs 16:26

The appetite of the laborer works for him, for the need of his mouth urges him on. Proverbs 16:26 AMP

Whatsoever thy hand findeth to do, do it with thy might; for there is no work, nor device, nor knowledge, nor wisdom, in the grave, whither thou goest. Ecclesiastes 9:10

And whatsoever ye do, do it heartily, as to the Lord, and not unto men.
Colossians 3:23

For God is not unrighteous to forget your work and labour of love, which ye have shewed toward his name, in that ye have ministered to the saints, and do minister. Hebrews 6:10

And in the same house remain, eating and drinking such things as they give: for the labourer is worthy of his hire. Go not from house to house.
Luke 10:7

I must work the works of him that sent me, while it is day: the night cometh, when no man can work. John 9:4

For we are labourers together with God: ye are God's husbandry, ye are God's building. 1 Corinthians 3:9

Wherefore, my beloved, as ye have always obeyed, not as in my presence only, but now much more in my absence, work out your own salvation with fear and trembling. Philippians 2:12

He also that is slothful in his work is brother to him that is a great waster.
Proverbs 18:9

Inspiration without perspiration leads to frustration and stagnation. - Bill Bright

The quality of your character is the measure of your leadership effectiveness.

1. Benefits of Working

Every man also to whom God hath given riches and wealth, and hath given him power to eat thereof, and to take his portion, and to rejoice in his labour; this is the gift of God. Ecclesiastes 5:19

He that tilleth his land shall be satisfied with bread: but he that followeth vain persons is void of understanding. Proverbs 12:11

Every man's work shall be made manifest: for the day shall declare it, because it shall be revealed by fire; and the fire shall try every man's work of what sort it is. If any man's work abide which he hath built thereupon, he shall receive a reward. If any man's work shall be burned, he shall suffer loss: but he himself shall be saved; yet so as by fire.
1 Corinthians 3:13-15

2. We are Commanded to Work

But let every man prove his own work, and then shall he have rejoicing in himself alone, and not in another. Galatians 6:4

That ye might walk worthy of the Lord unto all pleasing, being fruitful in every good work, and increasing in the knowledge of God.
Colossians 1:10

And that ye study to be quiet, and to do your own business, and to work with your own hands, as we commanded you; That ye may walk honestly toward them that are without, and that ye may have lack of nothing.
1 Thessalonians 4:11-12

For even when we were with you, this we commanded you, that if any would not work, neither should he eat. 2 Thessalonians 3:10

3. Consequences of Not Working

Slothfulness casteth into a deep sleep; and an idle soul shall suffer hunger. Proverbs 19:15

Good Works

Let your light so shine before men, that they may see your good works, and glorify your Father which is in heaven. Matthew 5:16

And God is able to make all grace abound toward you; that ye, always having all sufficiency in all things, may abound to every good work:
2 Corinthians 9:8

That ye might walk worthy of the Lord unto all pleasing, being fruitful in every good work, and increasing in the knowledge of God;
Colossians 1:10

And whatsoever ye do in word or deed, do all in the name of the Lord Jesus, giving thanks to God and the Father by him. Colossians 3:17

Servants, obey in all things your masters according to the flesh; not with eyeservice, as menpleasers; but in singleness of heart, fearing God: And whatsoever ye do, do it heartily, as to the Lord, and not unto men.
Colossians 3:22-23

For we are his workmanship, created in Christ Jesus unto good works, which God hath before ordained that we should walk in them.
Ephesians 2:10

When people do not mean business with Christ in their hearts they will not do business for Christ with their hands. - Vance Havner

Likewise also the good works of some are manifest beforehand; and they that are otherwise cannot be hid. 1 Timothy 5:25

Attempt something so impossible that unless God is in it, it is doomed to failure. - John Haggai

That they do good, that they be rich in good works, ready to distribute, willing to communicate; 1 Timothy 6:18

If a man therefore purge himself from these, he shall be a vessel unto honour, sanctified, and meet for the master's use, and prepared unto every good work. 2 Timothy 2:21

That the man of God may be perfect, throughly furnished unto all good works. 2 Timothy 3:17

In all things shewing thyself a pattern of good works: in doctrine shewing uncorruptness, gravity, sincerity. Titus 2:7

Who gave himself for us, that he might redeem us from all iniquity, and purify unto himself a peculiar people, zealous of good works. Titus 2:14

O Lord, let us not live to be useless, for Christ's sake. - John Wesley

Put them in mind to be subject to principalities and powers, to obey magistrates, to be ready to every good work. Titus 3:1

This is a faithful saying, and these things I will that thou affirm constantly, that they which have believed in God might be careful to maintain good works. These things are good and profitable unto men.
Titus 3:8

And let ours also learn to maintain good works for necessary uses, that they be not unfruitful. Titus 3:14

And let us consider one another to provoke unto love and to good works.
Hebrews 10:24

Make you perfect in every good work to do his will, working in you that which is wellpleasing in his sight, through Jesus Christ; to whom be glory for ever and ever. Amen. Hebrews 13:21

Having your conversation honest among the Gentiles: that, whereas they speak against you as evildoers, they may by your good works, which they shall behold, glorify God in the day of visitation. 1 Peter 2:12

For so is the will of God, that with well doing ye may put to silence the ignorance of foolish men; 1 Peter 2:15

For it is God's will and intention that by doing right [your] good and honest lives should silence (muzzle, gag) the ignorant charges and ill-informed criticisms of foolish persons. 1 Peter 2:15 AMP

1. Your Works Will Be Judged by Christ

For the Son of man shall come in the glory of his Father with his angels; and then he shall reward every man according to his works.
Matthew 16:27

Every man's work shall be made manifest: for the day shall declare it, because it shall be revealed by fire; and the fire shall try every man's work of what sort it is. If any man's work abide which he hath built thereupon, he shall receive a reward. If any man's work shall be burned, he shall suffer loss: but he himself shall be saved; yet so as by fire.
1 Corinthians 3:13-15

The work of each [one] will become (plainly, openly known-shown for what it is; for the day (of Christ) will disclose and declare it, because it will be revealed with fire, and the fire will test and critically appraise the character and worth of the work each person has done. If the work which any person has built on this Foundation-any product of his efforts whatever–survives (this test), he will get his reward. But if any person's work is burned up [under the test], he will get his reward. But if any person's

303

work is burned up [under the test], he will suffer the loss (of it all, losing his reward), though he himself will be saved, but only as [one who has passed] through fire. 1 Corinthians 3:13-15 AMP

When God crowns our merits, it is nothing other than his own gifts that he crowns. - Augustine of Hippo

For the Son of man shall come in the glory of his Father with his angels; and then he shall reward every man according to his works.

Matthew 16:27

And, behold, I come quickly; and my reward is with me, to give every man according as his work shall be. Revelation 22:12

PREPARING THE MIND AND HEART TO RECEIVE GOD'S BLESSINGS

God Wants You to Prosper Financially

But thou shalt remember the Lord thy God: for it is he that giveth thee power to get wealth, that he may establish his covenant which he sware unto thy fathers, as it is this day. Deuteronomy 8:18

For the Lord thy God blesseth thee, as he promised thee: and thou shalt lend unto many nations, but thou shalt not borrow; and thou shalt reign over many nations, but they shall not reign over thee. Deuteronomy 15:6

The Lord shall open unto thee his good treasure, the heaven to give the rain unto thy land in his season, and to bless all the work of thine hand: and thou shalt lend unto many nations, and thou shalt not borrow.
Deuteronomy 28:12

Thou preparest a table before me in the presence of mine enemies: thou anointest my head with oil; my cup runneth over. Psalms 23:5

Let them shout for joy, and be glad, that favour my righteous cause: yea, let them say continually, Let the Lord be magnified, which hath pleasure in the prosperity of his servant. Psalms 35:27

The biggest lie ever told is that God wants his children to be poor.

If they obey and serve him, they shall spend their days in prosperity, and their years in pleasures. Job 36:11

For the Lord God is a sun and shield: the Lord will give grace and glory: no good thing will he withhold from them that walk uprightly.
Psalms 84:11

That I may cause those that love me to inherit substance; and I will fill their treasures. Proverbs 8:21

I know that there is no good in them, but for a man to rejoice, and to do good in his life. And also that every man should eat and drink, and enjoy the good of all his labour, it is the gift of God. Ecclesiastes 3:12-13

Wherefore I perceive that there is nothing better, than that a man should rejoice in his own works; for that is his portion: for who shall bring him to see what shall be after him? Ecclesiastes 3:22

Fear not, little flock; for it is your Father's good pleasure to give you the kingdom. Luke 12:32

The thief cometh not, but for to steal, and to kill, and to destroy: I am come that they might have life, and that they might have it more abundantly. John 10:10

He that spared not his own Son, but delivered him up for us all, how shall he not with him also freely give us all things? Romans 8:32

And God is able to make all grace abound toward you; that ye, always having all sufficiency in all things, may abound to every good work.
2 Corinthians 9:8

Now unto him that is able to do exceeding abundantly above all that we ask or think, according to the power that worketh in us. Ephesians 3:20

For ye know the grace of our Lord Jesus Christ, that, though he was rich, yet for your sakes he became poor, that ye through his poverty might be rich. 2 Corinthians 8:9

According as his divine power hath given unto us all things that pertain unto life and godliness, through the knowledge of him that hath called us to glory and virtue. 2 Peter 1:3

God has given us two hands - one for receiving and the other for giving. - Billy Graham

Giving in the Right Attitude

Every man according as he purposeth in his heart, so let him give; not grudgingly, or of necessity: for God loveth a cheerful giver.
2 Corinthians 9:7

Let each one [give] as he has made up his own mind and purposed in his heart, not reluctantly or sorrowfully or under compulsion, for God loves

As in every seed there is a forest, so
in every follower there is a leader.

(that is, He takes pleasure in, prizes above other things, and is unwilling to abandon or to do without) a cheerful (joyous, prompt-to-do-it) giver– whose heart is in his giving. 2 Corinthians 9:7 AMP

He that observeth the wind shall not sow; and he that regardeth the clouds shall not reap. Ecclesiastes 11:4

He who observes the wind [and waits for all conditions to be favorable] will not sow, and he who regards the clouds will not reap.

Ecclesiastes 11:4 AMP

Self, service, substance is the Divine order and nothing counts until we give ourselves. - Vance Havner

Take heed that ye do not your alms before men, to be seen of them: otherwise ye have no reward of your Father which is in heaven. There-fore when thou doest thine alms, do not sound a trumpet before thee, as the hypocrites do in the synagogues and in the streets, that they may have glory of men. Verily I say unto you, They have their reward. But when thou doest alms, let not thy left hand know what thy right hand doeth: That thine alms may be in secret: and thy Father which seeth in secret himself shall reward thee openly. Matthew 6:1-4

Take ye from among you an offering unto the Lord: whosoever is of a willing heart, let him bring it, an offering of the Lord; gold, and silver, and brass, Exodus 35:5

And they came, every one whose heart stirred him up, and every one whom his spirit made willing, and they brought the Lord's offering to the work of the tabernacle of the congregation, and for all his service, and for the holy garments. And they came, both men and women, as many as were willing hearted, and brought bracelets, and earrings, and rings, and tablets, all jewels of gold: and every man that offered an offer-ing of gold unto the Lord. Exodus 35:21-22

The children of Israel brought a willing offering unto the Lord, every man and woman, whose heart made them willing to bring for all manner of work, which the Lord had commanded to be made by the hand of Moses. Exodus 35:29

True Riches

Lay not up for yourselves treasures upon earth, where moth and rust doth corrupt, and where thieves break through and steal: But lay up for yourselves treasures in heaven, where neither moth nor rust doth cor-

307

rupt, and where thieves do not break through nor steal: For where your treasure is, there will your heart be also. Matthew 6:19-21

By humility and the fear of the Lord are riches, and honour, and life.
Proverbs 22:4

A faithful man shall abound with blessings. Proverbs 28:20

But thou shalt have a perfect and just weight, a perfect and just measure shalt thou have: that thy days may be lengthened in the land which the Lord thy God giveth thee. Deuteronomy 25:15

You really save in this life only that which you spend for the Lord. Under the guidance of the Holy Spirit every expenditure is an investment. The Bank of heaven is sound and pays eternal dividends. - Vance Havner

Wisdom is good with an inheritance: and by it there is profit to them that see the sun. For wisdom is a defence, and money is a defence: but the excellency of knowledge is, that wisdom giveth life to them that have it.
Ecclesiastes 7:11-12

Do Not Put Your Trust or Hope in Money

For the love of money is the root of all evil: which while some coveted after, they have erred from the faith, and pierced themselves through with many sorrows. 1 Timothy 6:10

Charge them that are rich in this world, that they be not highminded, nor trust in uncertain riches, but in the living God, who giveth us richly all things to enjoy; That they do good, that they be rich in good works, ready to distribute, willing to communicate; Laying up in store for themselves a good foundation against the time to come, that they may lay hold on eternal life. 1 Timothy 6:17-19

They that trust in their wealth, and boast themselves in the multitude of their riches; None of them can by any means redeem his brother, nor give to God a ransom for him. Psalms 49:6-7

Trust not in oppression, and become not vain in robbery: if riches increase, set not your heart upon them. Psalms 62:10

Riches profit not in the day of wrath: but righteousness delivereth from death. Proverbs 11:4

He that trusteth in his riches shall fall: but the righteous shall flourish as a branch. Proverbs 11:28

There is that maketh himself rich, yet hath nothing: there is that maketh himself poor, yet hath great riches. Proverbs 13:7

He that loveth silver shall not be satisfied with silver; nor he that loveth abundance with increase: this is also vanity. When goods increase, they are increased that eat them: and what good is there to the owners thereof, saving the beholding of them with their eyes? The sleep of a labouring man is sweet, whether he eat little or much: but the abundance of the rich will not suffer him to sleep. Ecclesiastes 5:10-12

Two things have I required of thee; deny me them not before I die: Remove far from me vanity and lies: give me neither poverty nor riches; feed me with food convenient for me: Lest I be full, and deny thee, and say, Who is the Lord? or lest I be poor, and steal, and take the name of my God in vain. Proverbs 30:7-9

Money is a terrible master but an excellent servant. - P. T. Barnum

Contentment

Better is little with the fear of the Lord than great treasure and trouble therewith. Proverbs 15:16

Labour not to be rich: cease from thine own wisdom. Wilt thou set thine eyes upon that which is not? for riches certainly make themselves wings; they fly away as an eagle toward heaven. Proverbs 23:4-5

Let your conversation be without covetousness; and be content with such things as ye have: for he hath said, I will never leave thee, nor forsake thee. Hebrews 13:5

The Purpose for Finances

To Spread the Gospel of Jesus Christ

And it shall come to pass in the last days, that the mountain of the Lord's house shall be established in the top of the mountains, and shall be exalted above the hills; and all nations shall flow unto it. Isaiah 2:2

And this gospel of the kingdom shall be preached in all the world for a witness unto all nations; and then shall the end come. Matthew 24:14

Go ye therefore, and teach all nations, baptizing them in the name of the Father, and of the Son, and of the Holy Ghost. Matthew 28:19

And he said unto them, Go ye into all the world, and preach the gospel to every creature. Mark 16:15

And they went forth, and preached everywhere, the Lord working with them, and confirming the word with signs following. Amen. Mark 16:20

We can go to the mission field in person, by prayer, by provision, or by proxy as we help send someone else. - Vance Havner

Therefore said he unto them, The harvest truly is great, but the labourers are few: pray ye therefore the Lord of the harvest, that he would send forth labourers into his harvest. Luke 10:2

And the lord said unto the servant, Go out into the highways and hedges, and compel them to come in, that my house may be filled. Luke 14:23

And that repentance and remission of sins should be preached in his name among all nations, beginning at Jerusalem. And ye are witnesses of these things. Luke 24:47-48

And I, if I be lifted up from the earth, will draw all men unto me.

John 12:32

But ye shall receive power, after that the Holy Ghost is come upon you: and ye shall be witnesses unto me both in Jerusalem, and in all Judaea, and in Samaria, and unto the uttermost part of the earth. Acts 1:8

311

How then shall they call on him in whom they have not believed? and how shall they believe in him of whom they have not heard? and how shall they hear without a preacher? And how shall they preach, except they be sent? as it is written, How beautiful are the feet of them that preach the gospel of peace, and bring glad tidings of good things!
Romans 10:14-15

But I say, Have they not heard? Yes verily, their sound went into all the earth, and their words unto the ends of the world. Romans 10:18

Preach the word; be instant in season, out of season; reprove, rebuke, exhort with all longsuffering and doctrine. 2 Timothy 4:2

To Help the Poor

For the poor shall never cease out of the land: therefore I command thee, saying, Thou shalt open thine hand wide unto thy brother, to thy poor, and to thy needy, in thy land. Deuteronomy 15:11

He that despiseth his neighbour sinneth: but he that hath mercy on the poor, happy is he. Proverbs 14:21

Blessed is he that considereth the poor: the Lord will deliver him in time of trouble. Psalms 41:1

Defend the poor and fatherless: do justice to the afflicted and needy. Deliver the poor and needy: rid them out of the hand of the wicked.
Psalms 82:3-4

Whoso stoppeth his ears at the cry of the poor, he also shall cry himself, but shall not be heard. Proverbs 21:13

And if thou draw out thy soul to the hungry, and satisfy the afflicted soul; then shall thy light rise in obscurity, and thy darkness be as the noonday. Isaiah 58:10

He answereth and saith unto them, He that hath two coats, let him impart to him that hath none; and he that hath meat, let him do likewise.
Luke 3:11

The Bible is very clear on the point that if we have money enough to live well, and do not share with others in need, it is questionable whether God's love is in us at all. - G. S.

A leader must be able to reconcile opposing viewpoints without giving offense and without compromising principle.

Then said he also to him that bade him, When thou makest a dinner or a supper, call not thy friends, nor thy brethren, neither thy kinsmen, nor thy rich neighbours; lest they also bid thee again, and a recompence be made thee. But when thou makest a feast, call the poor, the maimed, the lame, the blind: And thou shalt be blessed; for they cannot recompense thee: for thou shalt be recompensed at the resurrection of the just.

Luke 14:12-14

If a brother or sister be naked, and destitute of daily food, And one of you say unto them, Depart in peace, be ye warmed and filled; notwithstanding ye give them not those things which are needful to the body; what doth it profit? Even so faith, if it hath not works, is dead, being alone. James 2:15-17

When you commit to giving finances for the spreading of the gospel of Christ and feeding the poor, God will supply all of your needs.

GOD'S FINANCIAL BUSINESS PLAN FOR YOU

Tithing and Offerings

And all the tithe of the land, whether of the seed of the land, or of the fruit of the tree, is the Lord's: it is holy unto the Lord. And if a man will at all redeem ought of his tithes, he shall add thereto the fifth part thereof.
Leviticus 27:30-31

And it shall be, when thou art come in unto the land which the Lord thy God giveth thee for an inheritance, and possessest it, and dwellest therein; That thou shalt take of the first of all the fruit of the earth, which thou shalt bring of thy land that the Lord thy God giveth thee, and shalt put it in a basket, and shalt go unto the place which the Lord thy God shall choose to place his name there. Deuteronomy 26:1-2

And he hath brought us into this place, and hath given us this land, even a land that floweth with milk and honey. And now, behold, I have brought the firstfruits of the land, which thou, O Lord, hast given me. And thou shalt set it before the Lord thy God, and worship before the Lord thy God: And thou shalt rejoice in every good thing which the Lord thy God hath given unto thee, and unto thine house, thou, and the Levite, and the stranger that is among you. Deuteronomy 26:9-11

Will a man rob God? Yet ye have robbed me. But ye say, Wherein have we robbed thee? In tithes and offerings. Ye are cursed with a curse: for ye have robbed me, even this whole nation. Bring ye all the tithes into the storehouse, that there may be meat in mine house, and prove me now herewith, saith the Lord of hosts, if I will not open you the windows of heaven, and pour you out a blessing, that there shall not be room enough to receive it. Malachi 3:8-10

Not because I desire a gift: but I desire fruit that may abound: but I desire fruit that may abound to your account. But I have all, and abound: I am full, having received of Epaphroditus the things which were sent from you, an odor of a swcct smell, a sacrifice acceptable, well pleasing to

315

God. But my God shall supply all your need according to his riches in glory by Christ Jesus. Philippians 4:17-19

Sowing Seeds

For as the rain cometh down, and the snow from heaven, and returneth not thither, but watereth the earth, and maketh it bring forth and bud, that it may give seed to the sower, and bread to the eater: So shall my word be that goeth forth out of my mouth: it shall not return unto me void, but it shall accomplish that which I please, and it shall prosper in the thing whereto I sent it. Isaiah 55:10-11

He that goeth forth and weepeth, bearing precious seed, shall doubtless come again with rejoicing, bringing his sheaves with him. Psalms 126:6

Give, and it shall be given unto you; good measure, pressed down, and shaken together, and running over, shall men give into your bosom. For with the same measure that ye mete withal it shall be measured to you again. Luke 6:38

> *Sow your financial seeds as soon as you receive your increase. Faster sowers have a faster harvest. - Dr. John Avanzini*

But this I say, He which soweth sparingly shall reap also sparingly; and he which soweth bountifully shall reap also bountifully.
2 Corinthians 9:6

Now he that ministereth seed to the sower both minister bread for your food, and multiply your seed sown, and increase the fruits of your righteousness. Being enriched in every thing to all bountifulness, which causeth through us thanksgiving to God. 2 Corinthians 9:10-11

Be not deceived; God is not mocked: for whatsoever a man soweth, that shall he also reap. Galatians 6:7

> *Know the spirit of the person that tills the soil that you plant your seed into.*

In the morning sow thy seed, and in the evening withhold not thine hand: for thou knowest not whether shall prosper, either this or that, or whether they both shall be alike good. Ecclesiastes 11:6

There is that scattereth, and yet increaseth; and there is that withholdeth more than is meet, but it tendeth to poverty. Proverbs 11:24

A leader must be found faithful in stewardship.

Cast thy bread upon the waters: for thou shalt find it after many days.
Ecclesiastes 11:1

Reaping the Harvest

And let us not be weary in well doing: for in due season we shall reap, if we faint not. Galatians 6:9

And Jesus answered and said, Verily I say unto you, There is no man that hath left house, or brethren, or sisters, of father, or mother, or wife, or children, of lands, for my sake, and the gospel's. But he shall receive an hundredfold now in this time, houses, and brethren, and sisters, and mothers, and children, and lands, with persecutions; and in the world to come eternal life. Mark 10:29-30

> *The Dead Sea is a dead sea because it continually receives and never gives. - Anonymous*

The End-Time Transfer of Wealth to Christians

For I was envious at the foolish, when I saw the prosperity of the wicked. For there are no bands in their death: but their strength is firm. They are not in trouble as other men; neither are they plagued like other men. Therefore pride compasseth them about as a chain; violence covereth them as a garment. Their eyes stand out with fatness: they have more than heart could wish. They are corrupt, and speak wickedly concerning oppression: they speak loftily. They set their mouth against the heavens, and their tongue walketh through the earth. Therefore his people return hither: and waters of a full cup are wrung out to them. And they say, How doth God know? and is there knowledge in the most High? Behold, these are the ungodly, who prosper in the world; they increase in riches. Verily I have cleansed my heart in vain, and washed my hands in innocency. For all the day long have I been plagued, and chastened every morning. If I say, I will speak thus; behold, I should offend against the generation of thy children. When I thought to know this, it was too painful for me; Until I went into the sanctuary of God; then understood I their end. Surely thou didst set them in slippery places: thou castedst them down into destruction. How are they brought into desolation, as in a moment! they are utterly consumed with terrors. Psalms 73:3-19

This is the portion of a wicked man with God, and the heritage of oppressors, which they shall receive of the Almighty. If his children be multiplied, it is for the sword: and his offspring shall not be satisfied with bread. Those that remain of him shall be buried in death: and his widows shall not weep. Though he heap up silver as the dust, and pre-

317

pare raiment as the clay; He may prepare it, but the just shall put it on, and the innocent shall divide the silver. Job 27:13-17

He that by usury and unjust gain increaseth his substance, he shall gather it for him that will pity the poor. Proverbs 28:8

For God giveth to a man that is good in his sight wisdom, and knowledge, and joy: but to the sinner he giveth travail, to gather and to heap up, that he may give to him that is good before God. This also is vanity and vexation of spirit. Ecclesiastes 2:26

If God can get it through you, God will give it to you. - E. V. Hill

Go to now, ye rich men, weep and howl for your miseries that shall come upon you. Your riches are corrupted, and your garments are motheaten. Your gold and silver is cankered; and the rust of them shall be a witness against you, and shall eat your flesh as it were fire. Ye have heaped treasure together for the last days. James 5:1-3

Loans

Owe no man any thing, but to love one another: for he that loveth another hath fulfilled the law. Romans 13:8

The rich ruleth over the poor, and the borrower is servant to the lender.
Proverbs 22:7

For the Lord thy God blesseth thee, as he promised thee: and thou shalt lend unto many nations, but thou shalt not borrow; and thou shalt reign over many nations, but they shall not reign over thee. Deuteronomy 15:6

If thou lend money to any of my people that is poor by thee, thou shalt not be to him as an usurer, neither shalt thou lay upon him usury.
Exodus 22:25

Thou shalt not give him thy money upon usury, nor lend him thy victuals for increase. Leviticus 25:37

Thou shalt not lend upon usury to thy brother; usury of money, usury of victuals, usury of any thing that is lent upon usury: Unto a stranger thou mayest lend upon usury; but unto thy brother thou shalt not lend upon usury: that the Lord thy God may bless thee in all that thou settest thine hand to in the land whither thou goest to possess it.
Deuteronomy 23:19-20

The Lord shall open unto thee his good treasure, the heaven to give the rain unto thy land in his season, and to bless all the work of thine hand: and thou shalt lend unto many nations, and thou shalt not borrow.
Deuteronomy 28:12

The wicked borroweth, and payeth not again: but the righteous sheweth mercy, and giveth. Psalms 37:21

Co-Signing for Others

My son, if thou be surety for thy friend, if thou hast stricken thy hand with a stranger, Thou art snared with the words of thy mouth, thou art taken with the words of thy mouth. Do this now, my son, deliver thyself, when thou art come into the hand of thy friend; go, humble thyself, and make sure thy friend. Give not sleep to thine eyes, nor slumber to thine eyelids. Deliver thyself as a roe from the hand of the hunter, and as a bird from the hand of the fowler. Proverbs 6:1-5

He that is surety for a stranger shall smart for it: and he that hateth suretiship is sure. Proverbs 11:15

A man void of understanding striketh hands, and becometh surety in the presence of his friend. Proverbs 17:18

Take his garment that is surety for a stranger: and take a pledge of him for a strange woman. Proverbs 20:16

The rich ruleth over the poor, and the borrower is servant to the lender.
Proverbs 22:7

Be not thou one of them that strike hands, or of them that are sureties for debts. If thou hast nothing to pay, why should he take away thy bed from under thee? Proverbs 22:26-27

Take his garment that is surety for a stranger, and take a pledge of him for a strange woman. Proverbs 27:13

319

FACING CHALLENGES AND WINNING

Facing Fear and Winning

Fear not, little flock; for it is your Father's good pleasure to give you the kingdom. Luke 12:32

Peace I leave with you, my peace I give unto you: not as the world giveth, give I unto you. Let not your heart be troubled, neither let it be afraid.

John 14:27

1. Fear is an evil spirit from satan

For ye have not received the spirit of bondage again to fear; but ye have received the Spirit of adoption, whereby we cry, Abba, Father.

Romans 8:15

For God hath not given us the spirit of fear; but of power, and of love, and of a sound mind. 2 Timothy 1:7

There is no fear in love; but perfect love casteth out fear: because fear hath torment. He that feareth is not made perfect in love. 1 John 4:18

2. Fear Brings the Problem to You

The fear of the wicked, it shall come upon him: but the desire of the righteous shall be granted. Proverbs 10:24

The fear of man bringeth a snare: but whoso putteth his trust in the Lord shall be safe. Proverbs 29:25

For the thing which I greatly feared is come upon me, and that which I was afraid of is come unto me. Job 3:25

3. Don't Fear! God is with You

And he answered, Fear not: for they that be with us are more than they that be with them. 2 Kings 6:16

For I the Lord thy God will hold thy right hand, saying unto thee, Fear not; I will help thee. Isaiah 41:13

Yea, though I walk through the valley of the shadow of death, I will fear no evil: for thou art with me; thy rod and thy staff they comfort me.
Psalms 23:4

The Lord is my light and my salvation; whom shall I fear? the Lord is the strength of my life; of whom shall I be afraid? Psalms 27:1

Though an host should encamp against me, my heart shall not fear: though war should rise against me, in this will I be confident. Psalms 27:3

God is our refuge and strength, a very present help in trouble.
Psalms 46:1

But whoso hearkeneth unto me shall dwell safely, and shall be quiet from fear of evil. Proverbs 1:33

When thou liest down, thou shalt not be afraid: yea, thou shalt lie down, and thy sleep shall be sweet. Be not afraid of sudden fear, neither of the desolation of the wicked, when it cometh. For the Lord shall be thy confidence, and shall keep thy foot from being taken. Proverbs 3:24-26

And it shall come to pass in the day that the Lord shall give thee rest from thy sorrow, and from thy fear, and from the hard bondage wherein thou wast made to serve. Isaiah 14:3

When thou passest through the waters, I will be with thee; and through the rivers, they shall not overflow thee: when thou walkest through the fire, thou shalt not be burned; neither shall the flame kindle upon thee.
Isaiah 43:2

Facing Death and Winning

Yea, though I walk through the valley of the shadow of death, I will fear no evil: for thou art with me; thy rod and thy staff they comfort me.
Psalms 23:4

Mark the perfect man, and behold the upright: for the end of that man is peace. Psalms 37:37

For this God is our God for ever and ever: he will be our guide even unto death. Psalms 48:14

Criticism is the leader's greatest test of maturity, conviction and commitment to his vision. If you are ready for criticism, you're ready for leadership.

But God will redeem my soul from the power of the grave: for he shall receive me. Selah. Psalms 49:15

My flesh and my heart faileth: but God is the strength of my heart, and my portion for ever. Psalms 73:26

The wicked is driven away in his wickedness: but the righteous hath hope in his death. Proverbs 14:32

He will swallow up death in victory; and the Lord God will wipe away tears from off all faces; and the rebuke of his people shall he take away from off all the earth: for the Lord hath spoken it. Isaiah 25:8

I will ransom them from the power of the grave; I will redeem them from death: O death, I will be thy plagues; O grave, I will be thy destruction: repentance shall be hid from mine eyes. Hosea 13:14

That whosoever believeth in him should not perish, but have eternal life.
John 3:15

Verily, verily, I say unto you, If a man keep my saying, he shall never see death. John 8:51

Much more then, being now justified by his blood, we shall be saved from wrath through him. Romans 5:9

O death, where is thy sting? O grave, where is thy victory? The sting of death is sin; and the strength of sin is the law. But thanks be to God, which giveth us the victory through our Lord Jesus Christ.
1 Corinthians 15:55-57

For which cause we faint not; but though our outward man perish, yet the inward man is renewed day by day. 2 Corinthians 4:16

Forasmuch then as the children are partakers of flesh and blood, he also himself likewise took part of the same; that through death he might destroy him that had the power of death, that is, the devil; And deliver them who through fear of death were all their lifetime subject to bondage. Hebrews 2:14-15

Facing Enemies and Winning

For the Lord your God is he that goeth with you, to fight for you against your enemies, to save you. Deuteronomy 20:4

The Lord shall cause thine enemies that rise up against thee to be smitten before thy face: they shall come out against thee one way, and flee before thee seven ways. Deuteronomy 28:7

And he answered, Fear not: for they that be with us are more than they that be with them. 2 Kings 6:16

But the Lord your God ye shall fear; and he shall deliver you out of the hand of all your enemies. 2 Kings 17:39

In famine he shall redeem thee from death: and in war from the power of the sword. Job 5:20

They that hate thee shall be clothed with shame; and the dwelling place of the wicked shall come to nought. Job 8:22

For in the time of trouble he shall hide me in his pavilion: in the secret of his tabernacle shall he hide me; he shall set me up upon a rock. And now shall mine head be lifted up above mine enemies round about me: therefore will I offer in his tabernacle sacrifices of joy; I will sing, yea, I will sing praises unto the Lord. Psalms 27:5-6

And the Lord shall help them and deliver them: he shall deliver them from the wicked, and save them, because they trust in him. Psalms 37:40

Through God we shall do valiantly: for he it is that shall tread down our enemies. Psalms 60:12

Ye that love the Lord, hate evil: he preserveth the souls of his saints; he delivereth them out of the hand of the wicked. Psalms 97:10

His heart is established, he shall not be afraid, until he see his desire upon his enemies. Psalms 112:8

The Lord taketh my part with them that help me: therefore shall I see my desire upon them that hate me. Psalms 118:7

For the rod of the wicked shall not rest upon the lot of the righteous; lest the righteous put forth their hands unto iniquity. Psalms 125:3

Be not afraid of sudden fear, neither of the desolation of the wicked, when it cometh. For the Lord shall be thy confidence, and shall keep thy foot from being taken. Proverbs 3:25-26

When a man's ways please the Lord, he maketh even his enemies to be at peace with him. Proverbs 16:7

Behold, all they that were incensed against thee shall be ashamed and confounded: they shall be as nothing; and they that strive with thee shall perish. Thou shalt seek them, and shalt not find them, even them that contended with thee: they that war against thee shall be as nothing, and as a thing of nought. Isaiah 41:11-12

Behold, they shall surely gather together, but not by me: whosoever shall gather together against thee shall fall for thy sake. Isaiah 54:15

But I will deliver thee in that day, saith the Lord: and thou shalt not be given into the hand of the men of whom thou art afraid. For I will surely deliver thee, and thou shalt not fall by the sword, but thy life shall be for a prey unto thee: because thou hast put thy trust in me, saith the Lord.
Jeremiah 39:17-18

That we should be saved from our enemies, and from the hand of all that hate us. Luke 1:71

That he would grant unto us, that we being delivered out of the hand of our enemies might serve him without fear. Luke 1:74

And shall not God avenge his own elect, which cry day and night unto him, though he bear long with them? Luke 18:7

For I am with thee, and no man shall set on thee to hurt thee: for I have much people in this city. Acts 18:10

1. How to Treat Your Enemies

If thine enemy be hungry, give him bread to eat; and if he be thirsty, give him water to drink. Proverbs 25:21

But I say unto you, Love your enemies, bless them that curse you, do good to them that hate you, and pray for them which despitefully use you, and persecute you. Matthew 5:44

But I say unto you which hear, Love your enemies, do good to them which hate you, Bless them that curse you, and pray for them which despitefully use you. Luke 6:27-28

But love ye your enemies, and do good, and lend, hoping for nothing again; and your reward shall be great, and ye shall be the children of the Highest: for he is kind unto the unthankful and to the evil. Be ye therefore merciful, as your Father also is merciful. Luke 6:35-36

Bless them which persecute you: bless, and curse not. Romans 12:14

Love worketh no ill to his neighbour: therefore love is the fulfilling of the law. Romans 13:10

Therefore if thine enemy hunger, feed him; if he thirst, give him drink: for in so doing thou shalt heap coals of fire on his head. Romans 12:20

And labour, working with our own hands: being reviled, we bless; being persecuted, we suffer it. 1 Corinthians 4:12

325

2. Do Not Rejoice When Your Enemies Suffer

Whoso mocketh the poor reproacheth his Maker: and he that is glad at calamities shall not be unpunished. Proverbs 17:5

Say not thou, I will recompense evil; but wait on the Lord, and he shall save thee. Proverbs 20:22

Rejoice not when thine enemy falleth, and let not thine heart be glad when he stumbleth: Proverbs 24:17

Facing Loneliness and Winning

And, behold, I am with thee, and will keep thee in all places whither thou goest, and will bring thee again into this land; for I will not leave thee, until I have done that which I have spoken to thee of. Genesis 28:15

Be strong and of a good courage, fear not, nor be afraid of them: for the Lord thy God, he it is that doth go with thee; he will not fail thee, nor forsake thee. Deuteronomy 31:6

The Lord also will be a refuge for the oppressed, a refuge in times of trouble. And they that know thy name will put their trust in thee: for thou, Lord, hast not forsaken them that seek thee. Psalms 9:9-10

I will be glad and rejoice in thy mercy: for thou hast considered my trouble; thou hast known my soul in adversities. Psalms 31:7

But I am poor and needy; yet the Lord thinketh upon me: thou art my help and my deliverer; make no tarrying, O my God. Psalms 40:17

God is our refuge and strength, a very present help in trouble.
Psalms 46:1

Cast thy burden upon the Lord, and he shall sustain thee: he shall never suffer the righteous to be moved. Psalms 55:22

For the people shall dwell in Zion at Jerusalem: thou shalt weep no more: he will be very gracious unto thee at the voice of thy cry; when he shall hear it, he will answer thee. Isaiah 30:19

Fear thou not; for I am with thee: be not dismayed; for I am thy God: I will strengthen thee; yea, I will help thee; yea, I will uphold thee with the right hand of my righteousness. Isaiah 41:10

Leadership is lonely, because to lead means you must be out in front, ahead of the followers.

Then shalt thou call, and the Lord shall answer; thou shalt cry, and he shall say, Here I am. If thou take away from the midst of thee the yoke, the putting forth of the finger, and speaking vanity. Isaiah 58:9

In all their affliction he was afflicted, and the angel of his presence saved them: in his love and in his pity he redeemed them; and he bare them, and carried them all the days of old. Isaiah 63:9

Am I a God at hand, saith the Lord, and not a God afar off?
Jeremiah 23:23

The Lord is good, a strong hold in the day of trouble; and he knoweth them that trust in him. Nahum 1:7

Teaching them to observe all things whatsoever I have commanded you: and, lo, I am with you alway, even unto the end of the world. Amen.
Matthew 28:20

Let not your heart be troubled: ye believe in God, believe also in me.
John 14:1

I will not leave you comfortless: I will come to you. John 14:18

Who shall separate us from the love of Christ? shall tribulation, or distress, or persecution, or famine, or nakedness, or peril, or sword? As it is written, For thy sake we are killed all the day long; we are accounted as sheep for the slaughter. Nay, in all these things we are more than conquerors through him that loved us. For I am persuaded, that neither death, nor life, nor angels, nor principalities, nor powers, nor things present, nor things to come, Nor height, nor depth, nor any other creature, shall be able to separate us from the love of God, which is in Christ Jesus our Lord. Romans 8:35-39

Let your conversation be without covetousness; and be content with such things as ye have: for he hath said, I will never leave thee, nor forsake thee. Hebrews 13:5

Casting all your care upon him; for he careth for you. 1 Peter 5:7

Ye are of God, little children, and have overcome them: because greater is he that is in you, than he that is in the world. 1 John 4:4

Facing Revenge and Winning

1. Revenge is God's Job

For we know him that hath said, Vengeance belongeth unto me, I will recompense, saith the Lord. And again, The Lord shall judge his people.
Hebrews 10:30

To me belongeth vengeance, and recompence; their foot shall slide in due time: for the day of their calamity is at hand, and the things that shall come upon them make haste. Deuteronomy 32:35

O Lord God, to whom vengeance belongeth; O God, to whom vengeance belongeth, shew thyself. Psalms 94:1

Therefore thus saith the Lord; Behold, I will plead thy cause, and take vengeance for thee; and I will dry up her sea, and make her springs dry.
Jeremiah 51:36

That no man go beyond and defraud his brother in any matter: because that the Lord is the avenger of all such, as we also have forewarned you and testified. 1 Thessalonians 4:6

2. Do Not Seek Revenge

Whoso rewardeth evil for good, evil shall not depart from his house.
Proverbs 17:13

And having in a readiness to revenge all disobedience, when your obedience is fulfilled. 2 Corinthians 10:6

Whoso rewardeth evil for good, evil shall not depart from his house.
Proverbs 17:13

The Lord judge between me and thee, and the Lord avenge me of thee: but mine hand shall not be upon thee. 1 Samuel 24:12

Say not, I will do so to him as he hath done to me: I will render to the man according to his work. Proverbs 24:29

Recompense to no man evil for evil. Provide things honest in the sight of all men. Romans 12:17

Dearly beloved, avenge not yourselves, but rather give place unto wrath: for it is written, Vengeance is mine; I will repay, saith the Lord.
Romans 12:19

Revenge is often like biting a dog because the dog bit you.- Austin O'Malley

Thou shalt not avenge, nor bear any grudge against the children of thy people, but thou shalt love thy neighbour as thyself: I am the Lord.
Leviticus 19:18

See that none render evil for evil unto any man; but ever follow that which is good, both among yourselves, and to all men.
1 Thessalonians 5:15

328

Facing Persecution and Winning

He that hideth hatred with lying lips, and he that uttereth a slander, is a fool. Proverbs 10:18

Blessed are they which are persecuted for righteousness' sake: for theirs is the kingdom of heaven. **B**lessed are ye, when men shall revile you, and persecute you, and shall say all manner of evil against you falsely, for my sake. **R**ejoice, and be exceeding glad: for great is your reward in heaven: for so persecuted they the prophets which were before you.
Matthew 5:10-12

But I say unto you, Love your enemies, bless them that curse you, do good to them that hate you, and pray for them which despitefully use you, and persecute you; Matthew 5:44

But he shall receive an hundredfold now in this time, houses, and brethren, and sisters, and mothers, and children, and lands, with persecutions; and in the world to come eternal life. Mark 10:30

> *When you are living right and doing something for God, you will be criticized by three types of people: those who are jealous, those who are ill-informed, and those who are influenced by or filled with the devil.*

But before all these, they shall lay their hands on you, and persecute you, delivering you up to the synagogues, and into prisons, being brought before kings and rulers for my name's sake. Luke 21:12

Remember the word that I said unto you, The servant is not greater than his lord. If they have persecuted me, they will also persecute you; if they have kept my saying, they will keep yours also. John 15:20

Who shall separate us from the love of Christ? shall tribulation, or distress, or persecution, or famine, or nakedness, or peril, or sword?
Romans 8:35

Bless them which persecute you: bless, and curse not. Romans 12:14

And labour, working with our own hands: being reviled, we bless; being persecuted, we suffer it: 1 Corinthians 4:12

Persecuted, but not forsaken; cast down, but not destroyed;
2 Corinthians 4:9

Therefore I take pleasure in infirmities, in reproaches, in necessities, in persecutions, in distresses for Christ's sake: for when I am weak, then am I strong. 2 Corinthians 12:10

329

But as then he that was born after the flesh persecuted him that was born after the Spirit, even so it is now. Galatians 4:29

So that we ourselves glory in you in the churches of God for your patience and faith in all your persecutions and tribulations that ye endure:
2 Thessalonians 1:4

We Christians are not called to respond to criticism; we are called to respond to God. - John Mason

Persecutions, afflictions, which came unto me at Antioch, at Iconium, at Lystra; what persecutions I endured: but out of them all the Lord delivered me. 2 Timothy 3:11

Yea, and all that will live godly in Christ Jesus shall suffer persecution.
2 Timothy 3:12

Facing Temptation and Winning

And lead us not into temptation, but deliver us from evil: For thine is the kingdom, and the power, and the glory, for ever. Amen. Matthew 6:13

Watch and pray, that ye enter not into temptation: the spirit indeed is willing, but the flesh is weak. Matthew 26:41

Watch ye and pray, lest ye enter into temptation. The spirit truly is ready, but the flesh is weak. Mark 14:38

And Jesus answering said unto him, It is said, Thou shalt not tempt the Lord thy God. And when the devil had ended all the temptation, he departed from him for a season. Luke 4:12-13

And when he was at the place, he said unto them, Pray that ye enter not into temptation. Luke 22:40

And said unto them, Why sleep ye? rise and pray, lest ye enter into temptation. Luke 22:46

Temptations either tests your ability to say no, or it tests your conscience to promptly repent.

Neither let us tempt Christ, as some of them also tempted, and were destroyed of serpents. 1 Corinthians 10:9

One of the greatest dangers to leaders is the temptation to measure all others by oneself.

There hath no temptation taken you but such as is common to man: but God is faithful, who will not suffer you to be tempted above that ye are able; but will with the temptation also make a way to escape, that ye may be able to bear it. 1 Corinthians 10:13

And my temptation which was in my flesh ye despised not, nor rejected; but received me as an angel of God, even as Christ Jesus. Galatians 4:14

Brethren, if a man be overtaken in a fault, ye which are spiritual, restore such an one in the spirit of meekness; considering thyself, lest thou also be tempted. Galatians 6:1

For this cause, when I could no longer forbear, I sent to know your faith, lest by some means the tempter have tempted you, and our labour be in vain. 1 Thessalonians 3:5

But they that will be rich fall into temptation and a snare, and into many foolish and hurtful lusts, which drown men in destruction and perdition.
1 Timothy 6:9

For in that he himself hath suffered being tempted, he is able to succour them that are tempted. Hebrews 2:18

For we have not an high priest which cannot be touched with the feeling of our infirmities; but was in all points tempted like as we are, yet without sin. Hebrews 4:15

My brethren, count it all joy when ye fall into divers temptations.
James 1:2

Blessed is the man that endureth temptation: for when he is tried, he shall receive the crown of life, which the Lord hath promised to them that love him. **L**et no man say when he is tempted, I am tempted of God: for God cannot be tempted with evil, neither tempteth he any man: **B**ut every man is tempted, when he is drawn away of his own lust, and enticed. James 1:12-14

Wherein ye greatly rejoice, though now for a season, if need be, ye are in heaviness through manifold temptations. 1 Peter 1:6

The Lord knoweth how to deliver the godly out of temptations, and to reserve the unjust unto the day of judgment to be punished. 2 Peter 2:9

Because thou hast kept the word of my patience, I also will keep thee from the hour of temptation, which shall come upon all the world, to try them that dwell upon the earth. Revelation 3:10

If you would master temptation, you must first
let Christ master you. - Anonymous

331

Facing Stress and Depression and Winning

He shall deliver thee in six troubles: yea, in seven there shall no evil touch thee. Job 5:19

The Lord also will be a refuge for the oppressed, a refuge in times of trouble. Psalms 9:9

For his anger endureth but a moment; in his favour is life: weeping may endure for a night, but joy cometh in the morning. Psalms 30:5

Be of good courage, and he shall strengthen your heart, all ye that hope in the Lord. Psalms 31:24

Many are the afflictions of the righteous: but the Lord delivereth him out of them all. Psalms 34:19

That ye be not soon shaken in mind, or be troubled, neither by spirit, nor by word, nor by letter as from us, as that the day of Christ is at hand.
2 Thessalonians 2:2

For this shall every one that is godly pray unto thee in a time when thou mayest be found: surely in the floods of great waters they shall not come nigh unto him. Thou art my hiding place; thou shalt preserve me from trouble; thou shalt compass me about with songs of deliverance. Selah.
Psalms 32:6-7

Though he fall, he shall not be utterly cast down: for the Lord upholdeth him with his hand. Psalms 37:24

But the salvation of the righteous is of the Lord: he is their strength in the time of trouble. Psalms 37:39

Though I walk in the midst of trouble, thou wilt revive me: thou shalt stretch forth thine hand against the wrath of mine enemies, and thy right hand shall save me. Psalms 138:7

He healeth the broken in heart, and bindeth up their wounds.
Psalms 147:3

The wicked is snared by the transgression of his lips: but the just shall come out of trouble. Proverbs 12:13

There shall no evil happen to the just: but the wicked shall be filled with mischief. Proverbs 12:21

Therefore the redeemed of the Lord shall return, and come with singing unto Zion; and everlasting joy shall be upon their head: they shall obtain gladness and joy; and sorrow and mourning shall flee away. Isaiah 51:11

The Lord is good, a strong hold in the day of trouble; and he knoweth them that trust in him. Nahum 1:7

And he spake a parable unto them to this end, that men ought always to pray, and not to faint. Luke 18:1

Let not your heart be troubled: ye believe in God, believe also in me.
John 14:1

I will not leave you comfortless: I will come to you. John 14:18

And we know that all things work together for good to them that love God, to them who are the called according to his purpose. Romans 8:28

> *We should glory in our infirmities but not*
> *glorify them. - Vance Havner*

For I reckon that the sufferings of this present time are not worthy to be compared with the glory which shall be revealed in us. Romans 8:18

For I am persuaded, that neither death, nor life, nor angels, nor principalities, nor powers, nor things present, nor things to come, Nor height, nor depth, nor any other creature, shall be able to separate us from the love of God, which is in Christ Jesus our Lord. Romans 8:38-39

There hath no temptation taken you but such as is common to man: but God is faithful, who will not suffer you to be tempted above that ye are able; but will with the temptation also make a way to escape, that ye may be able to bear it. 1 Corinthians 10:13

> *A Christian is like a teabag-he's not worth much until he's*
> *been through some hot water. - Anonymous*

Blessed be God, even the Father of our Lord Jesus Christ, the Father of mercies, and the God of all comfort; Who comforteth us in all our tribulation, that we may be able to comfort them which are in any trouble, by the comfort wherewith we ourselves are comforted of God.
2 Corinthians 1:3-4

We are troubled on every side, yet not distressed; we are perplexed, but not in despair; Persecuted, but not forsaken; cast down, but not destroyed.
2 Corinthians 4:8-9

Wherefore seeing we also are compassed about with so great a cloud of witnesses, let us lay aside every weight, and the sin which doth so easily beset us, and let us run with patience the race that is set before us.
Hebrews 12:1

My brethren, count it all joy when ye fall into divers temptations; **K**nowing this, that the trying of your faith worketh patience. **B**ut let patience have her perfect work, that ye may be perfect and entire, wanting nothing. James 1:2-4

Wherefore also it is contained in the scripture, Behold, I lay in Sion a chief corner stone, elect, precious: and he that believeth on him shall not be confounded. 1 Peter 2:6

Beloved, think it not strange concerning the fiery trial which is to try you, as though some strange thing happened unto you: **B**ut rejoice, inasmuch as ye are partakers of Christ's sufferings; that, when his glory shall be revealed, ye may be glad also with exceeding joy. 1 Peter 4:12-13

> *All the tribulations of this life are but incidents on the road from Groans to Glory. - Vance Havner*

Casting all your care upon him; for he careth for you. 1 Peter 5:7

And God shall wipe away all tears from their eyes; and there shall be no more death, neither sorrow, nor crying, neither shall there be any more pain: for the former things are passed away. Revelation 21:4

Facing Anxiety and Worry and Winning

Therefore I say unto you, Take no thought for your life, what ye shall eat, or what ye shall drink; nor yet for your body, what ye shall put on. Is not the life more than meat, and the body than raiment? **B**ehold the fowls of the air: for they sow not, neither do they reap, nor gather into barns; yet your heavenly Father feedeth them. Are ye not much better than they? **W**hich of you by taking thought can add one cubit unto his stature? **A**nd why take ye thought for raiment? Consider the lilies of the field, how they grow; they toil not, neither do they spin: **A**nd yet I say unto you, That even Solomon in all his glory was not arrayed like one of these. **W**herefore, if God so clothe the grass of the field, which to day is, and to morrow is cast into the oven, shall he not much more clothe you, O ye of little faith? **T**herefore take no thought, saying, What shall we eat? or, What shall we drink? or, Wherewithal shall we be clothed? **F**or after all these things do the Gentiles seek: for your heavenly Father knoweth that ye have need of all these things. **B**ut seek ye first the kingdom of God,

---

**Courage is resistance to and mastery
of fear, not the absence of fear.**

---

and his righteousness; and all these things shall be added unto you. Take therefore no thought for the morrow: for the morrow shall take thought for the things of itself. Sufficient unto the day is the evil thereof.

Matthew 6:25-34

Be careful for nothing; but in every thing by prayer and supplication with thanksgiving let your requests be made known unto God.

Philippians 4:6

My brethren, count it all joy when ye fall into divers temptations; **Know**ing this, that the trying of your faith worketh patience. James 1:2-3

Casting all your care upon him; for he careth for you. 1 Peter 5:7

> *Worry is like a rocking chair. It keeps you going but you don't get anywhere. - Anonymous*

JESUS WILL

Jesus Will Give You Love

The Lord openeth the eyes of the blind: the Lord raiseth them that are bowed down: the Lord loveth the righteous. Psalms 146:8

For as a young man marrieth a virgin, so shall thy sons marry thee: and as the bridegroom rejoiceth over the bride, so shall thy God rejoice over thee. Isaiah 62:5

The Lord hath appeared of old unto me, saying, Yea, I have loved thee with an everlasting love: therefore with lovingkindness have I drawn thee. Jeremiah 31:3

I will heal their backsliding, I will love them freely: for mine anger is turned away from him. Hosea 14:4

For God so loved the world, that he gave his only begotten Son, that whosoever believeth in him should not perish, but have everlasting life.
John 3:16

For the Father himself loveth you, because ye have loved me, and have believed that I came out from God. John 16:27

And the glory which thou gavest me I have given them; that they may be one, even as we are one: I in them, and thou in me, that they may be made perfect in one; and that the world may know that thou hast sent me, and hast loved them, as thou hast loved me. John 17:22-23

And I have declared unto them thy name, and will declare it: that the love wherewith thou hast loved me may be in them, and I in them.
John 17:26

But God commendeth his love toward us, in that, while we were yet sinners, Christ died for us. Romans 5:8

But God, who is rich in mercy, for his great love wherewith he loved us, Even when we were dead in sins, hath quickened us together with Christ, by grace ye are saved. And hath raised us up together, and made us sit together in heavenly places in Christ Jesus: That in the ages to come he might shew the exceeding riches of his grace in his kindness toward us through Christ Jesus. Ephesians 2:4-7

And to know the love of Christ, which passeth knowledge, that ye might be filled with all the fulness of God. Ephesians 3:19

Now our Lord Jesus Christ himself, and God, even our Father, which hath loved us, and hath given us everlasting consolation and good hope through grace, Comfort your hearts, and stablish you in every good word and work. 2 Thessalonians 2:16-17

Behold, what manner of love the Father hath bestowed upon us, that we should be called the sons of God: therefore the world knoweth us not, because it knew him not. 1 John 3:1

Beloved, let us love one another: for love is of God; and every one that loveth is born of God, and knoweth God. He that loveth not knoweth not God; for God is love. In this was manifested the love of God toward us, because that God sent his only begotten Son into the world, that we might live through him. Herein is love, not that we loved God, but that he loved us, and sent his Son to be the propitiation for our sins. Beloved, if God so loved us, we ought also to love one another. 1 John 4:7-11

And we have known and believed the love that God hath to us. God is love; and he that dwelleth in love dwelleth in God, and God in him.
1 John 4:16

We love him, because he first loved us. 1 John 4:19

Jesus Will Give You Hope

To whom God would make known what is the riches of the glory of this mystery among the Gentiles; which is Christ in you, the hope of glory.
Colossians 1:27

Now our Lord Jesus Christ himself, and God, even our Father, which hath loved us, and hath given us everlasting consolation and good hope through grace. 2 Thessalonians 2:16

You cannot really lead and help people if you don't like them.

Let thy mercy, O Lord, be upon us, according as we hope in thee.

Psalms 33:22

For in thee, O Lord, do I hope: thou wilt hear, O Lord my God.

Psalms 38:15

And now, Lord, what wait I for? my hope is in thee. Psalms 39:7

Why art thou cast down, O my soul? and why art thou disquieted in me? hope thou in God: for I shall yet praise him for the help of his countenance. Psalms 42:5

Why art thou cast down, O my soul? and why art thou disquieted within me? hope thou in God: for I shall yet praise him, who is the health of my countenance, and my God. Psalms 42:11

For thou art my hope, O Lord God: thou art my trust from my youth.

Psalms 71:5

But I will hope continually, and will yet praise thee more and more.

Psalms 71:14

That they might set their hope in God, and not forget the works of God, but keep his commandments. Psalms 78:7

Let Israel hope in the Lord: for with the Lord there is mercy, and with him is plenteous redemption. Psalms 130:7

Let Israel hope in the Lord from henceforth and for ever. Psalms 131:3

Happy is he that hath the God of Jacob for his help, whose hope is in the Lord his God. Psalms 146:5

The Lord is my portion, saith my soul; therefore will I hope in him.

Lamentations 3:24

There is not enough darkness in all the world to put out the light of one small candle. - Anonymous

The Lord also shall roar out of Zion, and utter his voice from Jerusalem; and the heavens and the earth shall shake: but the Lord will be the hope of his people, and the strength of the children of Israel. Joel 3:16

It is good that a man should both hope and quietly wait for the salvation of the Lord. Lamentations 3:26

And have hope toward God, which they themselves also allow, that there shall be a resurrection of the dead, both of the just and unjust. Acts 24:15

But sanctify the Lord God in your hearts: and be ready always to give an answer to every man that asketh you a reason of the hope that is in you with meekness and fear. 1 Peter 3:15

Hope means expectancy when things are otherwise hopeless.- G. K. Chesterton

By whom also we have access by faith into this grace wherein we stand, and rejoice in hope of the glory of God. Romans 5:2

Wherefore gird up the loins of your mind, be sober, and hope to the end for the grace that is to be brought unto you at the revelation of Jesus Christ. 1 Peter 1:13

Jesus Will Give You Joy

Then he said unto them, Go your way, eat the fat, and drink the sweet, and send portions unto them for whom nothing is prepared: for this day is holy unto our Lord: neither be ye sorry; for the joy of the Lord is your strength. Nehemiah 8:10

When the morning stars sang together, and all the sons of God shouted for joy? Job 38:7

Thou wilt shew me the path of life: in thy presence is fulness of joy; at thy right hand there are pleasures for evermore. Psalms 16:11

For his anger endureth but a moment; in his favour is life: weeping may endure for a night, but joy cometh in the morning. Psalms 30:5

Let them shout for joy, and be glad, that favour my righteous cause: yea, let them say continually, Let the Lord be magnified, which hath pleasure in the prosperity of his servant. Psalms 35:27

Restore unto me the joy of thy salvation; and uphold me with thy free spirit. Psalms 51:12

They that sow in tears shall reap in joy. Psalms 126:5

Let the saints be joyful in glory: let them sing aloud upon their beds.
Psalms 149:5

A man hath joy by the answer of his mouth: and a word spoken in due season, how good is it! Proverbs 15:23

It is joy to the just to do judgment: but destruction shall be to the workers of iniquity. Proverbs 21:15

Go thy way, eat thy bread with joy, and drink thy wine with a merry heart; for God now accepteth thy works. Ecclesiastes 9:7

And the ransomed of the Lord shall return, and come to Zion with songs and everlasting joy upon their heads: they shall obtain joy and gladness, and sorrow and sighing shall flee away. Isaiah 35:10

Therefore the redeemed of the Lord shall return, and come with singing unto Zion; and everlasting joy shall be upon their head: they shall obtain gladness and joy; and sorrow and mourning shall flee away. Isaiah 51:11

For ye shall go out with joy, and be led forth with peace: the mountains and the hills shall break forth before you into singing, and all the trees of the field shall clap their hands. Isaiah 55:12

And thou shalt have joy and gladness; and many shall rejoice at his birth. Luke 1:14

And the angel said unto them, Fear not: for, behold, I bring you good tidings of great joy, which shall be to all people. Luke 2:10

Rejoice ye in that day, and leap for joy: for, behold, your reward is great in heaven: for in the like manner did their fathers unto the prophets. Luke 6:23

Likewise, I say unto you, there is joy in the presence of the angels of God over one sinner that repenteth. Luke 15:10

And they worshipped him, and returned to Jerusalem with great joy. Luke 24:52

These things have I spoken unto you, that my joy might remain in you, and that your joy might be full. John 15:11

Verily, verily, I say unto you, That ye shall weep and lament, but the world shall rejoice: and ye shall be sorrowful, but your sorrow shall be turned into joy. John 16:20

A woman when she is in travail hath sorrow, because her hour is come: but as soon as she is delivered of the child, she remembereth no more the anguish, for joy that a man is born into the world. And ye now therefore have sorrow: but I will see you again, and your heart shall rejoice, and your joy no man taketh from you. And in that day ye shall ask me nothing. Verily, verily, I say unto you, Whatsoever ye shall ask the Father in my name, he will give it you. Hitherto have ye asked nothing in my name: ask, and ye shall receive, that your joy may be full. John 16:21-24

And now come I to thee; and these things I speak in the world, that they might have my joy fulfilled in themselves. John 17:13

341

Thou hast made known to me the ways of life; thou shalt make me full of joy with thy countenance. Acts 2:28

And the disciples were filled with joy, and with the Holy Ghost.

Acts 13:52

And not only so, but we also joy in God through our Lord Jesus Christ, by whom we have now received the atonement. Romans 5:11

For the kingdom of God is not meat and drink; but righteousness, and peace, and joy in the Holy Ghost. Romans 14:17

Now the God of hope fill you with all joy and peace in believing, that ye may abound in hope, through the power of the Holy Ghost.

Romans 15:13

Not for that we have dominion over your faith, but are helpers of your joy: for by faith ye stand. 2 Corinthians 1:24

And having this confidence, I know that I shall abide and continue with you all for your furtherance and joy of faith. Philippians 1:25

And ye became followers of us, and of the Lord, having received the word in much affliction, with joy of the Holy Ghost. 1 Thessalonians 1:6

My brethren, count it all joy when ye fall into divers temptations.

James 1:2

And these things write we unto you, that your joy may be full. 1 John 1:4

Jesus Will Give You Mercy

The Lord is longsuffering, and of great mercy, forgiving iniquity and transgression, and by no means clearing the guilty, visiting the iniquity of the fathers upon the children unto the third and fourth generation.

Numbers 14:18

And shewing mercy unto thousands of them that love me and keep my commandments. Deuteronomy 5:10

Know therefore that the Lord thy God, he is God, the faithful God, which keepeth covenant and mercy with them that love him and keep his commandments to a thousand generations. Deuteronomy 7:9

A leader must allow himself no indulgence in secrets that would undermine his character or mar his public witness.

And he said, Lord God of Israel, there is no God like thee, in heaven above, or on earth beneath, who keepest covenant and mercy with thy servants that walk before thee with all their heart. 1 Kings 8:23

O give thanks unto the Lord; for he is good; for his mercy endureth for ever. 1 Chronicles 16:34

And that he would shew thee the secrets of wisdom, that they are double to that which is! Know therefore that God exacteth of thee less than thine iniquity deserveth. Job 11:6

Surely goodness and mercy shall follow me all the days of my life: and I will dwell in the house of the Lord for ever. Psalms 23:6

All the paths of the Lord are mercy and truth unto such as keep his covenant and his testimonies. Psalms 25:10

I will be glad and rejoice in thy mercy: for thou hast considered my trouble; thou hast known my soul in adversities. Psalms 31:7

Many sorrows shall be to the wicked: but he that trusteth in the Lord, mercy shall compass him about. Psalms 32:10

Thy mercy, O Lord, is in the heavens; and thy faithfulness reacheth unto the clouds. Psalms 36:5

The wicked borroweth, and payeth not again: but the righteous sheweth mercy, and giveth. Psalms 37:21

But I am like a green olive tree in the house of God: I trust in the mercy of God for ever and ever. Psalms 52:8

Also unto thee, O Lord, belongeth mercy: for thou renderest to every man according to his work. Psalms 62:12

For thou, Lord, art good, and ready to forgive; and plenteous in mercy unto all them that call upon thee. Psalms 86:5

For great is thy mercy toward me: and thou hast delivered my soul from the lowest hell. Psalms 86:13

But thou, O Lord, art a God full of compassion, and gracious, longsuffering, and plenteous in mercy and truth. Psalms 86:15

Justice and judgment are the habitation of thy throne: mercy and truth shall go before thy face. Psalms 89:14

The Lord is merciful and gracious, slow to anger, and plenteous in mercy. Psalms 103:8

For as the heaven is high above the earth, so great is his mercy toward them that fear him. Psalms 103:11

Like as a father pitieth his children, so the Lord pitieth them that fear him. Psalms 103:13

But the mercy of the Lord is from everlasting to everlasting upon them that fear him, and his righteousness unto children's children.
Psalms 103:17

Help me, O Lord my God: O save me according to thy mercy.
Psalms 109:26

The earth, O Lord, is full of thy mercy: teach me thy statutes.
Psalms 119:64

The Lord is gracious, and full of compassion; slow to anger, and of great mercy. Psalms 145:8

Let not mercy and truth forsake thee: bind them about thy neck; write them upon the table of thine heart. Proverbs 3:3

He that despiseth his neighbour sinneth: but he that hath mercy on the poor, happy is he. Do they not err that devise evil? but mercy and truth shall be to them that devise good. Proverbs 14:21-22

He that followeth after righteousness and mercy findeth life, righteousness, and honour. Proverbs 21:21

He that covereth his sins shall not prosper: but whoso confesseth and forsaketh them shall have mercy. Proverbs 28:13

And therefore will the Lord wait, that he may be gracious unto you, and therefore will he be exalted, that he may have mercy upon you: for the Lord is a God of judgment: blessed are all they that wait for him.
Isaiah 30:18

For my name's sake will I defer mine anger, and for my praise will I refrain for thee, that I cut thee not off. Isaiah 48:9

Let the wicked forsake his way, and the unrighteous man his thoughts: and let him return unto the Lord, and he will have mercy upon him; and to our God, for he will abundantly pardon. Isaiah 55:7

Blessed are the merciful: for they shall obtain mercy. Matthew 5:7

As concerning the gospel, they are enemies for your sakes: but as touching the election, they are beloved for the fathers' sakes. For the gifts and calling of God are without repentance. For as ye in times past have not believed God, yet have now obtained mercy through their unbelief: Even so have these also now not believed, that through your mercy they also may obtain mercy. For God hath concluded them all in unbelief, that he might have mercy upon all. Romans 11:28-32

But God, who is rich in mercy, for his great love wherewith he loved us. Ephesians 2:4

Not by works of righteousness which we have done, but according to his mercy he saved us, by the washing of regeneration, and renewing of the Holy Ghost. Titus 3:5

Let us therefore come boldly unto the throne of grace, that we may obtain mercy, and find grace to help in time of need. Hebrews 4:16

Behold, we count them happy which endure. Ye have heard of the patience of Job, and have seen the end of the Lord; that the Lord is very pitiful, and of tender mercy. James 5:11

Blessed be the God and Father of our Lord Jesus Christ, which according to his abundant mercy hath begotten us again unto a lively hope by the resurrection of Jesus Christ from the dead. 1 Peter 1:3

Which in time past were not a people, but are now the people of God: which had not obtained mercy, but now have obtained mercy.
1 Peter 2:10

Mercy unto you, and peace, and love, be multiplied. Jude 1:2

Jesus Will Give You Peace

And, having made peace through the blood of his cross, by him to reconcile all things unto himself; by him, I say, whether they be things in earth, or things in heaven. Colossians 1:20

I will both lay me down in peace, and sleep: for thou, Lord, only makest me dwell in safety. Psalms 4:8

The Lord will give strength unto his people; the Lord will bless his people with peace. Psalms 29:11

Mark the perfect man, and behold the upright: for the end of that man is peace. Psalms 37:37

He hath delivered my soul in peace from the battle that was against me: for there were many with me. Psalms 55:18

In his days shall the righteous flourish; and abundance of peace so long as the moon endureth. Psalms 72:7

Lord, thou wilt ordain peace for us: for thou also hast wrought all our works in us. Isaiah 26:12

For ye shall go out with joy, and be led forth with peace: the mountains and the hills shall break forth before you into singing, and all the trees of the field shall clap their hands. Isaiah 55:12

He shall enter into peace: they shall rest in their beds, each one walking in his uprightness. Isaiah 57:2

To give light to them that sit in darkness and in the shadow of death, to guide our feet into the way of peace. Luke 1:79

Now the God of hope fill you with all joy and peace in believing, that ye may abound in hope, through the power of the Holy Ghost.

Romans 15:13

For God is not the author of confusion, but of peace, as in all churches of the saints. 1 Corinthians 14:33

And let the peace of God rule in your hearts, to the which also ye are called in one body; and be ye thankful. Colossians 3:15

Now the Lord of peace himself give you peace always by all means. The Lord be with you all. 2 Thessalonians 3:16

> *"There is no peace ....to the wicked." The world offers false peace to dull the senses, deaden the conscience, quiet the nerves, but it cannot give peace. - Vance Havner*

1. Peace through Jesus Christ

But now in Christ Jesus ye who sometimes were far off are made nigh by the blood of Christ. For he is our peace, who hath made both one, and hath broken down the middle wall of partition between us. Having abolished in his flesh the enmity, even the law of commandments contained in ordinances; for to make in himself of twain one new man, so making peace. Ephesians 2:13-15

Therefore being justified by faith, we have peace with God through our Lord Jesus Christ. Romans 5:1

Peace I leave with you, my peace I give unto you: not as the world giveth, give I unto you. Let not your heart be troubled, neither let it be afraid.

John 14:27

**You cannot fully conquer kingdoms
until you have conquered yourself.**

These things I have spoken unto you, that in me ye might have peace. In the world ye shall have tribulation: but be of good cheer; I have overcome the world. John 16:33

Then said Jesus to them again, Peace be unto you: as my Father hath sent me, even so send I you. John 20:21

We will not have peace without righteousness. We will never get rested until we get right. - Vance Havner

2. Peace from God's Word

My son, forget not my law; but let thine heart keep my commandments: For length of days, and long life, and peace, shall they add to thee.
Proverbs 3:1-2

Great peace have they which love thy law: and nothing shall offend them.
Psalms 119:165

And all thy children shall be taught of the Lord; and great shall be the peace of thy children. Isaiah 54:13

Let us therefore follow after the things which make for peace, and things wherewith one may edify another. Romans 14:19

And as many as walk according to this rule, peace be on them, and mercy, and upon the Israel of God. Galatians 6:16

Be careful for nothing; but in every thing by prayer and supplication with thanksgiving let your requests be made known unto God. And the peace of God, which passeth all understanding, shall keep your hearts and minds through Christ Jesus. Finally, brethren, whatsoever things are true, whatsoever things are honest, whatsoever things are just, whatsoever things are pure, whatsoever things are lovely, whatsoever things are of good report; if there be any virtue, and if there be any praise, think on these things. Those things, which ye have both learned, and received, and heard, and seen in me, do: and the God of peace shall be with you.
Philippians 4:6-9

Grace and peace be multiplied unto you through the knowledge of God, and of Jesus our Lord. 2 Peter 1:2

3. How to Have Peace

When a man's ways please the Lord, he maketh even his enemies to be at peace with him. Proverbs 16:7

For to be carnally minded is death; but to be spiritually minded is life and peace. Romans 8:6

347

Thou wilt keep him in perfect peace, whose mind is stayed on thee: because he trusteth in thee. Isaiah 26:3

For the kingdom of God is not meat and drink; but righteousness, and peace, and joy in the Holy Ghost. For he that in these things serveth Christ is acceptable to God, and approved of men. Let us therefore follow after the things which make for peace, and things wherewith one may edify another. Romans 14:17-19

And the work of righteousness shall be peace; and the effect of righteousness quietness and assurance for ever. Isaiah 32:17

Jesus Will Give You Comfort

I, even I, am he that comforteth you: who art thou, that thou shouldest be afraid of a man that shall die, and of the son of man which shall be made as grass. Isaiah 51:12

To proclaim the acceptable year of the Lord, and the day of vengeance of our God; to comfort all that mourn. Isaiah 61:2

As one whom his mother comforteth, so will I comfort you; and ye shall be comforted in Jerusalem. Isaiah 66:13

Blessed are they that mourn: for they shall be comforted. Matthew 5:4

And I will pray the Father, and he shall give you another Comforter, that he may abide with you for ever. John 14:16

> *God does not comfort us to make us comfortable but to make us comforters. - J. H. Jowett*

Blessed be God, even the Father of our Lord Jesus Christ, the Father of mercies, and the God of all comfort; Who comforteth us in all our tribulation, that we may be able to comfort them which are in any trouble, by the comfort wherewith we ourselves are comforted of God. For as the sufferings of Christ abound in us, so our consolation also aboundeth by Christ. 2 Corinthians 1:3-5

Great is my boldness of speech toward you, great is my glorying of you: I am filled with comfort, I am exceeding joyful in all our tribulation.
2 Corinthians 7:4

Nevertheless God, that comforteth those that are cast down, comforted us by the coming of Titus; And not by his coming only, but by the consolation wherewith he was comforted in you, when he told us your earnest desire, your mourning, your fervent mind toward me; so that I rejoiced the more. 2 Corinthians 7:6-7

Finally, brethren, farewell. Be perfect, be of good comfort, be of one mind, live in peace; and the God of love and peace shall be with you.
2 Corinthians 13:11

Bear ye one another's burdens, and so fulfil the law of Christ.
Galatians 6:2

Comfort your hearts, and stablish you in every good word and work.
2 Thessalonians 2:17

God often comforts us, not always by changing the circum-stances of our lives, but by changing our attitude toward them.
- S. H. B. Masterman

Jesus Will Deliver You

He shall deliver thee in six troubles: yea, in seven there shall no evil touch thee. Job 5:19

But know that the Lord hath set apart him that is godly for himself: the Lord will hear when I call unto him. Psalms 4:3

The angel of the Lord encampeth round about them that fear him, and delivereth them. Psalms 34:7

Many are the afflictions of the righteous: but the Lord delivereth him out of them all. Psalms 34:19

For the Lord loveth judgment, and forsaketh not his saints; they are pre-served for ever: but the seed of the wicked shall be cut off. Psalms 37:28

He that believeth on him is not condemned: but he that believeth not is condemned already, because he hath not believed in the name of the only begotten Son of God. John 3:18

And ye shall know the truth, and the truth shall make you free. John 8:32

Knowing this, that our old man is crucified with him, that the body of sin might be destroyed, that henceforth we should not serve sin. Romans 6:6

For sin shall not have dominion over you: for ye are not under the law, but under grace. Romans 6:14

There hath no temptation taken you but such as is common to man: but God is faithful, who will not suffer you to be tempted above that ye are able; but will with the temptation also make a way to escape, that ye may be able to bear it. 1 Corinthians 10:13

Grace be to you and peace from God the Father, and from our Lord Jesus Christ, **W**ho gave himself for our sins, that he might deliver us from this present evil world, according to the will of God and our Father:

Galatians 1:3-4

But the Lord is faithful, who shall stablish you, and keep you from evil.

2 Thessalonians 3:3

For in that he himself hath suffered being tempted, he is able to succour them that are tempted. Hebrews 2:18

For the eyes of the Lord are over the righteous, and his ears are open unto their prayers: but the face of the Lord is against them that do evil. And who is he that will harm you, if ye be followers of that which is good? 1 Peter 3:12-13

The Lord knoweth how to deliver the godly out of temptations, and to reserve the unjust unto the day of judgment to be punished: 2 Peter 2:9

Jesus Will Give You Perseverance

Definition or perseverance - persistence; continued efforts; to stick to a task or purpose, no matter how hard or troublesome.

Know ye not that they which run in a race run all, but one receiveth the prize? So run, that ye may obtain. 1 Corinthians 9:24

The righteous also shall hold on his way, and he that hath clean hands shall be stronger and stronger. Job 17:9

I had fainted, unless I had believed to see the goodness of the Lord in the land of the living. **W**ait on the Lord: be of good courage, and he shall strengthen thine heart: wait, I say, on the Lord. Psalms 27:13-14

The Lord will perfect that which concerneth me: thy mercy, O Lord, endureth for ever: forsake not the works of thine own hands.

Psalms 138:8

But the path of the just is as the shining light, that shineth more and more unto the perfect day. Proverbs 4:18

For a dream cometh through the multitude of business. Ecclesiastes 5:3

Whatsoever thy hand findeth to do, do it with thy might; for there is no work, nor device, nor knowledge, nor wisdom, in the grave, whither thou goest. Ecclesiastes 9:10

Leaders are people of faith, for faith is vision.

---

strength. Even the youths shall faint and be weary, and the young men shall utterly fall: But they that wait upon the Lord shall renew their strength; they shall mount up with wings as eagles; they shall run, and not be weary; and they shall walk, and not faint. Isaiah 40:29-31

Ask, and it shall be given you; seek, and ye shall find; knock, and it shall be opened unto you: Matthew 7:7

Wherefore seeing we also are compassed about with so great a cloud of witnesses, let us lay aside every weight, and the sin which doth so easily beset us, and let us run with patience the race that is set before us.
Hebrews 12:1

When God sees someone who doesn't quit, He looks down and says, "There is someone I can use." - John Mason

Therefore, my beloved brethren, be ye stedfast, unmoveable, always abounding in the work of the Lord, forasmuch as ye know that your labour is not in vain in the Lord. 1 Corinthians 15:58

And let us not be weary in well doing: for in due season we shall reap, if we faint not. Galatians 6:9

I press toward the mark for the prize of the high calling of God in Christ Jesus. Philippians 3:14

Thou therefore endure hardness, as a good soldier of Jesus Christ.
2 Timothy 2:3

Now the just shall love by faith: but if any man draw back, my soul shall have no pleasure in him. Hebrews 10:38

And whatsoever ye do, do it heartily, as to the Lord, and not unto men.
Colossians 3:23

And so, after he had patiently endured, he obtained the promise.
Hebrews 6:15

I have fought a good fight, I have finished my course, I have kept the faith: Henceforth there is laid up for me a crown of righteousness, which the Lord, the righteous judge, shall give me at that day: and not to me only, but unto all them also that love his appearing. 2 Timothy 4:7-8

Difficulties are stepping stones to success. - Anonymous

Let us hold fast the profession of our faith without wavering; for he is faithful that promised. Hebrews 10:23

Cast not away therefore your confidence, which hath great recompence of reward. For ye have need of patience, that, after ye have done the will of God, ye might receive the promise. Hebrews 10:35-36

Wherefore take unto you the whole armour of God, that ye may be able to withstand in the evil day, and having done all, to stand. Stand therefore, having your loins girt about with truth, and having on the breastplate of righteousness. Ephesians 6:13-14

Therefore, my brethren dearly beloved and longed for, my joy and crown, so stand fast in the Lord, my dearly beloved. Philippians 4:1

Rooted and built up in him, and stablished in the faith, as ye have been taught, abounding therein with thanksgiving. Colossians 2:7

Prove all things; hold fast that which is good. 1 Thessalonians 5:21

Watch ye, stand fast in the faith, quit you like men, be strong.
1 Corinthians 16:13

Of the Jews five times received I forty stripes save one. Thrice was I beaten with rods, once was I stoned, thrice I suffered shipwreck, a night and a day I have been in the deep; In journeyings often, in perils of waters, in perils of robbers, in perils by mine own countrymen, in perils by the heathen, in perils in the city, in perils in the wilderness, in perils in the sea, in perils among false brethren; In weariness and painfulness, in watchings often, in hunger and thirst, in fastings often, in cold and nakedness. 2 Corinthians 11:24-27

We are troubled on every side, yet not distressed; we are perplexed, but not in despair; Persecuted, but not forsaken; cast down, but not destroyed.
2 Corinthians 4:8-9

For which cause we faint not; but though our outward man perish, yet the inward man is renewed day by day. For our light affliction, which is but for a moment, worketh for us a far more exceeding and eternal weight of glory. 2 Corinthians 4:16-17

And we desire that every one of you do shew the same diligence to the full assurance of hope unto the end. Hebrews 6:11

PERTINENT TRUTHS OF THE GOSPEL

Who is God?

God is love; and he that dwelleth in love dwelleth in God, and God in him. 1 John 4:16

God is a Spirit: and they that worship him must worship him in spirit and in truth. John 4:24

Shall we not much rather be in subjection to the Father of spirits, and live? Hebrews 12:9

O God, the God of the spirits of all flesh. Numbers 16:22

Let the Lord; the God of the spirits of all flesh. Numbers 27:16

1. God is the Creator of Heaven and Earth

In the beginning God created the heaven and the earth. Genesis 1:1

Thus saith God the Lord, he that created the heavens, and stretched them out; he that spread forth the earth, and that which cometh out of it; he that giveth breath unto the people upon it, and spirit to them that walk therein. Isaiah 42:5

For thus saith the Lord that created the heavens; God himself that formed the earth and made it; he hath established it, he created it not in vain, he formed it to be inhabited: I am the Lord; and there is none else.

Isaiah 45:18

2. God is Sovereign and Omnipotent

For his eyes are upon the ways of man, and he seeth all his goings.

Job 34:21

Behold, God is great, and we know him not, neither can the number of his years be searched out. Job 36:26

353

Dost thou know the balancings of the clouds, the wondrous works of him which is perfect in knowledge? Job 37:16

Nature is the art of God. - Thomas Browne

He ruleth by his power for ever; his eyes behold the nations: let not the rebellious exalt themselves. Selah. Psalms 66:7

Lord, thou hast been our dwelling place in all generations. **B**efore the mountains were brought forth, or ever thou hadst formed the earth and the world, even from everlasting to everlasting, thou art God. **T**hou turnest man to destruction; and sayest, Return, ye children of men. **F**or a thousand years in thy sight are but as yesterday when it is past, and as a watch in the night. Psalms 90:1-4

He causeth the vapours to ascend from the ends of the earth; he maketh lightnings for the rain; he bringeth the wind out of his treasuries.
Psalms 135:7

When he uttereth his voice, there is a multitude of waters in the heavens, and he causeth the vapours to ascend from the ends of the earth; he maketh lightnings with rain, and bringeth forth the wind out of his treasures.
Jeremiah 10:13

Thy kingdom is an everlasting kingdom, and thy dominion endureth throughout all generations. Psalms 145:13

Great is our Lord, and of great power: his understanding is infinite.
Psalms 147:5

For the ways of man are before the eyes of the Lord, and he pondereth all his goings. Proverbs 5:21

The eyes of the Lord are in every place, beholding the evil and the good.
Proverbs 15:3

The king's heart is in the hand of the Lord, as the rivers of water: he turneth it whithersoever he will. Proverbs 21:1

Who hath ascended up into heaven, or descended? who hath gathered the wind in his fists? who hath bound the waters in a garment? who hath established all the ends of the earth? what is his name, and what is his son's name, if thou canst tell? Proverbs 30:4

The quality of tomorrow's leaders lie in the character of today's followers.

All nations before him are as nothing; and they are counted to him less than nothing, and vanity. To whom then will ye liken God? or what likeness will ye compare unto him? Isaiah 40:17-18

For my thoughts are not your thoughts, neither are your ways my ways, saith the Lord. For as the heavens are higher than the earth, so are my ways higher than your ways, and my thoughts than your thoughts.
Isaiah 55:8-9

Thus saith the Lord, The heaven is my throne, and the earth is my footstool: where is the house that ye build unto me? and where is the place of my rest? Isaiah 66:1

Am I a God at hand, saith the Lord, and not a God afar off? Can any hide himself in secret places that I shall not see him? saith the Lord. Do not I fill heaven and earth? saith the Lord. Jeremiah 23:23-24

For with God nothing shall be impossible. Luke 1:37

O the depth of the riches both of the wisdom and knowledge of God! how unsearchable are his judgments, and his ways past finding out!
Romans 11:33

Because the foolishness of God is wiser than men; and the weakness of God is stronger than men. 1 Corinthians 1:25

For when God made promise to Abraham, because he could swear by no greater, he sware by himself. Hebrews 6:13

Wherefore we receiving a kingdom which cannot be moved, let us have grace, whereby we may serve God acceptably with reverence and godly fear: For our God is a consuming fire. Hebrews 12:28-29

And when I saw him, I fell at his feet as dead. And he laid his right hand upon me, saying unto me, Fear not; I am the first and the last: I am he that liveth, and was dead; and, behold, I am alive for evermore, Amen; and have the keys of hell and of death. Revelation 1:17-18

And I heard as it were the voice of a great multitude, and as the voice of many waters, and as the voice of mighty thunderings, saying, Alleluia: for the Lord God omnipotent reigneth. Revelation 19:6

And he said unto me, It is done. I am Alpha and Omega, the beginning and the end. I will give unto him that is athirst of the fountain of the water of life freely. Revelation 21:6

I am Alpha and Omega, the beginning and the end, the first and the last.
Revelation 22:13

3. God is the Creator of Mankind

And God said, Let us make man in our image, after our likeness.
Genesis 1:26

So God created man in his own image, in the image of God created he him; male and female created he them. Genesis 1:27

And the Lord God formed man of the dust of the ground, and breathed into his nostrils the breath of life; and man became a living soul.
Genesis 2:7

And the Lord God said, It is not good that the man should be alone; I will make him an help meet for him. Genesis 2:18

And the Lord God caused a deep sleep to fall upon Adam and he slept: and he took one of his ribs, and closed up the flesh instead thereof; And the rib, which the Lord God had taken from man, made he a woman, and brought her unto the man. And Adam said, This is now bone of my bones, and flesh of my flesh: she shall be called Woman, because she was taken out of Man. Therefore shall a man leave his father and his mother, and shall cleave unto his wife: and they shall be one flesh.
Genesis 2:21-24

The Lord, which stretcheth forth the heavens, and layeth the foundation of the earth, and formeth the spirit of man within him. Zechariah 12:1

As thou knowest not what is the way of the spirit, nor how the bones do grow in the womb of her that is with child: even so thou knowest not the works of God who maketh all. Ecclesiastes 11:5

He hath made the earth by his power, he hath established the world by his wisdom, and hath stretched out the heavens by his discretion.
Jeremiah 10:12

The Trinity (The Father, The Son, and The Holy Spirit)

And God said, Let us make man in our image, after our likeness: and let them have dominion over the fish of the sea, and over the fowl of the air, and over the cattle, and over all the earth, and over every creeping thing that creepeth upon the earth. Genesis 1:26

And the Lord God said, Behold, the man is become as one of us, to know good and evil: and now, lest he put forth his hand, and take also of the tree of life, and eat, and live for ever: Genesis 3:22

Come ye near unto me, hear ye this; I have not spoken in secret from the beginning; from the time that it was, there am I: and now the Lord God, and his Spirit, hath sent me. Isaiah 48:16

Go ye therefore, and teach all nations, baptizing them in the name of the Father, and of the Son, and of the Holy Ghost: Matthew 28:19

> *The sun, in my opinion, is the best example of the Trinity. God is the sun; Jesus is the light of the sun; and the Holy Ghost is the heat of the sun. - Benny Hinn*

And the Holy Ghost descended in a bodily shape like a dove upon him, and a voice came from heaven, which said, Thou art my beloved Son; in thee I am well pleased. John 3:22

For he whom God hath sent speaketh the words of God: for God giveth not the Spirit by measure unto him. The Father loveth the Son, and hath given all things into his hand. John 3:34-35

I and my Father are one. John 10:30

And I will pray the Father, and he shall give you another Comforter, that he may abide with you for ever; Even the Spirit of truth; whom the world cannot receive, because it seeth him not, neither knoweth him: but ye know him; for he dwelleth with you, and shall be in you. John 14:16-17

But the Comforter, which is the Holy Ghost, whom the Father will send in my name, he shall teach you all things, and bring all things to your remembrance, whatsoever I have said unto you. John 14:26

But when the Comforter is come, whom I will send unto you from the Father, even the Spirit of truth, which proceedeth from the Father, he shall testify of me: John 15:26

What? know ye not that your body is the temple of the Holy Ghost which is in you, which ye have of God, and ye are not your own?
1 Corinthians 6:19

But to us there is but one God, the Father, of whom are all things, and we in him; and one Lord Jesus Christ, by whom are all things, and we by him. 1 Corinthians 8:6

Now he which stablisheth us with you in Christ, and hath anointed us, is God; Who hath also sealed us, and given the earnest of the Spirit in our hearts. 2 Corinthians 1:21-22

The grace of the Lord Jesus Christ, and the love of God, and the communion of the Holy Ghost, be with you all. Amen. 2 Corinthians 13:14

357

But when the fulness of the time was come, God sent forth his Son, made of a woman, made under the law, And because ye are sons, God hath sent forth the Spirit of his Son into your hearts, crying, Abba, Father. Galatians 4:4,6

That their hearts might be comforted, being knit together in love, and unto all riches of the full assurance of understanding, to the acknowledgment of the mystery of God, and of the Father, and of Christ;
Colossians 2:2

But we are bound to give thanks alway to God for you, brethren beloved of the Lord, because God hath from the beginning chosen you to salvation through sanctification of the Spirit and belief of the truth: Whereunto he called you by our gospel, to the obtaining of the glory of our Lord Jesus Christ. 2 Thessalonians 2:13-14

But after that the kindness and love of God our Saviour toward man appeared, Not by works of righteousness which we have done, but according to his mercy he saved us, by the washing of regeneration, and renewing of the Holy Ghost; Which he shed on us abundantly through Jesus Christ our Saviour; Titus 3:4-6

Elect according to the foreknowledge of God the Father, through sanctification of the Spirit, unto obedience and sprinkling of the blood of Jesus Christ: Grace unto you, and peace, be multiplied. 1 Peter 1:2

For Christ also hath once suffered for sins, the just for the unjust, that he might bring us to God, being put to death in the flesh, but quickened by the Spirit: 1 Peter 3:18

This is he that came by water and blood, even Jesus Christ; not by water only, but by water and blood. And it is the Spirit that beareth witness, because the Spirit is truth. For there are three that bear record in heaven, the Father, the Word, and the Holy Ghost: and these three are one.
1 John 5:6-7

How to Reach God

Jesus saith unto him, I am the way, the truth, and the life: no man cometh unto the Father, but by me. John 14:6

For there is one God, and one mediator between God and men, the man Christ Jesus. 1 Timothy 2:5

True leaders never forget from whence they came, and live to bring others to where they are.

Then said Jesus unto them again, Verily, verily, I say unto you, I am the door of the sheep. All that ever came before me are thieves and robbers: but the sheep did not hear them. I am the door: by me if any man enter in, he shall be saved, and shall go in and out, and find pasture.

John 10:7-9

Whosoever denieth the Son, the same hath not the Father: (but) he that acknowledgeth the Son hath the Father also. 1 John 2:23

He that hath the Son hath life; and he that hath not the Son of God hath not life. 1 John 5:12

How to Love and Please God

If ye love me, keep my commandments. John 14:15

He that hath my commandments, and keepeth them, he it is that loveth me: and he that loveth me shall be loved of my Father, and I will love him, and will manifest myself to him. John 14:21

Jesus answered and said unto him, If a man love me, he will keep my words: and my Father will love him, and we will come unto him, and make our abode with him. He that loveth me not keepeth not my sayings: and the word which ye hear is not mine, but the Father's which sent me. John 14:23-24

If ye keep my commandments, ye shall abide in my love; even as I have kept my Father's commandments, and abide in his love. John 15:10

Ye are my friends, if ye do whatsoever I command you. John 15:14

By this we know that we love the children of God, when we love God, and keep his commandments. 1 John 5:2

For this is the love of God, that we keep his commandments: and his commandments are not grievous. 1 John 5:3

Who is Jesus?

Who is the image of the invisible God, the firstborn of every creature:

Colossians 1:15

For by him were all things created, that are in heaven, and that are in earth, visible and invisible, whether they be thrones, or dominions, or principalities, or powers: all things were created by him, and for him: And he is before all things, and by him all things consist. And he is the head of the body, the church: who is the beginning, the firstborn from the dead; that in all things he might have the preeminence. For it pleased the Father that in him should all fulness dwell; Colossians 1:16-19

He was in the world, and the world was made by him, and the world knew him not. John 1:10

1. Jesus is the Mediator between God and Man

For there is one God, and one mediator between God and men, the man Christ Jesus. 1 Timothy 2:5

Jesus saith unto him, I am the way, the truth, and the life: no man cometh unto the Father, but by me. John 14:6

Whosoever denieth the Son, the same hath not the Father: (but) he that acknowledgeth the Son hath the Father also. 1 John 2:23

And, having made peace through the blood of his cross, by him to reconcile all things unto himself; by him, I say, whether they be things in earth, or things in heaven. Colossians 1:20

All things are delivered unto me of my Father: and no man knoweth the Son, but the Father; neither knoweth any man the Father, save the Son, and he to whomsoever the Son will reveal him. Matthew 11:27

All that the Father giveth me shall come to me; and him that cometh to me I will in no wise cast out. For I came down from heaven, not to do mine own will, but the will of him that sent me. And this is the Father's will which hath sent me, that of all which he hath given me I should lose nothing, but should raise it up again at the last day. And this is the will of him that sent me, that every one which seeth the Son, and believeth on him, may have everlasting life: and I will raise him up at the last day.
John 6:37-40

2. Jesus is the Son of God

Which were born, not of blood, nor of the will of the flesh, nor of the will of man, but of God. John 1:13

For he whom God hath sent speaketh the words of God: for God giveth not the Spirit by measure unto him. John 3:34

I came forth from the Father, and am come into the world: again, I leave the world, and go to the Father. John 16:28

And declared to be the Son of God with power, according to the spirit of holiness, by the resurrection from the dead. Romans 1:4

3. Jesus is God

I and my Father are one. John 10:30

And without controversy great is the mystery of godliness: God was manifest in the flesh, justified in the Spirit, seen of angels, preached unto the Gentiles, believed on in the world, received up into glory.

1 Timothy 3:16

But whosoever drinketh of the water that I shall give him shall never thirst; but the water that I shall give him shall be in him a well of water springing up into everlasting life. John 4:14

Therefore the Jews sought the more to kill him, because he not only had broken the sabbath, but said also that God was his Father, making himself equal with God. John 5:18

And he that seeth me seeth him that sent me. John 12:45

And Jesus said unto them, I am the bread of life: he that cometh to me shall never hunger; and he that believeth on me shall never thirst.

John 6:35

But if I do, though ye believe not me, believe the works: that ye may know, and believe, that the Father is in me, and I in him. John 10:38

Hath in these last days spoken unto us by his Son, whom he hath appointed heir of all things, by whom also he made the worlds; Who being the brightness of his glory, and the express image of his person, and upholding all things by the word of his power, when he had by himself purges our sins, sat down on the right hand of the Majesty on high;

Hebrews 1:2-3

4. Jesus Existed as God Before He Came to Earth

John bare witness of him, and cried, saying, This was he of whom I spake, He that cometh after me is preferred before me: for he was before me. John 1:15

He that cometh from above is above all: he that is of the earth is earthly, and speaketh of the earth: he that cometh from heaven is above all.

John 3:31

Who, being in the form of God, thought it not robbery to be equal with God: But made himself of no reputation, and took upon him the form of a servant, and was made in the likeness of men: And being found in fashion as a man, he humbled himself, and became obedient unto death, even the death of the cross. **W**herefore God also hath highly exalted him, and given him a name which is above every name. Philippians 2:6-9

And God said, Let us make man in our image, after our likeness: and let them have dominion over the fish of the sea, and over the fowl of the air, and over the cattle, and over all the earth, and over every creeping thing that creepeth upon the earth. Genesis 1:26

But thou art the same, and thy years shall have no end. Psalms 102:27

In the beginning was the Word, and the Word was with God, and the Word was God. John 1:1

Say ye of him, whom the Father hath sanctified, and sent into the world, Thou blasphemest; because I said, I am the Son of God? John 10:36

All things were made by him; and without him was not any thing made that was made. John 1:3

And the Word was made flesh, and dwelt among us, and we beheld his glory as of the only begotten of the Father, full of grace and truth.
John 1:14

Your father Abraham rejoiced to see my day: and he saw it, and was glad. John 8:56

Then said the Jews unto him, Thou art not yet fifty years old, and hast thou seen Abraham? **J**esus said unto them, Verily, verily, I say unto you, Before Abraham was, I am. John 8:57-58

Father, I will that they also, whom thou hast given me, be with me where I am; that they may behold my glory, which thou hast given me: for thou lovedst me before the foundation of the world. John 17:24

Who is the image of the invisible God, the firstborn of every creature: For by him were all things created, that are in heaven, and that are in earth, visible and invisible, whether they be thrones, or dominions, or principalities, or powers: all things were created by him, and for him: And he is before all things, and by him all things consist.
Colossians 1:15-17

Who being the brightness of his glory, and the express image of his person, and upholding all things by the word of his power, when he had by himself purged our sins, sat down on the right hand of the Majesty on high; Hebrews 1:3

> **Leaders are not born, but are created by life.**

But unto the Son he saith, Thy throne, O God, is for ever and ever: a sceptre of righteousness is the sceptre of thy kingdom. Thou hast loved righteousness, and hated iniquity; therefore God, even thy God, hath anointed thee with the oil of gladness above thy fellows. And, Thou, Lord, in the beginning hast laid the foundation of the earth; and the heavens are the works of thine hands: They shall perish; but thou remainest; and they all shall wax old as doth a garment; And as a vesture shalt thou fold them up, and they shall be changed: but thou art the same, and thy years shall not fail. Hebrews 1:8-12

Jesus Christ the same yesterday, and today, and forever. Hebrews 13:8

I am Alpha and Omega, the beginning and the end, the first and the last.
Revelation 22:13

5. Jesus is the Word of God

In the beginning was the Word, and the Word was with God, and the Word was God. John 1:1

And the Word was made flesh, and dwelt among us, and we beheld his glory, the glory as of the only begotten of the Father, full of grace and truth. John 1:14

For there are three that bear record in heaven, the Father, the Word, and the Holy Ghost: and these three are one. 1 John 5:7

And he was clothed with a vesture dipped in blood: and his name is called The Word of God. Revelation 19:13

6. Jesus is Wisdom

But unto them which are called, both Jews and Greeks, Christ the power of God, and the wisdom of God. 1 Corinthians 1:24

But of him are ye in Christ Jesus, who of God is made unto us wisdom, and righteousness, and sanctification, and redemption: 1 Corinthians 1:30

In whom are hid all the treasures of wisdom and knowledge.
Colossians 2:3

The Pre-Existence of Jesus Christ

John bare witness of him, and cried, saying, This was he of whom I spake, He that cometh after me is preferred before me: for he was before me. John 1:15

363

He that cometh from above is above all: he that is of the earth is earthly, and speaketh of the earth: he that cometh from heaven is above all.

John 3:31

Who, being in the form of God, thought it not robbery to be equal with God: But made himself of no reputation, and took upon him the form of a servant, and was made in the likeness of men: And being found in fashion as a man, he humbled himself, and became obedient unto death, even the death of the cross. Wherefore God also hath highly exalted him, and given him a name which is above every name. Philippians 2:6-9

And God said, Let us make man in our image, after our likeness: and let them have dominion over the fish of the sea, and over the fowl of the air, and over the cattle, and over all the earth, and over every creeping thing that creepeth upon the earth. Genesis 1:26

But thou art the same, and thy years shall have no end. Psalms 102:27

In the beginning was the Word, and the Word was with God, and the Word was God. John 1:1

Say ye of him, whom the Father hath sanctified, and sent into the world, Thou blasphemest; because I said, I am the Son of God? John 10:36

All things were made by him; and without him was not any thing made that was made. John 1:3

And the Word was made flesh, and dwelt among us, (and we beheld his glory as of the only begotten of the Father,) full of grace and truth.

John 1:14

Your father Abraham rejoiced to see my day: and he saw it, and was glad. John 8:56

Then said the Jews unto him, Thou art not yet fifty years old, and hast thou seen Abraham? Jesus said unto them, Verily,verily, I say unto you, Before Abraham was, I am. John 8:57-58

Father, I will that they also, whom thou hast given me, be with me where I am; that they may behold my glory, which thou hast given me: for thou lovedst me before the foundation of the world. John 17:24

Who is the image of the invisible God, the firstborn of every creature: For by him were all things created, that are in heaven, and that are in earth, visible and invisible, whether they be thrones, or dominions, or principalities, or powers: all things were created by him, and for him: And he is before all things, and by him all things consist.

Colossians 1:15-17

Who being the brightness of his glory, and the express image of his person, and upholding all things by the word of his power, when he had by himself purged our sins, sat down on the right hand of the Majesty on high; Hebrews 1:3

But unto the Son he saith, Thy throne, O God, is for ever and ever: a sceptre of righteousness is the sceptre of thy kingdom. Thou hast loved righteousness, and hated iniquity; therefore God, even thy God, hath anointed thee with the oil of gladness above thy fellows. And, Thou, Lord, in the beginning hast laid the foundation of the earth; and the heavens are the works of thine hands: They shall perish; but thou remainest; and they all shall wax old as doth a garment; And as a vesture shalt thou fold them up, and they shall be changed: but thou art the same, and thy years shall not fail. Hebrews 1:8-12

Jesus Christ the same yesterday, and to day, and for ever. Hebrews 13:8

I am Alpha and Omega, the beginning and the end, the first and the last.

Revelation 22:13

The Sufferings and Death of Jesus Christ

1. Prophecies of the Suffering and Death of Jesus Christ

Searching what, or what manner of time the Spirit of Christ which was in them did signify, when it testified beforehand the sufferings of Christ, and the glory that should follow. 1 Peter 1:11

They gaped upon me with their mouths, as a ravening and a roaring lion. I am poured out like water, and all my bones are out of joint: my heart is like wax; it is melted in the midst of my bowels. My strength is dried up like a potsherd; and my tongue cleaveth to my jaws; and thou hast brought me into the dust of death. For dogs have compassed me: the assembly of the wicked have inclosed me: they pierced my hands and my feet. I may tell all my bones: they look and stare upon me. They part my garments among them, and cast lots upon my vesture. But be not thou far from me, O Lord: O my strength, haste thee to help me. Psalms 22:13-19

365

He is despised and rejected of men; a man of sorrows, and acquainted with grief: and we hid as it were our faces from him; he was despised, and we esteemed him not. Surely he hath borne our griefs, and carried our sorrows: yet we did esteem him stricken, smitten of God, and afflicted. But he was wounded for our transgressions, he was bruised for our iniquities: the chastisement of our peace was upon him; and with his stripes we are healed. All we like sheep have gone astray; we have turned every one to his own way; and the Lord hath laid on him the iniquity of us all. He was oppressed, and he was afflicted, yet he opened not his mouth: he is brought as a lamb to the slaughter, and as a sheep before her shearers is dumb, so he openeth not his mouth. He was taken from prison and from judgment: and who shall declare his generation? for he was cut off out of the land of the living: for the transgression of my people was he stricken. And he made his grave with the wicked, and with the rich in his death; because he had done no violence, neither was any deceit in his mouth. Yet it pleased the Lord to bruise him; he hath put him to grief: when thou shalt make his soul an offering for sin, he shall see his seed, he shall prolong his days, and the pleasure of the Lord shall prosper in his hand. He shall see of the travail of his soul, and shall be satisfied: by his knowledge shall my righteous servant justify many; for he shall bear their iniquities. Isaiah 53:3-11

2. New Testament Fulfillment of Old Testament Prophecies

My God, my God, why hast thou forsaken me? why art thou so far from helping me, and from the words of my roaring? Psalms 22:1

And about the ninth hour Jesus cried with a loud voice, saying, Eli, Eli, lama sabachthani? that is to say, My God, my God, why hast thou forsaken me? Matthew 27:46

My lovers and my friends stand aloof from my sore; and my kinsmen stand afar off. Psalms 38:11

And all his acquaintance, and the women that followed him from Galilee, stood afar off, beholding these things. Luke 23:49

From the sole of the foot even unto the head there is no soundness in it; but wounds, and bruises, and putrifying sores: they have not been closed, neither bound up, neither mollified with ointment. Isaiah 1:6

Leaders learn from others, but they are not made by others.

I gave my back to the smiters, and my cheeks to them that plucked off the hair: I hid not my face from shame and spitting. Isaiah 50:6

As many were astonied at thee; his visage was so marred more than any man, and his form more than the sons of men: Isaiah 52:14

And the men that held Jesus mocked him, and smote him. Luke 22:63

Then did they spit in his face, and buffeted him; and others smote him with the palms of their hands, Matthew 26:67

Therefore will I divide him a portion with the great, and he shall divide the spoil with the strong; because he hath poured out his soul unto death: and he was numbered with the transgressors; and he bare the sin of many, and made intercession for the transgressors. Isaiah 53:12

And the scripture was fulfilled, which saith, And he was numbered with the transgressors. Mark 15:28

For I say unto you, that this that is written must yet be accomplished in me, And he was reckoned among the transgressors: for the things concerning me have an end. Luke 22:37

They gave me also gall for my meat; and in my thirst they gave me vinegar to drink. Psalms 69:21

My strength is dried up like a potsherd; and my tongue cleaveth to my jaws; and thou hast brought me into the dust of death. Psalms 22:15

After this, Jesus knowing that all things were now accomplished, that the scripture might be fulfilled, saith, I thirst. Now there was set a vessel full of vinegar: and they filled a spunge with vinegar, and put it upon hyssop, and put it to his mouth. John 19:28-29

Into thine hand I commit my spirit: thou hast redeemed me, O Lord God of truth. Psalms 31:5

And when Jesus had cried with a loud voice, he said, Father, into thy hands I commend my spirit: and having said thus, he gave up the ghost.
Luke 23:46

They part my garments among them, and cast lots upon my vesture.
Psalms 22:18

Then the soldiers, when they had crucified Jesus, took his garments, and made four parts, to every soldier a part; and also his coat: now the coat was without seam, woven from the top throughout. They said therefore among themselves, Let us not rend it, but cast lots for it, whose it shall be: that the scripture might be fulfilled, which saith, They parted my raiment among them, and for my vesture they did cast lots. These things therefore the soldiers did. John 19:23-24

He keepeth all his bones: not one of them is broken. Psalms 34:20

Then came the soldiers, and brake the legs of the first, and of the other which was crucified with him. But when they came to Jesus, and saw that he was dead already, they brake not his legs: But one of the soldiers with a spear pierced his side, and forthwith came there out blood and water. And he that saw it bare record, and his record is true: and he knoweth that he saith true, that ye might believe. For these things were done, that the scripture should be fulfilled, A bone of him shall not be broken. John 19:32-36

For dogs have compassed me: the assembly of the wicked have inclosed me: they pierced my hands and my feet. Psalms 22:16

And I will pour upon the house of David, and upon the inhabitants of Jerusalem, the spirit of grace and of supplications: and they shall look upon me whom they have pierced, and they shall mourn for him, as one mourneth for his only son, and shall be in bitterness for him, as one that is in bitterness for his firstborn. Zechariah 12:10

But he was wounded for our transgressions, he was bruised for our iniquities: the chastisement of our peace was upon him; and with his stripes we are healed. Isaiah 53:5

Who his own self bare our sins in his own body on the tree, that we, being dead to sins, should live unto righteousness: by whose stripes ye were healed. 1 Peter 2:24

And he made his grave with the wicked, and with the rich in his death; because he had done no violence, neither was any deceit in his mouth.
Isaiah 53:9

Who did no sin, neither was guile found in his mouth: Who, when he was reviled, reviled not again; when he suffered, he threatened not; but committed himself to him that judgeth righteously:
1 Peter 2:22-23

The Shed Blood of Jesus Christ

1. Redeemed by the Blood

For this is my blood of the new testament, which is shed for many for the remission of sins. Matthew 26:28

And hath made of one blood all nations of men for to dwell on all the face of the earth, and hath determined the times before appointed, and the bounds of their habitation. Acts 17:26

Take heed therefore unto yourselves, and to all the flock, over the which the Holy Ghost hath made you overseers, to feed the church of God, which he hath purchased with his own blood. Acts 20:28

For all have sinned, and come short of the glory of God; Being justified freely by his grace through the redemption that is in Christ Jesus. Whom God hath set forth to be a propitiation through faith in his blood, to declare his righteousness for the remission of sins that are past, through the forbearance of God. Romans 3:23-25

In whom we have redemption through his blood, the forgiveness of sins, according to the riches of his grace. Ephesians 1:7

But now in Christ Jesus ye who sometimes were far off are made nigh by the blood of Christ. Ephesians 2:13

Who hath delivered us from the power of darkness, and hath translated us into the kingdom of his dear Son: In whom we have redemption through his blood, even the forgiveness of sins. Colossians 1:13-14

And, having made peace through the blood of his cross, by him to reconcile all things unto himself; by him, I say, whether they be things in earth, or things in heaven. Colossians 1:20

But Christ being come an high priest of good things to come, by a greater and more perfect tabernacle, not made with hands, that is to say, not of this building. Neither by the blood of goats and calves, but by his own blood he entered in once into the holy place, having obtained eternal redemption for us. For if the blood of bulls and of goats, and the ashes of an heifer sprinkling the unclean, sanctifieth to the purifying of the flesh: How much more shall the blood of Christ, who through the eternal Spirit offered himself without spot to God, purge your conscience from dead works to serve the living God? And for this cause he is the mediator of the new testament, that by means of death, for the redemption of the transgressions that were under the first testament, they which are called might receive the promise of eternal inheritance. Hebrews 9:11-15

And almost all things are by the law purged with blood; and without shedding of blood is no remission. It was therefore necessary that the patterns of things in the heavens should be purified with these; but the heavenly things themselves with better sacrifices than these. For Christ

369

is not entered into the holy places made with hands, which are the figures of the true; but into heaven itself, now to appear in the presence of God for us: Nor yet that he should offer himself often, as the high priest entereth into the holy place every year with blood of others. For then must he often have suffered since the foundation of the world: but now once in the end of the world hath he appeared to put away sin by the sacrifice of himself. And as it is appointed unto men once to die, but after this the judgment. So Christ was once offered to bear the sins of many; and unto them that look for him shall he appear the second time without sin unto salvation. Hebrews 9:22-27

Having therefore, brethren, boldness to enter into the holiest by the blood of Jesus. Hebrews 10:19

And to Jesus the mediator of the new covenant, and to the blood of sprinkling, that speaketh better things than that of Abel. Hebrews 12:24

And they sung a new song, saying, Thou art worthy to take the book, and to open the seals thereof: for thou wast slain, and hast redeemed us to God by thy blood out of every kindred, and tongue, and people, and nation. Revelation 5:9

2. Sins Cleansed by the Blood

But if we walk in the light, as he is in the light, we have fellowship one with another, and the blood of Jesus Christ his Son cleanseth us from all sin. 1 John 1:7

And from Jesus Christ, who is the faithful witness, and the first begotten of the dead, and the prince of the kings of the earth. Unto him that loved us, and washed us from our sins in his own blood. Revelation 1:5

And I said unto him, Sir, thou knowest. And he said to me, These are they which came out of great tribulation, and have washed their robes, and made them white in the blood of the Lamb. Revelation 7:14

3. The Blood of Jesus as a Spiritual Weapon

And they overcame him by the blood of the Lamb, and by the word of their testimony; and they loved not their lives unto the death.
Revelation 12:11

> To be an effective leader, you may listen to all, but in the end, be responsible for your own decision.

The Resurrection of Jesus Christ

1. Prophecies of the Resurrection of Jesus Christ

From that time forth began Jesus to shew unto his disciples, how that he must go unto Jerusalem, and suffer many things of the elders and chief priests and scribes, and be killed, and be raised again the third day.
Matthew 16:21

And as they came down from the mountain, Jesus charged them, saying, Tell the vision to no man, until the Son of man be risen again from the dead. Matthew 17:9

And they shall kill him, and the third day he shall be raised again. And they were exceeding sorry. Matthew 17:23

And shall deliver him to the Gentiles to mock, and to scourge, and to crucify him: and the third day he shall rise again. Matthew 20:19

But after I am risen again, I will go before you into Galilee.
Matthew 26:32

2. The Resurrection

He is not here: for he is risen, as he said. Come, see the place where the Lord lay. And go quickly, and tell his disciples that he is risen from the dead; and, behold, he goeth before you into Galilee; there shall ye see him: lo, I have told you. Matthew 28:6-7

And he saith unto them, Be not affrighted: Ye seek Jesus of Nazareth, which was crucified: he is risen; he is not here: behold the place where they laid him. Mark 16:6

Jesus said unto her, I am the resurrection, and the life: he that believeth in me, though he were dead, yet shall he live. John 11:25

This is now the third time that Jesus shewed himself to his disciples, after that he was risen from the dead. John 21:14

He seeing this before spake of the resurrection of Christ, that his soul was not left in hell, neither his flesh did see corruption. This Jesus hath God raised up, whereof we all are witnesses. Acts 2:31-32

And killed the Prince of life, whom God hath raised from the dead; whereof we are witnesses. Acts 3:15

The God of our fathers raised up Jesus, whom ye slew and hanged on a tree. Acts 5:30

Him God raised up the third day, and shewed him openly; Not to all the people, but unto witnesses chosen before of God, even to us, who did eat and drink with him after he rose from the dead. Acts 10:40-41

But God raised him from the dead. Acts 13:30

But he, whom God raised again, saw no corruption. Acts 13:37

Opening and alleging, that Christ must needs have suffered, and risen again from the dead; and that this Jesus, whom I preach unto you, is Christ. Acts 17:3

That Christ should suffer, and that he should be the first that should rise from the dead, and should shew light unto the people, and to the Gentiles. Acts 26:23

Knowing that Christ being raised from the dead dieth no more; death hath no more dominion over him. Romans 6:9

And that he was buried, and that he rose again the third day according to the scriptures. 1 Corinthians 15:4

But now is Christ risen from the dead, and become the firstfruits of them that slept. 1 Corinthians 15:20

3. Benefits from the Resurrection of Jesus Christ

But for us also, to whom it shall be imputed, if we believe on him that raised up Jesus our Lord from the dead; Who was delivered for our offences, and was raised again for our justification. Romans 4:24-25

Therefore we are buried with him by baptism into death: that like as Christ was raised up from the dead by the glory of the Father, even so we also should walk in newness of life. For if we have been planted together in the likeness of his death, we shall be also in the likeness of his resurrection. Romans 6:4-5

But if the Spirit of him that raised up Jesus from the dead dwell in you, he that raised up Christ from the dead shall also quicken your mortal bodies by his Spirit that dwelleth in you. Romans 8:11

That if thou shalt confess with thy mouth the Lord Jesus, and shalt believe in thine heart that God hath raised him from the dead, thou shalt be saved. Romans 10:9

And God hath both raised up the Lord, and will also raise up us by his own power. 1 Corinthians 6:14

And that he died for all, that they which live should not henceforth live unto themselves, but unto him which died for them, and rose again.

2 Corinthians 5:15

And hath raised us up together, and made us sit together in heavenly places in Christ Jesus. Ephesians 2:6

And to wait for his Son from heaven, whom he raised from the dead, even Jesus, which delivered us from the wrath to come.

1 Thessalonians 1:10

Blessed be the God and Father of our Lord Jesus Christ, which according to his abundant mercy hath begotten us again unto a lively hope by the resurrection of Jesus Christ from the dead. 1 Peter 1:3

Who by him do believe in God, that raised him up from the dead, and gave him glory; that your faith and hope might be in God. 1 Peter 1:21

Eternal Life through Jesus Christ

For God so loved the world, that he gave his only begotten Son, that whosoever believeth in him should not perish, but have everlasting life.

John 3:16

But whosoever drinketh of the water that I shall give him shall never thirst; but the water that I shall give him shall be in him a well of water springing up into everlasting life. John 4:14

Verily, verily, I say unto you, He that heareth my word, and believeth on him that sent me, hath everlasting life, and shall not come into condemnation; but is passed from death unto life. John 5:24

Labour not for the meat which perisheth, but for that meat which endureth unto everlasting life, which the Son of man shall give unto you: for him hath God the Father sealed. John 6:27

Verily, verily, I say unto you, He that believeth on me hath everlasting life. John 6:47

I am the living bread which came down from heaven: if any man eat of this bread, he shall live for ever: and the bread that I will give is my flesh, which I will give for the life of the world. John 6:51

Whoso eateth my flesh, and drinketh my blood, hath eternal life; and I will raise him up at the last day. John 6:54

My sheep hear my voice, and I know them, and they follow me: And I give unto them eternal life; and they shall never perish, neither shall any man pluck them out of my hand. John 10:27-28

Jesus said unto her, I am the resurrection, and the life: he that believeth in me, though he were dead, yet shall he live: And whosoever liveth and believeth in me shall never die. Believest thou this? John 11:25-26

As thou hast given him power over all flesh, that he should give eternal life to as many as thou hast given him. John 17:2

And these shall go away into everlasting punishment: but the righteous into life eternal. Matthew 25:46

To them who by patient continuance in well doing seek for glory and honour and immortality, eternal life. Romans 2:7

But now being made free from sin, and become servants to God, ye have your fruit unto holiness, and the end everlasting life. For the wages of sin is death; but the gift of God is eternal life through Jesus Christ our Lord. Romans 6:22-23

For our light affliction, which is but for a moment, worketh for us a far more exceeding and eternal weight of glory; While we look not at the things which are seen, but at the things which are not seen: for the things which are seen are temporal; but the things which are not seen are eternal. 2 Corinthians 4:17-18

For he that soweth to his flesh shall of the flesh reap corruption; but he that soweth to the Spirit shall of the Spirit reap life everlasting.
Galatians 6:8

In hope of eternal life, which God, that cannot lie, promised before the world began. Titus 1:2

That being justified by his grace, we should be made heirs according to the hope of eternal life. Titus 3:7

And this is the promise that he hath promised us, even eternal life.
1 John 2:25

And this is the record, that God hath given to us eternal life, and this life is in his Son. 1 John 5:11

These things have I written unto you that believe on the name of the Son of God; that ye may know that ye have eternal life, and that ye may believe on the name of the Son of God. 1 John 5:13

And we know that the Son of God is come, and hath given us an understanding, that we may know him that is true, and we are in him that is true, even in his Son Jesus Christ. This is the true God, and eternal life.
1 John 5:20

The Return of Jesus Christ (The Rapture)

For the Son of man shall come in the glory of his Father with his angels; and then he shall reward every man according to his works.

Matthew 16:27

For as the lightning cometh out of the east, and shineth even unto the west; so shall also the coming of the Son of man be. Matthew 24:27

And then shall appear the sign of the Son of man in heaven: and then shall all the tribes of the earth mourn, and they shall see the Son of man coming in the clouds of heaven with power and great glory.

Matthew 24:30

And Jesus said, I am: and ye shall see the Son of man sitting on the right hand of power, and coming in the clouds of heaven. Mark 14:62

Verily, verily, I say unto you, The hour is coming, and now is, when the dead shall hear the voice of the Son of God: and they that hear shall live.

John 5:25

Marvel not at this: for the hour is coming, in the which all that are in the graves shall hear his voice. John 5:28

And if I go and prepare a place for you, I will come again, and receive you unto myself; that where I am, there ye may be also. John 14:3

Ye have heard how I said unto you, I go away, and come again unto you. If ye loved me, ye would rejoice, because I said, I go unto the Father: for my Father is greater than I. John 14:28

Which also said, Ye men of Galilee, why stand ye gazing up into heaven? this same Jesus, which is taken up from you into heaven, shall so come in like manner as ye have seen him go into heaven. Acts 1:11

Therefore judge nothing before the time, until the Lord come, who both will bring to light the hidden things of darkness, and will make manifest the counsels of the hearts: and then shall every man have praise of God.

1 Corinthians 4:5

When Christ, who is our life, shall appear, then shall ye also appear with him in glory. Colossians 3:4

For the Lord himself shall descend from heaven with a shout, with the voice of the archangel, and with the trump of God: and the dead in Christ shall rise first: Then we which are alive and remain shall be caught up together with them in the clouds, to meet the Lord in the air: and so shall we ever be with the Lord. 1 Thessalonians 4:16-17

375

Looking for that blessed hope, and the glorious appearing of the great God and our Saviour Jesus Christ. Titus 2:13

So Christ was once offered to bear the sins of many; and unto them that look for him shall he appear the second time without sin unto salvation. Hebrews 9:28

And when the chief Shepherd shall appear, ye shall receive a crown of glory that fadeth not away. 1 Peter 5:4

Beloved, now are we the sons of God, and it doth not yet appear what we shall be: but we know that, when he shall appear, we shall be like him; for we shall see him as he is. 1 John 3:2

Behold, he cometh with clouds; and every eye shall see him, and they also which pierced him: and all kindreds of the earth shall wail because of him. Even so, Amen. Revelation 1:7

And, behold, I come quickly; and my reward is with me, to give every man according as his work shall be. Revelation 22:12

He which testifieth these things saith, Surely I come quickly. Amen. Even so, come, Lord Jesus. Revelation 22:20

1. Are You Ready for the Rapture?

Watch therefore: for ye know not what hour your Lord doth come. Matthew 24:42

Watch ye therefore, and pray always, that ye may be accounted worthy to escape all these things that shall come to pass, and to stand before the Son of man. Luke 21:36

Behold, I show you a mystery; We shall not all sleep, but we shall all be changed, 1 Corinthians 15:51

In a moment, in the twinkling of an eye, at the last trump: for the trumpet shall sound, and the dead shall be raised incorruptible, and we shall be changed. 1 Corinthians 15:52

The Faithfulness of God

Know therefore that the Lord thy God, he is God, the faithful God, which keepeth covenant and mercy with them that love him and keep his commandments to a thousand generations. Deuteronomy 7:9

All great leaders are products of time and trophies of life's wars.

The Lord render to every man his righteousness and his faithfulness: for the Lord delivered thee into my hand to day, but I would not stretch forth mine hand against the Lord's anointed. 1 Samuel 26:23

Thy mercy, O Lord, is in the heavens; and thy faithfulness reacheth unto the clouds. Psalms 36:5

Shall thy lovingkindness be declared in the grave? or thy faithfulness in destruction? Psalms 88:11

I will sing of the mercies of the Lord for ever: with my mouth will I make known thy faithfulness to all generations. For I have said, Mercy shall be built up for ever: thy faithfulness shalt thou establish in the very heavens. Psalms 89:1-2

And the heavens shall praise thy wonders, O Lord: thy faithfulness also in the congregation of the saints. Psalms 89:5

O Lord God of hosts, who is a strong Lord like unto thee? or to thy faithfulness round about thee? Psalms 89:8

To shew forth thy lovingkindness in the morning, and thy faithfulness every night. Psalms 92:2

Thy faithfulness is unto all generations: thou hast established the earth, and it abideth. Psalms 119:90

He will not suffer thy foot to be moved: he that keepeth thee will not slumber. Behold, he that keepeth Israel shall neither slumber nor sleep.
Psalms 121:3-4

They are new every morning: great is thy faithfulness.
Lamentations 3:23

God is faithful, by whom ye were called unto the fellowship of his Son Jesus Christ our Lord. 1 Corinthians 1:9

There hath no temptation taken you but such as is common to man: but God is faithful, who will not suffer you to be tempted above that ye are able; but will with the temptation also make a way to escape, that ye may be able to bear it. 1 Corinthians 10:13

Faithful is he that calleth you, who also will do it. 1 Thessalonians 5:24

But the Lord is faithful, who shall stablish you, and keep you from evil.
2 Thessalonians 3:3

If we believe not, yet he abideth faithful: he cannot deny himself.
2 Timothy 2:13

Let us hold fast the profession of our faith without wavering; for he is faithful that promised. Hebrews 10:23

The Lord is not slack concerning his promise, as some men count slackness; but is longsuffering to us-ward, not willing that any should perish, but that all should come to repentance. 2 Peter 3:9

If we confess our sins, he is faithful and just to forgive us our sins, and to cleanse us from all unrighteousness. 1 John 1:9

And from Jesus Christ, who is the faithful witness, and the first begotten of the dead, and the prince of the kings of the earth. Unto him that loved us, and washed us from our sins in his own blood. Revelation 1:5

And I saw heaven opened, and behold a white horse; and he that sat upon him was called Faithful and True, and in righteousness he doth judge and make war. Revelation 19:11

Confessing Jesus Christ

Whosoever shall confess that Jesus is the Son of God, God dwelleth in him, and he in God. 1 John 4:15

Whosoever therefore shall confess me before men, him will I confess also before my Father which is in heaven. Matthew 10:32

Also I say unto you, Whosoever shall confess me before men, him shall the Son of man also confess before the angels of God. Luke 12:8

That if thou shalt confess with thy mouth the Lord Jesus, and shalt believe in thine heart that God hath raised him from the dead, thou shalt be saved. For with the heart man believeth unto righteousness; and with the mouth confession is made unto salvation. Romans 10:9-10

For it is written, As I live, saith the Lord, every knee shall bow to me, and every tongue shall confess to God. Romans 14:11

And that every tongue should confess that Jesus Christ is Lord, to the glory of God the Father. Philippians 2:11

Hereby know ye the Spirit of God: Every spirit that confesseth that Jesus Christ is come in the flesh is of God: And every spirit that confesseth not that Jesus Christ is come in the flesh is not of God: and this is that spirit of antichrist, whereof ye have heard that it should come; and even now already is it in the world. 1 John 4:2-3

1. Jesus Confessing the Word of His Father (God)

Then said Jesus unto them, When ye have lifted up the Son of man, then shall ye know that I am he, and that I do nothing of myself; but as my Father hath taught me, I speak these things. John 8:28

I speak that which I have seen with my Father: and ye do that which ye have seen with your father. John 8:38

And I know that his commandment is life everlasting: whatsoever I speak therefore, even as the Father said unto me, so I speak. John 12:50

Believest thou not that I am in the Father, and the Father in me? the words that I speak unto you I speak not of myself: but the Father that dwelleth in me, he doeth the works. John 14:10

Confessing the Word of God

And take not the word of truth utterly out of my mouth; for I have hoped in thy judgments. Psalms 119:43

My tongue shall speak of thy word: for all thy commandments are righteousness. Psalms 119:172

Bow down thine ear, and hear the words of the wise, and apply thine heart unto my knowledge. For it is a pleasant thing if thou keep them within thee; they shall withal be fitted in thy lips. Proverbs 22:17-18

We having the same spirit of faith, according as it is written, I believed, and therefore have I spoken; we also believe, and therefore speak.
2 Corinthians 4:13

Fight the good fight of faith, lay hold on eternal life, whereunto thou art also called, and hast professed a good profession before many witnesses.
1 Timothy 6:12

Seeing then that we have a great high priest, that is passed into the heavens, Jesus the Son of God, let us hold fast our profession. Hebrews 4:14

Let us hold fast the profession of our faith without wavering; for he is faithful that promised. Hebrews 10:23

But what saith it? The word is nigh thee, even in thy mouth, and in thy heart: that is, the word of faith, which we preach. Romans 10:8

Say unto them, As truly as I live, saith the Lord, as ye have spoken in mine ears, so will I do to you. Numbers 14:28

So then faith cometh by hearing, and hearing by the word of God.
Romans 10:17

379

1. The Power of Confession

And Jesus answering saith unto them, Have faith in God. For verily I say unto you, That whosoever shall say unto this mountain, Be thou removed, and be thou cast into the sea; and shall not doubt in his heart, but shall believe that those things which he saith shall come to pass; he shall have whatsoever he saith. Mark 11:22-23

Death and life are in the power of the tongue: and they that love it shall eat the fruit thereof. Proverbs 18:21

Confessing Sins

He that covereth his sins shall not prosper: but whoso confesseth and forsaketh them shall have mercy. Proverbs 28:13

And it shall be, when he shall be guilty in one of these things, that he shall confess that he hath sinned in that thing. Leviticus 5:5

If we confess our sins, he is faithful and just to forgive us our sins, and to cleanse us from all unrighteousness. 1 John 1:9

And the seed of Israel separated themselves from all strangers, and stood and confessed their sins, and the iniquities of their fathers. Nehemiah 9:2

I acknowledged my sin unto thee, and mine iniquity have I not hid. I said, I will confess my transgressions unto the Lord; and thou forgavest the iniquity of my sin. Selah. Psalms 32:5

And were baptized of him in Jordan, confessing their sins. Matthew 3:6

And many that believed came, and confessed, and shewed their deeds.
Acts 19:18

Confess your faults one to another, and pray one for another, that ye may be healed. The effectual fervent prayer of a righteous man availeth much.
James 5:16

Idolatry

Definition: The worship of false gods, whether by means of images or otherwise.

Thou shalt have no other gods before me. Exodus 20:3

Leaders do not make their work their God. Their work is guided out of their relationship with God.

Ye shall not make with me gods of silver, neither shall ye make unto you gods of gold. Exodus 20:23

For thou shalt worship no other god: for the Lord, whose name is Jealous, is a jealous God. Exodus 34:14

Turn ye not unto idols, nor make to yourselves molten gods: I am the Lord your God. Leviticus 19:4

Ye shall make you no idols nor graven image, neither rear you up a standing image, neither shall ye set up any image of stone in your land, to bow down unto it: for I am the Lord your God. Leviticus 26:1

And it shall be, if thou do at all forget the Lord thy God, and walk after other gods, and serve them, and worship them, I testify against you this day that ye shall surely perish. Deuteronomy 8:19

Wherefore, my dearly beloved, flee from idolatry. 1 Corinthians 10:14

1. The Consequences of Committing Idolatry

Know ye not that the unrighteous shall not inherit the kingdom of God? Be not deceived: neither fornicators, nor idolaters, nor adulterers, nor effeminate, nor abusers of themselves with mankind. 1 Corinthians 6:9

For this ye know, that no whoremonger, nor unclean person, nor covetous man, who is an idolater, hath any inheritance in the kingdom of Christ and of God. Ephesians 5:5

2. The Worship of demon spirits

And the rest of the men which were not killed by these plagues yet repented not of the works of their hands, that they should not worship devils, and idols of gold, and silver, and brass, and stone, and of wood: which neither can see, nor hear, nor walk. Revelation 9:20

But the fearful, and unbelieving, and the abominable, and murderers, and whoremongers, and sorcerers, and idolaters, and all liars, shall have their part in the lake which burneth with fire and brimstone: which is the second death. Revelation 21:8

3. Material and Human gods

Thou shalt have no other gods before me. Exodus 20:3

For where your treasure is, there will your heart be also. Matthew 6:21

4. Sins Related to Idolatry

For rebellion is as the sin of witchcraft, and stubbornness is as iniquity and idolatry. Because thou hast rejected the word of the Lord, he hath also rejected thee from being king. 1 Samuel 15:23

Mortify therefore your members which are upon the earth; fornication, uncleanness, inordinate affection, evil concupiscence, and covetousness, which is idolatry. Colossians 3:5

Unity in the Body of Christ

For as the body is one, and hath many members, and all the members of that one body, being many, are one body: so also is Christ. For by one Spirit are we all baptized into one body, whether we be Jews or Gentiles, whether we be bond or free; and have been all made to drink into one Spirit. For the body is not one member, but many. If the foot shall say, Because I am not the hand, I am not of the body; is it therefore not of the body? And if the ear shall say, Because I am not the eye, I am not of the body; is it therefore not of the body? If the whole body were an eye, where were the hearing? If the whole were hearing, where were the smelling? But now hath God set the members every one of them in the body, as it hath pleased him. And if they were all one member, where were the body? But now are they many members, yet but one body. And the eye cannot say unto the hand, I have no need of thee: nor again the head to the feet, I have no need of you. Nay, much more those members of the body, which seem to be more feeble, are necessary: And those members of the body, which we think to be less honourable, upon these we bestow more abundant honour; and our uncomely parts have more abundant comeliness. For our comely parts have no need: but God hath tempered the body together, having given more abundant honour to that part which lacked: That there should be no schism in the body; but that the members should have the same care one for another. And whether one member suffer, all the members suffer with it; or one member be honoured, all the members rejoice with it. Now ye are the body of Christ, and members in particular. 1 Corinthians 12:12-27

Endeavoring to keep the unity of the Spirit in the bond of peace. There is one body, and one Spirit, even as ye are called in one hope of your calling. Ephesians 4:3-4

From whom the whole body fitly joined together and compacted by that which every joint supplieth, according to the effectual working in the measure of every part, maketh increase of the body unto the edifying of itself in love. Ephesians 4:16

Wherefore putting away lying, speak every man truth with his neighbour: for we are members one of another. Ephesians 4:25

And not holding the Head, from which all the body by joints and bands having nourishment ministered, and knit together, increaseth with the increase of God. Colossians 2:19

God's Divine Protection

And of Benjamin he said, The beloved of the Lord shall dwell in safety by him; and the Lord shall cover him all the day long, and he shall dwell between his shoulders. Deuteronomy 33:12

I will both lay me down in peace, and sleep: for thou, Lord, only makest me dwell in safety. Psalms 4:8

The Lord is my light and my salvation; whom shall I fear? the Lord is the strength of my life; of whom shall I be afraid? Psalms 27:1

For in the time of trouble he shall hide me in his pavilion: in the secret of his tabernacle shall he hide me; he shall set me up upon a rock.
Psalms 27:5

He that dwelleth in the secret place of the most High shall abide under the shadow of the Almighty. I will say of the Lord, He is my refuge and my fortress: my God; in him will I trust. Surely he shall deliver thee from the snare of the fowler, and from the noisome pestilence. He shall cover thee with his feathers, and under his wings shalt thou trust: his truth shall be thy shield and buckler. Thou shalt not be afraid for the terror by night; nor for the arrow that flieth by day; Nor for the pestilence that walketh in darkness; nor for the destruction that wasteth at noonday. A thousand shall fall at thy side, and ten thousand at thy right hand; but it shall not come nigh thee. Only with thine eyes shalt thou behold and see the reward of the wicked. Because thou hast made the Lord, which is my refuge, even the most High, thy habitation; There shall no evil befall thee, neither shall any plague come nigh thy dwelling. For he shall give his angels charge over thee, to keep thee in all thy ways. They shall bear thee up in their hands, lest thou dash thy foot against a stone. Thou shalt tread upon the lion and adder: the young lion and the dragon shalt thou trample under feet. Because he hath set his love upon me, therefore will I deliver him: I will set him on high, because he hath known my name. He shall call upon me, and I will answer him: I will be with him in trouble; I will deliver him, and honour him. with long life will I satisfy him, and shew him my salvation.
Psalms 91:1-16

He suffered no man to do them wrong: yea, he reproved kings for their sakes; Saying, Touch not mine anointed, and do my prophets no harm.
Psalms 105:14-15

The Lord shall preserve thee from all evil: he shall preserve thy soul. The Lord shall preserve thy going out and thy coming in from this time forth, and even for evermore. Psalms 121:7-8

But whoso hearkeneth unto me shall dwell safely, and shall be quiet from fear of evil. Proverbs 1:33

The name of the Lord is a strong tower: the righteous runneth into it, and is safe. Proverbs 18:10

But now thus saith the Lord that created thee, O Jacob, and he that formed thee, O Israel, Fear not: for I have redeemed thee, I have called thee by thy name; thou art mine. When thou passest through the waters, I will be with thee; and through the rivers, they shall not overflow thee: when thou walkest through the fire, thou shalt not be burned; neither shall the flame kindle upon thee. Isaiah 43:1-2

And who is he that will harm you, if ye be followers of that which is good? 1 Peter 3:13

We know that whosoever is born of God sinneth not; but he that is begotten of God keepeth himself, and that wicked one toucheth him not.
1 John 5:18

Neither give place to the devil. Ephesians 4:27

Time on Earth

1. Human Life is Short

For he remembered that they were but flesh; a wind that passeth away, and cometh not again. Psalms 78:39

My days are like a shadow that declineth; and I am withered like grass. But thou, O Lord, shalt endure for ever; and thy remembrance unto all generations. Psalms 102:11-12

As for man, his days are as grass: as a flower of the field, so he flourisheth.

For the wind passeth over it, and it is gone; and the place thereof shall know it no more. Psalms 103:15-16

Criticism is the leader's greatest test of maturity, conviction and commitment to his vision. If you are ready for criticism, you're ready for leadership.

For all flesh is as grass, and all the glory of man as the flower of grass. The grass withereth, and the flower thereof falleth away: But the word of the Lord endureth for ever. And this is the word which by the gospel is preached unto you. 1 Peter 1:24-25

2. Man's Time Compared to God's Time

For a thousand years in thy sight are but as yesterday when it is past, and as a watch in the night. Psalms 90:4

While we look not at the things which are seen, but at the things which are not seen: for the things which are seen are temporal; but the things which are not seen are eternal. 2 Corinthians 4:18

But, beloved, be not ignorant of this one thing, that one day is with the Lord as a thousand years, and a thousand years as one day. 2 Peter 3:8

The Final Judgment of Mankind

And as it is appointed unto men once to die, but after this the judgment:
Hebrews 9:27

Some men's sins are open beforehand, going before to judgment; and some men they follow after. Likewise also the good works of some are manifest beforehand; and they that are otherwise cannot be hid.
1 Timothy 5:24-25

All the ways of a man are clean in his own eyes; but the Lord weigheth the spirits. Proverbs 16:2

I said in mine heart, God shall judge the righteous and the wicked: for there is a time there for every purpose and for every work.
Ecclesiastes 3:17

For if we would judge ourselves, we should not be judged.
1 Corinthians 11:31

For the time is come that judgment must begin at the house of God: and if it first begin at us, what shall the end be of them that obey not the gospel of God? 1 Peter 4:17

And through covetousness shall they with feigned words make merchandise of you: whose judgment now of a long time lingereth not, and their damnation slumbereth not. For if God spared not the angels that sinned, but cast them down to hell, and delivered them into chains of darkness, to be reserved unto judgment; 2 Peter 2:3-4

The Lord knoweth how to deliver the godly out of temptations, and to reserve the unjust unto the day of judgment to be punished: 2 Peter 2:9

But the heavens and the earth, which are now, by the same word are kept in store, reserved unto fire against the day of judgment and perdition of ungodly men. 2 Peter 3:7

And the angels which kept not their first estate, but left their own habitation, he hath reserved in everlasting chains under darkness unto the judgment of the great day. Jude 1:6

To execute judgment upon all, and to convince all that are ungodly among them of all their ungodly deeds which they have ungodly committed, and of all their hard speeches which ungodly sinners have spoken against him. These are murmurers, complainers, walking after their own lusts; and their mouth speaketh great swelling words, having men's persons in admiration because of advantage. Jude 1:15-16

But I say unto you, That every idle word that men shall speak, they shall give account thereof in the day of judgment. Matthew 12:36

1. Jesus Christ is Appointed by God to Judge the World

Behold my servant, whom I have chosen; my beloved, in whom my soul is well pleased: I will put my spirit upon him, and he shall shew judgment to the Gentiles. Matthew 12:18

For the Father judgeth no man, but hath committed all judgment unto the Son: John 5:22

And hath given him authority to execute judgment also, because he is the Son of man. John 5:27

I can of mine own self do nothing: as I hear, I judge: and my judgment is just; because I seek not mine own will, but the will of the Father which hath sent me. John 5:30

And yet if I judge, my judgment is true: for I am not alone, but I and the Father that sent me. John 8:16

And Jesus said, For judgment I am come into this world, that they which see not might see; and that they which see might be made blind.
John 9:39

But after thy hardness and impenitent heart treasurest up unto thyself wrath against the day of wrath and revelation of the righteous judgment of God; Romans 2:5

2. The Judgment Seat of Christ

But why dost thou judge thy brother? or why dost thou set at nought thy brother? for we shall all stand before the judgment seat of Christ.

Romans 14:10

For we must all appear before the judgment seat of Christ; that every one may receive the things done in his body, according to that he hath done, whether it be good or bad. 2 Corinthians 5:10

And I saw thrones, and they sat upon them, and judgment was given unto them: and I saw the souls of them that were beheaded for the witness of Jesus, and for the word of God, and which had not worshipped the beast, neither his image, neither had received his mark upon their foreheads, or in their hands; and they lived and reigned with Christ a thousand years. Revelation 20:4

Heaven

1. Who's Going to Heaven and Why

Blessed are they that do his commandments, that they may have right to the tree of life, and may enter in through the gates into the city.

Revelation 22:14

And these shall go away into everlasting punishment: but the righteous into life eternal. Matthew 25:46

Jesus answered and said unto his, Verily, verily, I say unto thee, Except a man be born again, he cannot see the kingdom of God. Nicodemus saith unto him, How can a man be born when he is old? can he enter the second time into his mother's womb, and be born? Jesus answered, Verily, verily, I say unto thee, Except a man be born of water and of the Spirit, he cannot enter into the kingdom of God. That which is born of the flesh is flesh; and that which is born of the Spirit is spirit. Marvel not that I said unto thee, Ye must be born again. John 3:3-7

> *Our Savior has gone to prepare a place, but there are places only for those who make reservations. The dying thief made a reservation: "Remember me." - Vance Havner*

But whosoever drinketh of the water that I shall give him shall never thirst; but the water that I shall give him shall be in him a well of water springing up into everlasting life. John 4:14

387

Verily, verily, I say unto you, He that heareth my word, and believeth on him that sent me, hath everlasting life, and shall not come into condemnation; but is passed from death unto life. John 5:24

Verily, verily, I say unto you, If a man keep my saying, he shall never see death. John 8:51

Jesus said unto her, I am the resurrection, and the life: he that believeth in me, though he were dead, yet shall he live: And whosoever liveth and believeth in me shall never die. Believest thou this? John 11:25-26

2. What is Heaven Like?

But as it is written, Eye hath not seen, nor ear heard, neither have entered into the heart of man, the things which God hath prepared for them that love him. 1 Corinthians 2:9

The Lord hath prepared his throne in the heavens; and his kingdom ruleth over all. Psalms 103:19

Thy sun shall no more go down; neither shall thy moon withdraw itself: for the Lord shall be thine everlasting light, and the days of thy mourning shall be ended. Thy people also shall be all righteous: they shall inherit the land for ever, the branch of my planting, the work of my hands, that I may be glorified. Isaiah 60:20-21

In my Father's house are many mansions: if it were not so, I would have told you. I go to prepare a place for you. And if I go and prepare a place for you, I will come again, and receive you unto myself; that where I am, there ye may be also. John 14:2-3

But now they desire a better country, that is, an heavenly: wherefore God is not ashamed to be called their God: for he hath prepared for them a city. Hebrews 11:16

There is only one thing better than going to heaven and that is to take someone with you. - Anonymous

Nevertheless we, according to his promise, look for new heavens and a new earth, wherein dwelleth righteousness. 2 Peter 3:13

Therefore are they before the throne of God, and serve him day and night in his temple: and he that sitteth on the throne shall dwell among

---

A leader who knows who he is does not depend on others to validate his sense of self-worth.

---

them. They shall hunger no more, neither thirst any more; neither shall the sun light on them, nor any heat. For the Lamb which is in the midst of the throne shall feed them, and shall lead them unto living fountains of waters: and God shall wipe away all tears from their eyes.

Revelation 7:15-17

He that hath an ear, let him hear what the Spirit saith unto the churches; To him that overcometh will I give to eat of the tree of life, which is in the midst of the paradise of God. Revelation 2:7

And the city had no need of the sun, neither of the moon, to shine in it: for the glory of God did lighten it, and the Lamb is the light thereof. And the nations of them which are saved shall walk in the light of it: and the kings of the earth do bring their glory and honour into it. And the gates of it shall not be shut at all by day: for there shall be no night there. And they shall bring the glory and honour of the nations into it.

Revelation 21:23-26

And he shewed me a pure river of water of life, clear as crystal, proceeding out of the throne of God and of the Lamb. In the midst of the street of it, and on either side of the river, was there the tree of life, which bare twelve manner of fruits, and yielded her fruit every month: and the leaves of the tree were for the healing of the nations. And there shall be no more curse: but the throne of God and of the Lamb shall be in it; and his servants shall serve him: And they shall see his face; and his name shall be in their foreheads. And there shall be no night there; and they need no candle, neither light of the sun; for the Lord God giveth them light: and they shall reign for ever and ever. Revelation 22:1-5

> *Christians are not citizens of earth trying to get to heaven but citizens of heaven making their way through this world. - Vance Havner*

3. Buildings in Heaven

For we know that if our earthly house of this tabernacle were dissolved, we have a building of God, an house not made with hands, eternal in the heavens. 2 Corinthians 5:1

For he looked for a city which hath foundations, whose builder and maker is God. Hebrews 11:10

Blessed and holy is he that hath part in the first resurrection: on such the second death hath no power, but they shall be priests of God and of Christ, and shall reign with him a thousand years. Revelation 20:6

389

And I saw a new heaven and a new earth: for the first heaven and the first earth were passed away; and there was no more sea. And I John saw the holy city, new Jerusalem, coming down from God out of heaven, prepared as a bride adorned for her husband. Revelation 21:1-2

Having the glory of God: and her light was like unto a stone most precious, even like a jasper stone, clear as crystal; And had a wall great and high, and had twelve gates, and at the gates twelve angels, and names written thereon, which are the names of the twelve tribes of the children of Israel: On the east three gates; on the north three gates; on the south three gates; and on the west three gates. And the wall of the city had twelve foundations, and in them the names of the twelve apostles of the Lamb. And he that talked with me had a golden reed to measure the city, and the gates thereof, and the wall thereof. And the city lieth foursquare, and the length is as large as the breadth: and he measured the city with the reed, twelve thousand furlongs. The length and the breadth and the height of it are equal. And he measured the wall thereof, an hundred and forty and four cubits, according to the measure of a man, that is, of the angel. And the building of the wall of it was of jasper: and the city was pure gold, like unto clear glass. And the foundations of the wall of the city were garnished with all manner of precious stones. The first foundation was jasper; the second, sapphire; the third, a chalcedony; the fourth, an emerald; The fifth, sardonyx; the sixth, sardius; the seventh, chrysolite; the eighth, beryl; the ninth, a topaz; the tenth, a chrysoprasus; the eleventh, a jacinth; the twelfth, an amethyst. And the twelve gates were twelve pearls; every several gate was of one pearl: and the street of the city was pure gold, as it were transparent glass. And I saw no temple therein: for the Lord God Almighty and the Lamb are the temple of it.
Revelation 21:11-22

4. Fellowship in Heaven

And I appoint unto you a kingdom, as my Father hath appointed unto me; That ye may eat and drink at my table in my kingdom, and sit on thrones judging the twelve tribes of Israel. Luke 22:29-30

And I say unto you, That many shall come from the east and west, and shall sit down with Abraham, and Isaac, and Jacob, in the kingdom of heaven. Matthew 8:11

To him that overcometh will I grant to sit with me in my throne, even as I also overcame, and am set down with my Father in his throne.
Revelation 3:21

Hell

For we must all appear before the judgment seat of Christ; that every one may receive the things done in his body, according to that he hath done, whether it be good or bad. 2 Corinthians 5:10

I am he that liveth, and was dead; and, behold, I am alive for evermore, Amen; and have the keys of hell and of death. Revelation 1:18

And fear not them which kill the body, but are not able to kill the soul: but rather fear him which is able to destroy both soul and body in hell.
Matthew 10:28

Hell is naked before him, and destruction hath no covering. Job 26:6

But I say unto you, That whosoever is angry with his brother without a cause shall be in danger of the judgment: and whosoever shall say to his brother, Raca, shall be in danger of the council: but whosoever shall say, Thou fool, shall be in danger of hell fire. Matthew 5:22

Hell is truth seen too late - duty neglected in its season.- Tryon Edwards

Ye serpents, ye generation of vipers, how can ye escape the damnation of hell? Matthew 23:33

But he that shall blaspheme against the Holy Ghost hath never forgiveness, but is in danger of eternal damnation. Mark 3:29

1. Who is Hell For?

Then shall he say also unto them on the left hand, Depart from me, ye cursed, into everlasting fire, prepared for the devil and his angels.
Matthew 25:41

And through covetousness shall they with feigned words make merchandise of you: whose judgment now of a long time lingereth not, and their damnation slumbereth not. For if God spared not the angels that sinned, but cast them down to hell, and delivered them into chains of darkness, to be reserved unto judgment. 2 Peter 2:3-4

And the beast was taken, and with him the false prophet that wrought miracles before him, with which he deceived them that had received the mark of the beast, and them that worshipped his image. These both were cast alive into a lake of fire burning with brimstone. Revelation 19:20

And I saw an angel come down from heaven, having the key of the bottomless pit and a great chain in his hand. And he laid hold on the dragon, that old serpent, which is the Devil, and Satan, and bound him a thousand years, And cast him into the bottomless pit, and shut him up, and set a seal upon him, that he should deceive the nations no more, till the thousand years should be fulfilled: and after that he must be loosed a little season. Revelation 20:1-3

And the devil that deceived them was cast into the lake of fire and brimstone, where the beast and the false prophet are, and shall be tormented day and night for ever and ever. Revelation 20:10

And death and hell were cast into the lake of fire. This is the second death. And whosoever was not found written in the book of life was cast into the lake of fire. Revelation 20:14-15

There are no humanists, agnostics or atheists in hell, because every soul in hell believes in Jesus, bows to Jesus, and confess that Jesus is Lord. Only after damnation awakes does reality break.

2. Who's Going to Hell and Why?

The wicked shall be turned into hell, and all the nations that forget God.
Psalms 9:17

He that believeth and is baptized shall be saved; but he that believeth not shall be damned. Mark 16:16

Whosoever therefore resisteth the power, resisteth the ordinance of God: and they that resist shall receive to themselves damnation. Romans 13:2

For the Lord knoweth the way of the righteous: but the way of the ungodly shall perish. Psalms 1:6

That they all might be damned who believed not the truth, but had pleasure in unrighteousness. 2 Thessalonians 2:12

That thou mayest give him rest from the days of adversity, until the pit be digged for the wicked. Psalms 94:13

Life is too short and hell is too hot to play games with your eternal future.

Nay, ye do wrong, and defraud, and that your brethren. Know ye not that the unrighteous shall not inherit the kingdom of God? Be not deceived: neither fornicators, nor idolaters, nor adulterers, nor effeminate, nor abus-

All leaders are the targets of criticism.

ers of themselves with mankind, Nor thieves, nor covetous, nor drunkards, nor revilers, nor extortioners, shall inherit the kingdom of God.

1 Corinthians 6:8-10

Envyings, murders, drunkenness, revellings, and such like: of the which
I tell you before, as I have also told you in time past, that they which do
such things shall not inherit the kingdom of God. Galatians 5:21

Having damnation, because they have cast off their first faith.

1 Timothy 5:12

3. How Serious is Hell?

And if thine eye offend thee, pluck it out, and cast it from thee: it is better
for thee to enter into life with one eye, rather than having two eyes to be
cast into hell fire. Matthew 18:9

And if thy right eye offend thee, pluck it out, and cast it from thee: for it
is profitable for thee that one of thy members should perish, and not that
thy whole body should be cast into hell. And if thy right hand offend
thee, cut if off, and cast it from thee: for it is profitable for thee that one
of thy members should perish, and not that thy whole body should be
cast into hell. Matthew 5:29-30

And if thy hand offend thee, cut it off: it is better for thee to enter into life
maimed, than having two hands to go into hell, into the fire that never
shall be quenched: Where their worm dieth not, and the fire is not
quenched. And if thy foot offend thee, cut it off: it is better for thee to
enter halt into life, than having two feet to be cast into hell, into the fire
that never shall be quenched: Where their worm dieth not, and the fire is
not quenched. And if thine eye offend thee, pluck it out: it is better for
thee to enter into the kingdom of God with one eye, than having two
eyes to be cast into hell fire: Where their worm dieth not, and the fire is
not quenched. Mark 9:43-48

4. An Example of Hell

And there was a certain beggar named Lazarus, which was laid at his
gate, full of sores, And desiring to be fed with the crumbs which fell
from the rich man's table: moreover the dogs came and licked his sores.
And it came to pass, that the beggar died, and was carried by the angels
into Abraham's bosom: the rich man also died, and was buried; And in
hell he lift up his eyes, being in torments, and seeth Abraham afar off,
and Lazarus in his bosom. And he cried and said, Father Abraham, have
mercy on me, and send Lazarus, that he may dip the tip of his finger in

393

water, and cool my tongue; for I am tormented in this flame. **B**ut Abraham said, Son, remember that thou in thy lifetime receivedst thy good things, and likewise Lazarus evil things: but now he is comforted, and thou art tormented. **A**nd beside all this, between us and you there is a great gulf fixed: so that they which would pass from hence to you cannot; neither can they pass to us, that would come from thence. **T**hen he said, I pray thee therefore, father, that thou wouldest send him to my father's house: **F**or I have five brethren; that he may testify unto them, lest they also come into this place of torment. **A**braham saith unto him, They have Moses and the prophets; let them hear them. And he said, Nay, father Abraham: but if one went unto them from the dead, they will repent. **A**nd he said unto him, If they hear not Moses and the prophets, neither will they be persuaded, though one rose from the dead. Luke 16:20-31

5. What is Hell Like?

And he opened the bottomless pit; and there arose a smoke out of the pit, as the smoke of a great furnace; and the sun and the air were darkened by reason of the smoke of the pit. Revelation 9:2

And the devil that deceived them was cast into the lake of fire and brimstone, where the beast and the false prophet are, and shall be tormented day and night for ever and ever. Revelation 20:10

As for thee also, by the blood of thy covenant I have sent forth thy prisoners out of the pit wherein is no water. Zechariah 9:11

The sinners in Zion are afraid; fearfulness hath surprised the hypocrites. Who among us shall dwell with the devouring fire: who among us shall dwell with everlasting burnings? Isaiah 33:14

Where their worm dieth not, and the fire is not quenched. Mark 9:48

6. Different Levels of Punishment in Hell

Woe unto you, scribes and Pharisees, hypocrites! for ye devour widows' houses, and for a pretence make long prayer: therefore ye shall receive the greater damnation. Matthew 23:14

But and if that servant say in his heart, My lord delayeth his coming; and shall begin to beat the menservants and maidens, and to eat and drink, and to be drunken; The lord of that servant will come in a day when he looketh not for him, and at an hour when he is not aware, and will cut him in sunder, and will appoint him his portion with the unbelievers. **A**nd that servant, which knew his lord's will, and prepared not himself, neither did according to his will, shall be beaten with many stripes. **B**ut he that knew not, and did commit things worthy of stripes, shall be beaten with few stripes. For unto whomsoever much is given, of him shall be much required: and to whom men have committed much, of him they will ask the more. Luke 12:45-48

7. The Location of Hell

When I shall bring thee down with them that descend into the pit, with the people of old time, and shall set thee in the low parts of the earth, in places desolate of old, with them that go down to the pit, that thou be not inhabited; and I shall set glory in the land of the living; **I** will make thee a terror, and thou shalt be no more: though thou be sought for, yet shalt thou never be found again, saith the Lord God. Ezekiel 26:20-21

I made the nations to shake at the sound of his fall, when I cast him down to hell with them that descend into the pit: and all the trees of Eden, the choice and best of Lebanon, all that drink water, shall be comforted in the nether parts of the earth. Ezekiel 31:16

But he knoweth not that the dead are there; and that her guests are in the depths of hell. Proverbs 9:18

The way of life is above to the wise, that he may depart from hell beneath. Proverbs 15:24

Therefore hell hath enlarged herself, and opened her mouth without measure: and their glory, and their multitude, and their pomp, and he that rejoiceth, shall descend into it. Isaiah 5:14

Wherefore he saith, When he ascended up on high, he led captivity captive, and gave gifts unto men. Now that he ascended, what is it but that he also descended first into the lower parts of the earth? He that descended is the same also that ascended up far above all heavens, that he might fill all things. Ephesians 4:8-10

8. Hell is a Bottomless Pit

And the fifth angel sounded, and I saw a star fall from heaven unto the earth: and to him was given the key of the bottomless pit. And he opened the bottomless pit; and there arose a smoke out of the pit, as the smoke of a great furnace; and the sun and the air were darkened by reason of the smoke of the pit. Revelation 9:1-2

And they had a king over them, which is the angel of the bottomless pit, whose name in the Hebrew tongue is Abaddon, but in the Greek tongue hath his name Apollyon. Revelation 9:11

And when they shall have finished their testimony, the beast that ascendeth out of the bottomless pit shall make war against them, and shall overcome them, and kill them. Revelation 11:7

And I saw an angel come down from heaven, having the key of the bottomless pit and a great chain in his hand. And he laid hold on the dragon, that old serpent, which is the Devil, and Satan, and bound him a thousand years, And cast him into the bottomless pit, and shut him up, and set a seal upon him, that he should deceive the nations no more, till the thousand years should be fulfilled: and after that he must be loosed a little season. Revelation 20:1-3

satan's Past

Thy pomp is brought down to the grave, and the noise of thy viols: the worm is spread under thee, and the worms cover thee. How art thou fallen from heaven, O Lucifer, son of the morning! how art thou cut down to the ground, which didst weaken the nations! For thou hast said in thine heart, I will ascend into heaven, I will exalt my throne above the stars of God: I will sit also upon the mount of the congregation, in the sides of the north: I will ascend above the heights of the clouds; I will be like the most High. Yet thou shalt be brought down to hell, to the sides of the pit. They that see thee shall narrowly look upon thee, and consider thee, saying, Is this the man that made the earth to tremble, that did shake kingdoms; That made the world as a wilderness, and destroyed the cities thereof; that opened not the house of his prisoners? All the kings of the nations, even all of them, lie in glory, every one in his own house. But thou art cast out of thy grave like an abominable branch, and as the raiment of those that are slain, thrust through with a sword, that go down to the stones of the pit; as a carcase trodden under feet. Thou shalt not be joined with them in burial, because thou hast destroyed thy land, and slain thy people: the seed of evildoers shall never be renowned.

Isaiah 14:11-20

And having spoiled principalities and powers, he made a shew of them openly, triumphing over them in it. Colossians 2:15

He that committeth sin is of the devil; for the devil sinneth from the beginning. For this purpose the Son of God was manifested, that he might destroy the works of the devil. 1 John 3:8

True leadership provides opportunity for others to find and fulfill their God-given purpose.

For the terrible one is brought to nought, and the scorner is consumed, and all that watch for iniquity are cut off: Isaiah 29:20

He was a murderer from the beginning, and abode not in the truth, because there is no truth in him. When he speaketh a lie, he speaketh of his own: for he is a liar, and the father of it. John 8:44

The thief cometh not, but for to steal, and to kill, and to destroy:
John 10:10

Be sober, be vigilant; because your adversary the devil, AS a roaring lion, walketh about, seeking whom he *may* devour. 1 Peter 5:8

He that committeth sin is of the devil; for the devil sinneth from the beginning. For this purpose the Son of God was manifested, that he might destroy the works of the devil. 1 John 3:8

For the accuser of our brethren is cast down, which accused them before our God day and night. Revelation 12:10

But if our gospel be hid, it is hid to them that are lost: In whom the god of this world hath blinded the minds of them which believe not, lest the light of the glorious gospel of Christ, who is the image of God, should shine unto them. 2 Corinthians 4:3-4

Wherein in time past ye walked according to the course of this world, according to the prince of the power of the air, the spirit that now worketh in the children of disobedience. Ephesians 2:2

satan's Eternal Future

Then shall he say also unto them on the left hand, Depart from me, ye cursed, into everlasting fire, prepared for the devil and his angels:
Matthew 25:41

Now is the judgment of this world: now shall the prince of this world be cast out. John 12:31

And the God of peace shall bruise Satan under your feet shortly. The grace of our Lord Jesus Christ be with you. Amen. Romans 16:20

For if God spared not the angels that sinned, but cast them down to hell, and delivered them into chains of darkness, to be reserved unto judgment; 2 Peter 2:4

These are wells without water, clouds that are carried with a tempest; to whom the mist of darkness is reserved for ever. 2 Peter 2:17

He that committeth sin is of the devil; for the devil sinneth from the beginning. For this purpose the Son of God was manifested, that he might destroy the works of the devil. 1 John 3:8

And the angels which kept not their first estate, but left their own habitation, he hath reserved in everlasting chains under darkness unto the judgment of the great day. Jude 1:6

And he opened the bottomless pit; and there arose a smoke out of the pit, as the smoke of a great furnace; and the sun and the air were darkened by reason of the smoke of the pit. Revelation 9:2

And prevailed not; neither was their place found any more in heaven.
Revelation 12:8

Therefore rejoice, ye heavens, and ye that dwell in them. Woe to the inhabiters of the earth and of the sea! for the devil is come down unto you, having great wrath, because he knoweth that he hath but a short time.
Revelation 12:12

And the third angel followed them, saying with a loud voice, If any man worship the beast and his image, and receive his mark in his forehead, or in his hand, The same shall drink of the wine of the wrath of God, which is poured out without mixture into the cup of his indignation; and he shall be tormented with fire and brimstone in the presence of the holy angels, and in the presence of the Lamb: And the smoke of their torment ascendeth up for ever and ever: and they have no rest day nor night, who worship the beast and his image, and whosoever receiveth the mark of his name. Revelation 14:9-11

And the beast was taken, and with him the false prophet that wrought miracles before him, with which he deceived them that had received the mark of the beast, and them that worshipped his image. These both were cast alive into a lake of fire burning with brimstone. Revelation 19:20

A lot of things seem in the devil's hand but there is no devil in the first two chapters of the Bible and there is no devil in the last two chapters either. He is out of business when the Book closes. Everything is in God's hand, including the future of the devil. - Vance Havner

And I saw an angel come down from heaven, having the key of the bottomless pit and a great chain in his hand. And he laid hold on the dragon, that old serpent, which is the Devil, and Satan, and bound him a thousand years, And cast him into the bottomless pit, and shut him up, and set a seal upon him, that he should deceive the nations no more, till the thousand years should be fulfilled: and after that he must be loosed a little season. Revelation 20:1-3

And they went up on the breadth of the earth, and compassed the camp of the saints about, and the beloved city: and fire came down from God out of heaven, and devoured them. And the devil that deceived them was cast into the lake of fire and brimstone, where the beast and the false prophet are, and shall be tormented day and night for ever and ever.

Revelation 20:9-10

And death and hell were cast into the lake of fire. This is the second death. And whosoever was not found written in the book of life was cast into the lake of fire. Revelation 20:14-15

Daily Bible Reading Plan

Day	Date	Text	Day	Date	Text
1	Jan. 1	Gen. 1-3	56	Feb. 25	Lev. 26-27
2	Jan. 2	Gen. 4:1—6:8	57	Feb. 26	Num. 1-2
3	Jan. 3	Gen. 6:9—9:29	58	Feb. 27	Num. 3-4
4	Jan. 4	Gen. 10-11	59	Feb. 28	Num. 5-6
5	Jan. 5	Gen. 12-14	60	Mar. 1	Num. 7
6	Jan. 6	Gen. 15-17	61	Mar. 2	Num. 8-10
7	Jan. 7	Gen. 18-19	62	Mar. 3	Num. 11-13
8	Jan. 8	Gen. 20-22	63	Mar. 4	Num. 14-15
9	Jan. 9	Gen. 23-24	64	Mar. 5	Num. 16-18
10	Jan. 10	Gen. 25-26	65	Mar. 6	Num. 19-21
11	Jan. 11	Gen. 27-28	66	Mar. 7	Num. 22-24
12	Jan. 12	Gen. 29-30	67	Mar. 8	Num. 25-26
13	Jan. 13	Gen. 31-32	68	Mar. 9	Num. 27-29
14	Jan. 14	Gen. 33-35	69	Mar. 10	Num. 30-31
15	Jan. 15	Gen. 36-37	70	Mar. 11	Num. 32-33
16	Jan. 16	Gen. 38-40	71	Mar. 12	Num. 34-36
17	Jan. 17	Gen. 41-42	72	Mar. 13	Deut. 1-2
18	Jan. 18	Gen. 43-45	73	Mar. 14	Deut. 3-4
19	Jan. 19	Gen. 46-47	74	Mar. 15	Deut. 5-7
20	Jan. 20	Gen. 48-50	75	Mar. 16	Deut. 8-10
21	Jan. 21	Job 1-3	76	Mar. 17	Deut. 11-13
22	Jan. 22	Job 4-7	77	Mar. 18	Deut. 14-17
23	Jan. 23	Job 8-11	78	Mar. 19	Deut. 18-21
24	Jan. 24	Job 12-15	79	Mar. 20	Deut. 22-25
25	Jan. 25	Job 16-19	80	Mar. 21	Deut. 26-28
26	Jan. 26	Job 20-22	81	Mar. 22	Deut. 29:1—31:29
27	Jan. 27	Job 23-28	82	Mar. 23	Deut. 31:30—34:12
28	Jan. 28	Job 29-31	83	Mar. 24	Josh. 1-4
29	Jan. 29	Job 32-34	84	Mar. 25	Josh. 5-8
30	Jan. 30	Job 35-37	85	Mar. 26	Josh. 9-11
31	Jan. 31	Job 38-42	86	Mar. 27	Josh. 12-14
32	Feb. 1	Ex. 1-4	87	Mar. 28	Josh. 15-17
33	Feb. 2	Ex. 5-8	88	Mar. 29	Josh. 18-19
34	Feb. 3	Ex. 9-11	89	Mar. 30	Josh. 20-22
35	Feb. 4	Ex. 12-13	90	Mar. 31	Josh. 23—Judg. 1
36	Feb. 5	Ex. 14-15	91	Apr. 1	Judg. 2-5
37	Feb. 6	Ex. 16-18	92	Apr. 2	Judg. 6-8
38	Feb. 7	Ex. 19-21	93	Apr. 3	Judg. 9
39	Feb. 8	Ex. 22-24	94	Apr. 4	Judg. 10-12
40	Feb. 9	Ex. 25-27	95	Apr. 5	Judg. 13-16
41	Feb. 10	Ex. 28-29	96	Apr. 6	Judg. 17-19
42	Feb. 11	Ex. 30-31	97	Apr. 7	Judg. 20-21
43	Feb. 12	Ex. 32-34	98	Apr. 8	Ruth
44	Feb. 13	Ex. 35-36	99	Apr. 9	1 Sam. 1-3
45	Feb. 14	Ex. 37-38	100	Apr. 10	1 Sam. 4-7
46	Feb. 15	Ex. 39-40	101	Apr. 11	1 Sam. 8-10
47	Feb. 16	Lev. 1:1—5:13	102	Apr. 12	1 Sam. 11-13
48	Feb. 17	Lev. 5:14—7:38	103	Apr. 13	1 Sam. 14-15
49	Feb. 18	Lev. 8-10	104	Apr. 14	1 Sam. 16-17
50	Feb. 19	Lev. 11-12	105	Apr. 15	1 Sam. 18-19; Ps. 59
51	Feb. 20	Lev. 13-14	106	Apr. 16	1 Sam. 20-21;
52	Feb. 21	Lev. 15-17			Pss. 56; 34
53	Feb. 22	Lev. 18-20	107	Apr. 17	1 Sam. 22-23;
54	Feb. 23	Lev. 21-23			1 Chron. 12:8-18;
55	Feb. 24	Lev. 24-25			Pss. 52; 54; 63;142

Daily Bible Reading Plan

Day	Date	Text
108	Apr. 18	1 Sam. 24; Ps. 57; 1 Sam. 25
109	Apr. 19	1 Sam. 26-29; 1 Chron. 12:1-7, 19-22
110	Apr. 20	1 Sam. 30-31; 1 Chron. 10; 2 Sam. 1
111	Apr. 21	2 Sam. 2-4
112	Apr. 22	2 Sam. 5:1—6:11; 1 Chron. 11:1-9; 12:23-40; 13:1—14:17
113	Apr. 23	2 Sam. 22; Ps. 18
114	Apr. 24	1 Chron. 15-16; 2 Sam. 6:12-23; Ps. 96
115	Apr. 25	Ps. 105; 2 Sam. 7; 1 Chron. 17
116	Apr. 26	2 Sam. 8-10; 1 Chron. 18-19; Ps. 60
117	Apr. 27	2 Sam. 11-12; 1 Chron. 20:1-3; Ps. 51
118	Apr. 28	2 Sam. 13-14
119	Apr. 29	2 Sam. 15-17
120	Apr. 30	Ps. 3; 2 Sam. 18-19
121	May 1	2 Sam. 20-21; 23:8-23; 1 Chron. 20:4-8; 11:10-25
122	May 2	2 Sam. 23:24—24:25; 1 Chron. 11:26-47; 21:1-30
123	May 3	1 Chron. 22-24
124	May 4	Ps. 30; 1 Chron. 25-26
125	May 5	1 Chron. 27-29
126	May 6	Pss. 5-7; 10;11;13;17
127	May 7	Pss. 23; 26; 28; 31; 35
128	May 8	Pss. 41; 43; 46; 55; 61; 62; 64
129	May 9	Pss. 69-71; 77
130	May 10	Pss. 83; 86; 88; 91; 95
131	May 11	Pss. 108-9; 120-21; 140; 143-44
132	May 12	Pss. 1; 14-15; 36-37; 39
133	May 13	Pss. 40; 49-50; 73
134	May 14	Pss. 76; 82; 84; 90; 92; 112; 115
135	May 15	Pss. 8-9; 16; 19; 21; 24; 29
136	May 16	Pss. 33; 65-68
137	May 17	Pss. 75; 93-94; 97-100
138	May 18	Pss. 103-4; 113-14; 117
139	May 19	Ps. 119:1-88
140	May 20	Ps. 119:89-176
141	May 21	Pss. 122; 124; 133-36
142	May 22	Pss. 138-39; 145;148; 150
143	May 23	Pss. 4; 12; 20; 25; 32; 38

Day	Date	Text
144	May 24	Pss. 42; 53; 58; 81; 101; 111; 130-31; 141; 146
145	May 25	Pss. 2; 22; 27
146	May 26	Pss. 45; 47-48; 87;110
147	May 27	1 Kings 1:1—2:12; 2 Sam. 23:1-7
148	May 28	1 Kings 2:13—3:28; 2 Chron. 1:1-13
149	May 29	1 Kings 5-6; 2 Chron. 2-3
150	May 30	1 Kings 7; 2 Chron. 4
151	May 31	1 Kings 8; 2 Chron. 5:1—7:10
152	June 1	1 Kings 9:1—10:13; 2 Chron. 7:11—9:12
153	June 2	1 Kings 4; 10:14-29; 2 Chron. 1:14-17; 9:13-28; Ps. 72
154	June 3	Prov. 1-3
155	June 4	Prov. 4-6
156	June 5	Prov. 7-9
157	June 6	Prov. 10-12
158	June 7	Prov. 13-15
159	June 8	Prov. 16-18
160	June 9	Prov. 19-21
161	June 10	Prov. 22-24
162	June 11	Prov. 25-27
163	June 12	Prov. 28-29
164	June 13	Prov. 30-31; Ps. 127
165	June 14	Song of Songs
166	June 15	1 Kings 11:1-40; Eccles. 1-2
167	June 16	Eccles. 3-7
168	June 17	Eccles. 8-12; 1 Kings 11:41-43; 2 Chron. 9 29-31
169	June 18	1 Kings 12; 2 Chron. 10:1—11:17
170	June 19	1 Kings 13-14; 2 Chron. 11:18—12:16
171	June 20	1 Kings 15:1-24; 2 Chron. 13-16
172	June 21	1 Kings 15:25—16:34; 2 Chron. 17; 1 Kings 17
173	June 22	1 Kings 18-19
174	June 23	1 Kings 20-21
175	June 24	1 Kings 22:1-40; 2 Chron. 18
176	June 25	1 Kings 22:41-53; 2 Kings 1; 2 Chron. 19:1—21:3
177	June 26	2 Kings 2-4
178	June 27	2 Kings 5-7

Daily Bible Reading Plan

Day	Date	Text
179	June 28	2 Kings 8-9;
		2 Chron. 21:4—22:9
180	June 29	2 Kings 10-11;
		2 Chron. 22:10—23:21
181	June 30	Joel
182	July 1	2 Kings 12-13;
		2 Chron. 24
183	July 2	2 Kings 14;
		2 Chron. 25; Jonah
184	July 3	Hos. 1-7
185	July 4	Hos. 8-14
186	July 5	2 Kings 15:1-7;
		2 Chron. 26;
		Amos 1-4
187	July 6	Amos 5-9;
		2 Kings 15:8-18
188	July 7	Isa. 1-4
189	July 8	2 Kings 15:19-38;
		2 Chron. 27; Isa. 5-6
190	July 9	Micah
191	July 10	2 Kings 16;
		2 Chron. 28; Isa. 7-8
192	July 11	Isa. 9-12
193	July 12	Isa. 13-16
194	July 13	Isa. 17-22
195	July 14	Isa. 23-27
196	July 15	Isa. 28-30
197	July 16	Isa. 31-35
198	July 17	2 Kings 18:1-8;
		2 Chron. 29-31
199	July 18	2 Kings 17;18:9-37;
		2 Chron. 32:1-19;
		Isa. 36
200	July 19	2 Kings 19;
		2 Chron. 32:20-23;
		Isa. 37
201	July 20	2 Kings 20;
		2 Chron. 32:24-33;
		Isa. 38-39
202	July 21	2 Kings 21:1-18;
		2 Chron. 33:1-20;
		Isa. 40
203	July 22	Isa. 41-43
204	July 23	Isa. 44-47
205	July 24	Isa. 48-51
206	July 25	Isa. 52-57
207	July 26	Isa. 58-62
208	July 27	Isa. 63-66
209	July 28	2 Kings 21:19-26;
		2 Chron. 33:21—34:7;
		Zephaniah
210	July 29	Jer. 1-3
211	July 30	Jer. 4-6
212	July 31	Jer. 7-9
213	Aug. 1	Jer. 10-13

Day	Date	Text
214	Aug. 2	Jer. 14-16
215	Aug. 3	Jer. 17-20
216	Aug. 4	2 Kings 22:1—23:28;
		2 Chron. 34:8—35:19
217	Aug. 5	Nahum;
		2 Kings 23:29-37;
		2 Chron. 35:20—36:5;
		Jer. 22:10-17
218	Aug. 6	Jer. 26; Habakkuk
219	Aug. 7	Jer. 46-47;
		2 Kings 24:1-4, 7;
		2 Chron. 36:6-7;
		Jer. 25, 35
220	Aug. 8	Jer. 36, 45, 48
221	Aug. 9	Jer. 49:1-33; Dan. 1-2
222	Aug. 10	Jer. 22:18-30;
		2 Kings 24:5-20;
		2 Chron. 36:8-12;
		Jer. 37:1-2; 52:1-3;
		24; 29
223	Aug. 11	Jer. 27-28, 23
224	Aug. 12	Jer. 50-51
225	Aug. 13	Jer. 49:34-39; 34:1-22;
		Ezek. 1-3
226	Aug. 14	Ezek. 4-7
227	Aug. 15	Ezek. 8-11
228	Aug. 16	Ezek. 12-14
229	Aug. 17	Ezek. 15-17
230	Aug. 18	Ezek. 18-20
231	Aug. 19	Ezek. 21-23
232	Aug. 20	2 Kings 25:1;
		2 Chron. 36:13-16;
		Jer. 39:1; 52:4;
		Ezek. 24;
		Jer. 21:1—22:9;
		32:1-44
233	Aug. 21	Jer. 30-31, 33
234	Aug. 22	Ezek. 25; 29:1-16;
		30; 31
235	Aug. 23	Ezek. 26-28
236	Aug. 24	Jer. 37:3—39:10;
		52:5-30;
		2 Kings 25:2-21;
		2 Chron. 36:17-21
237	Aug. 25	2 Kings 25:22;
		Jer. 39:11—40:6;
		Lam. 1-3
238	Aug. 26	Lam. 4-5; Obadiah
239	Aug. 27	Jer. 40:7—44:30;
		2 Kings 25:23-26
240	Aug. 28	Ezek. 33:21—36:38
241	Aug. 29	Ezek. 37-39
242	Aug. 30	Ezek. 32:1—33:20;
		Dan. 3
243	Aug. 31	Ezek. 40-42

Daily Bible Reading Plan

Day	Date	Text
244	Sept. 1	Ezek. 43-45
245	Sept. 2	Ezek. 46-48
246	Sept. 3	Ezek. 29:17-21;
		Dan. 4; Jer. 52:31-34;
		2 Kings 25:27-30;
		Ps. 44
247	Sept. 4	Pss. 74; 79-80; 89
248	Sept. 5	Pss. 85; 102; 106;
		123; 137
249	Sept. 6	Dan. 7-8; 5
250	Sept. 7	Dan. 9; 6
251	Sept. 8	2 Chron. 36:22-23;
		Ezra 1:1—4:5
252	Sept. 9	Dan. 10-12
253	Sept. 10	Ezra 4:6—6:13;
		Haggai
254	Sept. 11	Zech. 1-6
255	Sept. 12	Zech. 7-8;
		Ezra 6:14-22; Ps. 78
256	Sept. 13	Pss. 107; 116; 118
257	Sept. 14	Pss. 125-26; 128-29;
		132; 147; 149
258	Sept. 15	Zech. 9-14
259	Sept. 16	Esther 1-4
260	Sept. 17	Esther 5-10
261	Sept. 18	Ezra 7-8
262	Sept. 19	Ezra 9-10
263	Sept. 20	Neh. 1-5
264	Sept. 21	Neh. 6-7
265	Sept. 22	Neh. 8-10
266	Sept. 23	Neh. 11-13
267	Sept. 24	Malachi
268	Sept. 25	1 Chron. 1-2
269	Sept. 26	1 Chron. 3-5
270	Sept. 27	1 Chron. 6
271	Sept. 28	1 Chron. 7:1—8:27
272	Sept. 29	1 Chron. 8:28—9:44
273	Sept. 30	John 1:1-18; Mark 1:1;
		Luke 1:1-4; 3:23-38;
		Matt. 1:1-17
274	Oct. 1	Luke 1:5-80
275	Oct. 2	Matt. 1:18—2:23;
		Luke 2
276	Oct. 3	Matt. 3:1—4:11;
		Mark 1:2-13;
		Luke 3:1-23; 4:1-13;
		John 1:19-34
277	Oct. 4	John 1:35—3:36
278	Oct. 5	John 4; Matt. 4:12-17;
		Mark 1:14-15;
		Luke 4:14-30
279	Oct. 6	Mark 1:16-45;
		Matt. 4:18-25;
		8:2-4,14-17;
		Luke 4:31—5:16

Day	Date	Text
280	Oct. 7	Matt. 9:1-17;
		Mark 2:1-22;
		Luke 5:17-39
281	Oct. 8	John 5; Matt. 12:1-21;
		Mark 2:23—3:12;
		Luke 6:1-11
282	Oct. 9	Matt. 5; Mark 3:13-19;
		Luke 6:12-36
283	Oct. 10	Matt. 6-7;
		Luke 6:37-49
284	Oct. 11	Luke 7;
		Matt. 8:1, 5-13;
		11:2-30
285	Oct. 12	Matt. 12:22-50;
		Mark 3:20-35;
		Luke 8:1-21
286	Oct. 13	Mark 4:1-34;
		Matt. 13:1-53
287	Oct. 14	Mark 4:35—5:43;
		Matt. 8; 18, 23-34; 9;
		18-34; Luke 8;22-56
288	Oct. 15	Mark 6;1-30; Matt. 13;
		54-58; 9:35—11:1;
		14:1-12; Luke 9:1-10
289	Oct. 16	Matt. 14:13-36;
		Mark 6:31-56;
		Luke 9:11-17;
		John 6:1-21
290	Oct. 17	John 6:22—7:1;
		Matt. 15:1-20;
		Mark 7:1-23
291	Oct. 18	Matt. 15:21—16:20;
		Mark 7:24—8:30;
		Luke 9:18-21
292	Oct. 19	Matt. 16:21—17:27;
		Mark 8:31—9:32;
		Luke 9:22-45
293	Oct. 20	Matt. 18; 8:19-22;
		Mark 9:33-50;
		Luke 9:46-62;
		John 7:2-10
294	Oct. 21	John 7:11—8:59
295	Oct. 22	Luke 10:1—11:36
296	Oct. 23	Luke 11:37—13:21
297	Oct. 24	John 9-10
298	Oct. 25	Luke 13:22—15:32
299	Oct. 26	Luke 16:1—17:10;
		John 11:1-54
300	Oct. 27	Luke 17:11—18:17;
		Matt. 19:1-15;
		Mark 10:1-16
301	Oct. 28	Matt. 19:16—20:28;
		Mark 10:17-45;
		Luke 18:18-34

Daily Bible Reading Plan

Day	Date	Text
302	Oct. 29	Matt. 20:29-34; 26:6-13; Mark 10:46-52; 14:3-9; Luke 18:35—19:28; John 11:55—12:11
303	Oct. 30	Matt. 21:1-22; Mark 11:1-26; Luke 19:29-48; John 12:12-50
304	Oct. 31	Matt. 21:23—22:14; Mark 11:27—12:12; Luke 20:1-19
305	Nov. 1	Matt. 22:15-46; Mark 12:13-37; Luke 20;20-44
306	Nov. 2	Matt. 23; Mark 12:38-44; Luke 20:45—21:4
307	Nov. 3	Matt. 24:1-31; Mark 13:1-27; Luke 21:5-27
308	Nov. 4	Matt. 24:32—26:5, 14-16; Mark 13:28—14:2, 10-11; Luke 21:28—22:6
309	Nov. 5	Matt. 26:17-29; Mark 14:12-25; Luke 22:7-38; John 13
310	Nov. 6	John 14-16
311	Nov. 7	John 17:1—18:1; Matt. 26:30-46; Mark 14:26-42; Luke 22:39-46
312	Nov. 8	Matt. 26:47-75; Mark 14:43-72; Luke 22:47-65; John 18:2-27
313	Nov. 9	Matt. 27:1-26; Mark 15:1-15; Luke 22:66—23:25; John 18:28—19:16
314	Nov. 10	Matt. 27:27-56; Mark 15:16-41; Luke 23:26-49; John 19:17-30
315	Nov. 11	Matt. 27:57—28:8; Mark 15:42—16:8; Luke 23:50—24:12; John 19:31—20:10
316	Nov. 12	Matt. 28:9-20; Mark 16:9-20; Luke 24:13-53; John 20:11—21:25

Day	Date	Text
317	Nov. 13	Acts 1-2
318	Nov. 14	Acts 3-5
319	Nov. 15	Acts 6:1—8:1
320	Nov. 16	Acts 82—9:43
321	Nov. 17	Acts 10-11
322	Nov. 18	Acts 12-13
323	Nov. 19	Acts 14-15
324	Nov. 20	Gal. 1-3
325	Nov. 21	Gal. 4-6
326	Nov. 22	James
327	Nov. 23	Acts 16:1—18:11
328	Nov. 24	1 Thessalonians
329	Nov. 25	2 Thessalonians; Acts 18:12—19:22
330	Nov. 26	1 Cor. 1-4
331	Nov. 27	1 Cor. 5-8
332	Nov. 28	1 Cor. 9-11
333	Nov. 29	1 Cor. 12-14
334	Nov. 30	1 Cor. 15-16
335	Dec. 1	Acts 19:23—20:1; 2 Cor. 1-4
336	Dec. 2	2 Cor. 5-9
337	Dec. 3	2 Cor. 10-13
338	Dec. 4	Rom. 1-3
339	Dec. 5	Rom. 4-6
340	Dec. 6	Rom. 7-8
341	Dec. 7	Rom. 9-11
342	Dec. 8	Rom. 12-15
343	Dec. 9	Rom. 16; Acts 20:2—21:16
344	Dec. 10	Acts 21:17—23:35
345	Dec. 11	Acts 24-26
346	Dec. 12	Acts 27-28
347	Dec. 13	Eph. 1-3
348	Dec. 14	Eph. 4-6
349	Dec. 15	Colossians
350	Dec. 16	Philippians
351	Dec. 17	Philemon; 1 Tim. 1-3
352	Dec. 18	1 Tim. 4-6; Titus
353	Dec. 19	2 Timothy
354	Dec. 20	1 Peter
355	Dec. 21	Jude; 2 Peter
356	Dec. 22	Heb. 1:1—5:10
357	Dec. 23	Heb. 5:11—9:28
358	Dec. 24	Heb. 10-11
359	Dec. 25	Heb. 12-13; 2 John; 3 John
360	Dec. 26	1 John
361	Dec. 27	Rev. 1-3
362	Dec. 28	Rev. 4-9
363	Dec. 29	Rev. 10-14
364	Dec. 30	Rev. 15-18
365	Dec. 31	Rev. 19-22

Prayer Journal

DATE	REQUEST	ANSWER

Prayer Journal

DATE	REQUEST	ANSWER

Prayer Journal

DATE	REQUEST	ANSWER

Prayer Journal

DATE	REQUEST	ANSWER

Prayer Journal

DATE	REQUEST	ANSWER

Prayer Journal

DATE	REQUEST	ANSWER

Personal Goals

Personal Goals

Ministry Goals

Church Goals

Mission Statement

Personal Information

NAME _____

ADDRESS _____

CITY/STATE _____ ZIP _____

PHONE: HOME (   ) _____ WORK (   ) _____

PASSPORT NO _____ EXP. DATE _____

DRIVERS LICENCE # _____ EXP. DATE _____

CAR REGISTRATION # _____

INSURANCE POLICY # _____

CHURCH _____ PHONE _____

MINISTER _____ PHONE _____

PRAYER PARTNER _____ PHONE _____

MEDICAL INFORMATION

BLOOD TYPE _____

ALLERGIES _____

PHYSICIAN _____ PHONE _____

HEALTH INSURANCE _____

MEDICALERT _____

IN CASE OF EMERGENCY OR ILLNESS CONTACT:

_____

_____ PHONE: _____

Staff Phone Numbers

Name ______________________ Name ______________________

Phone (   ) ______________________ Phone (   ) ______________________

Name ______________________ Name ______________________

Phone (   ) ______________________ Phone (   ) ______________________

Name ______________________ Name ______________________

Phone (   ) ______________________ Phone (   ) ______________________

Name ______________________ Name ______________________

Phone (   ) ______________________ Phone (   ) ______________________

Name ______________________ Name ______________________

Phone (   ) ______________________ Phone (   ) ______________________

Name ______________________ Name ______________________

Phone (   ) ______________________ Phone (   ) ______________________

Name ______________________ Name ______________________

Phone (   ) ______________________ Phone (   ) ______________________

Name ______________________ Name ______________________

Phone (   ) ______________________ Phone (   ) ______________________

Name ______________________ Name ______________________

Phone (   ) ______________________ Phone (   ) ______________________

Name ______________________ Name ______________________

Phone (   ) ______________________ Phone (   ) ______________________

Name ______________________ Name ______________________

Phone (   ) ______________________ Phone (   ) ______________________

Phone Numbers

Name ______________________________

Phone (   ) ______________________

Name ______________________________

Phone (   ) ______________________

Name ______________________________

Phone (   ) ______________________

Name ______________________________

Phone (   ) ______________________

Name ______________________________

Phone (   ) ______________________

Name ______________________________

Phone (   ) ______________________

Name ______________________________

Phone (   ) ______________________

Name ______________________________

Phone (   ) ______________________

Name ______________________________

Phone (   ) ______________________

Name ______________________________

Phone (   ) ______________________

Name ______________________________

Phone (   ) ______________________

Name ______________________________

Phone (   ) ______________________

Name ______________________________

Phone (   ) ______________________

Name ______________________________

Phone (   ) ______________________

Name ______________________________

Phone (   ) ______________________

Name ______________________________

Phone (   ) ______________________

Name ______________________________

Phone (   ) ______________________

Name ______________________________

Phone (   ) ______________________

Name ______________________________

Phone (   ) ______________________

Name ______________________________

Phone (   ) ______________________

Name ______________________________

Phone (   ) ______________________

Name ______________________________

Phone (   ) ______________________

Phone Numbers

Name ______________________ Name ______________________

Phone (   ) ______________________ Phone (   ) ______________________

Name ______________________ Name ______________________

Phone (   ) ______________________ Phone (   ) ______________________

Name ______________________ Name ______________________

Phone (   ) ______________________ Phone (   ) ______________________

Name ______________________ Name ______________________

Phone (   ) ______________________ Phone (   ) ______________________

Name ______________________ Name ______________________

Phone (   ) ______________________ Phone (   ) ______________________

Name ______________________ Name ______________________

Phone (   ) ______________________ Phone (   ) ______________________

Name ______________________ Name ______________________

Phone (   ) ______________________ Phone (   ) ______________________

Name ______________________ Name ______________________

Phone (   ) ______________________ Phone (   ) ______________________

Name ______________________ Name ______________________

Phone (   ) ______________________ Phone (   ) ______________________

Name ______________________ Name ______________________

Phone (   ) ______________________ Phone (   ) ______________________

Name ______________________ Name ______________________

Phone (   ) ______________________ Phone (   ) ______________________

Phone Numbers

Name ______________________	Name ______________________
Phone ( ) ______________________	Phone ( ) ______________________
Name ______________________	Name ______________________
Phone ( ) ______________________	Phone ( ) ______________________
Name ______________________	Name ______________________
Phone ( ) ______________________	Phone ( ) ______________________
Name ______________________	Name ______________________
Phone ( ) ______________________	Phone ( ) ______________________
Name ______________________	Name ______________________
Phone ( ) ______________________	Phone ( ) ______________________
Name ______________________	Name ______________________
Phone ( ) ______________________	Phone ( ) ______________________
Name ______________________	Name ______________________
Phone ( ) ______________________	Phone ( ) ______________________
Name ______________________	Name ______________________
Phone ( ) ______________________	Phone ( ) ______________________
Name ______________________	Name ______________________
Phone ( ) ______________________	Phone ( ) ______________________
Name ______________________	Name ______________________
Phone ( ) ______________________	Phone ( ) ______________________
Name ______________________	Name ______________________
Phone ( ) ______________________	Phone ( ) ______________________

Phone Numbers

Name ______________________________

Phone (   ) ________________________

Name ______________________________

Phone (   ) ________________________

Name ______________________________

Phone (   ) ________________________

Name ______________________________

Phone (   ) ________________________

Name ______________________________

Phone (   ) ________________________

Name ______________________________

Phone (   ) ________________________

Name ______________________________

Phone (   ) ________________________

Name ______________________________

Phone (   ) ________________________

Name ______________________________

Phone (   ) ________________________

Name ______________________________

Phone (   ) ________________________

Name ______________________________

Phone (   ) ________________________

Name ______________________________

Phone (   ) ________________________

Name ______________________________

Phone (   ) ________________________

Name ______________________________

Phone (   ) ________________________

Name ______________________________

Phone (   ) ________________________

Name ______________________________

Phone (   ) ________________________

Name ______________________________

Phone (   ) ________________________

Name ______________________________

Phone (   ) ________________________

Name ______________________________

Phone (   ) ________________________

Name ______________________________

Phone (   ) ________________________

Name ______________________________

Phone (   ) ________________________

Name ______________________________

Phone (   ) ________________________

Phone Numbers

Name _____   Name _____

Phone (   ) _____   Phone (   ) _____

Name _____   Name _____

Phone (   ) _____   Phone (   ) _____

Name _____   Name _____

Phone (   ) _____   Phone (   ) _____

Name _____   Name _____

Phone (   ) _____   Phone (   ) _____

Name _____   Name _____

Phone (   ) _____   Phone (   ) _____

Name _____   Name _____

Phone (   ) _____   Phone (   ) _____

Name _____   Name _____

Phone (   ) _____   Phone (   ) _____

Name _____   Name _____

Phone (   ) _____   Phone (   ) _____

Name _____   Name _____

Phone (   ) _____   Phone (   ) _____

Name _____   Name _____

Phone (   ) _____   Phone (   ) _____

Name _____   Name _____

Phone (   ) _____   Phone (   ) _____

Helpful Toll Free Numbers

AIRLINES

Air Canada Airlines
U.S.A.   1-800-776-3000
America West
U.S.A.   1-800-235-9292
American Airlines
U.S.A.   1-800-433-7300
British Airways
U.S.A.   1-800-247-9297
Continental Airlines
U.S.A.   1-800-525-0280
Delta Airlines
U.S.A.   1-800-221-1212
Japan Airlines
U.S.A.   1-800-525-3663
KLM Royal Dutch Airlines
U.S.A.   1-800-374-7747
Lufthansa Airlines
U.S.A.   1-800-645-3880
Mexican Airlines
U.S.A.   1-800-531-7921
Northwest Airlines
U.S.A. and Canada   1-800-225-2525
Qantas Airlines
U.S.A.   1-800-227-4500
Sabena Belgian World Airlines
U.S.A. (except NY)   1-800-955-2000
Southwest Airlines
U.S.A.   1-800-435-9792
TWA
U.S.A.   1-800-221-2000
United Airlines
U.S.A. and Canada   1-800-241-6522
US Air
U.S.A. and Canada   1-800-428-4322
AMTRAK
U.S.A.   1-800-872-7245

HOTELS, MOTELS

Best Western
U.S.A.   1-800-528-1234
Beverly Wilshire
U.S.A.(except CA)   1-800-421-4354
California only   1-800-427-4354
Canadian Pacific Hotels International
U.S.A.   1-800-828-7447
Choice Hotels International
U.S.A. and Canada   1-800-424-6423
Courtyard By Marriott
U.S.A.   1-800-321-2211
Cunard Hotels and Resorts
U.S.A.   1-800-222-0939
Days Inns of America
U.S.A. and Canada   1-800-325-2525

Downtowner
U.S.A. and Canada   1-800-238-6161
Embassy Suites
U.S.A.   1-800-362-2779
Fairmont Hotels
U.S.A.   1-800-527-4727
Four Seasons
U.S.A.   1-800-332-3442
Helmsley Hotels
U.S.A.   1-800-221-4982
Hilton International
U.S.A.   1-800-445-8667
Holiday Inn
U.S.A.   1-800-465-4329
Howard Johnson
U.S.A.   1-800-654-2000
Hyatt Hotels
U.S.A. and Canada   1-800-233-1234
Intercontinental Hotels
U.S.A.   1-800-327-0200
Knights Lodging
U.S.A. and Canada   1-800-722-7220
La Quinta Motor Inns
U.S.A.   1-800-531-5900
Marriott Hotels
U.S.A. and Canada   1-800-228-9290
New Otani
U.S.A. (except CA)   1-800-421-8795
California only   1-800-273-2294
Nikko Hotels International
U.S.A.   1-800-645-5687
Omni International Hotels
U.S.A.   1-800-843-6664
Preferred Hotel Association
U.S.A.   1-800-323-7500
Princess Hotels International
U.S.A.   1-800-223-1818
Quality Inns
U.S.A.   1-800-228-5151
Radisson Hotels
U.S.A. and Canada   1-800-333-3333
Ramada Inn
U.S.A. and Canada   1-800-228-2828
Red Carpet Inn
U.S.A.   1-800-251-1962
Red Lion Hotels
U.S.A.   1-800-547-8010
Ritz-Carlton
U.S.A.   1-800-241-3333
Ritz-Carlton-Chicago
U.S.A.   1-800-332-3442
Sheraton Hotels
U.S.A. and Canada   1-800-325-3535
Sonesta Hotels
U.S.A. (except AK)   1-800-766-3782

St. Moritz On-The-Park
U.S.A.   1-800-221-4774
Stouffer Hotels
U.S.A.   1-800-468-3571
TraveLodge
U.S.A. and Canada   1-800-255-3050
Utell International
U.S.A.   1-800-448-8355
Westin Hotels & Resorts
U.S.A.   1-800-228-3000
Williamsburg Hotel
U.S.A.   1-800-446-9244

CREDIT CARDS—GENERAL

American Express
Customer Service
U.S.A.   1-800-528-4800
Diners Club/Carte Blanche
Customer Service
U.S.A.   1-800-234-6377
Discover Card
Customer Service
U.S.A.   1-800-347-2683
MasterCard International
Customer Service
U.S.A.   1-800-826-2181
Visa
"Lost or Stolen Cards"
U.S.A.   1-800-336-8472

RENT-A-CAR

Alamo
U.S.A.   1-800-327-9633
Avis
U.S.A.   1-800-331-1212
Budget
U.S.A.   1-800-527-0700
Hertz
U.S.A   1-800-654-3131
National
U.S.A.   1-800-227-7368
Thrifty
U.S.A.   1-800-367-2277

TRAVELER'S CHECKS

American Express
U.S.A   1-800-221-7282
CitiCorp
U.S.A.   1-800-645-6556
Interpayment
U.S.A.   1-800-221-2426
MasterCard International
U.S.A.   1-800-223-9920
Thomas Cook MasterCard
U.S.A.   1-800-223-7373
Visa
U.S.A.   1-800-227-6811

Travel Mileage Between Cities

FROM (columns) / **TO** (rows)

TO \ FROM	Albany, NY	Atlanta, GA	Baltimore, MD	Boston, MA	Buffalo, NY	Chicago, IL	Cincinnati, OH	Cleveland, OH	Columbus, OH	Dallas, TX	Denver, CO	Detroit, MI	Houston, TX	Indianapolis, IN	Kansas City, MO	Little Rock, AR
Albany, NY		1068	331	171	278	803	701	462	603	1717	1835	530	1829	757	1278	1403
Amarillo, TX	1817	1150	1669	1983	1501	1098	1136	1333	1207	362	438	1305	605	1033	583	611
Asheville, NC	890	230	504	900	525	589	349	603	457	799	1368	611	861	434	731	464
Atlanta, GA	1068		687	1083	914	707	472	726	580	814	1495	734	789	507	798	542
Baltimore, MD	331	687		399	353	685	502	351	395	1436	1617	511	1494	554	1062	1101
Birmingham, AL	1223	155	842	1228	939	667	497	751	605	659	1376	759	713	464	677	387
Bismarck, ND	1694	1586	1563	1873	1403	866	1153	1215	1171	1196	793	1153	1470	1042	816	1224
Boise, ID	2648	2288	2426	2807	2337	1820	2149	2119	2119	1684	831	1987	1877	1860	1202	1853
Boston, MA	171	1083	399		447	972	882	631	772	1837	2021	699	1857	907	1438	1500
Buffalo, NY	278	900	353	447		527	425	186	327	1421	1551	252	1592	507	984	1095
Calgary, AB	2555	2496	2404	2714	2280	1727	2008	2056	2026	1916	1116	1994	2159	1917	1645	2013
Charleston, WV	683	529	406	795	457	488	211	268	174	1111	1434	362	1238	321	790	819
Chattanooga, TN	1052	120	660	1085	791	589	349	603	457	799	1368	611	861	384	583	464
Cheyenne, WY	1817	1525	1663	1962	1492	975	1207	1318	1271	903	103	1242	1356	1097	612	1095
Chicago, IL	803	707	685	972	527		342	341	359	957	1034	293	1102	184	507	665
Cincinnati, OH	701	472	502	882	425	342		239	106	960	1161	255	1110	109	591	661
Cleveland, OH	462	726	351	631	186	341	239		141	1233	1363	167	1382	295	794	893
Colorado Spgs, CO	1875	1463	1672	2088	1583	1095	1213	1395	1282	731	69	1382	1102	1106	612	926
Columbia, SC	854	218	512	903	852	811	565	664	538	1032	1695	781	1210	637	1058	791
Columbus, OH	603	580	395	772	327	359	106	141		1068	1225	185	1238	173	670	756
Dallas, TX	1717	814	1436	1837	1421	957	960	1233	1068		800	1200	243	933	521	335
Denver, CO	1835	1495	1617	2021	1551	1034	1161	1363	1225	800		1321	1043	1051	644	967
Des Moines, IA	1152	945	1038	1331	881	344	578	673	664	731	721	608	1043	468	209	581
Detroit, MI	530	734	511	699	252	293	255	167	185	1200	1321		1355	295	766	865
Duluth, MN	1324	1203	1193	1503	974	496	797	847	815	1147	1075	756	1428	686	620	992
El Paso, TX	2237	1441	2063	2400	1941	1515	1556	1753	1627	627	721	1725	750	1453	1000	962
Evansville, IN	988	413	769	1104	678	297	236	490	344	764	1075	436	881	168	431	429
Fargo, ND	1498	1390	1367	1677	1207	670	957	1019	975	1136	955	910	1379	846	669	1077
Ft. Smith, AR	1422	696	1272	1602	1126	710	741	938	849	295	815	957	497	616	309	154
Ft. Wayne, IN	674	667	556	843	398	151	175	212	154	1046	1093	161	1148	121	607	706
Galveston, TX	1877	896	1550	1957	1592	1160	1150	1404	1258	293	1161	1355	50	1106	814	500
Great Falls, MT	2366	2174	2235	2525	1981	1538	1809	1867	1837	1556	756	1805	1799	1699	1323	1791
Greensboro, NC	675	352	320	716	688	786	479	536	422	1166	1686	630	1254	589	1042	852
Harrisburg, PA	338	762	74	398	284	655	484	321	382	1469	1695	481	1582	556	1046	1112
Hartford, CT	109	1011	301	104	393	918	784	577	682	1736	1974	645	1827	863	1357	1401
Helena, MT	2379	2197	2246	2536	2066	1549	1832	1878	1846	1612	812	1826	1855	1722	1346	1812

Travel Mileage Between Cities

TO \ FROM	Albany, NY	Atlanta, GA	Baltimore, MD	Boston, MA	Buffalo, NY	Chicago, IL	Cincinnati, OH	Cleveland, OH	Columbus, OH	Dallas, TX	Denver, CO	Detroit, MI	Houston, TX	Indianapolis, IN	Kansas City, MO	Little Rock, AR
Houston, TX	1829	868	1521	1928	1533	1110	1102	1356	1210	243	1043	1307		1035	764	452
Indianapolis, IN	757	554	568	926	481	184	109	295	173	933	1051	277	1035		494	593
Jacksonville, FL	1165	324	799	1198	1187	1036	796	984	875	1024	1789	1063	877	881	1175	810
Kansas City, MO	1278	799	1062	1444	1198	507	601	794	670	521	644	766	764	494		408
Knoxville, TN	911	192	548	944	722	568	280	534	388	890	1427	542	791	373	853	445
Las Vegas, NV	2756	2024	2519	2915	2424	1887	2010	2236	2225	1251	914	2174	1474	1951	1457	1485
Lexington, KY	875	387	598	987	527	372	85	339	193	919	1242	347	957	188	598	627
Lincoln, NE	1369	1076	1197	1535	1058	548	741	882	805	640	493	809	883	631	225	633
Little Rock, AR	1403	542	1052	1502	1081	661	665	893	756	335	967	865	452	593	408	
Los Angeles, CA	2941	2257	2793	3107	2645	2175	2260	2225	2331	1443	1059	2174	1541	2157	1728	1735
Louisville, KY	870	440	641	976	550	305	108	362	216	835	1170	452	928	114	524	557
Memphis, TN	1273	403	962	1363	953	549	511	744	619	474	1040	716	591	444	466	139
Miami, FL	1470	681	1159	1550	1450	1388	1132	1314	1210	1350	2056	1374	1187	1300	1516	1256
Milwaukee, WI	891	796	773	1060	615	91	429	429	447	1046	1050	381	1199	279	596	750
Minneapolis, MN	1242	1122	1112	1422	952	415	716	764	734	991	916	702	1228	605	464	836
Mobile, AL	1433	365	1052	1448	1218	870	742	850	850	599	1389	1038	537	748	853	445
Montgomery, AL	1245	177	864	1260	1018	767	588	842	696	659	1337	850	725	605	835	484
Montreal, PQ	228	1267	580	327	409	886	851	587	743	1808	1914	593	1900	855	1359	1458
Nashville, TN	1104	257	742	1138	775	451	291	587	399	694	1231	553	811	297	587	359
New Orleans, LA	1592	524	1211	1609	1296	941	841	962	941	507	1297	1116	385	847	868	460
New York, NY	169	875	187	216	445	841	654	507	551	1629	1807	667	1675	811	1220	1294
Oklahoma City, OK	1555	875	1407	1721	1239	826	876	1071	945	211	618	1043	454	724	358	349
Omaha, NE	1310	888	1056	1469	999	482	700	811	764	679	537	750	922	590	212	620
Philadelphia, PA	236	783	97	304	366	760	572	426	470	1537	1712	586	1572	643	1160	1198
Phoenix, AZ	2525	1839	2405	2717	2255	1793	1872	2067	1941	1040	827	2013	1163	1767	1276	1256
Pittsburgh, PA	492	752	230	598	220	459	284	125	182	1247	1410	285	1389	356	853	919
Portland, ME	238	1188	501	105	530	1053	972	722	850	1942	2073	782	2067	1022	1516	1607
Portland, OR	3073	2803	2935	3252	2768	2265	2478	2594	2564	2137	1337	2532	2385	2368	1952	2361
Providence, RI	166	1083	366	43	450	975	849	743	747	1808	2056	766	1899	921	1429	1473
Quebec, PQ	401	1440	753	402	582	1053	1024	616	522	1981	2087	710	2073	1028	1532	1641
Raleigh, NC	645	402	303	699	671	866	559	616	522	1216	1766	710	1304	669	1122	932
Rapid City, SD	1770	1592	1619	1929	1459	942	1252	1271	1241	1134	406	1209	1402	1137	761	1169
Richmond, VA	507	561	144	540	512	788	522	479	485	1341	1745	650	1406	632	1101	1008
Sacramento, CA	2919	2614	2792	3096	2626	2109	2336	2438	2403	1815	1181	2376	1961	2226	1810	2038
St. Joseph, MO	1274	905	1056	1440	905	500	600	790	664	581	561	767	818	490	54	462
St. Louis, MO	1070	587	506	1239	797	294	340	611	411	641	901	560	813	238	257	361

Travel Mileage Between Cities

TO \ FROM	Albany, NY	Atlanta, GA	Baltimore, MD	Boston, MA	Buffalo, NY	Chicago, IL	Cincinnati, OH	Cleveland, OH	Columbus, OH	Dallas, TX	Denver, CO	Detroit, MI	Houston, TX	Indianapolis, IN	Kansas City, MO	Little Rock, AR
Salt Lake City, UT	2276	1991	2122	2424	1954	1437	1666	1766	1730	1250	530	1704	1504	1556	1174	1478
San Antonio, TX	2012	1098	1706	2104	1692	1251	1250	1504	1358	274	954	1474	196	1183	795	600
San Diego, CA	2912	2184	2768	3082	2620	2191	2235	2432	2306	1370	1192	2375	1493	2132	1682	1556
San Francisco, CA	3008	2644	2881	3187	2717	2200	2425	2529	2492	1800	1270	2467	1991	2315	1899	2068
Santa Fe, NM	2110	1430	1959	2276	1801	1378	1428	1613	1487	642	391	1585	885	1313	832	881
Sault Ste. Marie	775	1074	899	940	553	491	604	513	530	1406	1453	352	1540	520	936	1088
Scranton, PA	175	884	219	310	248	777	564	369	462	1570	1761	500	1712	635	1166	1232
Seattle, WA	2979	2773	2849	3125	2687	2172	2435	2501	2471	2151	1381	2439	2394	2250	1994	2294
Shreveport, LA	1623	627	1312	1713	1303	890	862	1115	969	187	977	1066	241	794	565	211
Sioux City, IA	1318	1149	1207	1497	1027	510	782	839	819	785	613	777	1116	635	318	726
Sioux Falls, SD	1396	1237	1265	1555	1085	568	870	897	867	873	695	835	1028	712	406	814
Spokane, WA	2684	2478	2559	2863	2392	1882	2140	2211	2181	1837	1086	2149	2080	2072	1627	1999
Springfield, IL	969	600	754	1138	696	193	301	510	365	795	817	459	906	192	306	464
Springfield, MO	1245	725	1077	1411	949	522	564	761	635	472	674	733	674	461	174	234
Syracuse, NY	139	1014	327	309	153	685	595	344	490	1558	1704	405	1700	641	1137	1234
Tampa, FL	1370	482	1010	1396	1378	1194	954	1160	1071	1101	1901	1216	1057	1036	1292	941
Toledo, OH	572	678	454	741	296	239	198	110	128	1149	1254	57	1251	220	710	809
Toronto, ON	400	1014	468	570	100	542	500	288	426	1453	1559	238	1545	510	1004	1103
Tulsa, OK	1444	830	1276	1610	1128	720	765	960	834	278	701	932	521	660	249	291
Vancouver, BC	3121	2890	2971	3300	2830	2313	2594	2642	2612	2294	1498	2561	2537	2484	2075	2411
Washington, DC	369	648	38	437	361	685	492	351	395	1402	1614	511	1407	575	1059	1067
Wichita, KS	1496	1014	1348	1662	1200	741	815	1012	868	385	515	964	628	588	198	475
Wilmington, NC	757	441	398	796	776	961	682	739	645	1255	1876	836	1305	792	1234	994
Winnipeg, MB	1643	1584	1620	1808	1421	877	1178	1226	1196	1375	1105	1203	1618	1067	908	1316

Travel Mileage Between Cities

TO \ FROM	Los Angeles, CA	Louisville, KY	Memphis, TN	Miami, FL	Minneapolis, MN	New Orleans, LA	New York, NY	Omaha, NE	Philadelphia, PA	Richmond, VA	St. Louis, MO	Salt Lake City, UT	San Francisco, CA	Seattle, WA	Spokane, WA	Washington, DC
Albany, NY	2941	846	1273	1470	1242	1592	169	1310	236	507	1070	2276	3008	2979	2684	369
Amarillo, TX	1124	1059	747	1736	1042	869	1789	678	1699	1616	792	899	1457	1789	1524	1630
Asheville, NC	2396	371	525	733	1062	706	696	604	604	383	638	2042	2729	2814	2519	469
Atlanta, GA	2257	440	403	681	1122	524	875	1056	783	561	587	1991	2644	2644	2478	648
Baltimore, MD	2793	641	962	1159	1112	1211	187	950	97	144	806	2122	2881	2849	2559	38
Birmingham, AL	2102	394	244	796	1079	357	1030	1156	938	719	548	1864	2440	2678	2383	769
Bismarck, ND	1740	1156	1299	2267	437	1684	1720	604	1623	1864	1000	1000	1759	1263	968	1559
Boise, ID	900	1968	1934	2993	1477	2141	2646	1270	2557	2492	1864	373	653	510	396	2506
Boston, MA	3107	976	1363	1550	1422	1609	216	1469	304	548	1263	2424	3187	3125	2863	437
Buffalo, NY	2645	550	953	1450	952	1296	445	999	366	540	968	2151	2863	2685	2685	361
Calgary, AB	1624	2195	2135	3157	1329	2375	2553	1493	2464	2638	2506	1000	1076	760	437	2400
Charleston, WV	2449	266	647	1046	903	936	587	911	497	311	533	1877	2336	2687	2392	367
Chattanooga, TN	2196	320	325	801	1019	505	848	936	756	545	467	1871	2529	2501	2361	533
Cheyenne, WY	1194	1205	1231	2213	840	1400	1844	507	1750	1729	938	461	1281	1300	1086	1740
Chicago, IL	2175	305	549	1388	415	941	841	482	760	788	294	1437	2200	2172	1882	685
Cincinnati, OH	2260	108	511	1132	716	854	653	700	572	522	340	1666	2425	2435	2140	492
Cleveland, OH	2457	362	744	1314	764	1108	507	580	426	479	611	1766	2529	2501	2211	351
Colorado Spgs, CO	1172	1136	1018	2102	975	1238	1895	811	1768	1713	869	580	1339	1371	1076	1671
Columbia, SC	2495	544	649	650	1227	724	700	1227	603	363	794	2198	2882	2980	2685	468
Columbus, OH	2331	216	619	1210	734	962	551	764	470	485	411	1730	2471	2471	2181	395
Dallas, TX	1443	852	474	1350	991	507	1629	679	1537	1341	641	1250	1800	1800	1837	1402
Denver, CO	1265	1168	1103	2143	961	1297	1807	552	1712	1745	901	530	1270	1270	1086	1614
Des Moines, IA	1840	625	620	1626	255	1023	1189	139	1086	1122	358	1105	1864	1864	1549	1035
Detroit, MI	2429	370	716	1374	702	1116	667	750	586	650	560	1704	2467	2439	2149	511
Duluth, MN	2174	800	977	1884	156	1377	1342	520	1253	1284	676	1439	2198	1713	1418	1189
El Paso, TX	816	1476	1101	2001	1459	1135	2175	1095	2100	1968	1212	898	1241	1785	1654	2029
Evansville, IN	2090	128	280	1085	712	683	918	643	828	705	174	1571	2330	2353	2058	732
Fargo, ND	1925	960	1103	2058	241	1504	1516	457	1427	1458	803	1190	1949	1164	1164	1363
Ft. Smith, AR	1581	664	290	1330	773	576	1394	521	1304	1159	397	1326	1914	2140	1845	1233
Ft. Wayne, IN	2270	220	557	1316	576	960	712	646	631	639	354	1612	2371	2313	2023	556
Galveston, TX	1616	1042	639	1340	1278	372	1749	972	1646	1567	861	1544	2041	2395	2090	1468
Great Falls, MT	1323	1873	1811	2835	1007	2053	2053	2275	2316	1435	588	1292	706	411	331	2114
Greensboro, NC	2584	518	713	837	1201	876	508	1179	416	230	785	2230	2947	2964	2669	281
Harrisburg, PA	2740	598	995	1237	1072	1185	186	1143	105	219	785	2074	2833	2809	2519	112
Hartford, CT	3020	897	1262	1490	1354	1472	118	444	206	439	1185	2356	3119	3082	2787	339
Helena, MT	1229	1894	1834	2871	1030	2007	2415	1192	2286	2317	1603	494	1128	617	317	2242

Travel Mileage Between Cities

TO \ FROM	Los Angeles, CA	Louisville, KY	Memphis, TN	Miami, FL	Minneapolis, MN	New Orleans, LA	New York, NY	Omaha, NE	Philadelphia, PA	Richmond, VA	St. Louis, MO	Salt Lake City, UT	San Francisco, CA	Seattle, WA	Spokane, WA	Washington, DC
Houston, TX	1566	994	591	1300	1228	385	1675	922	1572	1406	813	1504	1991	2394	2080	1482
Indianapolis, IN	2157	114	444	1235	605	847	724	590	643	632	238	1556	2315	2250	2030	568
Jacksonville, FL	2467	764	671	356	1473	573	1031	1373	898	658	911	2287	2869	3101	2806	763
Kansas City, MO	1728	524	466	1516	447	868	1220	212	1160	1101	257	1174	1899	1994	1627	1059
Knoxville, TN	2287	259	415	871	983	617	736	985	644	433	526	1930	2620	2712	2417	509
Las Vegas, NV	289	1933	1621	2625	1729	1758	2707	1466	2617	2490	1666	436	596	1195	1088	2504
Lexington, KY	2257	74	445	1068	787	759	779	810	681	503	341	1738	2497	2520	2255	559
Lincoln, NE	1663	749	715	1757	423	1093	1359	59	1265	1263	482	928	1687	1697	1402	1194
Little Rock, AR	1735	715	139	1176	836	460	1294	620	1198	1008	361	1478	2068	2294	1999	1067
Los Angeles, CA		2183	1871	2817	2018	1951	2913	1701	2823	2740	1916	735	408	1190	1261	2754
Louisville, KY	2183		385	1121	719	751	790	704	700	577	267	1697	2423	2446	2151	604
Memphis, TN	1871	385		1030	863	403	1155	680	1059	869	301	1616	2204	2430	2135	928
Miami, FL	2817	1121	1030		1803	900	1350	1728	1247	1015	1259	2600	3219	3454	3159	1123
Minneapolis, MN	2018	719	863	1803		1261	1205	364	1172	1222	562	1216	1940	1638	1343	1073
Mobile, AL	2042	634	373	775	1304	152	1240	1062	1148	926	642	1877	2444	2701	2406	1013
Montgomery, AL	2102	491	345	730	1176	340	1052	1047	960	738	638	1961	2504	2775	2480	825
Montreal, PQ	3022	959	1309	1742	1150	1602	392	1348	495	724	1106	2303	3060	2747	2452	619
Nashville, TN	2091	183	220	929	868	568	930	806	840	628	330	1734	2424	2516	2221	703
New Orleans, LA	1951	751	403	900	1261		1365	1080	1261	1050	701	1808	2300	2658	2344	1138
New York, NY	2913	790	1155	1350	1205	1365		1300	92	332	962	2303	3062	2975	2708	225
Oklahoma City, OK	1386	797	485	1525	852	679	1517	488	1437	1354	530	1106	1719	1920	1625	1368
Omaha, NE	1701	704	680	1728	364	1080	1300		1300	1222	469	966	1725	1735	1440	1155
Philadelphia, PA	2823	700	1059	1247	1172	1261	92	1300		240	885	2209	2968	2875	2619	135
Phoenix, AZ	403	1793	1481	2414	1743	1548	2500	1349	2501	2350	1526	720	828	1535	1452	2364
Pittsburgh, PA	2547	395	795	1258	874	1125	386	950	305	352	596	1916	2675	2611	2321	230
Portland, ME	3179	1080	1468	1696	1480	1714	313	1515	406	645	1263	2470	3233	3016	2721	540
Portland, OR	1004	2489	2442	3482	1426	2634	3111	1778	3002	3000	2222	826	674	176	376	2931
Providence, RI	3195	969	1334	1562	1323	1544	183	1521	271	511	1295	2428	3183	3154	2859	404
Quebec, PQ	3159	1132	1482	1915	1426	1775	565	1521	565	897	1295	2470	3233	2920	2625	792
Raleigh, NC	2659	598	793	848	1281	926	491	1334	399	159	865	2310	2997	3044	2749	264
Rapid City, SD	1421	1272	1251	2293	597	1630	1772	332	1679	1789	844	686	1445	1197	902	1635
Richmond, VA	2740	577	869	1015	1222	1050	332	1222	240		869	2068	2868	2747	2554	105
Sacramento, CA	386	2334	2174	3189	1953	2322	2976	1636	2882	2868	2067	670	89	794	785	2789
St. Joseph, MO	1772	578	544	1586	436	922	1246	158	1156	1122	311	1072	1831	1866	1571	1053
St. Louis, MO	1916	267	301	1259	562	701	962	469	885	844		1397	2156	2251	1884	806

Travel Mileage Between Cities

The following chart lists the road mileage (TO cities across the top, FROM cities down the right side).

FROM \ TO	Salt Lake City, UT	San Antonio, TX	San Diego, CA	San Francisco, CA	Santa Fe, NM	Sault Ste. Marie	Scranton, PA	Seattle, WA	Shreveport, LA	Sioux City, IA	Sioux Falls, SD	Spokane, WA	Springfield, IL	Springfield, MO	Syracuse, NY	Tampa, FL	Toledo, OH	Toronto, ON	Tulsa, OK	Vancouver, BC	Washington, DC	Wichita, KS	Wilmington, NC	Winnipeg, MB
Los Angeles, CA	735	1379	124	408	896	2555	2860	1190	1630	1714	1752	1261	2034	1696	2798	2544	2373	2667	1497	1364	2754	1509	2698	2120
Louisville, KY	1664	1142	2158	2423	1339	634	718	2446	753	829	917	2151	280	487	703	922	314	608	686	2563	602	738	708	1223
Memphis, TN	1616	739	1846	2204	1027	964	1112	2430	350	808	896	2135	404	316	1109	802	660	954	427	2447	928	611	855	1343
Miami, FL	2600	1525	2744	3219	2016	1753	1366	3454	1187	1830	1918	3159	1296	1391	1489	272	1359	1630	1467	3607	1123	1659	778	2265
Minneapolis, MN	1283	1259	2068	2042	1307	537	1162	1642	1029	336	248	1347	502	602	1106	1633	637	957	713	1759	1108	678	1376	457
New Orleans, LA	1808	581	1878	2300	1149	1367	1415	2658	320	1186	1274	2344	804	694	1349	672	1060	1354	713	2840	1138	853	927	1746
New York, NY	2303	1894	2888	3062	2069	937	125	2975	1505	1336	1414	2708	944	1217	301	1229	610	527	1416	3144	225	1448	580	1773
Omaha, NE	966	953	1714	1725	905	901	1229	1735	777	106	194	1440	446	386	1147	1504	704	1004	401	1852	1155	314	1391	696
Philadelphia, PA	2191	1798	2798	2968	1992	941	122	2875	1409	1247	1325	2619	926	1127	262	1096	529	498	1326	3031	135	1358	477	1670
Richmond, VA	2209	1580	2715	2957	1896	988	341	2940	1191	1326	1414	2650	820	1132	471	863	590	612	1331	3062	105	1315	254	1665
St. Louis, MO	1397	966	2156	1891	1072	873	1072	2251	562	572	650	1884	101	220	882	1068	506	751	419	2296	806	471	975	1042
Salt Lake City, UT		1426	785	759	625	1820	2163	889	1465	996	889	756	1374	1314	2102	2383	1659	1957	1189	1032	2119	1003	2379	1385
San Francisco, CA	759	1804	556		1229	2579	2922	850	1755	2032	2850	939	2133	2029	2893	2946	2422	2705	1830	993	2878	1762	3085	2144
Seattle, WA	889	2305	1304	850	1514	2134	2919		1984	1203	1345	295	2238	2096	2840	3232	2414	2587	2003	143	2845	1817	3156	1473
Spokane, WA	756	2040	1344	939	1369	1839	2629	295	1984	1203	1345		1943	1801	2555	2937	2104	2292	1708	412	2555	1522	2861	1178
Washington, DC	2119	1667	2729	2878	1941	887	257	2845	1203	1241	1203	2555	751	1058	366	971	454	507	1257	2967		1309	359	1571

The God Factor
by James Giles

Is something missing in your life? Do you find yourself at the mercy of your circumstances? Is your self-esteem at an all-time low? Are your dreams only a faded memory? You could be missing the one element that could make the difference between success and failure, poverty and prosperity, and creativity and apathy. Knowing God supplies the creative genius you need to reach your potential and realize your dream. You'll be challenged as James Giles shows you how to tap into your God-given genius, take steps toward reaching your goal, pray big and get answers, eat right and stay healthy, prosper economically and personally, and leave a lasting legacy for your children.

The Biblical Principles of Success
Arthur L. Mackey Jr.

There are only three types of people in the world: People who make things happen, People who watch things happen, and People who do not know what in the world is happening. *The Biblical Principles of Success* will help you become one who makes things happen. Success is not a matter of "doing it my way." It is turning from a personal, selfish philosophy to God's outreaching, sharing way of life. This powerful book teaches you how to tap into success principles that are guaranteed – *the Biblical principles of success!*

Flaming Sword
by Tai Ikomi

Scripture memorization and meditation bring tremendous spiritual power, however many Christians find it to be an uphill task. Committing Scriptures to memory will transform the mediocre Christian to a spiritual giant. This book will help you to become addicted to the powerful practice of Scripture memorization and help you obtain the victory that you desire in every area of your life. *Flaming Sword* is your pathway to spiritual growth and a more intimate relationship with God.

Come, Let Us Pray
by Emmette Weir

Like an ocean, prayer is so vast that we will never plumb its depths. Are you content to walk along the shore, or are you ready to launch out into the deep? No matter what your stage of spiritual development, you can learn to pray with greater intimacy, gratitude, and power. Discover the secrets of personal prayer in *Come Let Us Pray.*

Available at your local bookstore